# Cases in Strategic Marketing Management

# *Cases in Strategic Marketing Management:*

## An Integrated Approach

**William J. McDonald, Ph.D.**
**Hofstra University**
**Winston Management Services**

Prentice Hall, Upper Saddle River, New Jersey 07458

*Acquisitions Editor:* Whitney Blake
*Associate Editor:* John Larkin
*Editorial Assistant:* Rachel Falk
*Vice President/Editorial Director:* Jim Boyd
*Marketing Manager:* John Chillingworth
*Production Editor/Liaison:* Michelle Rich
*Production Coordinator:* Carol Samet
*Managing Editor:* Dee Josephson
*Associate Managing Editor:* Linda DeLorenzo
*Manufacturing Buyer:* Diane Peirano
*Manufacturing Supervisor:* Arnold Vila
*Manufacturing Manager:* Vincent Scelta
*Cover Design:* Bruce Kenselaar
*Illustrator (Interior):* Maryland Composition
*Project Management and Composition:* Maryland Composition

Copyright © 1998 by Prentice-Hall, Inc.
A Simon & Schuster Company
Upper Saddle River, New Jersey 07458

*Library of Congress Cataloging-in-Publication Data*

McDonald, William J., Ph.D.
    Cases in strategic marketing management: an integrated approach /
    William J. McDonald.
        p.    cm.
    Includes bibliographical references and index.
    ISBN 0-02-379424-0 (hardcover)
    1. Marketing—Management—Case studies.   2. Marketing—Decision
making—Case studies.   3. Marketing—Management—Computer programs.
4. Marketing—Decision making—Computer programs.   I. Title.
HF5415.13.M369195 1998
658.8—dc21                                                              97-41735
                                                                            CIP

Prentice-Hall International (UK) Limited, London
Prentice-Hall of Australia Pty. Limited, Sydney
Prentice-Hall Canada, Inc., Toronto
Prentice-Hall Hispanoamericana, S.A., Mexico
Prentice-Hall of India Private Limited, New Delhi
Prentice-Hall of Japan, Inc., Tokyo
Simon & Schuster Asia Pte. Ltd., Singapore
Editora Prentice-Hall do Brasil, Ltda., Rio de Janeiro

Printed in the United States of America

10 9 8 7 6 5 4 3 2 1

# Contents

# *Preface*

The cases in this book are designed to enhance the learning experience and excite you about the real-world aspects of marketing strategy, especially those not usually conveyed well by the typical textbook. Cases play a real-world role by allowing you to work on the marketing problems of actual firms and, thereby, to develop an appreciation for the types of issues in marketing strategy management. Cases also help to develop the analysis and decision-making skills necessary for a successful career in marketing.

Normally, casebooks are used to supplement a textbook containing the definitions and descriptions of concepts fundamental to the content of a course. This casebook is designed to supplement the text of a marketing strategy or marketing management course at either the undergraduate or graduate level. It can also be a useful supplement to a marketing principles course text.

The 32 cases in this book represent a broad range of marketing problems, including consumer and industrial situations. Most of the cases are comprehensive enough to fit into any section of a course on strategic marketing or marketing management. The cases are long and complex enough to require some analysis depth, but are not overly burdensome. Within the casebook sections, cases vary in terms of length, difficulty, and complexity. This casebook is augmented by a computer program designed to enhance the learning associated with working through the cases.

As a user of this casebook, your task is to analyze a firm's situation and to develop solutions for the problems, opportunities, and threats confronting marketing decision makers. To help structure your analyses, a case analysis format is offered in chapter 3. You will be using this format, or some other framework suggested by your instructor, to analyze the cases. Through the case analyses, you will develop the analytic and thinking skills necessary to make good decisions in real-world marketing situations.

All the cases in this book were written by the author based on a combination of interactions with the firms and public sources. Thus, the cases contain experience from consulting work, interviews with company personnel, and information published in business periodicals.

I would like to thank Barry Berman at Hofstra University, Arthur Weinstein at Nova University, and the reviewers and editors of this casebook for their helpful comments. I would also like to acknowledge influences from several casebooks used during my many years of teaching marketing management and marketing strategy courses.

**William J. McDonald, Ph.D.**

# CHAPTER

# *Strategic Marketing Management and Decision Making*

The primary purpose of a marketing strategy is to effectively allocate resources, coordinate the firm's activities, and accomplish specific goals. Accordingly, marketing managers develop strategies to articulate the desired direction for a product or service based on profit objectives and the efficient allocation of resources. Decisions are made during all phases of the planning process about what is to be accomplished and how it will be accomplished. During this process, the impact of a firm's strengths and weakness; problems, opportunities, and threats; and competitive advantages are taken into consideration. Firms seek competitive advantages through well-integrated marketing programs that coordinate the pricing, promotion, product, and distribution of product or service offerings to satisfy the needs of target markets.

Strategic marketing decisions are often complex. There are four major reasons for this complexity:

1. *A large number of factors influence market outcomes.* When marketing managers reposition a product or service or introduce a new offering, a large number of factors, some of which are not controllable by marketing management, determine the success (or failure) of the marketing effort. Competitive reactions, changing economic conditions, and the willingness of consumers to try something new all influence ultimate sales and profitability.

2. *Many marketing influences are from external factors uncontrollable by marketing management.* For example, changes in consumer preferences or increased competition can adversely impact a marketing manager's plans. National or international economic conditions will also affect product or service sales and profitability.

3. *Factors affecting the outcome of marketing plans lack stability.* The uncontrollable factors sometimes change rapidly. These changes can occur in consumer preferences, economic conditions, or other factors over relatively short periods of time. Technology changes quickly in some markets, like the personal computer market, where major new products appear regularly. As these changes occur, they can have serious, adverse impacts on a firm's sales and profits.

4. *Responses to the allocation of marketing resources are not linear.* The underlying

forces that cause nonlinear responses to marketing moves are numerous. Frequently, the end result is diminishing returns for resource allocations. The so-called "s-curve" describes the relationship between many marketing efforts and their eventual results. For example, doubling a product or service's advertising budget rarely increases sales by a commensurate amount; the actual impact is usually more modest.

In addition to a high degree of complexity, marketing decisions frequently involve financial risks that can cost a significant amount of money. For example, when a marketing manager proposes the introduction of a new product, the effort may require funding in the multimillion dollar range. For some firms, the amount at risk may be equal to their entire revenue stream of the last several years.

Marketing decisions also have significant impacts beyond the marketing department. In a marketing driven firm, the approval of marketing plans and budgets determines the budgeting for other functional areas such as manufacturing and human resources. Thus, in fitting the organization to the business environment, strategic marketing management provides direction to the firm and influences production, financial, and human resource requirements.

While these financial and resource allocation consequences should be explicitly stated when the marketing plan is approved, they represent commitments that frequently detract from the other activities of a functional area. Normally, these departments are considered cost centers while only the marketing department has the dual role of revenue generation and cost management.

## WHO MAKES STRATEGIC MARKETING DECISIONS?

In most firms, marketing decisions are made in a hierarchy. The progression upward reflects a shift in focus from day-to-day operational considerations toward greater concern with long-run strategic issues. From the bottom to the top, common titles for a packaged-goods firm are: assistant brand manager, brand manager, group brand manager, vice president of marketing, and president. The former individuals are on the front line dealing with the day-to-day pressures of carrying out the strategic marketing tasks. Their job is to supervise the application of marketing efforts such as advertising and pricing. These are the controllable factors that marketing manages and manipulates in the face of uncontrollables, such as the competition, to achieve sales and profit results.

Time horizons in strategic marketing are usually about five years, although these longer term plans also have immediate effects that are reflected in short-term tactical plans. These may include promotional campaigns, distribution efforts, pricing, and dealing. Thus, the marketing plan for a product or service represents the strategic and tactical direction developed and implemented by the brand manager and his or her assistants. The plan is approved by higher ranked marketing and top management executives.

Plan details usually include the following:

**1.** An assessment of the current situation for the product or service, including its place in the industry, related macroenvironmental trends, firm strengths and weaknesses, and other details.

2. A description of problems, opportunities, and threats.

3. Specific objectives based on the first two items.

4. Alternative approaches to addressing the problems, pursuing the opportunities (given the strengths and weaknesses and the overall industry situation), and avoiding threats, and an evaluation of these alternatives, with associated sales and profitability forecasts.

5. A decision as to which alternative to pursue.

Regardless of format, a good strategic marketing plan must address a myriad of product, firm, industry, and general environmental factors in detail. How your actual analysis and decision making is structured will reflect the preferences of your instructor, although the approach discussed in chapter 3 is strongly recommended.

## MARKETING STRATEGY SELECTION AND DECISION MAKING

A recurrent issue in strategic marketing management is the determination of the consistency of product or service strategies with the organization's objectives and resources, relevant macroenvironmental forces, and competitor activities. Proper analysis of these factors depends on the availability and evaluation of information, including market size, buying behavior, and consumer requirements. Information on macroenvironmental forces such as sociocultural, political and legal, and economic changes is necessary to determine the future viability of the firm's offerings and the markets it serves. In recent years, for example, companies had to alter or adapt their strategies because of political and legal actions (regulation), sociocultural changes (increase in the number of employed women), and economic fluctuations (unemployment and declines in disposable personal income). Competitor activities must be monitored to ascertain to ascertain their existing or possible strategies and performance in satisfying needs.

In practice, the strategy selection decision is based on an analysis of the costs and benefits of alternative plans and their probability of success. For example, a marketing manager may compare the costs and benefits involved in further penetrating an existing market with those associated with introducing that product into a new market.

The product or service itself may dictate a strategy change. If the product has been purchased by all of the buyers it is going to attract in an existing market, opportunities for growth beyond replacement purchases are reduced. This situation would indicate a need to search out new buyers (markets) or to develop new products or services for presently served markets.

## CASEBOOK STRUCTURE

This casebook has five introductory chapters about analyzing cases and 32 individual cases about firms in a variety of industries.

Chapter 2 provides a rationale for the case method. It also describes the benefits you gain from doing case work. Chapter 3 addresses the specifics of how strategic analysis and marketing decision making should proceed based on a case analysis. It suggests that you apply that format in Table 1.1 to your case analysis and explains the details of

TABLE 1–1    Format for Case Analysis

I. Situation Analysis
   A. Extent of demand
   B. Nature of demand
   C. Strategy analysis
   D. Life cycle stage
   E. Macroenvironmental trends
   F. International issues
   G. Strengths and weaknesses
   H. Nature of competition
II. Problems, Opportunities, and Threats
   A. Problems
   B. Opportunities
   C. Threats
III. Objectives
IV. Alternatives
   A. Marketing alternatives
   B. Evaluation of alternatives
V. Decision
   A. Recommendation
   B. Implementation and control

each section in the format. It details the various components of the recommended case analysis approach and specific questions that you can ask yourself as you progress with a case analysis.

According to the case analysis format in Table 1–1, you begin by doing a complete analysis of the situation facing the organization in the case. This situation analysis includes an assessment of (A) the extent of the demand for the organization's product or service, (B) the nature of the demand in terms of the prospects or customers, (C) the business and marketing strategies of the case firm and major competitors, (D) the stage of the life cycle for the product or service, (E) the macroenvironmental trends, (F) the international issues, (G) the strengths and weaknesses of the firm and its competitors, and (H) the nature of how firms in the market compete.

Once the aforementioned work is completed, you are in a position to summarize the problems, opportunities, and threats arising from that situation analysis. Next, objectives are defined. This should all lead to a set of marketing alternatives that offer solutions to the problems, pursue the opportunities, and avoid the threats. They are evaluated relative to the situation analysis, the problems, opportunities, threats, and the feasibility and projected financial results from each alternative. The pros and cons of each alternative are weighed as part of this evaluation, and a decision is then reached that includes a plan for implementation and monitoring.

Chapter 4 includes a discussion of the importance of computer-based analyses in marketing decision making and an overview of the computer program that accompanies this casebook. Chapter 5 provides details about a financial analysis procedure recommended for analyzing cases. The remainder of the book contains the 32 marketing strategy cases and appendices describing how to use the computer program that comes with this book to analyze cases.

## Sources

Bernhardt, Kenneth L., and Thomas C. Kinnear. *Cases in Marketing Management.* 5th ed. Homewood, IL: Richard D. Irwin, 1991.

Cravens, David, and Charles W. Lamb, Jr. *Strategic Marketing Management Cases.* 4th ed. Homewood, IL: Richard D. Irwin, 1993.

David, Fred R. *Cases in Strategic Management.* 4th ed. New York: Macmillan Publishing Company, 1993.

Hill, Charles W. L., and Gareth R. Jones. *Strategic Management: An Integrated Approach.* 2nd ed. Boston: Houghton Mifflin Company, 1992.

Jain, Subhash C. *Marketing Planning & Strategy.* 4th ed. Cincinnati, OH: South-Western Publishing, 1993.

Kotler, Philip. *Marketing Management.* 7th ed. Upper Saddle River, NJ: Prentice Hall, 1991.

O'Dell, William F., Andrew C. Ruppe, and Robert H. Trent. *Marketing Decision Making: Analytical Framework and Cases.* Cincinnati, OH: South-Western Publishing, 1979.

Walker, Orville C. Jr., Harper W. Boyd, Jr., and Jean-Claude Larreche. *Marketing Strategy: Planning and Implementation.* Homewood, IL: Richard D. Irwin, 1992.

# CHAPTER

## The Case Method

**2**

Chapter 1 described how strategic marketing management and decision making address the specifics of how strategic analysis and decision making should proceed. It also covered the case orientation of this book and previewed a format for case analysis. This chapter provides an overview of the philosophy behind the case method, including a discussion of the role that cases play in the learning process. After carefully reading this material, you will be prepared to study the specifics of the case analysis format covered in the chapter 3.

A marketing strategy case describes an organization's external and internal situation and raises issues about that firm's strategies, objectives, and plans. Most of the information in a case is factual, but some may contain opinions, judgments, and beliefs. The cases are written to give you practice in applying marketing concepts and allow you to learn by doing.

A case study presents an account of what happened to a firm and industry over a number of years. It covers the wide range of issues and problems that managers had to confront, and, in some cases, the courses of action they selected. Each case is different because each industry, firm, and marketing situation is different. The underlying premise of all the cases is that strategic analysis and planning can help solve the marketing problems of a firm by providing it with a comprehensive road map for its future.

## THE CASE METHOD

The case method differs from other approaches to learning because it requires that you take an active rather than a passive role in the analysis of problems and the formation of alternative courses of action. The case places you in a situation where you are the substitute for the marketing manager in the decision-making process. Cases are descriptions of situations faced by firms and the surrounding facts and opinions that the managers depended on in their decision making. Thus, the real, and sometimes slightly fictionalized cases, are presented for thorough analysis, open discussion, and, ultimately, decision making.

Because case analysis is an applied skill, it is something you learn through experience. The more you practice, the more proficient you will become at identifying problems and formulating solutions. The benefits you receive from a case analysis are directly proportional to the effort you make. With the case method, the decisions you make and the process used to arrive at those decisions are important. You are expected to develop the ability to make decisions, to support those decisions with appropriate analysis, and to learn to communicate those choices, supporting facts, and opinions in discussions, presentations, and written reports.

Your responsibilities as a case analyst include active participation, interaction, critical evaluation, and effective communication. The case method requires individual participation in class discussions based on thorough preparation, entailing more than a casual reading of each case.

You will benefit from discussing cases with your fellow class members. These case discussions, whether in and/or out of class, are valuable because they provide feedback regarding your perspectives about the situations facing the firms and possible solutions you formulate. Another important aspect of these case discussions results from synergisms and new insights produced by group interactions.

## THE VALUE OF CASE ANALYSIS

Cases prove valuable in a strategic marketing course for several reasons. First, they provide you with experience addressing marketing problems that you probably have not had the opportunity to experience firsthand. While analyzing cases, you will have the chance to appreciate the problems faced by many different companies and understand how marketing managers tried to deal with them.

Second, cases illustrate the theory and content of strategic marketing. The meaning and implications of what you read in your textbook become clearer when applied to the cases. Marketing theory and concepts help reveal the complexities of the situations and problems, allowing you to evaluate solutions that specific firms adopted to deal with those issues.

The third advantage of case studies is that they provide you with class participation opportunities. Through classroom discussion the major issues and solutions to the problem(s), along with the strategy options, will emerge. In this class discussion, you may find that the opinions of other members of the class differ from your own. However, this should lead to a clearer perception of what is facing a firm and a greater awareness of the complexities associated with how management decisions are reached.

## PREPARING A CASE

The goal of your first reading of the case should be to become familiar with the scope of the situation for the firm and the problems, opportunities, and threats it faces, plus an overview of the organizational issues and resource base of the business involved. A second reading should be more thorough, focusing on understanding the specifics of what is happening to the firm and the details of its problems, opportunities, and threats, including potential strategic alternatives.

Question the data presented in the case frequently; only some of it is relevant. Decide what the case is really about. Is it competitive challenges, technological change, or a shift in consumer demand? As part of the process of mastering the case, it is sometimes desirable to use the numbers in the case to make calculations and comparisons that will help you analyze the situation.

You must add to the facts in a case by making reasonable assumptions regarding the situation in which the firm finds itself and the strategic options available to address any issues facing the firm. Note that marketing decision making is rarely based on perfect information. Even given a lack of complete information, reasonable assumptions are necessary in the face of uncertainty. It is better to make your assumptions explicit and incorporate them in your analysis than to use them implicitly or not make them at all. For example, the case may not describe the purchase decision process for the product or service. A poor analysis would either omit mentioning this or just state that no information is available. A good analysis attempts to delineate that process even if it means drawing on real-life experience rather than on case facts only. The ability to make decisions based on well-reasoned assumptions is a skill that must also be developed for effective case analysis and for effective marketing management.

The most important part of analyzing cases is how you support your decisions. In business, marketing strategists usually do not know if their decisions are right until resources have been allocated and the plan has been fully implemented. It is often too late then to reverse the decisions. This fact accents the need for careful integration of intuition and analysis in preparing your cases or in doing your job as a marketing manager.

## Sources

Bernhardt, Kenneth L., and Thomas C. Kinnear. *Cases in Marketing Management.* 5th ed. Homewood, IL: Richard D. Irwin, 1991.

Clark, Darrel G. *Marketing Analysis and Decision Making.* 2nd ed. San Francisco, CA: Scientific Press, 1993.

Cravens, David, and Charles W. Lamb, Jr. *Strategic Marketing Management Cases.* 4th ed. Homewood, IL: Richard D. Irwin, 1993.

David, Fred R. *Cases in Strategic Management.* 4th ed. New York: Macmillan Publishing Company, 1993.

Hill, Charles W. L., and Gareth R. Jones. *Strategic Management: An Integrated Approach*, 2nd ed. Boston: Houghton Mifflin Company, 1992.

Jain, Subhash C. *Marketing Planning & Strategy.* 4th ed. Cincinnati, OH: South-Western Publishing, 1993.

Kotler, Philip. *Marketing Management.* 7th ed. Upper Saddle River, NJ: Prentice Hall, 1991.

O'Dell, William F., Andrew C. Ruppe, and Robert H. Trent. *Marketing Decision Making: Analytical Framework and Cases.* Cincinnati, OH: South-Western Publishing, 1979.

Walker, Orville C. Jr., Harper W. Boyd, Jr., and Jean-Claude Larreche. *Marketing Strategy: Planning and Implementation.* Homewood, IL: Richard D. Irwin, 1992.

# CHAPTER

## *Format for Case Analysis*

This chapter expands on the case analysis format introduced in chapter 1. In a sense, the format resembles a comprehensive checklist because it contains a broad range of issues and questions that need to be addressed when analyzing the marketing situations in the cases. However, it is not necessarily intended to be applied in its totality to every case. Instead, the format is a framework that illustrates how any or all of the facts and options presented about the firms in the cases can be organized for decision making. A particularly large part of what you will learn from these case analyses is how to define, structure, and analyze problems, opportunities, and threats.

If your instructor does not assign an alternative analytical format, use the approach outlined in Table 3–1. A discussion of each area in the table follows, including detailed information about of the analytic issues and related questions for each case analysis format topic.

## SITUATION ANALYSIS

The first step in the case analysis process is basically a synopsis and evaluation of a firm's current situation, which leads to an identification of problems, opportunities, and threats. This helps you to prepare marketing alternatives and make a specific decision about what course of action to recommend. The situation analysis interprets and shows the relevance of important information, providing a diagnostic rather than a descriptive background for proceeding with the case analysis.

The breadth and depth of this analysis are determined by the nature and scope of the case situation and the specific instructions you receive on how to approach the case. Each case may require a situation analysis that is different from any of the others because the information available and the potential alternatives to be explored are unique.

TABLE 3–1 Format for Case Analysis

I. Situation Analysis
   A. Extent of demand
   B. Nature of demand
   C. Strategy analysis
   D. Life cycle stage
   E. Macroenvironmental trends
   F. International issues
   G. Strengths and weaknesses
   H. Nature of competition
II. Problems, Opportunities, and Threats
   A. Problems
   B. Opportunities
   C. Threats
III. Objectives
IV. Alternatives
   A. Marketing alternatives
   B. Evaluation of alternatives
V. Decision
   A. Recommendation
   B. Implementation and control

A good situation analysis includes a thorough and comprehensive assessment of the overall market; a profiling of present and potential customers; an examination of marketing objectives and strategies (including those for product, distribution, pricing, and promotion); a product or service life cycle assessment; a detailed review and evaluation of macroenvironmental trends; a specification of international issues, particularly those relating to competitive considerations; an analysis of the firm's and competitor's major strengths and weaknesses; and an understanding of the nature of the competition that describes the basis on which firms compete for attention and sales in a firm's market.

## Extent of Demand

The task of specifying the extent of demand in a market involves defining the actual size of that market and estimates of future sales potential. This is a quantitative exercise because it provides information on customer demand for a category of products or services.

To understand the extent of demand for a product or service category you need to estimate the size of the market (units and dollars) now and in the future; competitor market shares and trends in units and dollars; and the market position of competitors in terms of sales and share, including forecasts of market segment growth, usually for the next five years, for the segments in which firms compete. In addition to considering differences in demand at the primary (category level demand), you will need to understand selective demand (product or service specific demand) levels and make assumptions about related brand specific trends.

## Nature of Demand

In this section, the consumer or industrial market segment identifies buyers and their purchase decision-making process. This process encompasses specifics about how those purchases are influenced by factors external to the customer, including any joint decision making that may occur in families or business organizations. The key to conducting this analysis is to think about the implications of alternative marketing strategies and programs.

### Segmentation

Proper identification of the target market(s) is a key part of strategic marketing. As part of understanding the nature of demand, there should be interest in whether segments of the market are growing. Is the case firm's target segment large enough to support the product or service? Can the market be more meaningfully segmented into several homogenous groups, which identify what customers want and how they buy? Also, look at the buyer segment demographics, psychological characteristics, and decision-making processes in the context of influences from other entities such as family, friends, society, business organizations, and government.

Examine if and how the market has been segmented by competitors and the basis for those segmentations, include identification of which segments have the most potential. What key competitors serve each customer group? Are there segments currently not being served? Can the case firm successfully serve those markets? Think about whether a more effective marketing program might be developed for each segment versus having an overall program for all segments. Will tailoring a marketing strategy to a specific segment provide a competitive advantage?

### Decision Making

Determine the *who, what, where, when, why,* and *how* of the purchase decision. How do buyers (consumer or industrial) currently buy existing products or services? What are the more important types of behavior patterns and attitudes? In connection with decision making: how many stores are shopped or industrial sources considered in making the purchase; what is the degree of information seeking; what is the level of brand awareness and loyalty; what are the sources of product or service information; and who makes the purchase decision?

Is the purchase an individual or group decision and who influences the decision maker(s)? How frequently is the purchase decision made or repeated? What is the buyer's involvement in the decision-making process? Is it a routine decision made frequently (e.g., buying toothpaste) or is it a decision that occurs infrequently (e.g., buying a car)? What is the risk or uncertainty level associated with the purchase and what are the consequences of making a poor choice? What are the reasons for purchase behavior? What needs do buyers satisfy by purchasing the product or service? Are they emotional or rational? What are the most important sources of information used to make a decision and what criteria are used to evaluate the product or service?

## Strategy Analysis

An understanding of a case firm's strategy and the strategies of major competitors is an important aspect of the situation analysis. Start by delineating the objectives of the various marketing strategies. For each firm you analyze, be able to provide specific answers to the following questions:

1. What are the firm's objectives?
2. Have/are they been/being successfully achieved?

### Marketing Strategy

As you analyze the marketing strategy of each firm, you should address a series of specific questions about the case company and its major competitors. Does the firm (or major competitor) have an integrated marketing strategy made up of individual product, channel, price, advertising, and sales force strategies? Is the role selected for each mix element consistent with the overall program objectives, and does it complement other mix elements? Are adequate resources available to carry out the marketing strategy? Are resources committed to market to individual targets consistent with their importance? Is the effectiveness of the marketing strategy reviewed on a regular basis? To understand a firm's product or service marketing strategy, you need to delineate what is happening with each of the products, the distribution, and the prices.

### Product Strategy

Is the product mix geared to the needs that the firm wants to meet for each market? What branding strategy is being used? Are products properly positioned against competing brands? Does the firm have a sound approach to product planning and management, and is marketing involved in product decisions? Are additions to, modifications of, or deletions from the product mix needed to make the firm more competitive in the marketplace? Is the performance of each product evaluated on a regular basis?

### Distribution Strategy

Has the firm selected the type and intensity of distribution appropriate for each market it wants to serve? How well does each channel access its market target? Is an effective channel mix used? Are channel organizations carrying out their assigned functions properly? How is the channel(s) of distribution managed? Are improvements needed? Are desired customer service levels reached, and are the costs of reaching this level acceptable?

### Pricing Strategy

How responsive is each market target to price variation? What roles does price have in the marketing mix? Is price an active or passive part of the product or service positioning strategy? How do the firm's price strategy and tactics compare with those of competitors? How are prices established? Are there indications that changes are needed in price strategy or tactics?

Promotion Strategy

What are the roles and objectives for advertising and sales promotion in the marketing mix? Is the creative strategy consistent with the positioning strategy? Is the budget adequate enough to carry out the advertising and sales promotion objectives? Do the promotional plans represent the most cost-effective means of communicating with market targets? Do advertising copy and content effectively communicate the intended messages? How well does the promotional program meet its objectives?

## Life Cycle Stage

In this section you will make explicit assumptions about where a product or service market is in its life cycle. This reasoning is important because the effectiveness of specific marketing options and approaches tend to vary by stages of the life cycle.

In what stage of the life cycle is the product or service category? What market characteristics support your life cycle stage evaluation? Be sure to describe the category in which the case firm is competing and not just the product or service the firm is selling. The product life cycle is the description of a whole category of products or services and not just of the offerings of individual firms in a category.

## Macroenvironmental Trends

Six components of the macroenvironment are critical from a marketing point of view: the sociocultural, demographic, political and legal, technological, economic, and competitive environments (Table 3–2). Clearly, these components interact in complex ways. Government actions on taxes impact economic growth and the distribution of incomes. Technological changes influence the nature of competition among firms. For example, today, many companies use computers in their marketing efforts to directly promote to households rather than with newspaper coupons or flyers.

Macroenvironmental trends are particularly important to the marketing strategy formulation process because any plan unfolds in some future macroenvironment. In that sense, a marketing strategy is a business plan based on a scenario about what the future will be like. Because of the importance of this prediction, the next part of this

---

**TABLE 3–2   Macroenvironmental Areas**

1. Sociocultural environment
2. Demographic environment
3. Political and legal environment
4. Technological environment
5. Economic environment
6. Competitive environment

---

chapter provides an in-depth analysis of some of the major U.S. and global macro-environmental trends.

Sociocultural Environment

Sociocultural environment represents the cultural, attitudinal, and behavioral aspects of the macroenvironment. Changes in this environment tend to be more evolutionary than revolutionary, but, to many in a society, the pace of change can appear excessive. Usually the changes occur with generations more than with individuals from a given generation. Of particular interest to marketers are changes in individual values, family structure, leisure-time activities, and expectations about the future. These changes affect the sale of personal consumer goods; the advertising of products and services; the marketing of political candidates; and almost every other area of social, economic, and political life related to business activities. Two of the more important trends involve generation values and the structure of American families.

**Generational Change and Conflict**     The role of generational change in the evolution of a society is highlighted by conflicts over values and resources. Each new generation makes its claims to be different from the last by espousing its own agenda and priorities. The baby busters (or generation 13 or the X-generation or the repair generation or the dysfunctional generation) are not different. And, for all the talk of the baby bust, this not a small group. Compared with those born from 1951 through 1962, the core of the baby boom, this generation of 18 to 29 year olds is the second largest group of young adults in U.S. history.

When their elders think of this generation, they see them as uppity, mischievous, and poorly educated whiners, with sound-bite attention spans. So why does this post-baby-boom generation think it is going to save the world? Because it has no other choice. Americans born between 1961 and 1981 will be left with the "dirty work" of fixing inherited problems that other generations, including those selfish baby boomers and those greedy seniors, are unable or unwilling to resolve. Members of this "sacrificial generation" will be those most hurt by the debt crisis, disintegrating families, growing racial disharmony, and a damaged environment.

What most motivates this group is the fear that the "American Dream" is over, at least for their generation. They believe that they will be the first generation to fail to match their parents' economic success. Already, they are the adults most likely to live with their parents (58 percent of all unmarried singles ages 20 to 24), the least likely to own a home (home ownership among those under age 25 dropped by 35 percent between 1973 and 1990), and the least likely to see their incomes keep up with inflation.

The concerns of the twentysomethings are supported by economic data about changes in the economy and income during the last decade. Between 1980 and 1990, the median income of Americans under age 25 declined by 10.8 percent. For all others, it grew by 6.5 percent. Today's college students graduate with the fear that their expensive education may not be enough to keep them out of low pay, low skill *McJobs*.

***The economic shaft.***     Most annoying to twentysomethings is their belief that a massive redistribution of wealth is taking place. It is not so much a gap between the rich and poor as it is a widening gulf between the young and old. For people age 65 and older, income grew by 21 percent in the 1980s, in part because Social Security checks are in-dexed for inflation, while the minimum wage failed to climb with inflation. These young people will pay a higher percentage of their incomes to Social Security taxes than any generation before them, but less than 30 percent expect that they will ever draw out of Social Security what they put in.

***Unique experiences.*** There are experiences unique to twentysomethings that give them generational identity. Most of all, post-boomers make up a survivor generation. They are the children of divorce. (Some 40 percent grew up in broken families.) They are the children of neglect. (Through the 1970s, 12 percent of elementary school chil-dren and 30 percent of middle school kids were latchkey children, triple the rate of the previous decade.) They attended school during a period of declining educational standards.

Still, what makes this generation potentially powerful is that its members share a generational identity that can be used to reclaim the American Dream. To gain some measure of economic justice, they need to change the course of American society by demanding that the older generations stop living off their future.

**The Changing Family Structure** The traditional "nuclear family" (or *Father Knows Best* family) with husband-dominant and 2.2 children represents a minority of house-holds in American society. The rising divorce rate has made one-parent households commonplace; many chose not to marry at all or to not remarry after divorce; and some are attracted to members of their own sex.

This family structure evolution has considerably changed the buying process for many goods and services. Often today, a variety of different influences operate on the purchase of such routine consumer products and services and on the purchase of major durables such as housing, cars, furniture, and appliances.

Single's market growth in the United States illustrates how the nature of family life has evolved. The 1990 census shows that about 23 million Americans live by them-selves, a 91 percent jump for women since 1970, and a 156 percent increase for men over the same period. Two trends are behind this singles surge. Unprecedented num-bers of adults are never marrying, and, by some estimates, 60 percent of all couples di-vorce.

Middle-aged singles are among the fastest growing of these groups. But, the mar-ket is even larger than these numbers suggest. Some 18 million adults aged 18 to 34 live with their parents or in college dormitories and, therefore, have plenty of spending money. Throw in these other singles and estimates are that this group has an earning power of $660 billion. And, as married baby boomers evolve into budget-conscious par-ents, the affluent singles may prove to be the last big spenders.

This is an attractive target, but a tough one. Studies show that singles share such traits as a tendency to spend more on travel, eat convenience foods, and frequent more restaurants than married adults. But, this vast, fragmented group includes carefree 21 year olds to elderly widows, groups having very diverse interests and needs. There is also the delicate task of getting a message across without offending.

However, too often marketers have treated singles as if they were just some sort of extramarital aberration. Campbell Soup made that mistake with its Soup for One line. Soup for One is a lonely name. Singles eat alone but do not need to be reminded. After years of mediocre sales, the Soup for One label was removed. Single-serving sizes now come without the offending label, and sales have improved.

Other marketers with appeals that are apparently aimed at singles do not like to talk about it. A print ad for Haagen-Dazs ice cream has a woman finding her ice cream bar more appealing than conversation. Haagen-Dazs ice cream is a high-indulgence food that appeals to singles who are a little less price-sensitive.

Many companies, however, admit to chasing the unattached. MCI Telecommunications Corp. is a good example. Single people do not have nuclear families. So they are more emotionally connected to family and friends elsewhere. That means high phone usage. To reach them, MCI does not use the word "single" in its singles-oriented campaigns. Instead, several "Friends and Family" ads show attractive adults of varying ages in nonfamily settings making lists of friends to phone. If customers get their friends and family to join MCI with them, both parties get 20 percent discounts on calls made to each other.

Other marketers want older singles. Recently, Colgate ran a television ad showing a 40-year-old single mother of two brushing her teeth while getting ready for her first date in years. Royal Cruise Line, which caters to an older crowd, has a successful program that gets men over 50 to act as dance partners and social hosts to single women. Despite all the activity, many singles' markets remain largely unexploited.

Demographic Environment

Changing demographics are a major influence on all aspects of American society. In addition, the American population's age distribution is skewing older, marketers have a particular interest in changes in the income and social structure of the United States because they directly affect the nature of demand from consumer and industrial markets.

Those income and social class changes are being driven largely by international competition. In a 1993 Senate committee hearing on the NAFTA treaty, the dean of the Harvard Business School described the plight of the U.S. labor force in a very competitive international environment. He characterized the top one-third of all U.S. workers as "world class" and the other two-thirds as "positively third world." In the future, the "American labor premium" will completely disappear in the face of low-wage workers in other countries. Thus, the projection is that because this two-thirds of the U.S. labor force does not warrant a wage rate higher than that paid to comparable workers in Korea or Mexico, these U.S. worker's wages will systematically fall over the next 10 to 20 years, as they have done for the last 12 years.

The dean's scenario is widely accepted in government and academia as a major reason for the declining incomes and lower living standards of most less skilled workers. It is also consistent with theories about the way the social class structure in the United States is changing. The message is that the U.S. middle class is in trouble and that the future class structure of the United States will essentially be third world, with the highly educated and trained at the top, a small number in the middle, and the majority of the population at the bottom. Those who analyze this phenomenon say that the top group will be about 25 percent of households, while the bottom will represent close to 65 percent, with the remainder in the middle. This also says that the majority of the current middle class is downwardly, not upwardly, mobile.

The future also holds more taxes for those at the top as the government attempts to compensate for the aforementioned phenomenon. In this modern age, the primary role of the government is to make income transfers and those transfers will accelerate in the future. Those changes may also hold the seeds of a social and political revolution that threatens American democracy. Some believe that in an attempt to redistribute income and resources, the federal government will destroy the economy and individual initiative. That economic implosion will likely occur in the next 10 to 15 years.

Marketers should be particularly concerned about the implications of a changing social class structure and income distribution. If the middle class has substantially less money to spend, the impact will be felt by all businesses serving that group. These businesses will have to change their targeting to more upscale consumers or lower their sights to target the less affluent.

The notion that a majority of U.S. citizens are in decline both occupationally and in their standard of living is a statistical reality. Another reality is the new macroenvironment being created for U.S. firms by these changes. That environment has significant economic, sociocultural, and other implications for marketing strategies in the 1990s and beyond.

### Political and Legal Environment

The political and legal environment includes all the factors controlled by public authorities, the interest groups, and other forces that operate on the legislative process. It defines the regulatory environment within which business must operate. The political and legal process has the ability to impose mandatory constraints on a firm's operations and on the behavior of consumers. As with any other external force, this environment presents both opportunities and threats to a firm. Major elements of that environment that have a potential impact on marketing activities are government regulation, consumer protection legislation, and other politically driven influences.

The intricacies and sheer number of laws and regulations make it difficult for marketing executives to fully comprehend the regulatory elements that may affect them. However, government, business, and the general public are increasingly aware of the negatives of over regulation that protect inefficiencies, restrict entry by new competitors, and create inflationary pressures.

The regulatory burden is especially rough on small companies, which are considered the nation's job generators. The National Federation of Independent Business, a Washington trade group representing some 600,000 smaller employers, has been polling its members about their biggest problems for two decades. In 1993, for the first time, regulation rose to the top of the list—ahead of taxes, the quality of labor, and the availability of credit. The smallest businesses are so overwhelmed now that they are taking to ignoring all the laws. For example, we are very close to a breakdown in the banking regulations Congress passed in 1989. Bank regulators now insist that lending institutions pay a federally certified appraiser to value real estate put up as collateral for any loan over $100,000. The average $5,000 cost of such an appraisal can price a small business out of the market. Typically, the entrepreneurs put up their homes, and, therefore, the default rate on small business loans poses little risk to the banks. The banks themselves could do the appraisals at a tenth of the cost.

Just trimming back the regulatory overgrowth would be difficult. But, there are many well intentioned new laws, such as the 1990 Clean Air Act, that have yet to be fully translated into rules for business and local governments. The Clean Air Act is one reason Americans will be spending 2.8 percent of Gross National Product (GNP) to comply with federal environmental mandates by the end of the decade. Germans are no less green and face a monumental challenge in cleaning up the former East Germany. Yet, Germany will be spending 1.6 percent to 1.8 percent of GNP.

### Technological Environment

Technology is the driving force behind the development of many new products and markets, but it is also a major reason for the decline of some products and markets. Dramatic acceleration has occurred in identifying the commercial potential of technological developments. Thus, the time between ideas, invention, and commercialization has decreased. In particular, new technologies affecting production will be adopted more quickly.

**The Rapidity of Technological Change**     A major example of the rapidity of technological change is the transformation of the personal computer (PC) industry. For three decades that industry seemed to epitomize the marriage of technological wizardry and business acumen. Led by IBM, the industry exploited a pace of technological change that produced many significant innovations, from powerful desktop computers to extremely light and sophisticated hand-held models. The PC industry revolutionized the way nearly all other businesses worked. And, it consistently made profits.

In the early 1990s, the computer industry went into turmoil as profits plummeted, sales flatted, tens of thousands lost their jobs, and vicious price wars began. The industry's reversal of fortune was so abrupt that it left many of its leading companies floundering.

IBM, the biggest computer maker and long one of the most successful companies in the world, lost $4.9 billion in 1992, one of the biggest corporate losses in history. In that same year, it shed 40,000 of its 340,000 employees in an effort to control costs. And IBM was not alone. DEC, the world's second-biggest computer firm lost $2.8 billion in 1992. Olivetti, Siemens-Nixdorf, Group Bull, Bujitsu, Hitachi, and NEC all saw profits collapse. Wang, a success story in the early 1980s, fell into bankruptcy.

But global recession was not the only, or even the primary, cause for the industry's traumas. Recession-accelerated changes, which were already reshaping the industry, had a deeper impact. Until the mid-1980s the computer business was dominated by a few large firms, foremost among them IBM, whose marketing and technological resources let them educate, reassure, and control the corporate customers who bought most computers. Smaller companies often introduced the latest technology to the market, but usually their innovations were not widely accepted until adopted by IBM. These smaller firms seldom posed much of a threat.

Beginning in the early 1990s, technological change swept away the established computer industry. Firms scrambled to find their place in the market, but even for those that survived, the turmoil continues. And, far from slowing the pace of innovation, as might be expected, hard times have quickened it. An unprecedented number of new products came to market in the early 1990s. With chip technology improving faster than ever, a plethora of new products will reach the market during the remainder of the decade: pen-based PCs, hand-held computing and communication devices, ever more powerful versions of today's desktop and notebook computers, sophisticated network and database software, and cheaper and fancier supercomputers.

Moreover, a growing part of the computer market shows many of the classic characteristics of a commodity business: there are few discernible differences between products except price, low barriers to entry, and thin profit margins. The large amount of intellectual property contained in computer products, and their complexity, ought to make it easy for companies to keep out new rivals, differentiate their products, and command fat margins. Instead, even in many niches of the industry, growing competition is eroding margins.

**Five Hundred Channels**     A second important example of technological change is occurring in the communications and home entertainment industry. In the past decade, channel capacity in the average home quadrupled, from 9 to 38, due to the growth of cable and independent stations. With digital compression and the development of electronic superhighways, many experts expect 500 channels in every home. Not only will this proliferation of channels change viewer habits, it will also change television as a marketing and advertising medium.

*A new mix of competitors.*     Members of the television industry that rely on advertising revenues will be affected by these changes, but not equally. The broadcast networks will suffer further audience losses, and while they will still draw large audiences relative to cable, this will not be enough to keep them profitable, forcing drastic measures such as massive cost cutting, withdrawal from time periods, specialization in news or sports, and mergers with program creators.

The networks have already been severely hurt by audience fragmentation. During the past 10 years, as channel capacity has quadrupled, the big three network prime time ratings have fallen by 40 percent. In daytime, a key source of profitability, ratings have fallen by 30 percent. Viewers are going to cable (all dayparts), to Fox (prime time and kids), and syndication (especially kids, daytime and late fringe).

Local television stations will also suffer audience losses. But, they should actually gain in relative strength because of their unique ability to establish and build on a strong local identity with local news and programming. They will assert themselves more strongly versus the networks.

Established cable networks will find their small ratings diminished further, especially those without clear niches. New networks will have to be more reliant than older ones on scarce advertising revenues. Cable will grow as an industry as it attracts more households, both to view television and to take advantage of other services such as interactive games and new ways of shopping.

Advertisers will need to adapt to the loss of concepts such as day/date/time scheduling, which no longer suits viewer's preferences. Rather than buying a medium, they may need to select certain shows on the basis of viewer/environmental compatibility, and to advertise on each show in all its various runs within a given time range.

***Programming.*** This technological breakthrough raises a key question: If a programming is the lifeblood of television, who is going to pay for it? Specifically, if programmers have trouble funding programming for today's 36 channels, how can they fund programming for 500, especially the big, expensive action dramas for which American television is known?

Channel capacity may be increasing rapidly, but the advertising money to pay for programming is not, nor is viewership. That means lower average ratings, and hence, for advertiser-supported programming, less advertising money for each channel.

What kind of programming would fill up a 500-channel system? It is clear that broad-based, advertiser-supported programming will only be a small part of it. Cable systems will experiment with new services, such as interactive home shopping, banking, etc. They will also use much of the new capacity for Pay-Per-View channels. In each case, the programming or services can be paid for out of consumer revenues—but that reduces the audience for free television still further. In addition, new cable networks that have been blocked for lack of available space will also start up. Some will aim at tiny-but-loyal niches, such as the Golf Channel. Others may try to compete with existing channels in news, sports, and music.

For marketers, these developments open an unlimited number of advertising opportunities. Most likely, many of these channels will be occupied by home shopping or Pay-Per-View services and not by program-oriented networks. One main reason, these options generate revenue for local operators, whose rates are under government regulation.

***Targeting.*** As the communications market becomes fragmented, there is more opportunity for advertisers to target their consumers. The ability of niche networks to deliver a targeted audience in an age of viewer fragmentation should lead to higher efficiencies, as audiences will contain less waste. But, in comparison, what an advertiser pays on a cost-per-thousand readers basis for the specialty magazines will be higher than a broad-based magazine.

The development of cable technologies should also let marketers reach consumers in ways other than new programming ventures. Some envision the day when commercials can be targeted to households, as is now done with personalized mass-market magazines. The overall effect of such a development is that marketers can place ads not by show but by audience.

Economic Environment

The economic situation in the United States is undergoing dramatic transformations. Some of the changes are attributable to the recent recession but the most important changes are actually systemic; the developed countries, including the United States, Canada, and Western European nations are "averaging" their economies (and standard of living) with the less developed world. Worldwide technological change is also resulting in more worker productivity and, therefore, less of a need for workers, causing massive social and economic dislocations.

Years ago nearly everyone worked on farms; next, few worked on farms but many labored in manufacturing related activities; subsequently, few were on farms or in manufacturing but many worked at service jobs (that tend to be lower paid than those in manufacturing); finally, many will not work at all because it only takes a finite number of workers (many of whom may be in the "third world") to serve the total consumer population of the globe, as was the case with the transition from an agricultural to a manufacturing and service based economy. In fact, the largest growth segment of "workers" is people who "do nothing," including those who retired, were forced to re-tire early, or those who just cannot find another job. And, of those who do work, many are underemployed.

**What Happened?**     Since 1973, America's basic engine of prosperity, productivity, or output per worker, has grown at one-third the rate of the previous 25 years. When productivity lags, employers struggle to keep their costs in line, and in doing so hold down pay. This has happened especially in the part of the economy that has created most of America's new jobs over the last two decades—the service industries. In man-ufacturing, meanwhile, foreign competition erased millions of jobs in the 1980s, and employers clamped down on pay for the ones they kept.

In other cases, the jobs disappeared, but not the work. Machinery has replaced workers since the Model T, but rarely so dramatically as in recent years. At the GE Fanue Automation plant in Charlottesville, Virginia, state-of-the-art wizardry places electronic components onto circuit boards in half the time of the older technology. General Motors bumped 750 workers in its Livonia, Michigan, plant when it decided that producing bumpers in-house was simply too expensive. Adman Jim Patterson of J. Walter Thompson starts his days at 5 A.M.—like several colleagues at the newly stream-lined agency he is now responsible for the work two executives used to do. Many jobs have been moved to Mexico where wages are a fraction of those in the United States, there are few unions, and environmental laws are poorly enforced. Some of the United State's best known corporations, such as GM and Pillsbury, are conducting business there with operating policies that would result in fines and imprisonment if done here. However, American consumers benefit from those behaviors through lower prices.

**The Future Economic Landscape**     The economic landscape is undergoing more than a slow, cyclical change; instead a fundamental transformation is occurring. The question is: What new post-industrial world will emerge? Because the answers are so important, social and economic forecasters across the United States are busily charting scenarios for the future. Governments and major corporations base long-range plans on such scenarios. While anything can happen, most forecasters adhere to one of four alternatives.

A small minority of forecasters say the remainder of the 1990s will bring a full-scale boom, with much lower unemployment and economic growth averaging 5 percent to 6 percent annually. These optimists base much of their analysis on the U.S. econ-omy's current strengths, particularly low interest and inflation rates, plus indications that consumers and business are turning away from 1980s-style financial management approaches.

The most optimistic futurists predict that the U.S. economy will be lifted to un-precedented heights as the baby-boom generation reaches its peak spending years. Some believe that things improve as each new generation progresses up a predictable curve of earning and spending, until its consumption peaks between ages 45 and 49. The inevitable aging of the 78-million-strong baby boomer crowd will result in a massive increase in consumer demand, producing in a spending wave that lifts the economy to new heights by the end of the century.

Those dramatic changes are also possible because the increase in baby boomer spending power will be joined by a surge of new technologies, which represents an innovation wave that will send ripples throughout the U.S. economy. Past generations produced inventions that prompted major economic growth spurts. The Abraham Lincoln generation had their railroads, the telegraph, and basic steel production. The Henry Ford generation gave us the automobile, the telephone, electrical energy, canned foods, movies, radio, and the phonograph. And Bob Hope's generation contributed the television, jet engine, mainframe computer, radar, and home appliances, such as washers and dryers. Each of these surges came 40 to 50 years apart and another is due now.

Some are convinced that the United States will emerge from the 1990s far stronger than its current global competitors. Many are particularly bearish on Japan's prospects, citing that country's limited natural resources and a rigid social structure. They see enhanced U.S. competitiveness leading to strong export gains, lush corporate profits, especially for capital goods manufacturers, and a robust stock market.

However, most of the forecasters take only a moderately bullish view. According to that outlook, the U.S. economy is likely to settle into a steady annual growth rate of slightly more than 2 percent, which will edge up to slightly under 3 percent in the latter part of the 1990s.

The key reason these forecasters do not think there will be a sprightly expansion is that two crucial elements of economic expansion, increases in population and productivity, have slowed in recent years. The U.S. population overall will probably grow around 1.8 percent annually through the 1990s, with no big increase in the working age population either. So there simply will not be all that many more people entering the labor force to force production of more goods and services. Productivity improvements are unlikely because most businesses have already made many advances in that area. The only change that would significantly boost the work force, an enormous influx of immigrants, is unlikely. Productivity growth would probably have to double to produce GDP increases in the 4 percent range, and that too is improbable.

However, these modestly optimistic forecasters do find some signs of economic vigor, especially in the corporate sector. Widespread restructuring and downsizing may have wreaked havoc with people's lives, but they have produced thousands of far more efficient and flexible enterprises. Corporate profits should be strong because payroll costs are down and interest rates on short-term corporate debt have tumbled, providing a lift to earnings.

Nearly all forecasters who predict solid if unspectacular growth through the 1990s add a caveat or two. Most stress that a series of strong economic shocks, however unlikely, could upset their predictions. Commercial banking is a particular concern. New laws that would shut down institutions with insufficient funds have prompted warnings about a wave of bank closings and another raid on the Treasury, as the Federal Deposit Insurance Corp. pays off hordes of depositors. But the banking business has been reasonably good for some time now, and many balance sheets have improved markedly.

A few seers, particularly those of a conservative political bent, take a dimmer view of the 1990s. They envision a decade of little if any economic growth and rising unemployment, punctuated by intermittent recessions. The cause of their moderately grim vision is the Democrats.

President Clinton's conservative critics have grave doubts about his promise to keep a tight grip on spending in order to halve the budget deficit by the end of his first term. The private sector, especially smaller businesses, would suffer from higher interest rates for capital while sectors crucial to the country's living standards, education, health research, and law enforcement among them, would be starved for funding.

These pessimists are especially concerned about a cascade of costly new regulations that could flow out of Washington and stifle growth. Clinton's health insurance proposals could put 710,000 to 965,000 people out of work because of higher costs to employers, and new mandatory worker-training programs could cost another 175,000 to 350,000 jobs. The Clean Air Act will cost $150 billion per year and lead to the loss of one million jobs when fully implemented. The mandatory family leave package will cost businesses about $10,000 in replacement costs each time a worker departs for a 12-week stint. New costs of an OSHA reform package will be $50 billion a year.

Employers of all sizes are dreading the effects of these new laws, and the stiff penalties for noncompliance. The Better Business Bureau reports that the new Americans with Disabilities Act spawned dozens of dubious enterprises that offer seminars and other services to small businesses struggling to figure out their potential liabilities under the statute.

On top of everything else, there is the possibility of a global trade war. An all-out trade war could have terrible consequences for the U.S. economy and Americans' living standards in the 1990s. Not only would U.S. exports slump and Americans wind up paying more than in the past for imported goods, but the very industries supposedly being protected could lose their edge in the race to remain globally competitive. Those with the impending collapse perspective seem to agree that an economic disaster could be touched off during the next few years by some momentous happening overseas.

A subtext in the gloomy scenarios is the potential for a social upheaval that would thoroughly undermine the American way of life. What most concerns analysts is the widening social and economic gap between rich and poor in the United States. The core of the problem is that the population is becoming increasingly segregated by income level. Inner cities and rural areas are more and more home only to the underclass, while the more affluent concentrate in suburban enclaves. As a result, the poor are shut off from good schools, good jobs, and all sorts of economic opportunities.

Competitive Environment

Competition in the United States and internationally is intense. The United States no longer enjoys competitive advantages in many of the industries it once dominated. In the United States, competition between firms for customers and market share is resulting in major industry shakeouts. Satisfying consumer needs is key; new and innovative products play a critical role.

Even if the U.S. economy completes its long-awaited recovery, there is good reason to believe that the upturn will not cure all that ails it and the U.S. labor market. This outcome is traceable to the most powerful economic force of all, which is global competition. In the 1980s, manufacturing companies bore the brunt of America's competitiveness battles. Confronted with a massive foreign-trade deficit and the attendant loss of market share at home and abroad, the factory sector went through a wrenching restructuring.

Yet as America saw the decline of its smokestack industries, many pointed to the potential of the service sector. Banks, retailers, insurance companies, telecommunications giants, and airlines were viewed as industries of great scope and diversity, that could more than compensate for the steady decline of the factory sector. The hope was for a smooth transition to the postindustrial era. And, initially, those hopes seemed well founded. During the 1980s, service companies generated about 18 million new jobs, accounting for 96 percent of total employment growth.

Unfortunately, something critical was missing in this hiring trend, meaningful increases in worker productivity. While American manufacturers were facing serious market pressures, regulation shielded services from foreign competition. As a result, service companies became burdened with high costs and low productivity, caused in part by loose, undisciplined hiring practices.

But, in the 1990s, the pressures of global competition have significantly impacted the service sector. Government deregulation lowered the barriers to entry in many service industries, including airlines, trucking, cable TV, telecommunications, and finance. Moreover, foreign firms have joined the battle for market share in America's service sector—not through cross-border trade, as was the case in manufacturing, but by strengthening a number of large U.S. service companies through direct investment. Unfortunately, America's service companies were ill-prepared to meet that global competition. As a consequence, the service sector was compelled to embark on a campaign of intense restructuring.

As the pressures of global competition spread from capital-intensive manufacturing companies to people-intensive service organizations, American workers faced a painful reality. A process of restructuring focused on reducing white-collar labor expenses, which is the single largest component of the service sector's high cost structure.

## International Issues

In this section of the analysis format, you need to delineate the international issues relevant to the case firm's business and marketing activities. This outline may include a discussion of products and services from international competitors; changes in international market opportunities, including shifts in demand; international competitive trends that have implications for the case firm; and others.

International market opportunities and competitive issues dominate the discourse about the future of businesses in the United States and, more generally, the American economy. Most firms have greater opportunities in overseas markets than in the United States because those populations are growing and incomes and standards of living are on the rise. How these firms address their international opportunities and threats will shape the future of both the United States and world economies.

One major issue in international business is the degree to which firms marketing abroad should customize versus standardized their offerings. Within the last decade, many companies have moved from an emphasis on customizing items to offering globally standardized products that are advanced, functional, reliable, and low priced. However, multinational companies that concentrated on idiosyncratic consumer preferences have had difficulty, taking advantage of opportunities for growth in multiple countries.

A powerful force drives the world toward a converging commonality, and that force is technology. The result is a new business and marketing reality about global markets and the standardization of many consumer products. With the globalization of markets, strategy selection, with an emphasis on standardization, is becoming much more common. Corporations geared toward this new reality benefit from economies of scale in production, distribution, marketing, and management.

## Strengths and Weaknesses

The next step in the case analysis process is to identify a firm's internal strengths and weaknesses and the strengths and weaknesses of major competitors. These attributes should emerge during the situation analysis. Take all the events you have analyzed and use them to develop a profile of the case firm's strengths and weaknesses. Examine each of the firm's functional areas and identify those that are strong or weak. For example, some companies are weak in marketing, and others are strong in manufacturing.

A full list of firm strengths and weaknesses might include: strengths in product lines; market coverage; manufacturing competence; marketing skills; materials management; R&D; information systems; human resource; product cost or differentiation; financial position; among many others. And, a list of weaknesses might include an obsolete or narrow product line; manufacturing costs; inadequate R&D innovations; poor marketing skills; poor materials management systems; poor customer service, inadequate information systems; loss of brand loyalty; poor financial management; and many others.

Overall, your thinking should cover the strengths and weaknesses in an analysis that includes questioning whether the case firm and its key competitors have the skills and experience to perform the functions necessary to compete in their product or service category. During your analysis, look especially at each of the following areas:

1. Marketing skills
2. Production skills
3. Management skills
4. Financial skills
5. R&D skills

How do the case firm's skills compare to those of competitors? Does the firm in the case have the funds to support an effective marketing program and the resources to successfully execute that plan?

## Nature of Competition

The purpose of this section is to evaluate the present and future nature of competition. The key is to understand how buyers evaluate alternative products or services relative to their needs by considering the critical success factors in a market and whether the case firm is strong in those areas. The firm's probability of success with a particular opportunity depends on whether its business strengths (i.e., distinctive competencies) not only match the key success requirements for operating in a market but also exceed those of its competitors. The best-performing company will be the one that is strong on what customers value and can sustain a differential advantage in that competence over time. Thus, having a competence is not enough; the firm must bring a superior competence in order to attain a sustainable competitive advantage.

## PROBLEMS, OPPORTUNITIES, AND THREATS

Here you prepare a definite analysis of key problems, opportunities, and threats identified from your situation analysis.

### Problems

A major pitfall in defining problems occurs in confusing symptoms with problems. Thus, learning to separate problems from symptoms is an important aspect of the case analysis process. Such things as declining sales, low morale, high turnover, or increasing costs are symptoms that are often incorrectly identified as problems. You can frequently avoid incorrectly defining a symptom as a problem by thinking in terms of causes and effects.

Problems are causes, and symptoms are effects. For example, you might list two problems such as sales are down and distributors are dropping the firm's products. That would not be correct. They are symptoms. The real problems are identified by answering the questions: Why are sales declining? Why are the distributors dropping the firm's products? The key question is "why." What is the cause or causes? Sales may be declining because product quality is low and distributors do not want to carry the product because of the resulting reduction in consumer demand. But, why is product quality down? This quality reduction may be due to inadequate production worker training or a shift in the sourcing of ingredients for the product. But, that in turn, may not yet be the root problem. You still need to ask: Why is worker training inadequate? And, why was the sourcing of product ingredients changed? You need to keep asking why until you have identified the root problem(s) and not just another symptom. Often there will be a number of subissues involved, and it will be necessary to break the problem down into component parts.

Once you have identified more than one major problem in a case, ask yourself whether or not the problems are related enough to be consolidated into one problem. You may not yet have reached the central problem. If, however, you have identified two or more problems that are not directly associated with one another, rank them in the order of their importance and address them in that order. You may find that although the problems do not appear to be closely linked, the solutions are related, where one solution may solve multiple problems.

## Opportunities

One of the major purposes of the situation analysis is to discern opportunities. A marketing opportunity is an attractive arena for marketing action in which the firm can expect to enjoy a competitive advantage. Each opportunity should be classified according to its attractiveness and the probability of success by the firm. However, do not confuse opportunities with taking action. You can recognize an opportunity but not take any action related to it. For example, a large market for a product may exist. This is an opportunity. However, a firm may decide not to compete in that market due to a lack of resources or skills or the existence of strong competition.

It is one thing to identify attractive opportunities in the environment; it is another to have the necessary competencies to succeed in those opportunities. The analysis of firm strengths and weaknesses in the marketing, financial, manufacturing, and organization forms the basis for determining if opportunities can and should be pursued. Of course, not all factors are equally important for succeeding in a business or with a new marketing opportunity.

Ask the following types of questions about potential opportunities: Will pursuing the opportunity expand core business(es)? Exploit new market segments? Widen product range? Extent a differential advantage? Diversify into new growth businesses? Expand into foreign markets? Apply R&D skills in new areas? Enter new related businesses? Vertically integrate forward? Vertically integrate backward? Overcome barriers to entry? Or apply brand name equity in new areas?

## Threats

Some of the developments in the external environment represent threats. A threat is a challenge posed by an unfavorable trend or development in the environment external to the firm that would lead, in the absence of purposeful marketing action, to an erosion of the firm's position. The various identified threats should be classified according to their seriousness and probability of occurrence.

Potential environmental threats to the firm include domestic competition, increased foreign competition, changing consumer tastes, new or substitute products, new forms of competition, changes in demographics, changes in economic trends, government legislation, consumer pressure groups, recession, slower market growth, and many others.

# OBJECTIVES

Before marketing alternatives can be developed, you need to specify your overall objectives. These objectives should be specific and explicitly point to where the firm is expected to be at a particular time in the future, usually in five years. If the objectives are not explicitly stated, there is a need to speculate about them because they will be the standards against which the success or failure of a particular strategy will be evaluated.

Many cases in this book include descriptions of objectives, but you need to critically evaluate those assertions and revise them if necessary. Then, you will use those revised objectives as part of the argument about which marketing alternatives to develop and which alternative to select. A poor analysis either ignores the stated objectives or accepts them at face value.

When constructing or modifying objectives, be sure they are as measurable as possible. Decision makers use them to reflect firm priorities and to determine how to set their own personal and professional goals. Make sure that the objectives are feasible and attainable. Moreover, because strategic marketing is futuristic and no one can predict the future with complete accuracy, objectives should always be adaptable to the changing conditions taking place in the organization, marketplace, and industry.

Objectives are usually classified in terms of sales, market share growth, and/or financial targets, which are symptoms of successful marketing efforts. For example, you may decide that the firm needs to grow sales by 10 percent per year for each of the next five years, with a market share growth of 5 points at the end of that five-year period. At the same time, you expect pre-tax profits to increase by 12 percent annually. Other objectives are also appropriate, including an increase in consumer advertising awareness and brand preference.

In general, there are two types of objectives:

* *Quantifiable behavioral objectives.*   Marketing objectives are invariably behavioral. They are concerned with the immediate response such as an order for a product, a request for information, or a sales call. That behavior is quantifiable. Objectives should be specific about actionable results to accomplish such as the number of orders or number of units sold. Once these levels are set, the plans can be evaluated as to whether the objectives are being met.
* *Unquantifiable nonbehavioral objectives.*   A marketing plan usually contains nonbehavioral objectives for marketing. Nonbehavioral objectives many include product image enhancements or attitudinal changes.

## EVALUATION OF ALTERNATIVE MARKETING PROGRAMS

Marketing alternatives are the strategic options or actions that appear to be viable solutions to the problem(s) that you identified, which also pursue opportunities while avoiding threats. Often, there are two or more seemingly appropriate actions available. Sometimes these are explicitly identified in the case, and usually they are not.

Prepare your list of alternatives in two stages. First, develop an initial list of alternatives that includes all the actions that you feel might be appropriate. After you have generated your initial list, begin refining it by combining similar actions. Use the information that you organized in your situation analysis to help you identify which alternatives to keep and which to eliminate. Ask yourself whether each alternative is feasible given existing financial, productive, managerial, marketing, and other constraints and whether each will produce the desired results.

Be sure that your descriptions of problems, opportunities, and threats and your alternatives are consistent. To help avoid any mistake, be explicit in showing the connections between the situation analysis, the problem(s), opportunities, and threats, and the final set of alternatives. Include an assessment of the advantages and limitations associated with each alternative. A poor analysis has no explicit discussion of the pros and cons of each alternative.

## Marketing Alternatives

"Doing nothing" and "collecting more data" are two alternatives often suggested by those with limited case experience. These are rarely the best actions to take. If you have identified a problem, ignoring it probably will not help. Likewise, recommending a survey, hiring a consultant, or employing some other option associated with gathering more data is rarely a viable solution. In some circumstances, a solution may include further study, but this will normally be part of the implementation plan rather than the solution. If complete information were available, decisions would be easy. This is not the true in most business situations, so it helps to become familiar with making decisions under conditions of uncertainty.

Your alternatives should address as many topic areas as appropriate in terms of strategy-related marketing mix and program decisions (along with marketing objectives and target market selection). These marketing mix and program decisions should cover: product line breath and depth, positioning, and branding issues; price points and discounting; promotion mix in terms of advertising, sales promotion, and personal selling; distribution channels, including intensity and types (wholesalers and retailers).

## Evaluation of Alternatives

A key to effective marketing decision making is to evaluate the financial viability of each marketing alternative. These calculations can be done with the computer program that comes with this casebook. Whatever way the financial analysis is done, it needs to provide sales and expense analyses and forecasts, including estimates of the profit contribution from each marketing alternative.

For the purpose of classroom exercises, most instructors only require that you submit the full sales and financial analysis for the marketing alternative that you choose as your decision. Marketing managers frequently operate in a similar fashion when they evaluate many alternative strategies in spreadsheet models before presenting their management with one or two recommended directions for the brand of product or service they manage.

## DECISION

The last part of the case analysis process involves making a decision based on your analysis of the case and your possible alternative courses of action. Obviously, the quality of your decision is dependent on the thoroughness with which you prepared your analysis. Decisions should be in line with your situation analysis and with the problems, opportunities, and threats you identified. The decision should also follow logically from the objectives you define and your discussion of the merits of each marketing alternative.

Your decision should have two parts. The first part covers your recommended course of action. The second involves issues in the implementation and control of your decision through monitoring its progress and insuring that adjustments are made to the strategy if unforeseen events impact your assumptions and predicted results.

## Recommendations

Your decision and associated recommendations are specific to each case. They address what actions should be taken and why. State the main reasons you believe your recommended course of action is best, but avoid rehashing the other sections of your case analysis. It is important that your recommendation be specific and operational. Such a recommendation often includes several parts such as an increase in spending on promotional efforts and the introduction of a new product.

The single most important factor in most decisions is profitability. Because profits are the principal goal in all commercial organizations, nearly every marketing decision is influenced by monetary considerations, which ultimately affect profits (or expected profits).

Avoid just recommending the course of action that the case firm actually undertook, even if those actions resulted in improved revenues and earnings. The aim of the case analysis is for you to consider all the facts and information relevant to the case firm at the time, generate feasible alternative strategies, choose among those alternatives, and defend your recommendations. Put yourself back in time to the point when the marketing decisions were being made by the firm. Based on information available then, what would you have done?

Avoid recommending a course of action beyond a firm's means. Be realistic. No organization can possibly pursue all the strategies that could potentially benefit it.

Reach a clear decision. You might like to hedge your bets and say "maybe this, maybe that." However, part of the skill of decision making is being forced to make a choice under ambiguous circumstances and then be prepared to defend what you recommend. This does not mean that you do not recognize the limitations of your position or the positive aspects of other positions. It just means that despite all that, you must reach a decision.

The real test for a strategy and plan decision, whether you are in the classroom or in an office, is how reasonable the strategy looks to those who review and evaluate it. Does it appear to be based on sound assumptions? Are the expectations for results realistic? Are the resources needed for the plan available? And, is this the best option for how those resources can be used? Are the mechanisms in place to implement and monitor the plan?

## Implementation and Control

The second part of your decision section should address strategy implementation and control issues. An implementation plan shows that your decision is both possible and practical. The aim is to identify what control systems to use when executing and monitoring your plan. Improper implementation of an excellent plan may doom it to failure, so it is important to follow through with appropriate analysis at this stage.

## IN CLOSING

Remember that case analysis is designed to develop your skills in making well-supported and reasoned marketing decisions. Generally, if your situation analysis is strong, your problems, opportunities, and threats well defined, your objectives well stated, and your alternatives logically determined and supported, you should make a good (and defensible) decision.

## Sources

Baker, Stephen, and Geri Smith. "The Mexican Worker." *Business Week* (April 19, 1993): 84–92.

Bernhardt, Kenneth L., and Thomas C. Kinnear. *Cases in Marketing Management.* 5th. ed. Homewood, IL: Richard D. Irwin, 1991.

Bernstein, Aaron, et al. "What Happened to the American Dream?" *Business Week* (August 19, 1991): 80–85.

"The Computer Industry." *The Economist* (February 27, 1993) (special insert survey).

Cravens, David, and Charles W. Lamb, Jr. *Strategic Marketing Management Cases.* 4th. ed. Homewood, IL: Richard D. Irwin, 1993.

David, Fred R. *Cases in Strategic Management.* 4th ed. New York: Macmillan Publishing Company, 1993.

Fierman, Jaclyn. "What Happened To The Jobs." *Fortune* (July 12, 1993): 40–41.

Fisher, Chisty. "Wooing Boomer's Babies." *Advertising Age* (July 22, 1991): 3, 30.

Hill, Charles W.L., and Gareth R. Jones. *Strategic Management: An Integrated Approach.* 2nd ed. Boston: Houghton Mifflin Company, 1992.

Jain, Subhash C. *Marketing Planning & Strategy.* 4th. ed. Cincinnati: South-Western Publication Company, 1993.

Kim, Bryan Junu. "Step Aside for the 500-Channel Elephant." *Advertising Age* (April 19, 1993): S-3–S-4.

Kotler, Philip. *Marketing Management.* 7th. ed. Upper Saddle River, NJ: Prentice Hall, 1991.

Labich, Kenneth. "Four Possible Futures." *Fortune* (January 25, 1993): 40–48.

Levitt, Theodore. "The Globalization of Markets." *Harvard Business Review* (May–June 1983): 92–102.

Nussbaum, Bruce. "Hot Products." *Business Week* (June 7, 1993): 54–57.

O'Reilly, Brian. "Preparing for Leaner Times." *Fortune* (January 27, 1992): 40–47.

Richman, Louis S. "The Truth About the Rich and Poor." *Fortune* (September 21, 1992): 134–146.

Richman, Louis S. "Bringing Reason to Regulation." *Fortune* (October 19, 1992): 94–96.

Rogers, Michael. "Brave New TV." *TV Guide* (January 23, 1993): 36–30.

Shapio, Joseph P. "Just Fix It." *U.S. News & World Report* (February 22, 1993): 50–56.

Spiers, Joseph. "Let's Get Real About Taxes." *Fortune* (October 19, 1992): 78–81.

Walker, Orville C. Jr., Harper W. Boyd, Jr., and Jean-Claude Larreche. *Marketing Strategy Planning and Implementation.* Homewood, IL: Richard D. Irwin, 1992.

# CHAPTER

# Computer Analysis for Strategic Marketing Management

**M**anagers acquire analytical skills to facilitate their decision making. These skills include the ability to do sound, rigorous business analysis that explicitly integrates marketing plans, market responses, and financial consequences.

Marketing decision models can be developed using most financial spreadsheets or other computer-based decision support tools. Spreadsheets such as *Lotus 1-2-3* or *Excel* are obvious resources and computer programs, such as the one associated with this casebook, represent more advance tools for marketing decision making. Using the computer program that comes with this casebook, you can analyze individual cases and examine relationships between marketing plan alternatives and financial results. That computer program also includes case-related exercises that explore various issues in case analysis.

## MAKING EFFECTIVE MARKETING MANAGEMENT DECISIONS

Managers face three important problems in making more effective marketing decisions: (1) obtaining the information they need from the volume of data available. (2) interpreting that data, and (3) determining what action(s) to take. Even though most marketing managers believe they understand the factors that influence the sales of their product or service, determining an effective course of action in any particular situation is still difficult. There are many variables to consider, and those variables interact to produce multiple results. Therefore, computer analysis helps to develop plans where complex effects are difficult to conceptualize and understand.

Typically, managers try to overcome the uncertainty inherent in marketing decision making by acquiring an extensive, detailed knowledge about their markets and products. This helps shape an intuitive model of how multiple factors influence sales volume and market share. Thus, these managers develop theories about all the details related to their products and competitors and create explanations for how they interact. Eventually, those managers produce marketing strategies and plans for influencing product sales and market share.

A well-designed tool for marketing management decision making requires an integration of market response and financial planning models. Such a system should include strategy and financial planning capabilities, graphics, and the ability to do sensitivity and scenario analysis. Additionally, this system needs database management functions and statistical analysis and forecasting capabilities.

However, decision support tools do not make decisions—that is the role of the manager. Therefore, the response of such a tool to a manager's marketing alternatives is limited to providing the market and financial consequences of each proposed action and not which specific alternative to select. Although the manger has the capability to make a better decision with these tools, experience and intuition still play major roles.

One of the most important contributions that such an analysis system makes is in providing the ability to relate marketing strategies and plan elements, such as advertising expenditures, to market performance. Such relationships are called market responses. They are quantitative representations of interactions between marketing plans and market situations. For example, if a marketing manager seeks to reposition a brand in a highly competitive market, he or she needs to produce estimates of the sales impact, costs, and profit results of this plan. These estimates form the basis for obtaining upper management's approval for the marketing effort.

## THE IMPORTANCE OF QUANTITATIVE AND QUALITATIVE ANALYSIS

Marketing managers frequently have problems utilizing decision support tools to their full potential because their analysis of the situation is often inadequate to define problems or what information is required to make a decision. The first step in a quantitative analysis is a qualitative analysis of the issues in a decision-making situation. This approach to analytical decision making can be summarized in five steps (they are the same areas involved in case analysis, see Table 3.1):

1. Carefully analyze the situation.
2. Define the problems, opportunities, and threats.
3. Develop objectives.
4. Develop marketing alternatives. Input the marketing alternatives into the analysis system to examine plan dynamics and market and financial results. If necessary, do a sensitivity analysis and more scenarios beyond the alternatives originally developed to refine and improve the marketing results.
5. Make the decision about which alternative to propose to upper management based on the analytical process.

## THE BENEFITS OF ANALYTICAL DECISION MAKING

A number of benefits result from this analytical decision-making experience:

1. An increased understanding of the decision situations and analytical process required to make fact-based choices.

**2.** An increased ability to understand the relative importance of multiple market variables and lesser tendency to believe that markets and product results are single factor driven.

**3.** An increased capacity to consider and evaluate alternative marketing programs.

**4.** An increased capacity to analyze alternatives more completely and better understand the likely financial consequences of those marketing efforts.

However, managers only receive these benefits by being personally involved in the analysis. This type of participation is the most crucial factor in appreciating the importance of analytical work in marketing decision making.

## Sources

Applegate, Lynda M., James I. Cash, and Quinn D. Mills. "Information Technology and Tomorrow's Manager." *Harvard Business Review* 66 (November/December 1988) 128–136.

Clark, Darrel G. *Marketing Analysis and Decision Making.* 2nd ed. San Francisco, CA: Scientific Press, 1993.

Goslar, Martin D., and Stephen W. Brown. "Decision Support Systems: Advantages in Consumer Marketing Settings." *Journal of Consumer Marketing* 3 (Summer 1986) 43–50.

Jain, Subhash C. *Marketing Planning & Strategy.* 4th ed Cincinnati: South-Western Publication Company, 1993.

Kotler, Philip. *Marketing Management.* 7th. ed. Upper Saddle River, NJ: Prentice Hall, 1991.

Mayros, Van, and D. Michael Werner. *Marketing Information Systems: Design & Application for Marketers.* Chilton: Radnor, 1987.

McCann, John M. *The Marketing Workbench: Using Computers for Better Performance.* Irwin: Homewood, 1986.

McDonald, William J. "The Use of Knowledge Workers in Marketing Organizations: An Exploratory Study," in *Developments in Marketing Science* Michael Levy, and Dhruv Grewal, eds. (Coral Gables: Academy of Marketing Science, 16, 1993), pp. 533–537.

Walker, Orville C. Jr., Harper W. Boyd, Jr., and Jean-Claude Larreche. *Marketing Strategy: Planning and Implementation.* Homewood, IL: Richard D. Irwin, 1992.

# CHAPTER

# *Financial Analysis for Strategic Marketing Management*

T he first test of any marketing alternative is whether or not it is "reasonable." You must ask yourself if the projected outcome is likely to occur based primarily on historical precedent. If all the strategic, competitive, and resource assumptions look reasonable, you are ready to conduct a financial analysis of the projected returns from the proposed alternative.

This financial analysis of alternatives is a critical aspect of any strategy evaluation. The ultimate goal of all marketing activities is financial, and because companies need returns on the investment of their resources, all such proposed activities must be evaluated for their financial implications. Firms should not invest in a new $5 million marketing information system or in a $35 million advertising program without closely examining the financial implications of such resource allocations. Because a financial justification for a marketing program is "real-world" marketing, it is also an important part of a good case analysis.

Although financial analysis can be complex, it can be simplified by focusing on a particular technique. This text, and the accompanying computer software, emphasizes the *discounted cash flow analysis* approach exclusively. There are other sophisticated and complex approaches, many of which are covered in finance classes, but the discounted cash flow method is both efficacious and efficient in its ability to characterize the relative value of alternatives. Your instructor may prefer another approach and will instruct you about how to use it.

Because financial considerations are ultimately the most important factor in evaluating marketing alternatives, these alternatives must be reduced to a set of numbers or they are of limited value to the decision makers of a firm. However, there are circumstances where the qualitative aspects of marketing objectives, derived from a situation analysis, are also relevant because, for example, the long-term benefits of particular sustained strategies are hard to reliably quantify.

This chapter assumes that you are familiar with introductory financial management concepts. More detailed treatments than the one described here are available in books on corporate finance and capital budgeting.

35

## CASH FLOW ANALYSIS

One of the most important tasks in capital budgeting for marketing is estimating future cash flows for a proposed strategy alternative. However, the final results obtained from these forecasts are really only as good as the accuracy of the initial estimates. A firm invests cash now in the hope of receiving cash returns in greater amounts in the future. Only cash receipts can be reinvested in the firm or paid to stockholders in the form of dividends. Thus, cash, not income, is what is important in evaluating alternatives, and the reason for expressing expected benefits from a project as cash flows rather than as income is that cash is central to all decisions of a firm.

For each marketing proposal created in your case analysis, you need to consider information on expected future cash flows on an after-tax basis. In addition, the information must be developed for incremental changes only, so that you only analyze the difference between the cash flows of the firm with and without the proposed marketing alternative. For example, if a firm contemplates a new product that is likely to compete with existing products, it is not appropriate to express cash flows only in terms of the estimated sales of the new product. There will probably also be some "cannibalization" of existing products, which needs to be included in your cash-flow estimates. The key is to analyze the situation with and without the new marketing proposal. Only incremental cash flows matter.

To illustrate the information needed for approving a proposed marketing effort, consider the following situation. Suppose a marketing manager is asking the company president to support the introduction of a new product. In order to launch the product, that manager needs to spend $11.5 million for special equipment. The manager envisions the product's life to be five years and expects incremental net sales revenue (after cost of goods) to be (in millions):

| Year 1 | Year 2 | Year 3 | Year 4 | Year 5 |
|--------|--------|--------|--------|--------|
| $25.1  | $36.4  | $60.4  | $80.1  | $86.5  |

The cash outflow includes marketing, sales, and various other expenses associated with the new product introduction and management. As with sales, these costs must be estimated on an incremental basis only. In addition to these outflows, the firm will need to pay higher taxes if the new product generates higher profits.

Suppose that on the basis of these considerations the firm estimates the incremental cash outflows to be:

| Year 1 | Year 2 | Year 3 | Year 4 | Year 5 |
|--------|--------|--------|--------|--------|
| $20.6  | $25.4  | $45.1  | $55.5  | $59.8  |

The expected net cash flows from the project are:

| | Initial Cost | Year 1 | Year 2 | Year 3 | Year 4 | Year 5 |
|---|---|---|---|---|---|---|
| Cash inflows | | $25.1 | $36.4 | $60.4 | $80.1 | $86.5 |
| Cash outflows | $11.5 | $20.6 | $25.4 | $45.1 | $55.5 | $59.8 |
| Net cash flows | −$11.5 | $ 4.5 | $11.0 | $15.3 | $24.6 | $26.7 |

Thus, for an initial cash outflow of $11.5, the firm expects to generate net cash flows of $4.5, $11.0, $15.3, $24.6, and $26.7 over the five years. These cash flows represent the kind of relevant information needed to judge the attractiveness of the marketing proposal.

Recognize that the returns on all marketing programs are subject to varying degrees of uncertainty. Assume constant dollars in your analysis. Despite potential problems with some of the data required for the estimates, your proposal must include calculations of the probable outcome if it is to receive upper management consideration.

# EVALUATING EXPECTED PROFITABILITY

To evaluate the cash flow from a marketing proposal, calculate the net present value of the future cash from the investment. This is the discounted cash-flow approach to investment analysis. With this approach, the value of a proposal is the sum of all future cash flows discounted to present value (using a required rate of return) minus the initial investments. A marketing proposal is either accepted or rejected based on the result of this calculation (sometimes versus the calculated values from other marketing proposals).

The minimal acceptance criterion is that an alternative must have a discounted present value of cash inflows that exceeds the present value of cash outflows (with the value of the initial investment removed). The rationale behind the acceptance criterion is that the firm expects to earn a positive, adjusted return on your marketing proposal, and, thus, it expects your proposal to have a net present value greater than zero.

When actually calculating the net present value, you discount expected future payoffs by the rate of return offered for comparable investment alternatives. This rate of return is often referred to as the *discount rate, hurdle rate*, or *opportunity cost of capital*. It is called the opportunity cost because it is the return forgone by investing in your marketing alternative rather than investing in securities or some other investment where both a return rate and risk are already known.

If you assume a required rate of return of 10 percent after taxes, the net present value of the new product marketing proposal discussed previously is:

$$\text{NPV(marketing proposal)} = \text{NPV}(4.5 + 11.0 + 15.3 + 24.6 + 26.7) - 11.5$$
$$= \$44.6$$

Thus, based on the calculation above, you would say that this marketing proposal provides a positive investment return to the firm because its net present value is greater than zero.

Because a marketing manager cannot be *certain* about the competitive environment, the direction of the economy, or the nature of consumer demand, the $44.6 million figure represents the best *forecast* and not a sure thing.

However, the conclusion about whether or not to invest in the new product is dependent on achieving $44.6 million with certainty versus, for example, buying U.S. government securities with a certain rate of return.

Always remember that a *safe dollar is worth more than a risky one.* Many firms will avoid risk when they can even if they sacrifice small increments in return. The concepts of present value and the opportunity cost of capital still make sense for risky investments. But, it is proper to discount the payoff by the rate of return offered by a comparable investment. You need to think of expected payoffs and the expected rates of return on alternative investments. In reality, not all investments are equally risky nor are their outcomes equally likely.

Once you have developed the necessary net present value estimates, you have quantified the attractiveness of your marketing proposal. For the case analyses in this text, you should assume that your proposed marketing alternatives do potentially differ on their risk of investment or on the certainty of their expected outcome but that this is frequently a non-quantifiable issue. In financial terms, therefore, the decision is to either accept or reject each marketing alternative based on projected returns to the firm.

## THE ROLE OF THE CASEBOOK COMPUTER PROGRAM IN FINANCIAL ANALYSIS

The computer program included with this casebook, automatically does all the financial calculations just discussed. It takes the elements of your marketing strategy alternative as sales and expense forecasts and computes cash flows, profitability, and the net present value of your proposal(s). See Appendix B of this text for a complete description of the analysis program.

# C H A P T E R

## Strategic Marketing Management Cases

**6**

# CASE 1
## MTV Networks

A music video is a brief performance on videotape that accompanies a song, featuring the vocalists and musicians of the recording. It is generally meant to embellish the song and present it visually in an unusual way. The major outlet is television, although music videos are available on videocassettes and are shown in nightclubs and theaters. Although music videos became a significant artistic and social phenomenon in the early 1980s, televised music is as old as television itself.

In the late 1970s, European record companies began using videos to promote their artists. These music videos were shown in nightclubs and on television. The resulting sales persuaded United States record companies to use that same promotional vehicle. In 1981 the USA Network, a cable television company, introduced *Night Flight,* a weekend program featuring music videos. In that same year, Warner Amex Satellite Entertainment Company launched MTV as the first 24-hour music video channel.

MTV patterned itself after Top-40 radio, its on-air announcers, called "VJs" (video jockeys), ran contests and promotions and developed playlists that manipulated audience moods. MTV quickly became recognized as an effective way to promote record sales and introduce new artists, such as Cyndi Lauper, Madonna, and Duran Duran.

Although rock still predominates, MTV and the other channels featuring music videos now offer a variety of music to broaden their audiences. In that competitive environment, the videos try to meet the constant demands for originality, humor, and visualization. Many display groundbreaking efforts in style and presentation. The most widely imitated examples are well crafted and stylized, with quick camera cuts timed to the music and dreamlike, fantasy images. Over the years, these music-video styles have influenced the look and pace of television shows, commercials, and even feature films.

Only five years after the launch of MTV, the popularity of music videos began to diminish, and viewer ratings peaked. At the same time, record companies, who were spending heavily on promotional videos, began to question the practice of automatically producing a video to accompany every record album release.

The MTV Networks, which also includes the adult music channel Video Hits One (VH-1) and the kids' channel Nickelodeon, changed hands in 1987. By then, the novelty of rock videos had faded, and revenues slid. The new owner, Viacom International Inc., an entertainment conglomerate, put new management in charge. The channel became innovative again by introducing animated graphics and unusual promotions. It gave away fantasy prizes such as 24 hours with the Rolling Stones and a Caribbean island. It also began programming similar to that offered by the national networks, but with MTV's own special brand of humor and excitement. Today, MTV Networks targets a broad, diverse audience (those 12 through 34 years old) with a combination of music and entertainment.

## VIACOM

Viacom International owns 76 percent of MTV Networks, which includes MTV, VH-1, and Nickelodeon. Together, MTV and Nickelodeon provide unrivaled access to millions of young American television viewers. Viacom is also taking its youthful message around the world, expanding MTV into Europe, Australia, Latin America, and Russia. In 1991, the network announced a joint venture with an Asian satellite company to beam MTV into Hong Kong, China, Korea, and Taiwan. In December, 1992, MTV went back on the air in Japan, a market abandoned in 1991 because it could not get enough airtime.

As of 1992, MTV was bringing its music videos to 210 million television households in 71 countries. Cable News Network (CNN) is available in more than 130 countries, but CNN reaches an audience of fewer than 100 million households. While CNN is recording annual revenue gains of 16 percent to 18 percent, MTV's revenue is growing at an even faster rate of 18 percent to 22 percent.

Viacom's Nickelodeon channel, too, plans to go international. This will expand Viacom's ability to distribute films and television programs from its library, including new cartoons and kids' shows.

Viacom is developing plans to create three channels each for MTV and Nickelodeon that will cater to segments of their current audiences. MTV may offer separate channels for rap-music and heavy-metal fans, for example, while Nick may have one channel for children and another for teenagers. Overseas, Viacom is trying to consolidate MTV's growth and establish the groundwork for Nickelodeon. In 1991, it bought the 50 percent of MTV Europe did not own.

To bring Nick into Europe, Viacom is creating partnerships with European media companies. For example, the network coproduces one of its cartoons, *Doug,* with France's Canal Plus, and is working on original programming in various languages for several of its overseas markets.

In the United States, Viacom is spending heavily to produce more of the nontraditional programming that gives MTV and Nickelodeon their distinctive images. It invested $40 million in four new animated shows for Nick. Another of the network's offerings is *Clarissa Explains It All,* a sitcom about being a 13-year-old girl. In the evening, Nickelodeon becomes Nick at Nite when it reruns classic television shows such as *Get Smart* and *Mr. Ed.*

While Viacom had consistent increases in sales but erratic net income during the last several years (see Figures 6.1–1 and 6.1–2), MTV Networks has emerged as the firm's outstanding performer. In 1991, MTV Networks accounted for $411 million of Viacom's revenues and $162 million of its cash flow and was growing more than 20 percent a year. More than 65 percent of 1991 revenues came from advertisers such as Procter & Gamble, Nike, and Pepsi and the rest from subscriber fees.

## VIACOM'S AGGRESSIVE MARKETING EFFORT

Viacom's marketing is highly segmented in comparison with the national television networks. NBC, CBS, and ABC are mass-consumption vehicles; a show for one can run on any of the others. In contrast, MTV Networks has a certain style, aestheticism, and point of view. It stresses building each of the three networks as brands rather than boosting an individual performer or program.

Because its viewers dominate the record-buying audience, MTV has been able to negotiate exclusivity contracts, at minimal cost, that give it first option to play most major record companies' videos. With two music channels, MTV Networks can air only a

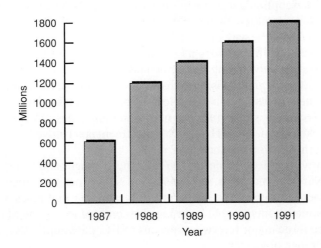

**FIGURE 6.1–1** Viacom International Sales

*Source: Viacom International 1991 Annual Report.*

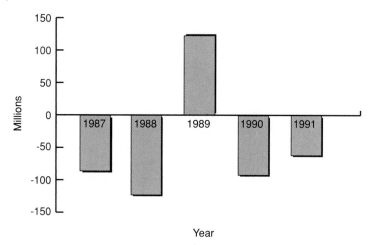

**FIGURE 6.1–2** Viacom International Net Income

*Source: Viacom International 1991 Annual Report.*

fraction of them. New digital technology will allow it to target its music programming to specialized target audiences.

## MTV'S COMPETITIVE ADVANTAGE

So, why do advertisers flock to cable's 24-hour rock video channel? It is certainly not because of the number of viewers. MTV's household ratings, the average percentage of subscribers who tune in have been flat for several years. Why does Levi Strauss advertise? Why does Coca-Cola sponsor a tour of the Club MTV dancers? The answer is that MTV's viewers are young, affluent, and loyal. MTV has persuaded advertisers that MTV's brand loyalty will benefit them.

MTV's niche lies in its youthful and innovative image. It was the first major television channel to combine stereophonic sound with its music visuals by using advanced techniques. The sound was transmitted through the cable subscriber's stereo tuner, providing a whole new concept of the way to listen to music.

With its market growing, MTV provides its service to 50 percent of all youths. This, in turn, attracts substantial advertising accounts, making MTV one of the most profitable cable services in American television history. To keep a hold on its market share, MTV relies on the help of its Creative Services Department. The department consists of dedicated professionals supporting the marketing and sales efforts of all three networks (MTV, Nickelodeon, and VH-1). The department is sensitive to the demographics and images of the networks it serves.

The mission of Creative Services' projects is to take these images and transform them into newsletters, advertising materials, stationery, and sales brochures. Spending has been increased to produce more of the irreverent programming that gives MTV and Nickelodeon their distinctive images. MTV's image was created to narrow MTV's audience as opposed to the three major television stations (NBC, CBS, and ABC) that program to attract a wide range of viewers.

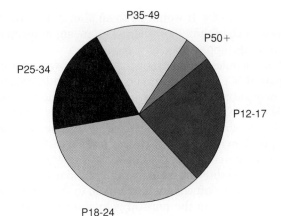

P35-49

P50+

P25-34

P12-17

P18-24

**FIGURE 6.1–3** MTV's Audience Age Distribution

*Source:* Estimated from various sources.

However, MTV is hardly at the top of the ratings and will never be so because of its specialized programming directed at a narrow audience. It has a smaller audience than CNN, ESPN, HBO, and many other channels. At the same time, it must constantly change its image in order not to grow old with its current audience. While MTV has captured the audience of the 18 through 34 year old (see Figure 6.1–3), once the audience ages, it hopefully moves on to VH-1. Also, changes in the musical tastes of society must always be taken into consideration. In 1985, Viacom introduced VH-1 for the audience ranging in age from 25 through 49. It decided that as the MTV viewers matured, they would be drawn to VH-1 with its video clips of adult contemporary, soft rock, and classic oldies. The advent of VH-1 succeeded in making the market more difficult for others to enter.

In reality, MTV serves three major target groups, each difficult to reach, each with tremendous spending power: teens spend $80 billion each year; college students spend $30 billion; and young adults (those age 18 to 34) spend $700 billion. Based on ratings, the MTV audience is 79 percent age 12 through 34 (U.S. population 43 percent), 53 percent is age 18 through 34 (U.S. population 33 percent), and 74 percent is over age 18 (U.S. population 90 percent).

MTV is not alone anymore; and the competition is very active. Some saw the creation of The Country Music Television Channel (CMT) and The Nashville Network (TNN) almost simultaneously in 1983 as a threat to MTV. CMT grew from a small station with little more than 20 videos and a small but faithful viewing audience to a major 24-hour cable presence. TNN has grown to more than 56 million cable television households. Through a series of moves, TNN acquired CMT with the ambition to do with country music what MTV did with pop and rock. The audience for country music stations has grown significantly. In just the last few years the number of country radio stations has almost doubled. The time is right for TNN because it's the nation's 76 million baby boomers who enjoy country music.

## A NEW DIRECTION

Although the halo effect and an audience that is hard to reach elsewhere has lured a blue-chip roster of advertisers to MTV, apparently that is not enough anymore. Late in

1989, MTV announced a change for the 1990s. It would go to an almost all-show format. This is a significant switch from much of the 1980s when MTV meant nonstop music videos, broken up only by the periodic appearance of video jockeys.

Evidence of MTV's expansion includes a game show, a dance show, and a pop-culture news program. This is all part of MTV's effort to act more like a traditional television network and, ultimately, boost ratings. The strategy is to create shows around appealing personalities and get viewers to stay tuned longer. MTV viewers, inveterate channel-flippers, often seek out the channel as a second choice. When they're bored, they zap over to watch MTV. The problem is that they zap away just as readily. As a result, the channel draws an average 0.6 percent (300,000) of its 50.4 million U.S. subscribers at any given time, which is a so-so showing even by cable standards.

In 1993, MTV plans to launch two spin-off channels to appeal to the varying musical tastes of its viewers. It has not settled on the musical genres for each channel, which will be called MTV 2 and MTV 3. Still, the network wants to be ready for the day when digital compression and fiber-optic technology vastly expand the number of cable channels.

Lest it lose its cutting-edge style, MTV is also undergoing a casting and programming change. It retired its thirty-something veejays in favor of fresh faces, and it introduced new programs that tackle issues like racism and the environment. MTV is now trying to cover issues that are of more importance than just music. However, MTV remembers why it became popular in the United States and with millions abroad; 85 percent of its airtime is still devoted to music.

The new MTV is not just about music anymore; it's about all the issues associated with pop culture. MTV has become more of a full service network for young adults rather that a 24-hour music video station. However, MTV executives are quick to point out that the 4-minute rock video is still the heart of their programming. The new half-hour vidcoms, for instance, feature three rock videos, sandwiched between comedic bits. Is there danger in such a strategy? Does MTV have to be careful not to become too much like broadcast television? Some argue that MTV's appeal comes from being defined as not normal television but as something else.

All this work should spur growth and revenue. Clever marketing of the MTV brand will play a major part. But, MTV's image is about being outrageous, on the edge. The question now is whether it can mimic traditional television and preserve that edge with it viewers. Advise MTV about what marketing strategy to pursue.

## Sources

Duffy, Susan. "Will A little Less Rock Get MTV Rolling Faster?" *Business Week* (April 30, 1990): 62–6.

Harris, Kathryn. "Mind Over Rock Videos." *Forbes* (January 21, 1991): 49–51.

Lander, Mark. "I Want My MTV—Stock." *Business Week* (May 18, 1992): 55.

Lander, Mark, and Geoffrey Smith. "The MTV Tycoon." *Business Week* (September 21, 1992): 56–62.

Newcomb, Peter. "Music Video Wars." *Forbes* (March 4, 1991): 68–70.

Schifrin, Matthew. "I Can't Even Remember the Old Star's Name." *Forbes* (March 16, 1992): 44–5.

*The Software Toolworks Multimedia Encyclopedia.* Danbury, CT: Grolier Electronic Publishing, 1992.

*Viacom International 1991 Annual Report.*

Welsh, Tricia. "America's Hottest Export: Pop Culture." *Fortune* (December 31, 1990): 50–60.

---

# CASE 2
## *MicroProse, Inc.*

Some consider the current crop of video and computer games the precursor to a new entertainment medium where the line between illusion and reality is blurred and where movies, games, and other forms of entertainment such as television merge into a virtual world. The signs of this revolution are all around us. A vision of how it will develop is available to those who follow the progress of computer technology, software innovations, and the evolution of personal computer (PC) games.

However, this revolution is still in its beginning stages. The PC is only a little more than a decade old. PC-based computer games are just beginning to appear life-like and reality oriented. Currently, the media that will eventually merge hold separate turfs which are aggressively protected. Mass-market games such as those from Nintendo and Atari are popular but rely on the weak computing power of cheap home-oriented control units. Some games are available over online services, but those offerings are crippled by slow telephone transmission rates and poor program designs.

The real power for running games lies in PCs. Their processing speed, storage capacity, and graphics make them the clear winner in the current game delivery competition. However, there is a real cost issue. Most PC games require a state-of-the-art machine (with many accessories) to perform at their maximum. That means a $2,500 to $3,000 machine to play a $50 game.

Nevertheless, the PC game makers deserve credit for constantly pushing the game frontier. During the last 10 years, small entrepreneurial companies contributed to the birth of an entire industry, complete with magazines, clubs, and conventions. And, for the PC, game playing is near the top of PC uses.

One pioneer in the PC games industry has been MicroProse, Inc. Over the last dozen years, this firm produced some of the most innovative and ground-breaking games available on the market. However, as the industry changes, MicroProse faces challenges, particularly those coming from new technologies and increased competition. The firm has never really made any money, and, recently, it had to make a deal with a competitor to obtain cash for operations. During the next few years, MicroProse will have to address its current problems and develop plans for the future that will determine if it will survive.

## VIDEO AND COMPUTER GAMES

Video games (those played on a television or in an arcade) and computer games (those played on a PC) are a contest between a player and a program on a machine equipped with a screen and a joystick or buttons that control the game's action. The machine may be designed to play one game, as are those in video game arcades, or many games, as with game consoles or home PCs.

Many of the games played on PCs are more or less identical to those in video arcades. Increasingly, however, PC games are more sophisticated, more difficult, and no longer dependent on elapsed time (as are arcade games); a few such games go on for many hours. Graphics have improved to the point where they almost resemble movies rather than rough, jagged video screens of past games. Some of the newest games generate their graphics through CD-ROMs. Many include complicated sounds, music, and video sequences. A sophisticated game has the potential for offering an almost limitless array of exotic worlds and fantastic situations. The player is the game's protagonist, the persona who must work his or her way through a web of possible actions, interact with the game's reactions, and win through a combination of dexterity and strategy.

## TYPES OF PC GAMES

For the PC, there are seven major classes of games. Each class represents a distinctive playing mode that places specific demands on the player and responds with a specific pattern of play. *Adventure games* involve finding things, roaming around, and solving clues and puzzles. In *role-playing games* the player assumes the role of a character in the plot. Usually, the player sees the action thorough the eyes of the person he or she portrays. *Simulation games* may be the most popular type of PC game. They tend to be action-oriented games of skill and strategy where the player is flying a plane, driving a race car, or piloting a helicopter. The emphasis is on combat and destruction, with the consequence of failure being death. The most highly rated such game is *X-Wing* from LucasArts. It is an excellent *Star Wars* simulation where players pilot rebel fighters against the Empire. The newly released *Rebel Assault* is by far the best simulation on the market. It sold out at CompUSA in two days. *Strategy games* are much more methodical and less action oriented than simulations. In such a game, a player must develop a plan and execute it systematically to accumulate enough successes to win the game. It takes a dedicated player to enjoy a game that may take days to finish. Currently, the second most highly rated such game is *Dune II* from Virgin. *Dune II* is patterned after the movie of the same name. *War games* involve strategy-oriented plots where the game player manipulates armies and battle fields. These games recreate historical situations or present the player with new scenarios. *Action games* tend to be arcade-like. Players are either shooting or running or dying during the process of trying to defeat an enemy. Some of these games are not violent, but the premise of the majority is kill or be killed. *Sports games* are, as might be expected, games that simulate sporting activities. The most highly rated such game is a golf simulation; others include football, baseball, and tennis.

## THE PC GAMES INDUSTRY

A recent directory of PC game firms, from a magazine dedicated to this type of entertainment, listed 50 companies involved in software development and marketing and online services. While that sounds like a lot, only a few are dominant players in the industry. Because most are privately held, information about sales and profits or market share are unavailable. Only a few firms appear repeatedly in the list of top 100 games as identified by *Computer Gaming World* in its readers poll. LucasArts excels in adventure games and simulation games; ElectronicArts at adventure games, simulation games, strategy games, and sports games; Spectrum HoloByte at simulation games and action games; Origin at role playing games and action games; and, MicroProse at simulation games, adventure games, and strategy games.

Individual games become popular because of plots, graphics, and playability. Games are advertised in magazines only because the sales volume involved is too specialized and small to justify any other medium. In-store displays and packaging play an important role in sales as do game reviews in the gaming magazines. Game producers must continually come out with new titles and, to a lesser extent, upgrades of existing games. The PC technology used to play the games is moving very quickly. Only games that make use of the power of new computer models can expect to do well.

## MICROPROSE

MicroProse develops, publishes, and markets entertainment software for use on PCs such as the IBM and compatibles, the Commodore Amiga, Atari ST, and Apple Macintosh, as well as home videogame systems, including Nintendo and Sega. The MicroProse team includes over 100 dedicated professionals. From its start, MicroProse became known for its high-quality simulation software targeted at a sophisticated adult audience.

MicroProse was established in 1982 by Bill Stealey and Sid Meier. After its inception as the moonlighting venture of two entrepreneurs, MicroProse catapulted to the top of the entertainment software industry (Fig. 6.2–1). Today, MicroProse designs and markets a full line of entertainment software, including such hits as *F-15 Strike Eagle, Silent Service, Gunship, Airborne Ranger*, and *Pirates!* The MicroProse name is synonymous with sophistication, quality, realism, detail, and playability. Its award-winning products are available nationally and internationally through distributors, retailers, and mass merchandisers.

MicroProse is unique in the entertainment software industry, using primarily an in-house software development staff. Development depends on a team approach with professional game designers, programmers, sound engineers, and screen graphics artists working on specific projects. Producing a new title, *Gunship 2000,* for example, can take as long as eight man-years over a three-year period for initial development and

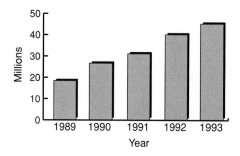

FIGURE 6.2–1 MicroProse Revenues

*Source: MicroProse, Inc. 1993 Annual Report.*

conversion to various computer systems, representing a multimillion dollar development and marketing investment.

In 1986, MicroProse established a U.K. subsidiary, MicroProse Software, Ltd., to manufacture and market its products throughout Europe. MicroProse U.K. has grown rapidly and now employs more than 75 people. The U.K. subsidiary was recently named "Software House of the Year." MicroProse also opened offices in Paris and Frankfurt, with additional operations planned for Scandinavia in the near future. MicroProse K.K. operates in Japan through its offices in Tokyo. Six other U.S. firms, noting the success of MicroProse's marketing strategy, joined the team and signed joint ventures to market their products overseas.

MicroProse's best-selling products include: *F-15 Strike Eagle,* with more than 500,000 computer pilots enjoying this in-depth simulation of the F-15 Eagle jet fighter plane; *Silent Service,* an international award-winning simulation of World War II submarine warfare in the Pacific, which sold more than 300,000 copies, and *Gunship*, a simulation of the U.S. Army's AH-64A attack helicopter.

The firm's marketing efforts are oriented toward print advertising in game magazines and promotional materials in their product packaging. The appendix to this case summarizes the product line. You will also find examples of MicroProse's advertising at the end of this case.

## OPERATING PROBLEMS AT MICROPROSE

During 1993, MicroProse experienced a significant loss from operations, primarily as a result of expansion into products out of its core niche. These products did not meet sales expectations, and had higher costs for manufacturing and development, and higher operating expense levels. Due to these losses and MicroProse's sizable investment in software development costs, it experienced a significant cash drain.

In an effort to improve operations and liquidity, management implemented several strategic initiatives. In 1993, it restructured operations. In particular, MicroProse decided to focus on its core PC entertainment market of simulation and strategy games. It reduced development and manufacturing costs by including such things as an emphasis on restricting the number of disks in future PC products and designing PC products that did not require the reconfiguration of user systems. In connection with this restructuring, it terminated 10 percent of its workforce at a savings of approximately $400,000. Management believed these steps would reduce future operating expenses and software development expenditures by approximately $2.5 million on an annual basis.

Also in 1993, in contemplation of a subsequent merger, MicroProse entered into a purchase agreement with Spectrum HoloByte, Inc. Under the terms of the agreement, MicroProse received $10 million and issued a 7.5 percent note.

The note is due in 1998, but the agreement contains provisions for the acceleration of maturity under certain circumstances, including a material adverse change in MicroProse's financial position. MicroProse's management believes that a merger with Spectrum will occur, and that Spectrum's default rights will terminate.

MicroProse's net revenues (Fig. 6.2–2) are derived from the sales of entertainment software games, licenses of MicroProse products and, in 1992 and 1993, shipments of videogame products. MicroProse's international market continues to account for a significant amount of company sales.

Revenues in 1993 increased from 1992 primarily as a result of increased sales of existing titles converted to additional hardware platforms and increased sales of products released in prior fiscal years. These increases were, however, partially offset by a year to year decline in revenue from new product introductions resulting from a delay in the release of new products and lower than anticipated sales of certain products.

Computer software product revenues in 1993, which represented 86.9 percent of net revenues, increased to $40.4 million from $37.6 million. Computer software revenues in Europe remained the same with most of the increase in computer software revenues coming from North America. Videogame product revenues, which represented 7.7 percent of net revenues, increased to $3.6 million from $1.3 million. Licensing revenues remained the same at $2.5 million and represented 5.4 percent of net revenues.

In 1993, MicroProse derived 58 percent of net revenues from North America, 37 percent from Europe, and 5 percent from Japan, as compared with 56 percent, 41 percent, and 3 percent, respectively, for 1992, and 53 percent, 43 percent, and 4 percent respectively, for 1991.

An increase in marketing and sales expenses from fiscal 1992 to 1993 was primarily the result of increased sales promotion and advertising associated with the number of new titles in development and expenses related to those products that had delayed release. MicroProse also increased expenses related to its initial launch into the 16-bit videogame business as well as two additional new areas of the PC entertainment market—animated graphics adventure and fantasy role-playing.

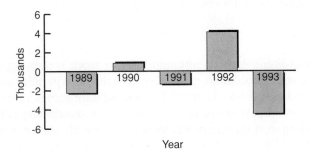

**FIGURE 6.2–2** MicroProse Net Income

*Source: MicroProse, Inc. 1993 Annual Report.*

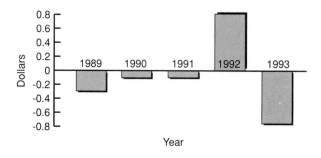

**FIGURE 6.2–3** MicroProse Earnings per Share

*Source: MicroProse, Inc. 1993 Annual Report.*

A decrease in operating income from 1992 to 1993 was due to higher cost of sales and operating expenses as well as delays in releases of new products and lower than anticipated sales of certain products, as discussed previously. MicroProse's income from continuing operations declined from fiscal 1992 to 1993 (Fig. 6.2–3).

## A FRESH START

Armed with new funding, freshly reorganized, and with a full stock of recent and impending releases, MicroProse looks poised to make quite a splash in 1994 (especially in the submarine simulation arena where ElectronicArts, Dynamix, and MicroProse will all be competing head-to-head). With *The Legacy, Pirates Gold!, Railroad Tycoon Deluxe*, and *Return of the Phantom* out of the way, efforts will be concentrated on *Fields of Glory*, a Napoleonic war game out of the U.K. office; *Bloodnet*, a fascinating, sci-fi noire role-playing game, which takes place out in cyberspace (a world where game playing occurs) and features vampires, some incredibly beautiful graphic artwork, and a sophisticated storyline; *Dragon Sphere,* an adventure game using Micro Prose's very effective adventuring interface and focused on a "medievalistic" fantasy world; *Master of Orion*, a complex stellar resource management and political role-playing game that may invite favorable comparison with some of the best strategy gaming work MPS has done in the recent past; *Starlord,* which looks to be the computerization of a long-standing pen-and-paper role-playing game by Mike Singleton; Sid Meier's upcoming *Civil War* game, of course; *Football,* a simulation to compete for the stakes raised by Dynamix' successful efforts; and finally, and perhaps most fascinatingly, *SubWars 2050,* a deep, highly developed, futuristic submarine tactical/strategic simulation that could combine the joys of games such as *Silent Service II* and *Red Storm Rising* in the framework of cutting-edge graphics, simulation, and sound technology.

## CONSUMERS

PC games are primarily an at-home activity, although play at work is also popular (Table 6.2–1). In fact, next to word processing, game playing is the most popular use of PCs at home. Table 6.2–2 shows that those who own a PC and use it for games have very distinctive demographics. Generally, they are male, middle-aged, married, upper income, and parents with children over the age of six. Most likely, the children are play-

| TABLE 6.2–1   Uses of Personal Computers: At Home and At Work (respondents are all adults) | | | |
| --- | --- | --- | --- |
| For which of the following purposes personally use a computer: | At home or work (%) | Own at home (%) | Use at work (%) |
| Accounting | 8.8 | 4.4 | 5.7 |
| Business analysis/forecasting | 4.5 | 1.4 | 3.4 |
| Computer games | 8.1 | 7.4 | 1.1 |
| Desktop publishing | 3.8 | 2.2 | 2.2 |
| Education | 6.3 | 4.8 | 2.0 |
| Filing/data base management | 8.3 | 3.5 | 6.0 |
| Graphics/presentation | 4.5 | 1.9 | 3.1 |
| Personal networking/electronic mail | 2.2 | 0.7 | 1.7 |
| Programming | 4.8 | 3.1 | 2.6 |
| Online information retrieval | 3.9 | 1.0 | 3.2 |
| Word processing | 14.3 | 8.8 | 9.2 |

*Source:* Simmons Market Research Bureau, Inc., 1991.

ing the games, but the themes and content of a larger number of PC games are clearly too sophisticated for children. Most 8-year-olds, for example, could never understand or play many of the strategy games. Unofficial estimates are that better than half of the PC games market is based on adult players and 90 percent or more of the time adults are the game buyers.

## THE EVOLUTION OF COMPETITION

The PC game industry is unique in that many of its most formidable competition is just on the horizon. While other game makers have always been a threat to a firm such as MicroProse, online networks and cable-related products that do not require a PC are probably the greatest long-term concern.

However, the most immediate threat to game makers are partnerships between game making companies and movie industry firms. LucasArts is a prime example. Because the latter firm owns all the rights to the *Star Wars* films, it is able to create PC games that have stunning visual effects and highly popular plots. But, firms such as LucasArts are also master game producers for original titles not based on movies. The special effects and other related cinematic skills of the movie industry people are emerging as a formidable force in PC games.

In 1993, LucasArts released *Indiana Jones and the Fate of Atlantis,* not as a movie but as a CD-ROM title. The *disc,* with 40 computer characters, numerous alternative outcomes, crisp sound, and more than 8,000 spoken lines, allowed the player to change the story with every move. Technicians at the firm also rendered the three-dimensional intergalactic thugs and pockmarked asteroids of the *Star Wars*-based game *Rebel Assault.* Lucas is not alone.

The game market totaled an estimated $7 billion in 1993, far exceeding the esti-

**TABLE 6.2–2 Personal Computer: Own, Games Usage, and Joystick/Paddles**
(respondents are all adults)

| | Own home personal computer (%) | Index | Use for games (%) | Index | Own joystick/ paddles (%) | Index |
|---|---|---|---|---|---|---|
| Total | 21.4 | 100 | 7.4 | 100 | 4.9 | 100 |
| *Gender* | | | | | | |
| Male | 22.7 | 106 | 7.9 | 102 | 5.4 | 109 |
| Female | 20.2 | 94 | 6.9 | 94 | 4.5 | 92 |
| *Age* | | | | | | |
| 18–24 | 19.7 | 92 | 7.4 | 101 | 4.5 | 92 |
| 25–34 | 21.8 | 102 | 7.0 | 95 | 4.2 | 85 |
| 35–44 | 28.9 | 135 | 12.8 | 173 | 9.0 | 183 |
| 45–54 | 24.3 | 113 | 8.5 | 115 | 6.5 | 131 |
| 55–64 | 19.6 | 92 | 4.7 | 64 | 3.0 | 60 |
| 65 and older | 11.5 | 54 | 1.8 | 25 | 1.3 | 25 |
| *Marital Status* | | | | | | |
| Single | 20.9 | 97 | 6.3 | 85 | 3.7 | 75 |
| Married | 24.1 | 113 | 9.1 | 124 | 6.3 | 127 |
| Divorced, etc. | 13.4 | 62 | 3.0 | 41 | 2.1 | 43 |
| Parents | 26.7 | 125 | 11.9 | 161 | 8.4 | 170 |
| *Region* | | | | | | |
| Northeast | 20.7 | 97 | 8.2 | 111 | 5.5 | 111 |
| Midwest | 22.1 | 103 | 8.1 | 109 | 5.8 | 118 |
| South | 20.1 | 94 | 6.0 | 81 | 4.0 | 80 |
| West | 23.5 | 110 | 8.1 | 110 | 5.0 | 101 |
| *Income* | | | | | | |
| $75+ | 32.5 | 152 | 13.2 | 179 | 8.1 | 164 |
| $60+ | 30.7 | 143 | 12.8 | 173 | 7.8 | 158 |
| $50+ | 30.3 | 141 | 12.3 | 167 | 7.4 | 149 |
| $40+ | 29.6 | 138 | 12.0 | 162 | 7.2 | 145 |
| $30+ | 27.8 | 130 | 10.8 | 147 | 6.7 | 136 |
| $30–$39 | 22.7 | 106 | 7.7 | 104 | 5.4 | 109 |
| $20–$29 | 17.1 | 80 | 4.4 | 59 | 3.4 | 69 |
| $10–$19 | 10.8 | 51 | 2.5 | 33 | 2.3 | 47 |
| Less than $10 | 11.3 | 53 | 1.7 | 23 | 2.1 | 43 |
| *Presence of children* | | | | | | |
| Under 2 years | 20.6 | 96 | 7.7 | 105 | 4.3 | 88 |
| 2–5 | 22.9 | 107 | 8.0 | 108 | 4.9 | 98 |
| 6–11 | 26.6 | 124 | 12.0 | 162 | 9.0 | 182 |
| 12–17 | 29.6 | 138 | 13.9 | 188 | 10.4 | 210 |

Note: Index values above are computed by dividing the proportion in a particular grouping by their proportion of the population. For example, if an age group has 20.2% of the products users and represents 18.3% of the population, the index value for the grouping is 110. Index values over 100 signify above average usage and index values below 100 signify below average usage. However, values over 110 or under 90 are the most significant.

*Source:* Simmons Market Research Bureau, Inc., 1991.

mated $5.3 billion Americans spent on movie tickets. A blockbuster video game can earn more than $500 million, a figure only blockbuster movies can match. Recently, the movie industry also made the disturbing discovery that it is losing some of its best customers in the 13- to 22-year-old age group to video games and computer games.

Those kinds of numbers have opened a lot of eyes in the movie industry. Producers, directors, actors, agents, writers, and cinematographers are scrambling to jump on the bandwagon. They hope to use their skills and savvy to stretch the creative boundaries of computer games and bring a new sophistication to interactive entertainment.

The movie industry's arrival promises to change the very nature of the game market, transforming high-end games from the special province of a small coterie of devoted fans to the mass-market products for the middle class. However, right now there is a big gap between what makes a good game and what makes a good movie.

## THE FUTURE

Before the next computer revolution can occur, Hollywood writers and performers must transfer their storytelling and character-building talents to the new medium. Traditionally, computer games have focused on a few themes, such as fantasy worlds, flight simulators, and sports, which appeal to a relatively narrow audience. However, Hollywood storytellers hope to draw new customers by expanding the range of topics to include the whole range of human experience.

Hollywood must also learn the complicated issues associated with games programming and player psychology. Computer games are much more than movies on computers. They are interactive; they include puzzles and challenges; and they must be interesting enough to have replay value. Also, game players are not movie goers sitting at their computers. Generally, movie attendance is a social experience—how many people go to the movies alone? But, computer game play, at least now, is more of an individual experience.

Regardless of how the newly emerging competitors position themselves in the game market, MicroProse faces some real challenges. Although the firm remains a key competitor in the PC games arena, recent events have not been favorable. And, the future appears to hold even greater threats (and opportunities). MicroProse has several entries on the list of all-time favorite PC games from *Computer Gaming World,* all produced in the late 1980s and early 1990s. However, in November 1993, MicroProse had just nine games on the *Computer Gaming World* top 100 list of games, with two as high as the number eleven position. All this implies that MicroProse may need a new marketing strategy, including a better understanding of the competition, the problems, opportunities and threats facing the firm, and, of course, a plan to survive and prosper in a rapidly changing gaming market.

The real questions for firms in this category revolve around marketing issues: how to develop and keep a differential advantage in a highly competitive and dynamic market, while maintaining sales growth and, above all, profitability. What marketing strategy would you recommend? What specific price, distribution, promotion, and product elements would you propose and why? How would you deal with the growth competition in the PC game market?

## Sources

"Broadening the Spectrum." *Computer Gaming World* (September 1993): 36–37.

"Computer Gaming World Hall of Fame." *Computer Gaming World* (November 1993).

Daly, James. "The Hollywood Connection." *Electronic Entertainment* (February 1994): 41–51.

*MicroProse, Inc. 1993 Annual Report.*

MicroProse, Inc. promotional materials and PR releases.

Simmons Market Research Bureau, Inc. 1991.

*The Software Toolworks Multimedia Encyclopedia.* Danbury, CT: Grolier Electronic Publishing, 1992.

"Top 100 Games." *Computer Gaming World* (November 1993).

APPENDIX A: **MICROPROSE 1993 PC PRODUCT LINE**
(in its own words)

## F-15 STRIKE EAGLE III (FIG. 6.2–4)

Squeeze into the cockpit of the *F-15 Strike Eagle III* and prepare yourself for the most thrilling flight simulator you'll ever pilot! Because MPS Labs has filled this F-15 with more spectacular features than ever before!

You'll experience a revolutionary new visual system! Incredible new photorealistic starting and ending screens! Amazing two-player capabilities! And modern high-tech opponents as ruthless as those faced by real F-15 pilots! It's nothing short of striking!

- Enhanced gameplay for experienced pilots, as well as easy-to-learn qualities for beginners!
- Unprecedented visual system for breathtaking air combat action!
- All-new war theaters!

## REX NEBULAR

### and the Cosmic Gender Bender

A priceless vase is lost on a distant planet that doesn't exist! An irate colonel wants the vase back! And only one man is experienced enough—skilled enough—and foolish enough to retrieve it! *Rex Nebular*—interstellar adventurer and bungling bachelor extraordinaire!

In the most far-out animated graphic adventure ever to land on store shelves, *Rex*

FIGURE 6.2–4 *F-15 Strike Eagle III* advertisement

*Nebular* will have you journeying through strange locations to unravel the myriad of puzzles and mysteries on Terra Androgena—a planet populated entirely by bizarre alien women!

- A multitude of puzzles to unlock!
- Unprecedented, state-of-the-art graphics to astound even the most experienced animated graphic adventure players!
- All-new MADS (MicroProse Adventure Development System) interface lets players control specific actions of Rex Nebular!

# TASK FORCE 1942 (FIG. 6.2–5)

## Surface Naval Action in the South Pacific

The first in a new series of spectacular WW II Pacific War Simulations, *Task Force 1942* is your chance to command a fleet of destroyers, cruisers, and battleships against enemy forces in the 1942–43 Solomons Campaign!

**FIGURE 6.2–5** *Task Force 1942* advertisement

Throughout your campaign, you'll issue commands to ships or entire units! You'll deliver devastating blows upon enemy battleships! You'll take control of crucial battle positions! And, through incredible special effects, you'll experience thrilling night combat, blinding explosions, burning and sinking ships, flares, and torpedo wakes. All bringing to life your battle for control of the Pacific Theater!

- Command U.S. or Japanese forces!
- More than 150 ships faithfully reproduced!
- Take control of Gun Director or Torpedo Mount for more effective ship-to-ship combat!
- Control actions of individual ships, groups of ships, or the whole task force!

## GREENS

### The Instructional 3-D Golf Simulation

David Leadbetter's *Greens* is the first golf game designed to help players improve their golf game while having fun.

David Leadbetter, the pro that teaches the pros, will accompany players on their rounds and provide invaluable advice on club selection, stance, swing and shot making.

"Greens" is the only 3-D golf game that provides players free movement around the course, instant screen redraws and animated "televisual" presentation with six camera positions, including a unique follow-the-ball option.

## JUMP JET

### The AV8B Harrier II in Explosive Front Line Action

Strap yourself into the cockpit of the AV8B Harrier II, the fearsome low-level strike plane specifically designed for the rigors of quick, tenacious aerial assaults.

Through three perilous battle theaters, you'll fly up to six close air support sorties. Each brought to life by dazzling state-of-the-art graphics and fast-paced gameplay.

Vertical take-off, hovering, and reverse capabilities! Pre-flight sequences! Ski-jump assisted take-offs! Incredible state-of-the-art 3-D graphics! MicroProse has pulled out all the stops in this flight simulation. No detail has been sacrificed to surround you in the complete experience of operating one of the world's incredible strike fighters.

- Varying difficulty levels for each battle theater as well as each Harrier model.
- New targets and missions generated as you fly.
- Players can choose from three different Harrier models: AV8B; GR; or an easy-to-fly 'MPS' Harrier. Each with its own unique instruments and HUDs.

## THE ANCIENT ART OF WAR IN THE SKIES

### The Fun World War I Strategy & Action Game

Finally, a strategy war game that requires arcade game skills, as well as brain power! With *The Ancient Art of War in the Skies* you'll get to do everything from dictating campaign strategy to flying World War I fighters and bombers in acrobatic aerial dogfights. You'll attempt to push back enemy lines from an exciting strategy perspective. And you'll compete against famous military leaders of the world in more than 40 historical and fictional campaigns. *The Ancient Art of War in the Skies* from MicroProse. It's a challenging World War I strategy game and a fun arcade game all wrapped up in one!

- Defeat the enemy by destroying or capturing their capital or airfields, wiping out their air force, or forcing them to surrender.
- Command a force of World War I fighters and bombers, stationed at one of your airfields, on strategic bombing and dogfighting missions.

## WORLD CIRCUIT

### The Grand Prix Race Simulation

Can overtaking a rival on the streets of Monaco compare to the adrenaline rush of a hairpin turn on the Suzuka Circuit? Well, aside from purchasing a Formula One race car, there's only one way to find out. And that's by driving the thrilling *World Circuit* race simulation garne from MicroProse.

    *World Circuit* allows you to compete against world class drivers on all 16 of the premiere Grand Prix racetracks. You'll fend off challengers . . . execute savage hairpin turns . . . and experience frighteningly realistic crashes on your way to becoming Grand Prix Champion of the Year.

## ATAC

### Advanced Tactical Air Command

A furious tide of drug cartels blankets the world in the year 2001. At the request of nations all over the world, the United States is asked to put an end to this juggernaut.

    Their answer? Advanced Tactical Air Command an elite paramilitary task force commanded by you!

    Leading a squadron of fierce, high performance F-22 fighters, you'll unleash devastating aerial assaults on drug plantations and strategic targets! You'll develop strategies to break the tight grip drug bosses have on politicians, judges, and military establishments! And you'll lead 250 undercover agents against drug runners in the mountains, cities, and plantations of the world!

## B-17 FLYING FORTRESS

### World War II Bombers in Action

What did the courageous flyboys of the Memphis Belle really experience as they plowed through relentless anti-aircraft fire over Nazi-occupied Europe?

Find out for yourself as you lead a 10-man crew to victory . . . or defeat . . . in the most complete and accurate bomber simulation ever produced!

You'll assign crew members to their specific tasks! You'll fly in authentic formation with other B-17s! And you'll destroy strategic targets like canals, bridges, dockyards, and factories in dangerous bombing runs!

Fly the *B-17 Flying Fortress* and become a legend before your own time!

## XF5700 MANTIS

### Experimental Fighter

Earth is ambushed by a hostile alien race. The Fist of Earth world government is formed to fight the aliens before humanity is conquered. The only hope: an experimental starfighter code-named Mantis that's armed to the teeth with the latest firepower. You're the pilot. Mantis is packed with an unprecedented array of eye-popping digitized graphics and scintillating sounds. Get ready for an outer space action extravaganza that will keep you on the edge of your seat!

## SILENT SERVICE II

*Silent Service* won critical and popular acclaim as the definitive World War II submarine simulation. *Silent Service II* picks up where its predecessor left off with enhanced, digitized graphics and thrilling new game options—including campaign play—that give you even more decisions, even more intense action.

## RAILROAD TYCOON (FIG. 6.2–6)

### Empire Building in the Golden Age of Railroads

Big business. Tough decisions. Excitement, challenge and compelling attention to detail. *Railroad Tycoon* re-creates the Golden Age of Railroads in any of four regions in America and Europe, and gives you complete control over every aspect of your industrial empire. But be careful: the world's other tycoons—like J. P. Morgan, Vanderbilt and Carnegie—are fierce competitors, determined to crush you or brush you from their path. Named Best Strategy Game by the Software Publishers' Association!

**FIGURE 6.2–6** Strategy Games advertisement

## M1 TANK PLATOON

Command a full platoon of America's armored juggernauts and their soldiers into explosive land combat against USSR forces! With a tremendous arsenal of laser rangefinders, wire-guided missiles, and other high-tech treats, you'll roll through thousands of battlefields in varying weather conditions!

## PIRATES! GOLD (FIG. 6.2–7)

Bombarding enemy ships with hull-crushing cannonballs. Crossing swords with scurvy rogues. It's the life of high-seas adventure when you journey through the swashbuckling world of *Pirates! Gold*.

In this fabulous upgrade of the MicroProse classic *Pirates!*, you'll lead hundreds of hotblooded buccaneers into all-new harbor towns. Battle new foes with enhanced

FIGURE 6.2–7 *Pirates* advertisement

swordfighting capabilities. And navigate your ships through rough Caribbean waters in search of magnificent treasure!

## SPECIAL FORCES

Cutting off enemy supply lines. Rescuing a POW. Sabotaging enemy headquarters. It's all in a day's work when you're part of *Special Forces* . . . the elite commandos sent into the world's hot spots" to restore order and make the world safe for democracy. With the pick of the military's elite to help you, you'll be creating diversions, sniping, jumping enemies, and setting off powerful explosives. Anything to complete your mission and carry out your master strategy. *Special Forces* from MicroProse . . . defeat is not an option!

## FIELDS OF GLORY

### The Road to Waterloo

The immortal Napoleon. The quick-tempered Wellington. The crude, relentless Field Marshal Blucher. Three of the most feared generals in the Napoleonic Wars. And three generals who you'll do battle with in *Fields of Glory*. Recreating the battles leading to the great Waterloo confrontation, you'll command French, British, or Prussian troops. Contend with harsh weather and rough terrain in 6 battles and the complete campaign. And zoom in and out of the action using battlefield and campaign maps. *Fields of Glory* . . . an action and strategy game as powerful as the men who inspired it.

## DR. FLOYD'S DESKTOP TOYS

### Entertainment Pack Vol #1

Finally, Windows users can enjoy MicroProse gaming excitement with this engaging collection of stress-smashing games. With the zany, irreverent Dr. Floyd as your talking guide, you can drop cages on slippery sharks in Shark Hunt. Unlock startling truths in Cryptograms. Pound penguins, poodles, or even your boss in Wallop! And spark intricate and colorful spider webs with the touch of your finger in Web Spinners!

    *Dr. Floyd's Desktop Toys* for Windows. They're the perfect prescription for fun!

## RETURN OF THE PHANTOM

The legendary Phantom of the Opera has returned to the Paris Opera House! As Inspector Raoul Montand, you're the only one who can pursue The Red Death into the past and prevent him from terrorizing the present!

    This animated graphic adventure will have you searching for clues along the catwalks, wings, and backstage rooms of the opera house. Interviewing witnesses and suspects. Pursuing the Phantom through a labyrinth of subterranean catacombs. And finally confronting the Phantom face-to-face!

It's a backstage pass to mystery and intrigue in *Return of the Phantom!*

## THE LEGACY

### Realm of Terror

Moving is a harrowing experience when you're the sole inheritor of the bloodcurdling Winthrop House.

In this role-playing horror movie, you'll encounter the petrifying puzzles of the Winthrop House. Battle hair-raising, grotesque creatures. And discover magical items and forbidden books as you explore hundreds of surreal rooms!

Can you take the tension? Will your magic combat skills work against loathsome gargoyles or death leeches? Will your new house drive you completely insane?

Find out for yourself by playing *The Legacy: Realm of Terror.*

## KNIGHTS OF THE SKY

Become a World War I flying ace in thrilling aerial dogfights against some of the greatest combat pilots ever—including the infamous Red Baron. Battle for the title of Ace of Aces, and also help the Allies win World War I in this comprehensive campaign game. Super 3-D graphics capture every heart-pounding moment, intelligent opponents and challenging scenarios pose the ultimate test to your dogfighting skills.

## F-15 STRIKE EAGLE II

If you liked the first *F-15 Strike Eagle,* you'll love *F-15II.* The classic of aerial combat roars back to life in the 90's, loaded with fast action and vivid graphics that make MicroProse the leader in combat flight simulations.

Operation Desert Storm Scenario Disk. . . Owners of *F-15 Strike Eagle II* can now experience the challenge of the Persian Gulf War with this add on scenario disk. Take on eight specific missions from Desert Storm or randomly-generated missions. Also includes the North Cape and Central Europe scenarios in *F-19 Stealth Fighter* (*F-15II* required).

## SEA ROGUE

Silver bars plundered by Spain in the New World. Gold doubloons that were once a pirate's prize. These treasures and many more await in this authentic undersea treasure hunt. Search for history's most famous buried treasures. Command a crew of five skilled treasure hunters, rising from a diver on a rickety scow to the commander of a high-tech treasure probe! You'll face claim jumpers, hijackers, drug smugglers and the elements themselves in your search for wealth.

## COVERT ACTION

Special agent Max Remington goes to work in an international espionage simulation that portrays this clandestine world the way it really is. Espionage in the 1990s thrives on technology. Tap phone lines, crack complex codes, defeat computerized defense systems. Track suspects around the globe as you put together the pieces to a worldwide criminal plot in the shrouded world of Covert Action, ingenuity is the best weapon you can have.

## DARKLANDS

Who says a fantasy role-playing game can't be realistic? *Darklands* places the player into a land of magic, intrigue and heroic adventure—medieval Germany, depicted as Europeans at that time thought it to be: filled with sorcerers and witches, hypocritical clerics and religious power mongers, mysterious and potent artifacts, and endless opportunities for fame and fortune. A role-playing epic begins.

## CHALLENGE OF THE FIVE REALMS

### Spellbound in the World of Nhagardia

The multi-dimensional world of Nhagardia is quickly becoming paralyzed by the evil lord Grimnoth's terrifying plague of darkness. As Prince of Alonia, you now have 100 days to keep the world from being cast into eternal despair!

Accept the *Challenge of the Five Realms* and you'll experience a fantasy role-playing adventure that will take you through hundreds of wondrous and unpredictable scenarios. Scenarios brought to life by compelling animations, captivating digitized speech, streamlined character generation, and graphics that are nothing short of spellbinding!

## GLOBAL CONQUEST

*Command HQ* creator Dan Bunten has done it again: created a compelling, addictive strategy game that's easy to learn yet difficult to master. *Global Conquest* is the first computer strategy game to support up to four players (human or computer), all of whom compete while exploring randomly-generated worlds via modem, direct link or LAN! In *Global Conquest* the emphasis is on exploration, as you conquer untamed regions of your world and prevent your opponents from doing the same.

## CIVILIZATION (FIG. 6.2–8)

The creator of the award-winning *Railroad Tycoon* (Fig. 6.2–6) now turns his attention to the construction of true empires: civilizations. As the guiding spirit of a new civilization, can you guide your people toward survival, expansion and dominance from the founding of the first cities through the space age? And can you do it while competing against history's greatest leaders, including Ghengis Khan, Napoleon.

FIGURE 6.2–8 Civilization advertisement

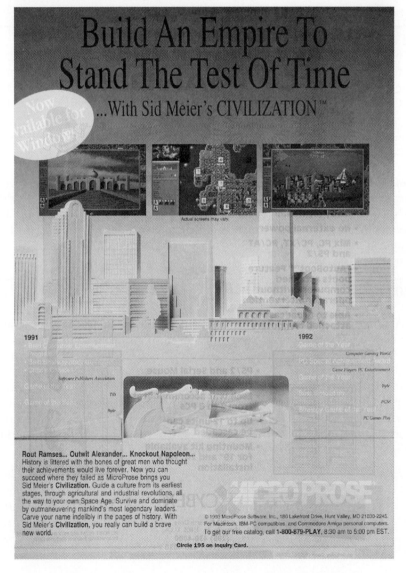

Voted Software Publishers Association's Best Strategy Game, Best Consumer Product and Best Entertainment Program in 1991.

## RED STORM RISING

Tom Clancy and MicroProse join forces for the most challenging military simulation ever. *Red Storm Rising* makes you an American nuclear attack submarine commander during World War III, charged with keeping the North Atlantic clear of Warsaw Pact forces. Includes 11 different scenarios, five types of radar and sonar for tracking and firing, five different U.S. sub classes and 37 different Soviet warship classes.

## F19 STEALTH FIGHTER

Fly the jet fighter no enemy can detect! Engage opponents in tenacious aerial dogfights as you soar through four explosive war theaters in Libya, the Persian Gulf, the North Cape, and Central Europe! All brought to life by spellbinding graphics from MPS Labs!

## HYPERSPEED

An updated and enhanced version of MicroProse's interstellar action and adventure epic, *Lightspeed*. Race through star clusters in a desperate search for a new world for Mankind. Negotiate with alien races for resources and political alliances. Battle those hostile to humanity. Hyperspeed features four progressively harder star clusters, an animated opening sequence, dazzling 3-D graphics, alien animation and more.

## GUNSHIP 2000

The original *Gunship* put you in the cockpit of the awesome AH-64A Apache attack helicopter. *Gunship 2000* gives you control of five gunships, from among seven different classes, for high tech battles around the world. Choose from Apaches, Blackhawks, Kiowas and more, and see every detail in the most detailed, Super 3-D Graphics yet.

GUNSHIP 2000 SCENARIO DISK AND MISSION BUILDER: Your career As A Gunship Pilot Has Just Been Extended. With this thrilling scenario disk, the best selling *Gunship 2000* multi-helicopter simulation will provide even more hours of enjoyment for old pros and entice the novice to climb aboard. There are new worlds to test your flight skills and new enemies to test your mettle.

## F117-A

### Stealth Fighter 2.0

Voted Best Simulation of the Year by the Software Publishers' Association in 1988, *F-19 Stealth Fighter* was a game the critics said could not be improved. It has been. *F-117A* features several thrilling new combat scenarios, even hotter 3-D graphics and more up-to-date information on the world's most elusive jet.

## COMMAND HQ

Take charge of a Superpower's high-tech military nerve center during World War I, II, III or IV. Deploy armies, air power and naval forces across the globe. See front-line action in colorful animation. *Command HQ* features an easy, intuitive interface and a realistic but uncomplicated approach to global warfare. Special two-player (modem) capability.

## TWILIGHT: 2000

Based on the award-winning RPG by Game Designers' Workshop, *Twilight: 2000* thrusts you into the brutal aftermath of World War III. Create and control one character, while commanding a squadron of hopeful survivors attempting to free the city of Krakow, Poland. Scaled 2-D and polygon-based 3-D action sequences: exciting role-playing opportunities.

## MEGATRAVELLER 2

### The Quest for the Ancients

More than just a continuation of an acclaimed series, *Mega Traveller 2* is a new, exciting direction in computer role-playing technology. Control one character but command four others—each responding to your orders according to the personalities and objectives you give them. Over 100 detailed worlds, hundreds of fascinating characters, and a challenging mystery to unravel. Game design by *Traveller* creator Marc Miller!

SOURCE: MicroProse, Inc. 1993 promotional materials.

# Subway Sandwich Shops

Success in the sandwich segment requires operators to work significantly harder than they did just a few years ago. There was a noticeable slowdown in the opening of new submarine sandwich shops in 1992, although the growth rate still exceeds most other restaurant segments. Competition has intensified, with hamburger chains such as Hardee's and Burger King experimenting with sub sandwiches as menu additions. Subs seem to be a category anyone can participate in. Subs offer easy entry into the food-service business and a simple, low-cost route to menu expansion, plus health appeal. Market data indicates that the sandwich is firmly established as a nationwide food item and there is plenty of room for growth in all areas. Many operators also see opportunities for sub-like concepts. For example, one variety of sandwich shop that continues to expand specializes in Philadelphia-style cheese-steak subs.

For sub shops, the Subway chain is the undisputed market leader, with 10 times more locations than any other competitor and more than 75 percent of all United States sub chain outlets. As of mid-1993, Subway operated 7,825 units worldwide, with about 7,750 units in North America. When it reached 8,400 stores in 1993, Subway was the No. 2 fast-food chain in the United States. By opening its small sandwich shops at break-neck speed, Subway grew from $360 million in sales in 1987 to $2.2 billion in sales in 1992 (Figure 6.3–1), while income increased substantially (Fig. 6.3–2). The former No. 2 was Pizza Hut, which operated 7,929 units in North America and expected to have 8,355 by the end of 1992. However, in terms of sales, Subway ranks 12th among chains nationwide. Sales are about 15 percent of McDonald's.

Subway is also looking to expand its nontraditional sites. The chain has about 150 outlets in colleges, convenience stores, hospitals, bus terminals, railway stations, and convention centers. Other future areas of emphasis include improving business during the dinner hour and late night and more marketing to children. About 4,000 outlets

**FIGURE 6.3–1** Worldwide Sales of Subway Sandwich Shops

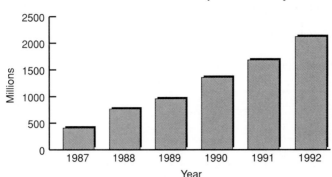

*Source:* Estimated from various sources.

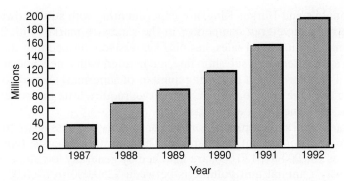

**FIGURE 6.3–2** Worldwide Income from Subway Sandwich Shops

*Source:* Estimated from various sources.

now feature kids packs, which include food items and a premium gift. In 1994 Subway also made a concerted effort to spend marketing dollars against teens and pre-teens.

However, Subway's rapid expansion has brought with it some problems. Franchisees are upset about the location of many new stores, claiming that these additions are cannibalizing sales at existing units. Some disgruntled franchisees have also charged the chain with making unrealistic financial projections during sales pitches. The Federal Trade Commission is looking into the complaints.

Among sub operators, Blimpie is running second to Subway in both unit totals and expansion plans. The New York-based firm opened about 100 restaurants in 1992, for a total of 575. It planned to reach 1,000 units by 1995. Blimpie has broken out of the Northeast over the past three years, with stores now open in 32 states, and it has begun to focus on international development.

Virtually all of Subway's competitors agree that the chain's main vulnerability is its product quality. Whether their version is an upscale, quasi-deli restaurant operation, or a more traditional, basic sub shop such as Blimpie, these other operators stress quality advantages over Subway in their efforts to attract customers and prospective franchisees.

## THE SANDWICH RESTAURANT INDUSTRY

Although sub and sandwich shops offer some of the best growth opportunities in fast food today, there are signs that the category is not what it used to be. Subway's rapid growth in recent years put sub sandwiches on the fast-food map and served to attract tremendous attention as well as investment dollars into the category. In part due to the increased competition, fewer operators and franchise prospects today view the name-brand sub shop as the easy way to success, compared with a couple of years ago.

### Growing Competition

Competition is growing not just from other subsandwich places, but from numerous other sources. Seeking to take advantage of their rising popularity and the public perception of subs as lighter, healthier alternatives to hamburgers and fried foods, the burger chains, McDonald's and Burger King, are experimenting with sub sandwiches as menu additions. Arby's, a veteran competitor in the sandwich market with 2,570 restaurants and $1.6 million in annual sales, has also aggressively pushed into the sub business. It launched a four-item cold sub shop line, augmented with a new hot sub offering. Subs are also a popular item at a growing number of supermarkets and convenience stores because they are easy to prepare and serve, require little investment in expensive equipment, and generate good profits.

However, for traditional sub shop operators whose primary business is strictly sub sandwiches, there are questions about profitability. The low start-up costs, typically ranging from as little as $50,000 to $130,000, are matched by generally low store sales. Segment leader Subway's annual unit volume is between $250,000 to $260,000, although the company claimed sales at mature units averaged closer to $280,000 in 1992. Then, even with the units' low operating costs, it is a close call as to whether such modest sales volumes provide a decent return on investment (ROI).

Neither Subway nor competitors with similar volumes are satisfied with their numbers, and many operators are focusing their attention on ways to boost unit sales. Common efforts include adding more higher-priced hot sandwiches and some non-sandwich items, expanding beyond lunch into other dayparts, and marketing office and party catering services.

## Upscale Shops

There is a growing trend toward upscale sub sandwich shops. Rather than remaining a stripped-down location designed primarily to provide working people with a quick take-out lunch, some shops, such as Quizno's Classic Subs, are styled as casual deli restaurants that aim to attract substantial eat-in business, including families.

Most Quizno's units seat 70 to 80 and average 65 percent of sales as eat-in traffic. The menu, which features a wide selection of fresh-made, oven-warmed subs, is augmented by chef salads, pasta dinners, extras such as soups and desserts, plus special QuizKidz meals. These additions have contributed to a 20 percent gain in unit sales and boosted evening business from 10 percent of volume to 30 percent. They have also helped Quizno's substantially increase weekend business.

Togo's Eatery, with 155 locations, manages higher volumes, in the $450,000 per year range, by highlighting quality ingredients in its menu of 30 hot and cold sandwiches, salads, fresh soups, and homemade chili. Also, it features an upscale decor package, including touches such as Italian tile, marble, and oak furnishings.

## Nontraditional Sub Offerings

Outside the traditional sub category, some sandwich chains are planning aggressive growth. One example is Miami Subs, which despite its name offers a broad-based menu of gourmet burgers, gyros, and chicken and shrimp platters, as well as hot and cold subs. The latter account for about 40 percent of sales.

Miami Sub sees itself as positioned somewhere between Chili's and McDonald's. Its service style is that of a fast-food shop, but in terms of food quality, quantity, presentation, and the fact that everything is made fresh puts it closer to a Chili's or other similar casual theme restaurant.

Schlotzsky's, which after struggling for a few years, plans to completely revamp its concept. Originally conceived as a fast-food outlet featuring a distinctive sandwich based on New Orleans' Muffuletta, Schlotzsky's recast itself as The Original Schlotzsky's Deli, serving an expanded menu of sandwiches, pizza, and salads, in a noticeably upscale, deli/market atmosphere.

Schlotzsky's customers perceive the chain as offering a quality product at a convenient location, and they are willing to pay for that difference. Schlotzsky's also upscaled its offerings and raised prices by 33 percent, increased the quality and quantity and broadened the menu. The strategy paid off, with converted locations boosting annual sales from an average of just $300,000 to $450,000 today.

Another variety of sandwich shop that continues to expand specializes in Philadelphia-style cheese steak subs. With their higher product and operating costs, most concentrate on developing mall units, sites in transportation centers, downtown office complexes, and selected other locations where they are guaranteed high pass-by traffic.

The cheese steak purveyors and other shops that feature hot, grilled sandwiches are reaching for ways to build stronger evening business. One chain that has been successful is Jerry's Subs & Pizza, which features Philly cheesesteak sandwiches and other subs for lunch and draws dinner business with a full pizza operation. Unit sales average in excess of $550,000.

This is a concept that many other sandwich chains are exploring. Schlotzsky's began offering pizza several years ago and kept it an integral part of its revised concept. Blimpie and D'Angelo's are currently testing pizza, and Quizno's offers it as part of its kids' menu.

### New Dayparts

A growing number of sandwich chains are also following fast food's move into breakfast in an attempt to build unit volumes. Subway now offers breakfast in 500 stores. Blimpie, D'Angelo's, and Great Steak & Fry are among the chains testing this concept.

### Value Pricing

With its intention of going head-to-head against McDonald's and Taco Bell, Subway committed itself to offering value items. It started by introducing a line of 79 cents Rounds sandwiches. Arby's is also focusing on Value Melts priced at 99 cents: roast beef sandwiches with melted cheddar or Swiss cheese.

Likewise, Jerry's Subs finds it's impossible not to address value pricing. Jerry's main value offering is a new $1.99 Philly Double Cheesesteak Junior, targeted at price-conscious customers. Blimpie, too, offers a value menu of Quik Bite sandwiches priced 99 cents to $1.69, credited with attracting some new business. However, as with several other sandwich chains, Blimpies' main focus is building value perceptions with specially-priced meal combos. Taking a different strategy, most of the more upscale chains have sought to avoid price competition completely by positioning themselves above standard fast food.

## FRED DELUCA'S SUBWAY

When Fred DeLuca, the founder of Subway, opened the first Subway Sandwiches & Salads shop in Bridgeport, Connecticut in 1965, his primary goal was to just stay in business. When he managed to make it through his second year without declaring bankruptcy, he became more ambitious. By 1982, DeLuca was planning to open at least 5,000 Subways by 1994. When he hit that mark early, in 1990, he upped the ante. When the chain approached its next goal of 5,000 stores, it thought its growth would begin to slow, but that has not happened, expansions has been very steady.

However, a chain with thousands of stores does not just happen by accident. Since Subway last topped the *Entrepreneur* list of top franchises in 1991, the company has taken a more aggressive approach to international franchising. Although most of Subway's stores are located in the United States, there are nearly 400 locations in Canada. People in countries as far afield as Australia, Japan, Israel, Ireland, Mexico, Portugal, and South Korea are also discovering the all-American taste of Subway's submarine sandwiches.

DeLuca's most important goal is to increase average sales volume per store, while decreasing operational costs. Thus, although growth is still a priority, Subway is placing an even greater emphasis on each individual store's volume and profitability.

## CUSTOMER ANALYSIS

A surprising 78.7 percent of all adults have patronized a fast-food or drive-in restaurant in the last 30 days (Table 6.3–1). And, some 31 percent of those same adults went 14 or more times to such a restaurant during that same time period (Table 6.3–1), making heavy users of the category. Demographically, heavy users are also more likely to be male, young, single, and live in the Northeast (Table 6.3–2).

In general, fast-food or drive-in restaurants appeal to a younger crowd who are single or young adults with children (Table 6.3–3). Subway has some unique customer demographics in comparison with Arby's, McDonald's, and the other fast-food or drive-in restaurants. These demographics skew much younger and single than those of major competitors (assuming that Arby's and McDonald's are competitors). In contrast to Arby's and McDonald's, Subway also has a much stronger franchise in the western United State. Both Arby's and Subway are more skewed toward middle to upper income customers than McDonald's. However, McDonald's does much better with adults who have children (Table 6.3–3).

The fast-food category has four main eating occasions each day: breakfast, lunch, dinner, and/or snack times (Table 6.3–1). Lunch is the most popular occasion for heavy users. Among all those who go to these restaurants, many go alone or with a spouse (Table 6.3–3). Eating with friends is also popular, as is taking the children.

Subway is low on the list of major fast-food or drive-in restaurants patronized in the last 30 days (Table 6.3–4). McDonald's, Burger King, and KFC are each several times more likely to be visited than is a Subway location.

## PROMOTION

Advertising plays an important part in the success of any business and Subway is no exception. In addition to individual location efforts to increase sales, all Subway franchisees contribute 2.5 percent (some markets elect to contribute more than this percentage) of weekly sales to the Subway Franchisee Advertising Fund Trust (SFAFT).

SFAFT is governed by a Board of Trustees consisting of 12 elected franchise own-

| TABLE 6.3–1 | Fast-Food and Drive-In Restaurants (respondents are all adults) |
|---|---|

| User of | (%) |
|---|---|
| Yes | 78.7 |
| No | 16.0 |
| Don't know | 5.3 |
| **Total** | **100.0** |

**Frequency of Use in Last 30 Days**

| Number of Times | (%) |
|---|---|
| 14 or more | 30.9 |
| 10–13 | 13.2 |
| 6–9 | 17.6 |
| 5 | 4.2 |
| 4 | 4.7 |
| 3 | 2.9 |
| 2 | 2.5 |
| 1 | 1.0 |
| None | 1.7 |
| **Total** | **78.7** |

**Frequency of Use in Last 30 Days by Occasion**

| Number of Times | Breakfast (%) | Lunch (%) | Dinner (%) | Snack (%) |
|---|---|---|---|---|
| 14 or more | 3.1 | 6.7 | 4.8 | 4.2 |
| 10–13 | 2.0 | 4.4 | 3.6 | 3.0 |
| 6–9 | 4.3 | 8.6 | 8.2 | 5.3 |
| 5 | 3.5 | 7.9 | 8.1 | 4.4 |
| 4 | 5.0 | 9.6 | 10.5 | 5.1 |
| 3 | 7.6 | 10.9 | 10.8 | 6.9 |
| 2 | 10.7 | 13.4 | 13.0 | 9.8 |
| 1 | 12.1 | 7.9 | 9.2 | 9.1 |
| None | 30.3 | 9.1 | 10.4 | 30.9 |
| **Total** | **78.6** | **78.5** | **78.6** | **78.7** |

*Source:* Simmons Market Research Bureau, Inc., 1991.

ers from across the chain. The SFAFT Board meets each quarter to discuss all aspects of future chain-wide advertising.

The owners of stores located in the same market work together to purchase advertising that benefits the entire group. Each market also elects an Ad Chairperson to preside over all local meetings and to provide input on chain-wide SFAFT proposals.

TABLE 6.3–2   Fast-Food and Drive-In Restaurants Category User Demographics
(respondents are all adults)

| | All Users | | Heavy Users 14 or More | |
|---|---|---|---|---|
| | % | Index | % | Index |
| **Total** | **78.6** | **100** | **30.9** | **100** |
| *Gender* | | | | |
| Male | 79.7 | 101 | 35.5 | 115 |
| Female | 77.7 | 99 | 26.7 | 86 |
| *Age* | | | | |
| 18–24 | 80.6 | 102 | 34.7 | 112 |
| 25–34 | 84.7 | 108 | 32.2 | 104 |
| 35–44 | 85.4 | 109 | 32.3 | 104 |
| 45–54 | 80.4 | 102 | 31.0 | 100 |
| 55–64 | 73.9 | 94 | 29.1 | 94 |
| 65 and older | 60.8 | 77 | 25.1 | 81 |
| *Marital Status* | | | | |
| Single | 79.7 | 101 | 34.0 | 110 |
| Married | 80.3 | 102 | 30.1 | 97 |
| Divorced, etc. | 72.2 | 92 | 29.8 | 96 |
| Parents | 86.2 | 110 | 31.6 | 102 |
| *Region* | | | | |
| Northeast | 69.8 | 89 | 39.4 | 127 |
| Midwest | 84.4 | 107 | 34.6 | 112 |
| South | 80.1 | 102 | 29.6 | 96 |
| West | 78.5 | 100 | 19.9 | 64 |
| *Income* | | | | |
| $75+ | 80.8 | 103 | 29.7 | 96 |
| $60+ | 80.0 | 102 | 30.2 | 98 |
| $50+ | 81.6 | 104 | 30.8 | 100 |
| $40+ | 81.6 | 104 | 31.6 | 102 |
| $30+ | 82.0 | 104 | 31.7 | 103 |
| $30–$39 | 83.1 | 106 | 32.1 | 104 |
| $20–$29 | 80.1 | 102 | 32.0 | 104 |
| $10–$19 | 75.2 | 96 | 31.1 | 101 |
| Less than $10 | 64.5 | 82 | 24.9 | 80 |
| *Presence of children* | | | | |
| Under 2 years | 86.2 | 110 | 32.3 | 104 |
| 2–5 | 87.4 | 111 | 30.4 | 98 |
| 6–11 | 85.2 | 108 | 31.6 | 102 |
| 12–17 | 84.2 | 107 | 34.0 | 110 |

Note: Index values above are computed by dividing the proportion in a particular grouping by their proportion of the population. For example, if an age group has 20.2% of the products users and represents 18.3% of the population, the index value for the grouping is 110. Index values over 100 signify above average usage and index values below 100 signify below average usage. However, values over 110 or under 90 are the most significant.

*Source:* Simmons Market Research Bureau, Inc., 1991.

TABLE 6.3–3   **Fast-Food and Drive-In Restaurants (respondents are all adults)**

*With Whom Do You Usually Go to These Restaurants?*

|  | Total (%) | Breakfast (%) | Lunch (%) | Dinner (%) | Snack (%) |
|---|---|---|---|---|---|
| Alone | 26.3 | 11.6 | 15.0 | 7.8 | 8.3 |
| With husband/wife | 29.6 | 9.5 | 13.8 | 21.3 | 6.3 |
| With children under 12 | 17.1 | 4.6 | 8.7 | 11.7 | 3.9 |
| With children 12–17 | 7.9 | 1.7 | 3.3 | 5.4 | 1.9 |
| With friends | 20.4 | 5.6 | 11.4 | 11.9 | 6.3 |
| With coworkers | 11.2 | 1.8 | 9.2 | 1.7 | 1.2 |
| Other | 7.8 | 2.4 | 3.7 | 4.5 | 2.4 |
| Don't know | 4.3 | 26.2 | 21.0 | 23.8 | 51.6 |
| **Total** | **124.6** | **63.4** | **86.1** | **88.1** | **81.9** |

*Restaurants Visited in the Last 30 Days (selected firms)*

|  | All (%) | Sole (%) | Primary (%) | Secondary (%) |
|---|---|---|---|---|
| Burger King | 28.6 | 1.8 | 21.7 | 5.1 |
| Domino's Pizza | 9.2 | 0.1 | 6.4 | 2.7 |
| Godfather's Pizza | 1.7 | 0.0 | 1.2 | 0.5 |
| KFC | 19.8 | 0.6 | 14.3 | 4.9 |
| McDonald's | 44.0 | 5.2 | 34.1 | 4.7 |
| Pizza Hut | 19.6 | 0.4 | 13.9 | 5.3 |
| Subway | 4.6 | 0.1 | 3.1 | 1.4 |
| Taco Bell | 15.9 | 0.3 | 11.9 | 3.7 |
| Wendy's | 15.9 | 0.6 | 11.8 | 3.5 |
| **Total** | **159.3** | **9.1** | **118.4** | **31.8** |

*Source:* Simmons Market Research Bureau, Inc., 1991.

To help develop the chain's advertising campaigns, SFAFT retains an advertising agency. That agency produces all the materials needed by franchisees to get consistent messages to consumers. Agency representatives attend all SFAFT Board meetings to propose campaigns and communicate with the SFAFT office. To inform consumers about Subway's advertising messages, SFAFT has commercials on the national television networks.

### Spending Level

Some 99 percent of Subway advertising is on television, with the rest spread over radio, outdoor, newspapers, and magazines. The advertising budget for 1992 was about $38.7 million. In comparison, Arby's budget was $26.3 million and Blimpies spent a total of $0.2 million; McDonald's spent about $413.5 million.

TABLE 6.3–4   Fast-Food and Drive-In Restaurants by Firm User Demographics (respondents are all adults)

| | Subway | | McDonald's | | Arby's | |
|---|---|---|---|---|---|---|
| | % | Index | % | Index | % | Index |
| **Total** | **4.6** | **100** | **44.0** | **100** | **10.7** | **100** |
| *Gender* | | | | | | |
| Male | 5.0 | 109 | 44.3 | 101 | 11.0 | 100 |
| Female | 4.2 | 92 | 43.8 | 99 | 10.4 | 97 |
| *Age* | | | | | | |
| 18–24 | 8.1 | 177 | 49.3 | 112 | 12.4 | 116 |
| 25–34 | 5.7 | 124 | 51.3 | 117 | 12.2 | 114 |
| 35–44 | 5.4 | 117 | 48.9 | 111 | 11.7 | 109 |
| 45–54 | 3.7 | 80 | 43.8 | 99 | 10.4 | 99 |
| 55–64 | 2.3 | 51 | 37.2 | 84 | 8.9 | 83 |
| 65 and older | 1.2 | 26 | 27.1 | 61 | 7.0 | 65 |
| *Marital Status* | | | | | | |
| Single | 7.8 | 170 | 46.2 | 105 | 12.8 | 120 |
| Married | 3.6 | 79 | 44.9 | 102 | 10.1 | 94 |
| Divorced, etc. | 3.9 | 86 | 38.7 | 88 | 10.2 | 95 |
| Parents | 4.9 | 107 | 53.3 | 121 | 11.4 | 107 |
| *Region* | | | | | | |
| Northeast | 1.7 | 38 | 42.4 | 96 | 5.6 | 52 |
| Midwest | 5.3 | 116 | 51.2 | 116 | 13.9 | 130 |
| South | 4.5 | 98 | 41.0 | 93 | 11.5 | 108 |
| West | 6.8 | 148 | 42.2 | 96 | 10.9 | 102 |
| *Income* | | | | | | |
| $75+ | 5.1 | 111 | 46.3 | 105 | 13.2 | 123 |
| $60+ | 5.5 | 119 | 46.8 | 106 | 13.6 | 127 |
| $50+ | 5.4 | 118 | 48.2 | 109 | 13.0 | 121 |
| $40+ | 5.5 | 121 | 47.7 | 108 | 12.2 | 114 |
| $30+ | 5.3 | 116 | 47.8 | 108 | 12.2 | 114 |
| $30–$39 | 4.7 | 103 | 48.0 | 109 | 12.1 | 113 |
| $20–$29 | 4.2 | 92 | 42.7 | 97 | 9.5 | 88 |
| $10–$19 | 3.6 | 78 | 41.2 | 94 | 10.0 | 93 |
| Less than $10 | 2.8 | 61 | 31.0 | 70 | 6.0 | 56 |
| *Presence of children* | | | | | | |
| Under 2 years | 5.1 | 112 | 55.5 | 126 | 10.6 | 99 |
| 2–5 | 5.0 | 109 | 58.1 | 132 | 10.2 | 95 |
| 6–11 | 4.8 | 105 | 53.3 | 121 | 10.9 | 102 |
| 12–17 | 5.3 | 115 | 47.6 | 108 | 12.6 | 118 |

Note: Index values above are computed by dividing the proportion in a particular grouping by their proportion of the population. For example, if an age group has 20.2% of the products users and represents 18.3% of the population, the index value for the grouping is 110. Index values over 100 signify above average usage and index values below 100 signify below average usage. However, values over 110 or under 90 are the most significant.

*Source:* Simmons Market Research Bureau, Inc., 1991.

### Campaigns

Subway Sandwich Shops broke a new campaign in 1993 that summed up the chain's rapid rise to the top of the sub market. The promotion, called the "No. 2¢ Sale," symbolized the submarine sandwich chain's claim that it will soon be the second largest fast-food chain in North America.

The campaign, which featured black and white visuals with color product shots, starred Subway franchisees. It helped drive Subway's best sales year ever, while spurring a few copycat campaigns from other chains. The four-week "No. 2¢ Sale" offered game-card winners sandwiches and other items for 2¢. The campaign ran on network and cable prime time, as well as on sports and syndicated programs, carrying Subway's new theme: "Subway is the place where fresh is the taste."

The campaign was followed by a tie-in with the Paramount Pictures film "The Coneheads" and a "Consume Mass Quantities Meal Deal" promotion. Subway's most popular sandwich, the turkey sub, and chips and a Coneheads collector cup were offered at a special price, varying by markets.

## PROBLEMS IN FRANCHISE LAND

Charges of broken promises and hidden costs are just some of the problems plaguing franchising today. Throughout the $246 billion industry, defined to exclude auto dealers and gas stations, franchisees are battling franchisors for more control over their businesses. The franchisors are fighting back to preserve their profits. At stake is the 12.7 percent of retail sales accounted for by franchises.

Anything these days can be, and is, a franchise, from steel bungee jumping towers (Air Boingo) to gun shops (Strictly Shooting). For small-business owners, franchising offers an alternative way of raising capital, which speeds growth. For more laid-off managers and early retirees, it is a way to pursue the American dream of owning a business.

Bad management and poor locations have resulted in many franchises failing in past years. And, the recession, over saturation in many markets, and huge debt loads from leveraged buyouts put new pressures on franchisors to squeeze franchisees. As franchisors burrow into new market, they are also increasingly vying for the franchisees' customers.

The industry claims are that fewer than 5 percent of franchises fail or close annually. In comparison, the U.S. Small Business Administration says that 63 percent of new businesses fail after six years. Most experts would agree that more franchises survive than other new businesses. The actual franchise annual failure rate is probably between 10 and 12 percent.

## DIFFERENTIAL ADVANTAGE

Even with a recession and intense competition, the fast-food and drive-in restaurant category has a bright future. It is popular with consumers mainly because it satisfies their needs for convenient, value-oriented products that taste good. While they may change the mix of the fast foods they consume (pizza versus subs versus burgers), there is not any indication that consumers are about to descend on the supermarkets in mass so that they can go home and cook from scratch.

The real questions for firms in this category revolve around marketing issues: how to develop and keep a differential advantage in a highly competitive and dynamic market, while maintaining sales growth and, above all, profitability. What marketing strategy would you recommend to Subway? What specific price, distribution, promotion, and product elements would you propose and why? How would you deal with the growth competition in the sub market?

## Sources

Caminiti, Susan. "Look Who Likes Franchising Now." *Fortune* (September 23, 1991): 125–130.

Casper, Carol. "Market Segment Report: Sandwiches." *Restaurant Business* (December 10, 1992): 79–102.

Cortez, John P. "Subway Builds its Way to No. 2." *Advertising Age* (July 5, 1993): 32.

DeGeorge, Gail. "Fed-up Franchisees: They're Mad as Hell and . . ." *Business Week* (November 13, 1989): 83–85.

*Franchise* (an internal Subway communications letter to franchises and prospective franchisees), various issues in 1993. *Franchise* is published monthly by Franchise World Headquarters, Inc. Subway is owned by Doctor's Associates, Inc.

Simmons Market Research Bureau, Inc., 1991.

"Sub-stantial Success." *Success* (January 1993): 54, 126.

---

# *Prodigy Services Company*  CASE 4

When Prodigy was first introduced, online services were still a novelty and primarily the province of only the most computer literate. The first services targeted the "computer crowd" and not the general public.

In those early days, Prodigy also thought that those with computers and modems were the most appropriate audience for their new product. One clearly identifiable segment were the personal computer (PC) user's groups members around the country. These groups are easy to identify; there is even a national organization of user groups. Prodigy gave away software with a month's free membership in the service to those PC user group members to generate trial. Later, they asked for the regular price from those interested in remaining with the service.

However, there were a couple of things Prodigy had not counted on. In 1988, the telecommunications field was still in its infancy. Modems were expensive and slow. The people who did own them were mostly users of sophisticated online services, private bulletin board systems, and specialized online networks. To this market, and to the columnists in the trade press, Prodigy looked like "the Fisher-Price toy of online services."

Prodigy also misjudged the direction and likely growth of the home computer market. As Prodigy planned its nationwide rollout, industry indicators pointed to "the year of the home computer." Computer hardware vendors, including IBM and Apple, came out with new models targeted directly at the home market. What nobody predicted was that 1989 would find a nervous buying public, shying away from major "luxury" purchases such as home computers.

Although Prodigy had found an easily identifiable segment, it could not secure its patronage and loyalty. In retrospect, the outcome is understandable, if not obvious. The members of the computer community targeted by Prodigy were accustomed to the sophisticated online services such as CompuServe, Delphi, and Genie, not to a visual and extremely user-friendly environment like Prodigy. The older services ran all sessions on their main computers; users talked to one another as a group experience. Thus, they could communicate with others who were "there" with them at their keyboard. In contrast, Prodigy was a more solitary experience. The other services also offered vast collections of programs to download—but, Prodigy did not. A "macho factor" also operated. Those who understood the sophisticated services had a certain superiority complex, felling a sense of accomplishment for having mastered the telecommunication software and a complex series of commands. To this market segment, Prodigy was too easy.

Similarly, small numbers of PC users controlled the computers and held sway over those wanting access. During the 1980s and early 1990s, PCs, both at home and in the workplace, were the province of "experts." By 1994, computers had been democratized; they are everywhere and used by almost everyone.

Until very recently, most home PCs were there for business reasons; their owners either worked at home or routinely brought work home from the office. Most of those home PCs had a single "owner," specifically men working at office tasks. Other family members were largely excluded for a number of reasons. First, they did not know how to use PCs and the "owner" did not want to spare the time and energy to teach them. Second, not many of them were really interested in designing databases or using spreadsheets, which are common business applications available for PCs, and most word processors were hard to learn. And, finally, games for PCs were slow to be developed and, until recently, expensive.

With the emergence of more user friendly software and operating environments, PC use expanded, but still, only the "owner" was using the PC on a regular basis. Prodigy helped change that with its easy access and use. In a way, it was a revolution, if only in terms of putting the power of the PC in the hands of everyone.

By 1994, a significant percentage of new computer purchases were for home use. It was probably not that consumers felt any richer than they did in late 1989; it was more likely that a home computer was perceived as a useful, if not necessary, tool and less as a luxury. Another major factor, computers were a lot less expensive.

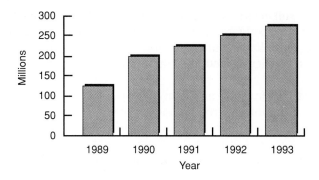

FIGURE 6.4–1 Prodigy Services Revenues

*Source:* Estimated from various sources.

## PRODIGY'S ONLINE SERVICES

By 1993, Prodigy had more than 2,000,000 members. CompuServe, the closest competition in the online arena had less than a million members. Prodigy is accessible with a local call by 95 percent of the households in the United States. The company has nearly half of the $500 million annual market for consumer online information services. Figure 6.4–1 shows the firm's dramatic revenue growth over the last five years. However, as can been seen in Figure 6.4–2, that growth has not been accompanied by any positive net income.

Initially, Prodigy took a big risk by selling the product through the consumer market rather than through software vendors. However, as retailers and computer makers have promoted PCs, as pricing has come down, and as consumers have become more familiar with computers through their jobs, the home computer market has opened up. Prodigy's main selling point is its ease of use and value. Prodigy offers numerous services, including news, weather, sports, and financial and business news (updated throughout the day), an online encyclopedia, banking, and stock quotes, among others.

### Online Shopping Services

Prodigy's online shopping mall provides customers with a wide range of products at prices that are usually about the same as retail outlets. The malls are open around the clock, seven days a week. For example, Comp-u-Store Online is a shopping club

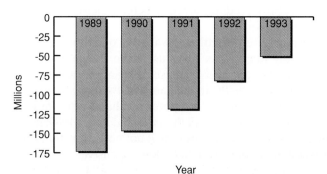

FIGURE 6.4–2 Prodigy Services Income

*Source:* Estimated from various sources.

that is available on several online services, including Prodigy, CompuServe, and America Online. Included in Comp-u-Store's product list of 250,000 items are books and magazines, home electronics, and automobile accessories.

Prodigy can put consumers in touch with name brand clothing at Spiegel, or executives can even obtain attaché cases. From their modems, users can stock their offices with everything from paper clips to fax machines. Sears, through Prodigy, offers a wide selection of items online.

### Online Travel Planning

Prodigy can assist in the hassles of business travel to cities such as New York. Prodigy's guide to New York includes information on nightlife, attractions, events, shopping, the weather, the lottery, dining, and lodging. Prodigy's Mobil Travel Guide lists restaurants by cuisine.

### Online Banking

About 15 banks offer home banking through Prodigy. Prodigy allows customers to pay bills, receive statements, transfer funds, and open accounts. However, major banks have had limited success in encouraging customers to bank electronically. Four things are changing that:

1. Automated teller machines and touch-tone telephone services provided by many banks have educated consumers.
2. As the prices of PCs have dropped, more customers have them and can now link up with banks.
3. As more banks merge or fail, there will be fewer branches and longer lines.
4. New software and computer services make electronic banking cheaper and easier.

### Online Investing

More than 3,000 mutual funds can be researched through Prodigy. However, even though 25 percent of all U.S. households have money in funds, few use PCs to manage their money. The American Association of Individual Investors has found that 64 percent of its 110,000 members own computers, but only about 40 percent do any investment analysis with them, and just one-third of that group use the computers for fund investing.

## A PROFILE OF PRODIGY MEMBERS

Prodigy is now targeting the many millions of people who have PCs in their homes who have not tried, or stayed with, an online service but not the million or fewer serious information customers who are regular users of electronic information and who made a serious effort to master communications software, online searching, electronic mail, and online user groups.

On an average Prodigy day, there are 500,000 "sessions." (A session lasts from sign-on to sign-off on a single ID.) On that same average day, somewhere between 20 and 30 percent of Prodigy members will sign on at least once.

Some 60 percent of Prodigy users are adult males, 30 percent are adult females, and 10 percent are kids under 18 years old. About 72 percent are married, with 17 percent single and 10 percent divorced. These numbers seem to bear out Prodigy's orientation as a family service. Prodigy touts the attractive demographics of its audience, whose average household income is $70,000, to advertisers.

## PRODIGY INSTALLS NEW PROGRAMS

Many Prodigy customers log on to check stock quotes, get news, or consult an electronic encyclopedia. But such customers have been a problem for Prodigy. Why? Prodigy says the $12.95 that such customers pay each month does not cover the costs of delivering service to them. So Prodigy counts on advertising revenues for goods and services sold online as well as commissions from those transactions, to make up the difference. But even though Prodigy vendors sell everything from airline tickets to designer jeans, many users seldom, if ever, buy anything, meaning that they are probably on Prodigy's "bad-consumer list."

With so many "bad" customers among its members, Prodigy is revamping its business strategy, particularly because it is losing money. By contrast, the number two competitor, CompuServe has been profitable since 1981. To meet its own deadline of profitability by the "early 1990s," Prodigy must reconsider its marketing strategy, with special attention to its pricing, the nature of its product offering, and how it promotes its service.

As a result, a new Prodigy is emerging with new features for its online users. And, instead of simply charging one low price for the basic service and hoping to make up the difference with ads and commissions, Prodigy is adding extra-cost options, similar to a cable television company's premium channels. These new premium services include action games for kids and the ability to download public domain software. Also, for an extra fee, customers have the option of using faster baud modems to speed up Prodigy's on-screen graphics, which many users say change too slowly.

In addition to boosting revenue, these new premium services may help Prodigy better compete with rivals such as Sierra Network, which specializes in games, and America On-line Inc., which caters to specific markets. They have received unintended help from Prodigy, which has spent about $50 million in advertising and promotions since 1990 to get ordinary consumers to log on to its service.

Still, Prodigy has not turned enough people into electronic shoppers. One reason, Prodigy displays cartoon-like graphics, not photographic images of merchandise. That is not a problem if it is selling a mutual fund, but people will not buy a designer dress that way.

In time, new technology should open up the market for interactive home shopping. Prodigy is looking at new ways to enhance its service with photos, video, and sound. One possibility is to transmit Prodigy to television sets rather than to PCs using interactive cable systems. Another idea is to mail members CD-ROM disks that can store well-designed and colorful electronic catalogs.

In the meantime, Prodigy is eliminating many of its online merchandisers. Instead of having dozens of retailers doing a little business, Prodigy believes that it is better to have a smaller number of happy retailers. Spiegel is staying because it is happy with the business it does selling sheets, towels, and other similar items. Among merchants that have already left are Contact Lense Supply, Sharon Luggage, and Buick, which had offered brochures. In general, successful Prodigy merchants sell known, branded items such as magazine subscriptions or compact discs.

Each day, Prodigy's members now send out about 65,000 private electronic mail notes and post an average of 80,000 messages to bulletin boards. Members have unlimited access to bulletin boards dealing with every topic from cooking tips to the television show *Northern Exposure*.

To reduce its telecommunications costs, Prodigy is encouraging subscribers to write and edit their messages and memos before logging on. Previously, Prodigy subscribers had to be online while they wrote. If enough members cooperate, Prodigy may be able to delay further expansion of its already massive, nationwide network. Big capital projects are getting harder to fund because IBM and Sears, the owners of Prodigy, have been cutting their annual investment in the service since 1990.

## SEGMENTING THE ONLINE SERVICES MARKET

In online services marketing, the diffusion process refers to the way a service is communicated to potential adopters. Mass media advertising to the target market and direct mail creates awareness and provides information sources during the introductory stage. Testimonials can help establish credibility. Evaluation depends on trial subscriptions and word-of-mouth, as the consumer weighs the benefits of the service versus its cost. After adoption, consumers seek information to relieve postpurchase anxiety and, therefore, look again to the mass media or online for reassurance.

Target market segmentation takes place along demographic, lifestyle, and benefit criteria. Examples of psychographic segments include: risk takers; innovators opinion leaders (others listen to and respect their judgment, about products); educated consumers able to utilize the services to their full potential; family-oriented consumers who allow their children to use PCs; those used to drawing information from new and unusual sources; those who do not view computers as "big brother and 1984"; people who exhibit a degree of trust in banks that they would not lose their money and will protect their privacy; and, those able to afford such services.

Several needs are being satisfied by online services. These include:

1. Prestige—being first on your block with the newest in electronic gadgetry.
2. Convenience—everything available at your fingertips and you do not have to leave your living room to shop.
3. Instant gratification—formation available when you want it, rather than when it is available.
4. Novelty/excitement—being part of a new craze sweeping the country.
5. Efficiency—one-stop shopping.
6. Ease of use—just press the buttons.
7. Timeliness—advantage of "real time" information, e.g., when buying stocks.

Online promotional strategies focus on services and benefits, target markets, and the appropriate media to tell the story. These strategies emphasize the benefits of convenience, value for the money, excitement, ease of use, and innovation without risk. The services do not want to suffer from a "gadget" image. The messages need to be copy-heavy to explain product features, pointing to advertising in the print medium, although not necessarily using such narrow vehicles as computer magazines. Some online services find a wider target audience by using more general publications such as *Fortune* or *Time*.

## SOME ISSUES TO THINK ABOUT

Given the benefits of hindsight, how would you have introduced Prodigy in 1988? What services would you have offered and how would you have segmented the market? What additional market segments should Prodigy consider targeting to expand its subscriber base? And, what services will it need to offer to appeal to those new markets? Given that most households in the United States do not own a PC, what additional markets could Prodigy attract if it was offered via television cable lines? How would Prodigy have to change its offering to appeal to that new market(s)?

Some industry experts argue that in the future, households will have access to a vast array of entertainment and information services from local cable and telephone lines. Some discuss the emergence of 500 channels with movies, information, shopping, and other services in an interactive marketplace between households and service providers. What is the most appropriate place for Prodigy in the scenario? What marketing strategy would you recommend? What specific price, distribution, promotion, and product elements would you propose and why?

## Sources

"CompuServe: Videotex Services," in *Cases and Exercises in Marketing* ed. W. Wayne Talarzyk (Chicago, IL: Dryden Press, 1987), pp. 273–285.

Kane, Pamela. *Prodigy Made Easy* 2nd. ed. Berkeley, CA: Osborne McGraw-Hill, 1993.

Kirkpatrick, David. "Hot New PC Serves." *Fortune* (November 2, 1992): 108–114.

Schepp, Brad and Debra Schepp. *The Complete Guide to CompuServe*. Berkeley, CA: Osborne McGraw-Hill, 1990.

Schwartz, Evan I. "Can GTE Outdo Prodigy?" *Business Week* (December 28, 1992): 42D.

Schwartz, Evan I. "Prodigy Installs a New Program." *Business Week* (September 14, 1992): 96–97.

# CASE *Hasbro Toys* 5

Hasbro Inc. is a very diverse company with lines of toys, games, and puzzle products, combined with the company's wide geographical distribution, advertising support, and with toy successes stemming from popular television shows and movies. Hasbro may also be the toy industry's licensing king. In 1994, with 15 percent of the domestic U.S. toy market, Hasbro was the world's largest toy company. In that year, it had $2.67 billion in sales and net income of $175 million.

Over the years, Hasbro has produced such megahits as a talking Barney (based on the popular *Barney & Friends* show) and *Jurassic Park's* Tyrannosaurus Rex (based on the popular movie *Jurassic Park*). It has also acquired a large number of other toy companies, including Milton Bradley, Playskool, Tonka, Kenner, Parker Brothers, Coleco, Knickerbocker, and Child Guidance. In the process, it moved ahead of its main rival Mattel, which makes such well-known toy brands as Barbie.

Hasbro's success with *Barney & Friends* is especially noteworthy. *Barney & Friends* is the second most popular children's show on the Public Broadcasting Service (PBS), enjoying a fanatical following among preschoolers. Hasbro produces over 20 Barney-related toys, games, and puzzles under a variety of brands, including Playskool, which markets the talking Barney, a Barney replica that says over 500 simple phrases.

The *Barney & Friends* television show features eight multiethnic children from 7 to 14 years old who sing and dance on a schoolyard set carpeted with fake grass, a concrete tree, from which hangs a tire swing. Inside the tire, or sometimes on top of a tree stump, rests the children's little stuffed mascot, the dinosaur doll named Barney.

The Barney episodes revolve around problem solving (a sharing dispute, stage fright before a recital, concerns about a "nontraditional" family, etc.), or game playing situations. As the kids use their imaginations in their simple schoolyard, the Barney doll comes to life in a rainbow shower of stars. Barney, and sometimes Baby Bop (a squeaky-voiced, bow-wearing triceratops who makes frequent appearances), talk and sing with the kids, including tunes they have heard a million times before. Everything about Barney's television show is geared toward young children. Adults rarely appear in Barney's schoolyard. The repetition of songs and key words appeals to kids, but not to adults.

## HASBRO'S PERFORMANCE

A few years ago, Hasbro never thought it would be disappointed about producing $175 million in earnings. But, then again, it had become accustomed to seeing significant growth year after year. On the plus side, 1994 was still Hasbro's second best year ever in terms of revenues and earnings. For the year, net revenues were $2.67 billion compared with the $2.75 billion reported in 1993 (Fig. 6.5–1), but income dropped during the same period (Fig. 6.5–2).

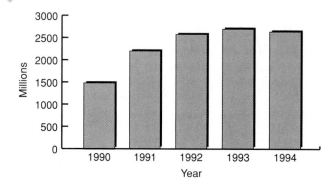

**FIGURE 6.5–1** Hasbro Total Sales

*Source: Hasbro 1994 Annual Report.*

There were two big reasons why Hasbro's growth slowed in 1994 and both were dinosaur related. Hasbro saw a dramatic fall in sales of Jurassic Park- and Barney-related products of some $170 million in combined revenue. However, Barney still remains popular with children, and with an international rollout, Hasbro expects Barney products to be in its line for years to come. Without the "dinosaur" numbers, Hasbro's business for the year was up almost 4 percent worldwide.

In 1994, Hasbro's games group enjoyed another year of record revenues. New products, including Elefun and Gator Golf, received very favorable consumer acceptance, while the classics, such as Monopoly and Scrabble, again demonstrated their staying power. Within the toy group, boy's toys were led by the continued strength of the Batman action figures and the new Ricochet remote-controlled vehicle. In the girl's activity area, the Fantastic Sticker Maker enjoyed a successful first year while the Littlest Pet Shop items continued to be strong. And the redesigned Easy Bake Oven was well accepted. In the infant and preschool arena, Playskool's In-Line Skates had a good second year and its new 4-in-1 Busy Center was well received.

## THE BARNEY EXPERIENCE

When PBS added *Barney & Friends* to its programming lineup in April 1992, no one could have anticipated the impact of that move. Now, *Barney & Friends* is the most watched children's program on PBS, with a weekly audience of about 14 million viewers.

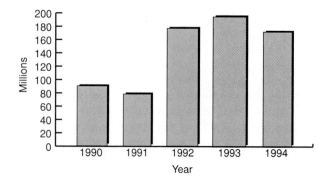

**FIGURE 6.5–2** Hasbro Net Income

*Source: Hasbro 1994 Annual Report.*

In just three years, Barney's promoters released 18 home videos. At the same time, The Barney Fan Club grew to more than 700,000 members. Barney's first album, "Barney's Favorites, Vol. 1," sold through double platinum. Not surprisingly, PBS extended broadcast rights for *Barney & Friends* through 1998.

*Barney & Friends* is successful because the show exudes warmth, simplicity, and the message that kid's concerns count. Barney appears, sings, dances, hugs, reassures, preaches a bit, and then he is gone. He never scolds or orders. He never tells the kids what to do.

Why do kids clamor for Barney videos, beg to watch Barney on television, plead for Barney t-shirts, puppets, and books? And how come parents just do not understand? The answer to those questions lie in Barney's ability to charm and mesmerize his young audience and his inability to captivate the older set. Barney's success comes from motivating the kids, while the parents go along to make them happy.

Unlike *Sesame Street,* which charms grown-ups as well as kids with spoofs such as *Twin Beaks* and *Monsterpiece Theater*, the *Barney & Friends* formula is unappetizing to many parents. But that is by design. Although their reactions to the show run from appreciation to mild astonishment to just plain caustic disgust, parents one and all bow to children's intense appreciation of Barney.

Barney's public appearances rival those of a popular musical group in the enthusiasm and audiences they produce. A recent Barney appearance at 8:30 A.M. on a Saturday morning in the biggest mall in Augusta, Georgia tells the story. Even before the stores opened, the parking lot was crowed with Barney fans, and their parents.

Inside the mall, a crowd estimated at 10,000 pushes toward the line of white plastic ribbon that separates Barney from his fans. These kids are imitating his gestures and, if they can talk, singing his songs. When Barney claps, sings, dances, they all do it along with him. After Barney leaves and the good-byes die down, fans stampede the J.C. Penney Barney boutique just across the mall from which they emerge with brand-new Barney and Baby Bop dolls.

## THE BARNEY BOOM

*Barney & Friends* is a marketing phenomenon, with videos, records, books, clothing, fan clubs, and, recently, even a special on NBC. Barney's corner in the J.C. Penney stores contains Barney coloring books, Barney bedsheets, Barney belts, Barney nightlights, Barney suspenders, and even Barney underpants, with that large, grinning purple presence bringing up the rear.

Over 4 million videos and nearly 3 million plush Barneys and Baby Bops have been rung up at cash registers since 1988. During one Christmas season, J.C. Penney sold more than a million stuffed Barneys. Hasbro's talking Barney sells in the millions at retail, and Barney stuffed animals also sell millions of dollars worth of merchandise.

Barney has captured both the adoration of 2- to 5-year-old children and of retailers, who frequently cannot seem to keep up with the demand for licensed products. However, with the growth in Barney mania, Lyons Group, which manages Barney's merchandising rights, is trying to control the marketing of related Barney products. The Lyons Group has earned a reputation for being vigilant about where the character appears and how he is presented. Some retailers have even complained about the stringent hold the Lyons Group maintains on the property and the fact that it insists on approving every aspect of selling, including artwork.

Until recently, sales of Barney licensed goods were phenomenal. At Macy's department stores, supply could not meet the demand. Customers literally bought the merchandise right out of the cartons. Many supply problems stemmed from J.C. Penney's agreement to have the Barney products exclusively through much of 1993. Those who were producing goods could not manufacture them fast enough. J.C. Penney stores did more than $50 million in Barney business in 1992.

However, after an extraordinary three-year run, some say licenses of Barney are struggling. Barney's popularity is definitely not over. Despite the downturn in sales, Barney is always going to be part of the retail store's product mix. In 1993 retailers may have had 100 feet of shelf space for Barney products. By 1995, they had about 20 feet.

Barney's creators have handed out 42 licenses to produce about 100 products with Barney's image. But, overexposure can be fatal. Barney's PBS television show is still a hit, his second album just came out, he has a radio talk show syndicated in 65 markets, and he recently signed a movie deal with Geffen pictures and Warner Brothers. Nevertheless, elsewhere Barney's products are in trouble. And, the Lyons Group has issued a moratorium on any new licenses and has decide to focus more on Baby Bop and her brother, BJ.

The popularity of a licensed character like Barney is often meteoric, featuring a swift rise that ends with a rapid decline in popularity. In 1993, retailers sold about $500 million worth of licensed merchandise bearing the likeness of Barney. *Forbes* magazine ranked Barney as that year's third-highest-earning entertainer, bringing in roughly $84 million in royalties and gross earnings. By 1994, sales of Barney merchandise were estimated by one industry source at less than a third of that total.

What happened? Industry experts guarantee that almost any licensed character is destined to be replaced by a new licensed character or to fall victim to poorly executed marketing plans. In addition, failure to properly manage such elements as distribution, timing, or even quality control can quickly put a licensed character in consumer disfavor.

Signs of an imminent Barney burnout were everywhere in 1994, with rampant "Barney Bashing," the incessant reruns, the counterfeit "knock-off" products or a dozen equally plausible reasons for the slide in sales. The peculiar thing is that as a television personality, the dinosaur himself is far from fossilized. The show still has a weekly audience of millions of viewers.

The Lyons Group 1994 sales certainly did not compare with 1993, but compared with other brands in the business, it did rather well. Many people fall into the trap of comparing Barney today and what it was in 1993. Barney was so big that it could not have possibly stayed at that level much longer. Gauging the performance of a licensed character to what it did in its biggest year will be disappointing all the time. Every license does not stay forever at its peak.

Retailers are very skittish about seeing rates of Barney sales drop versus their inventory positions. If they do not see it moving off the shelf at the rate they want to see, then they will basically back away. There are sales left in Barney, and once the oversupply of Barney merchandise moves through the marketplace, then it will probably do well again.

## THE FUTURE

The toy market is one of the most highly competitive consumer products areas. While the industry is dominated by two large competitors, Hasbro and Mattel, there are many small firms that have the potential for producing and marketing innovative new toys. There are also firms in the entertainment industry, such as Disney, which have the choice of licensing the rights to their products or to do their own manufacturing and marketing. There are also threats from the "edutainment" (combining education and entertainment) industry, which is focusing on titles for entertaining children.

What marketing strategy would you advise Hasbro to pursue in marketing its *Barney & Friends* line of products? How would you stimulate the sales of *Barney & Friends* products? What specific price, distribution, promotion, and product elements would you propose and why? How would you deal with the growth competition in the toy industry, which focuses on similar products, particularly dinosaurs?

## Sources

"America's Toy Industry: Nightmare." *Economist*, 337, 7945 (December 16, 1995). 58, 62; UK 78, 84.

Chanil, Debra. "Toys: Playing with Basics." *Discount Merchandiser*, 34, 2 (February 1994): 26–30.

"Film, TV Licenses Animate New Products at Toy Fair." *Discount Store News*, 33, 6 (March 21, 1994): 37–38.

Hample, Scott. "Endangered Species." *American Demographics Marketing Tools Supplement* (May 1995): 22–28.

*Hasbro Inc. 1994 Annual Report.*

Hayden, Chaunce. "Barney." *Stepin' Out* (March 30–April 5, 1994): 22–23, 26, 28.

Kimelman, John. "How Hasbro Snagged Barney." *Financial World*, 163, 1 (January 4, 1994): 36.

Kimelman, John. "No Babe in Toyland." *Financial World*, 163, 1 (January 4, 1994): 34–36.

La Franco, Robert. "Milking a Dinosaur." *Forbes*, 154, 8 (October 10, 1994): 122.

LaMonica, Paul R. "Mattel and Hasbro: Toy Stories." *Financial World*, 165, 1 (January 2, 1996): 20–22.

Liebeck, Laura. "Licensing is Not Mere Child's Play." *Discount Store News*, 33, 11 (June 6, 1994): 19, 45.

Lubove, Seth. "The Growing Gets Tough." *Forbes* (April 13, 1992): 68–70.

Maremont, Mark and Greg Bowens. "Brawls in Toyland." *Business Week* (December 21, 1992): 35–36.

Miller, Cyndee. "Finding Next Big Toy is Not Child's Play." *Marketing News*, 28, 11 (May 23, 1994): 2.

"Not Toying Around." *Forbes* (January 3, 1994): 131.

Overbeck, Joy. "I Love You. . . You Hate Me?" *TV Guide* (April 23, 1994): 30–32.

Reda, Susan. "The Barney Boom." *Stores*, 75, 6 (June 1993): 56–57.

Reeks, Ann. "Barney *The* Dino-Star." *Parenting* (April 1993): 88–93.

Teitelbaum, Richard S. "Children a Mixed Blessing? Not to These Stocks." *Fortune* (November 29, 1993): 27–28.

Touby, Laurel. "Suddenly, Tyco Is Playing with the Big Boys." *Business Week* (June 15, 1992): 124–125.

Weiner, Stewart. "Purple Passion." *TV Guide* (February 27, 1993): 22–23.

# *Lotus Development* 6

In 1989, Lotus Development Corporation took a risk by entering a new category of software called "groupware." Since, 1994, sales of Notes, Lotus' groupware offering, approached $200 million annually. This gave the software maker a significant lead in this innovative form of computing where corporations use personal computer (PC) networks controlled by groupware to help employees share information and work more closely with one another.

Companies report both quantitative and qualitative gains from the use of Lotus Notes, including an average return on investment of 179 percent over three years. Lotus Notes supports a broad class of business-process applications that require ongoing action by participants. It enables enterprise-wide collaboration and the sharing of work-flow applications over local networks and WANs. Lotus Notes users include an impressive list of blue chip corporations such as Bank of America, Price Waterhouse, and General Motors. The Notes starter kit of software for two users and a server cost $995 in 1994. Pricing for bigger networks was typically about $300 per PC computer.

Lotus Notes users say that this innovative software has brought about strong support for team work, a huge reduction in paper usage, better information access, more productive decisions, and improved internal communications (Fig. 6.6–1). Notes also leads naturally to business process re-engineering and to work teams consisting of people in different departments across different countries. These abilities surpass those of such old communication tools as mail, fax, and phones.

Lotus Notes has more than 5,000 customers (or about 1.3 million users). An entire industry has built up around Notes, with more than 8,000 new products and services designed to enhance the operations of Lotus Notes. Notes runs on Windows and OS/2 PCs, Macintoshes, and many UNIX machines. It incorporates elements of e-mail, bulletin boards, and databases to give workers, regardless of location, access to a wide variety of information. While Notes looks superficially like just another communications program, its real benefit is in how it can change business practices in a way that enhances white-collar productivity through better business information exchange and communications.

Computer networks have revolutionized intraoffice communications. But many employees spend much of their time away from the office, disconnected from the in-

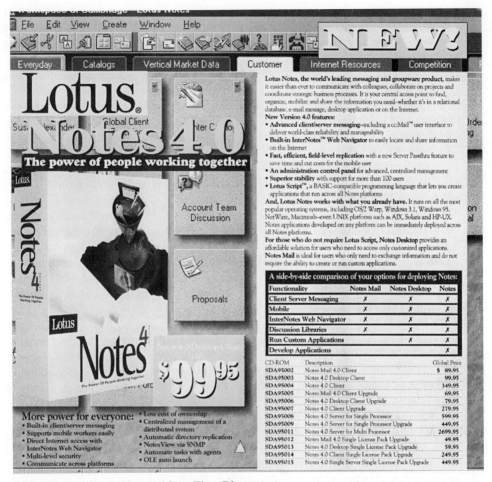

**FIGURE 6.6–1** Lotus Notes ad from Tiger Direct

formation on a firm's main computer hubs. Notes is the answer because it allows identical copies of information to be stored on multiple computers, including remote laptops. During each remote access, Notes sends only what has changed since the last time the user accessed the office network. With this technology, sales representatives only need access to phone lines to keep their inventory lists up to date. Notes provides multiple levels of security, an excellent model for interaction and response, and add-in tools for extensive customization. Software retailer Egghead uses Notes to handle orders from its corporate customers, and Compaq Computer uses the system to give product and price information to customers.

## THE POWER OF GROUPWARE

Because groupware enables users to share information, it is the perfect tool for the 1990s cooperative cultures promoted by many firms. Run on a client server or PC network, groupware allows unstructured information such as text to be disseminated throughout an organization. User departments design databases to hold the information that they need to do business. Users can then enter, search, share, and organize this information in ways which better suite their information needs and work habits. The replication function of groupware enables information held in the same databases to be synchronized regularly.

Groupware is commonly confused with messaging but differs in one vital respect: in messaging users have to specify to whom e-mail messages are sent. With groupware, users enter information into a common interest database that anyone can access and then enter his or her comments.

Groupware managed information can be divided into three categories: library, discussion, and activity tracking. Library information is for reference only. There is an enormous amount of information and experience locked up in people's heads, files, and libraries that can be shared. A variety of databases can be designed and employees can both feed information into the system and use it. With discussion databases, comments, questions, or ideas are entered into a database in order to attract good quality responses. Activity tracking is the most common Lotus Notes application. This involves constant contact with sales representatives and the recording of prospect and customer contacts, which are accessible to all users. This way all sales representatives know of every contact that has been made.

Typically, the inside representative creates a document, usually by filling out an electronic form, when an account is contacted. The outside representative adds follow-up comments from a face-to-face meeting. Accounting can include a document disclosing the account's payment history and creditworthiness. And the sales manager can review all of this information together to determine if the level of sales activity is appropriate.

The ability of Lotus Notes to replicate information is a major aspect of its competitive advantage. This technology allows servers to update each other by communicating across a network or telephone lines. Notes' replication coordinates data from multiple servers or distributes a database across a firm. This allows multiple users to work on the same database simultaneously. Conflicting information is automatically reconciled based on predetermined rules and date/time stamping. Other changes are also chronicled, creating an audit trail or "thread" of discussion.

A major drawback for Lotus Notes is the tendency to attempt to use it for everything. The ease with which end-users are able to build their own applications can result in expensive experiments, including failures. Users will often attempt to build applications better suited for a relational database or some more sophisticated programming effort. While the Notes application may seem to work well initially, it may not work when scaled up to meet the needs of a large department or organization. For example, many early Notes users tried to build travel expense systems only to discover that the systems got too slow once more than a few hundred forms were stored in the database.

## GROUPWARE COMPETITION

Although Notes was launched in 1989, roughly half of its total sales were made in 1994. By the end of 1994, of the 60 million computers in the United States some 1.3 million, had Notes installed, a market penetration of just over 2 percent. That left a major opportunity for other groupware manufacturers, and for Lotus. The marketing battle over groupware products is likely to be intense as several more firms, including Microsoft, Novell, and Netscape, have products aimed at this groupware market.

Part of Microsoft's plan is to make the switch to groupware easier. Because Notes is very comprehensive, installing it requires a significant amount of planning, programming, and training. Microsoft's approach allows customers to build their system using modules for e-mail, forms generation, and scheduling. Microsoft's offerings are easier to customize and make tracking system use simpler. Its offering beats Notes' per-PC price. However, some question whether Microsoft's collection of modules, rather than Lotus' single program, is the best approach. To stay competitive, Notes is being adapted to run on more brands of computers, adding a new forms program, a better programming language, and the ability to store video clips.

## THREATS TO GROUPWARE

Today, groupware, and particularly Lotus Notes, faces a new potential threat from the World Wide Web or Internet. As with groupware, the World Wide Web can be used for information sharing and communications between workers. At the end of 1994, the Internet had 30,000 Web sites, and it was growing rapidly. The main appeal of the Web is its ease of use. As with Notes, the Web is document based, and the broadcast nature of the Web makes it a good arena for developing applications that involve document publishing.

The core of any Notes application is a database of documents that appear to the user as forms that can be viewed with a browser. These documents can have any arbitrary structure for content. Notes is also able to store and manage collections of data that do not readily lend themselves to traditional database system approaches. Notes can easily support such facilities as passing information as formatted text, tabular data, graphics, linked or embedded objects, and multimedia objects, such as scanned images and faxes, voice, sound, and video. Notes also incorporates a full text search engine, allowing users to index and search documents. It can also implement version control to track multiple changes that different users make to a single document.

Lotus Notes advocates were the innovators of the early 1990s, unleashing the then new technology of document-oriented groupware to deliver real benefits. However, by 1995, the innovators on the Internet raised the question of whether or not Notes was a needlessly expensive and proprietary way of doing what the World Wide Web already did. Nevertheless, some recognized the strengths of both approaches and sought to learn how to make them work together for maximum effect. Notes supporters say that the Web lacks many of the features that make Notes such a powerful a tool; however, it is only a matter of time before those capabilities are added to the Web.

Another major threat to groupware comes from corporations creating "Intranets," which involve using Internet technology both within an office and to interact with the outside world, creating environments for more productive worker collaboration.

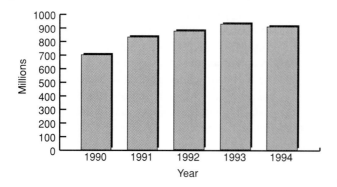

**FIGURE 6.6–2** Lotus Development Corporation Total Sales

*Source: Lotus Development Corporation 1994 Annual Report.*

## LOTUS DEVELOPMENT CORPORATION PERFORMANCE

Lotus Development Corporation has three major businesses. The first two, desktop and communications applications, are well established. As the firm transitions toward communications continues, the desktop business remains substantial, generating revenues and profits that enable Lotus to invest in growth. The third business, public networks and interenterprise computing, is growing and has significant potential.

Lotus' commitment to the desktop remains strong. As a result, it continues to release applications such as 1-2-3 Release 5, SmartSuite, Approach, Organizer, Freelance Graphics, and Ami Pro. But this is no longer an easy business. There are factors, such as the maturity of the business and intense competition, which have changed it forever. Renewed growth in this market will depend on Lotus' ability to reinvent it through team computing, which is at the heart of the groupware concept.

Overall, Lotus' worldwide revenue decreased one percent to $971 million in 1994 (Fig. 6.6–2), while profits declined (Fig. 6.6-3). But, revenue from desktop applications declined by 20 percent. Revenue from desktop applications represented 64 percent of total revenue in 1994, as compared with 79 percent in 1993.

In contrast, revenue from communications products and services grew by 94 percent. Revenue from communications products and services represented 36 percent of total revenue in 1994 as compared with 19 percent in 1993. The primary component of the communications revenue growth was a substantial increase in Lotus Notes sales.

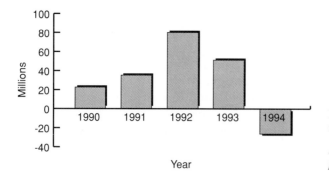

**FIGURE 6.6–3** Lotus Development Corporation Net Income

*Source: Lotus Development Corporation 1994 Annual Report.*

Notes revenue increased by more than 100 percent during 1994, and the number of Notes users more than doubled worldwide.

Lotus believes that its Notes performance was driven by several elements. As the client-server market expands and there is a greater availability of networked PCs, demand for networked applications, such as Notes, increases. In addition, end-user demand for Notes has grown dramatically as customers have begun to understand how the product's workgroup computing capabilities can enable them to become more productive.

## IBM'S ACQUISITION OF LOTUS DEVELOPMENT

In 1995, IBM agreed to pay $3.5 billion to acquire Lotus Development, mainly to grab Lotus Notes. IBM hopes to use Notes as its way of establishing a presence in collaborative computing. However, if Notes is going to justify its price tag, IBM has to do a better job than Lotus of marketing it to corporate America. IBM faces the same problems Lotus had explaining the benefits of Notes. Notes is also difficult and costly to implement. Because Notes is based on the concepts of information sharing and team computing, it often poses challenges to a company's established culture, especially those with hierarchical organizational structures in which employees are accustomed to rewards based on individual contributions.

After the acquisition, IBM quickly began marketing a new version of Notes, which allows it to read and create information for the World Wide Web, making it a far more useful tool for electronic commerce. This new version also facilitates electronic data interchange between companies or individuals via the Internet in two ways. Web pages can be created using Notes, and individuals can click onto the Web while reading e-mail from a colleague. However, IBM did not drop the price for its Notes software. Instead it introduced a stripped-down desktop version for between $69 and $155.

This latest version of Notes, release 4.0, has the following features for integrating with the Internet.

### InterNotes Server

This is a gateway to the Internet that runs on a Notes server (the software that coordinates communications for all PCs with Notes). It provides security limits on inbound traffic from the Internet, and it controls outbound Internet access.

### InterNotes Publisher

This application translates Notes documents into Hyper Text Markup Language (HTML), which is widely used on the World Wide Web. This allows Notes applications to produce Web documents as output.

### InterNotes Web Navigator

The Notes Web browser (for interacting with the World Wide Web) works within Notes. Users can control it with the usual Notes macros and scripts, which are tools for customizing how Notes operates.

With these tools, users can construct and manage applications that include unique features of both Notes and the Web and, thereby, benefit from the integration of the two technologies.

The big challenge for IBM is to counter competition from Microsoft, which has already convinced a large number of Notes third parties to develop products for its exchange messaging server. Novell is also gaining market share with its GroupWise messaging system. And, Netscape Communications' Collabra has a groupware user interface that effectively connects users to the Internet.

## THE FUTURE OF GROUPWARE

With Notes, Lotus educated the marketplace, and it made the competition aware of the potential for groupware sales. However, some argue that it could have done more and that it did a delinquent marketing job over a period of five years when it had no competition. IBM may bring more marketing know-how to the groupware arena and make more of the potential for Notes sales.

Some in the industry also doubt the long-term viability of Lotus Notes. They point to the promising coupling of the Internet and groupware capabilities. Lotus Notes may still however have a window of opportunity to exploit based on its lead in group-oriented collaborative software technology, but IBM needs to bring new and more innovative Notes offerings to market.

Even without strong groupware competitors such as Microsoft, the World Wide Web is a significant potential threat to Notes. It is easier to set up collaborative applications on the Web than it is to establish a network of Notes servers, create applications, devise replication schemes, and then manage that system. IBM hopes to address the threat by tightly meshing Notes with the Web, allowing Notes clients to browse the Web and Web browsers to access Notes, and by positioning Notes as a Web authoring and management system.

Both the Web and Notes have server environments designed for information distribution. However, to view data on a Notes server requires both a Notes client (Notes software on a PC) and permission to view the desired documents. This rigid control can make it difficult to create public domain documents or to share information with members of the general public, some of whom might not have the required Notes software.

Putting information from Notes on the Web solves the problem of giving access to non-Notes users. Anyone with a Web browser can access the Notes documents put on the Web. An organization can publish information on the Web to capitalize on its graphical nature and ready public access. This increase in visibility can aid overall firm marketing efforts. But the Web's ability to integrate itself into a company's core business applications is weak.

No organization wants to expose its confidential information to public access. Internet access to a firm's information can result in unauthorized viewing or possible tampering. While techniques for implementing security on the Internet are still evolving, Notes has good security features.

Both Notes and the Web (with the aid of additional software) can be programmed to search for and retrieve data from a variety of sources. Notes 4.0 includes the use of the InterNotes Web Navigator to create applications to monitor the Web, which allows firms to monitor Web sites for changes and create summaries of those changes.

What marketing strategy would you advise IBM to pursue in the selling of Lotus Notes to businesses? What specific price, distribution, promotion, and product elements would you propose and why? How would you deal with the growth competition from such firms as Microsoft, Novell, and Netscape? What do you think about IBM's concern with the competitive threat of the Internet?

## Sources

Baldwin, Howard. "Lotus Notes: More Power, Less Hassle." *Macworld*, 13, 1 (January 1996): 120–121.

Barney, Doug. "Notes 4.0 Promises to be Better at Being Bigger." *Network World*, 12, 40 (October 2, 1995): 10.

Baum, David. "Groupware: Is it Notes or Nothing?" *Datamation*, 41, 8 (May 1, 1995): 45–48.

Booker, Ellis. "The Web vs. Notes vs. Microsoft Exchange: World-Wide Web Emerges as a Viable Notes Alternative for Some." *Computerworld*, 29, 22 (May 29, 1995): 26.

Brandt, Richard. "The Battle of the Network Stars Boots Up." *Business Week* (April 5, 1994): 128–129.

Davis, Jessica. "Lotus Grooms Notes for Internet Glory." *InfoWorld*, 17, 47 (November 20, 1995): 8.

Davis, Jessica. "Lotus Will Leverage Notes with Web Links." *InfoWorld*, 17, 38 (September 18, 1995): 1, 20.

Davis, Jessica, and Ed Scannell. "Lotus Jockeys Notes into Better Spot in On-line Race." *InfoWorld*, 17, 51 (December 18, 1995): 6.

Frye, Colleen. "Lotus Buyout Raises Groupware Awareness." *Software Magazine*, 15, 10 (October 1995): 100.

Glyn-Jones, Frank. "The Groupware Grapevine." *Management Today* (April 1995): 83–86.

Hawkins, Donald T. "The Evolving Lotus Notes Information Industry." *Online*, 19, 5 (September/October 1995): 64–73.

Hummel, Robert L. "Net-Surfing with Notes." *BYTE* (March 1996): 96, DM 13.

Kirkpatrick, David. "Groupware Goes Boom." *Fortune* (December 27, 1993): 99–106.

Kirkpatrick, David. "Why Microsoft Can't Stop Lotus Notes." *Fortune* (December 12, 1994): 141–157.

Landau, Nilly. "Managing Information Overload." *International Business* (March 1995): 18–20.

*Lotus Corporation 1994 Annual Report.*

"Lotus Stays The Course." *ComputerWorld* (November 13, 1995): 41.

Mohan, Suruchi. "Lotus Goes Both Ways." *ComputerWorld*, 29, 41 (October 9, 1995): 60.

Mohan, Suruchi. "The Web vs. Notes vs. Microsoft Exchange: Users Plan for Dual Environments." *Computerworld*, 29, 22 (May 29, 1995): 26.

Rabinovitch, Eddie. "Will IBM Help or Hinder Notes?" *Communications Week* (July 24, 1995): 65.

Sliwa, Carol, and Peggy Watt. "Exchange Copies Notes." *Network World*, 12, 49 (December 4, 1995): 1, 74.

Timmins, Annmarie. "Web Moves in on Notes' Turf." *Network World*, 12, 30 (July 24, 1995): 29.

Van Kirk, Douglas. "The Lowdown on Lotus Notes." *CFO: The Magazine for Senior Financial Executives*, 11, 4 (April 1995): 77–79.

Vaughan, Jack. "Whither Lotus Notes?" *Software Magazine*, 16, 1 (January 1996): 28–29.

Verespej, Michael A. "Gutsy Decisions of 1995: IBM Goes Shopping." *Industry Week*, 245, 2 (January 22, 1996): 27.

Wildstrom, Stephen H. "The Year To Go Nuts About Notes." *Business Week* (January 23, 1995): 22.

---

# *Hilton Hotels* CASE 7

Hilton Hotels Corporation owns, manages and/or franchises hotels, casino-hotels and inns; sells furnishings, equipment, and supplies to hotels, motels, and inns; and operates a computerized reservation system for the hotel industry. After two major takeover attempts in the early 1990s, Hilton Hotels decided that it had to change by becoming a more aggressive business operation. The result was the decision to move heavily into gambling. This change of strategic direction represented a significant shift in Hilton's business focus and marketing objectives. Already the owner of four casinos in Nevada, the Los Angeles hotelier began pushing projects in New Orleans, Chicago, Egypt, Turkey, Uruguay, and Australia.

While gaming accounted for about 34 percent of Hilton's overall sales in the early 1990s, its four casinos contributed nearly two-thirds of Hilton's operating earnings. Nevertheless, Hilton's new emphasis on gambling carried a large element of risk. Competition for the gaming dollar is intense, and the degree of investment needed to be successful is high. Hilton has had to put more than $6 million into renovating the Las Vegas Hilton to keep up with such rivals as the Mirage and the Excalibur, and it has also renovated the Flamingo Hilton to keep pace with other new places. To lure high rollers away from other casinos, the Las Vegas Hilton has had to be more generous about extending credit, resulting in bad gaming debts and reductions in operating income from gaming.

## HILTON 1994 PERFORMANCE

The year 1994 was transitional for Hilton Hotels because, in a sharp reversal from the previous four year, hotels prospered while gaming struggled. This was true for Hilton

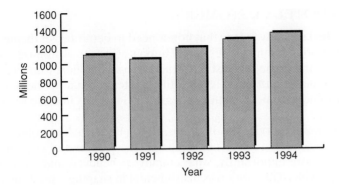

FIGURE 6.7–1 Hilton Hotels Total Revenues

*Source: Hilton Hotels Corporation 1994 Annual Report.*

and for the industry (Fig. 6.7–1). Hilton's net income for 1994 was $121.7 million, up 18 percent from $102.7 million in 1993 (Fig. 6.7–2). Total gaming revenue increased 2 percent to $889.2 million in 1994 compared with $873.5 million in 1993. Casino revenue, a component of gaming revenue, was $480.6 million in 1994 compared with $502.1 million in 1993. Gaming operating income was $159.0 million in 1994, a 7 percent decline from $170.5 million in 1993. Excluding the results of the company's gaming facilities in New Orleans and Windsor, both of which commenced operations in 1994, revenue increased 1 percent and operating income decreased 12 percent from the prior year.

For 1994, Hilton hotels showed system-wide occupancy of 70 percent, a three-point increase over 1993, while the U.S. hotel industry as a whole had occupancy of 65 percent. Equally as important as the increase in occupancy was the significant improvement in average daily rate. For the year, that rate jumped 7 percent over last year.

As of the end of 1994, Hilton's gaming segment included five wholly-owned Nevada hotel-casinos, equity income and management fees from partially owned hotel-casinos in Queensland, Australia and Istanbul, Turkey, and equity income and management fees from gaming operations in New Orleans, Louisiana and Windsor, Ontario, Canada. Its Nevada gaming operations offered a diversified product and service mix, which appeals to a broad spectrum of customers. The Flamingo Hilton-Las Vegas caters to the broad Las Vegas middle market, while the Las Vegas Hilton caters to premium players and the convention market. The Flamingo Hilton-Reno focuses on middle-market activity, while the Reno Hilton targets both convention and middle-market activity. The Flamingo Hilton-Laughlin targets the budget-market segment.

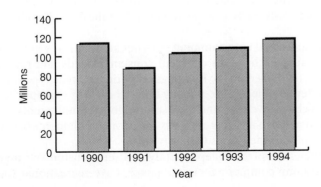

FIGURE 6.7–2 Hilton Hotels Corporation Net Income

*Source: Hilton Hotels Corporation 1994 Annual Report.*

## UNDERSTANDING HOTEL CUSTOMERS

The abundance of spare bed capacity means that hotels need to better target the needs of customer segments and offer distinctive services. Hilton's efforts to customize hotel services by purpose of visit and origin of guest is instructive to all hoteliers who want to increase their service, and hence customer, levels. Hilton International provides a diversity of services to customers from 130 nationalities at 150 locations in more than 50 countries around the world.

To determine the optimum service for the 1990s, Hilton undertook customer and employee surveys to identify market needs and expectations, the views of employees on job-related issues and, more importantly, what employees believed that their customers wanted them to provide. This work was instrumental in shaping a program designed to create a more contemporary service-led organization. It led, in part, to the Hilton Promise that every Hilton employee would give superior and distinctive service, which guests would remember and for which they would return.

Hilton's research highlighted the need for a product development approach that would enable customers to match their needs easily against a specially adapted style or area of hotel service. This led to attempts to define the concept of a service brand, which might support the kinds of innovation fundamental to Hilton's planned growth. The adopted approach was to consider different service clusters that combined, would provide key benefits to customers. The underlying assumption is that, if the majority of customers feel comfortable with the hotel service environment, that leads to additional guest satisfaction and to new business.

## THE HOTEL INDUSTRY FOCUSES ON GAMING AND ENTERTAINMENT

By mid-1994, Las Vegas operators had spent some $3.2 billion on the concept of packaging gaming with theme entertainment to create a destination resort. The same amount or more is likely to be committed by the year 2000. While this extends the Las Vegas tradition of having entertainment in show rooms as a sideline, these new offerings represent a significantly different concept and greater expenses.

Yet, despite huge investments, some casino operators are offering entertainment as a central attraction without much success. Some of these projects have been successful, while others were misconceived and perform below optimum levels. Part of the reason for this uneven performance is the disparate nature of entertainment and games and the difficulty in making them work together. However, the cost of providing entertainment is justified by its effectiveness in attracting people to the gaming tables and machines.

The diverse nature of games and entertainment does not automatically guarantee successful combinations because each serves different consumer needs and requires different management strategies. Based on the Las Vegas experience, some types of entertainment constitute a better complement to gaming than others. For example, location-based entertainment such as revenues and circuses are good complements, as is shopping. However, interactive video and feature films are poor complements because they provide experiences similar to the games themselves.

Gaming and entertainment evolved independently and serve customers in very different ways. Games, including commercial casino games, have recreational value only when people actively engage in them. Playing a game involves behaving according to the rules of the game. In contrast, entertainment is not usually defined by formal rules and is not normally interactive. Commercial entertainment is presented to consumers in a finished, ready-to-be-enjoyed form. Because games and entertainment are leisure pastimes, many casino operators seem to assume that gaming is just another form of entertainment. The distinction between games and entertainment is particularly nebulous in Nevada because games have been packaged as fantasy and presented in conjunction with spectacular floor shows; inexpensive or free food and alcoholic beverages; and outdoor recreation such as golf courses, swimming pools, and tennis courts. The core purpose of entertainment at gaming locations is to attract people to the games and any entertainment that detracts from that purpose is a bad fit.

## PURSUING MARKETS

What strategies would you advise Hilton to pursue in the hotel and gaming markets? What specific price, distribution, promotion, and product elements would you propose and why? How would you deal with the growth in competition from other gaming and hotel concerns? What balance would you strike between hotel and gaming operations and why?

## Sources

Casper, Carol. "Confirmed Reservations." *Restaurant Business*, 94, 17 (November 20, 1995): 104–118.

Christiansen, Eugene, Martin Brinkerhoff-Jacobs, and Julie Cornell. "Gaming and Entertainment: An Imperfect Union?" *Hotel & Restaurant Administration Quarterly*, 36, 2 (April 1995): 79–94.

Grover, Ronald and Eric Schine. "Can Hilton Draw a Full House?" *Business Week* (June 8, 1992): 88–89.

Gubernick, Lisa. "Moving on Vegas," *Forbes*, 154, 8 (October 10, 1994): 116–118.

*Hilton Hotels Corporation 1994 Annual Report.*

"Hilton's Home Away From Home." *Health Manpower Management*, 20, 4 (1994): 15–16.

Machan, Dyan. "'We Sell Sleep'." *Forbes* (September 14, 1992): 421–422.

Martin, Richard. "Caesars, Planet Hollywood Bet on Casino Hotels." *Nation's Restaurant News*, 28, 40 (October 10, 1994): 7.

Rice, Faye. "Competition." *Fortune* (October 4, 1993): 125–128.

Rice, Faye. "Where The Bargains Are in Hotels." *Fortune* (April 20, 1992): 91–98.

Stone, Amey. "Hotels With Corporate Room Service." *Business Week* (January 24, 1994): 110.

Walkup, Carolyn. "Cost-Cutting Hotel Chains Check in With New Brands, Value Formats." *Nation's Restaurant News*, 29, 31 (August 7, 1995): 130–134.

Walkup, Carolyn. "Hotels Key in One New Concepts for Tired Restaurants." *Nation's Restaurant News,* 29, 17 (April 24, 1995): 37–40.

# *Fox Broadcasting* CASE 8

In 1994, New World Communications Group Inc. shocked the television broadcast industry when it signed 12 of its network affiliations, 8 of them from CBS, with the Fox Broadcasting Co. network. New World's move from CBS to Fox was designed to give it more flexibility in its program scheduling. At the time, CBS and its rivals each produced 99 hours of primetime programming a week while Fox only produced 15 hours. The difference freed up time for such New World productions as a sequel to Jacqueline Susann's *Valley of the Dolls*, which it planned to show at night. On CBS affiliates, that show would have conflicted with *David Letterman*. Fox, though, produced no late-night programming. So New World could now air the program when it wanted.

This new arrangement also allowed New World stations to produce more local programming, which generates a higher profit because the affiliates can keep all the advertising revenue from those shows. Normally, affiliates serve as conduits for the networks, turning over the bulk of their airtime to network news, sports, and entertainment. With just three predominant networks, affiliates had few options in deciding about their programming.

A switch like that made by New World hurts any network severely. The network loses audience and, therefore, has less advertising to sell for a season. Fox, on the other hand, emerges a big winner by moving into the same league as the big three networks. Fox now reaches nearly the same number of U.S. households as the other networks. One solution if a major network wants to keep affiliates from moving to Fox is to give them more money or more airtime for their own programming.

With the advent of cable, the need for major television networks was called into question. Concurrently, cost-conscious networks, notably CBS, slashed its compensation, confident that its affiliates had no choice but to accept. Fox's emergence as a deep-pocketed suitor changed all that. The Fox and New World deal made the networks realize the importance of distribution, which is something that they had been ignoring recently. Instead of continuing a campaign to cut the cash compensation they pay affiliates, which can total about $2 million in such large markets as Atlanta, the networks have reversed course. They are now more likely to promise better compensation checks or give affiliates more time to air local ads.

## NEWS CORPORATION AND FOX BROADCASTING

The year 1995 was one in which News Corporation, the owner of Fox Broadcasting, *TV Guide*, and other entertainment entities, continued to improve its overall earnings (Fig. 6.8–1). Despite costly price wars and higher paper prices, consolidated revenues grew to $9 billion (Fig. 6.8–2). For 1995, earnings increased by 11 percent to $991 million, led, in part, by continuing growth in its television businesses both in the United States and the United Kingdom.

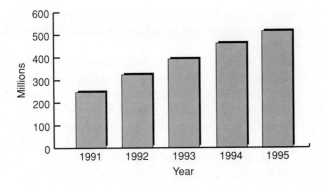

**FIGURE 6.8–1** News Corporation Television Segment Operating Income

*Source: News Corporation 1995 Annual Report and estimates.*

Television is an area of primary focus for News Corp., and fiscal year 1995 was no exception. In 1995, it combined the Fox spirit and edge with the excitement and action of the National Football League to launch the much anticipated *The NFL on FOX*. The critics and competitors said it would never work, but it was a great success.

Fox made significant gains versus the three older networks, emerging at the end of 1995 as fully competitive in many key areas, including program performance, distribution capabilities, and sales. Fueled by successful series such as *The X-Files* and *Melrose Place*, Fox ranked third for the broadcast season in primetime ratings among adults 18–49, beating CBS. Fox was also the only network to show significant year-on-year growth in primetime as 70 percent of those hours had ratings growth versus 1994. In all, Fox improved its distribution through 24 television station affiliation switches. Based on this improved distribution, and the ratings growth, Fox was able to reach sales pricing parity with the other three networks. In the recently completed upfront sales market for the 1995–96 broadcast season, Fox achieved a revenue milestone surpassing the $1 billion mark. This figure represents a 40 percent increase over 1994 and Fox's strongest upfront sales ever.

## TARGETING CHILDREN

The formerly sleepy world of children's television has become very competitive as nearly every broadcast and cable entity seeks to become a major player. At the top of

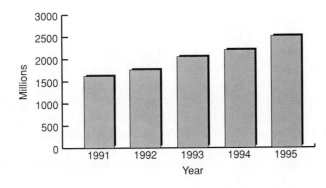

**FIGURE 6.8–2** News Corporation Television Segment Revenues

*Source: News Corporation 1995 Annual Report and estimates.*

the list is the Disney/ABC merger, with its shockwaves being felt everywhere. Meanwhile, fledgling network WB became an instant hit with kids, and cable's Nickelodeon and the Cartoon Network posted large gains.

Several companies, including Disney/ABC, Fox, Nickelodeon, and Discovery, are planning to offer new kids cable networks. But, before any of these new kids channels can succeed, they must first be launched, and there is some question about how many of the plans will actually result in new offerings. Entertainment for children is a growth business and there is room for two or three more basic kid's channels. Naturally, any expansion will increase the war for children's program talent. The high-end talent is commanding historic fees, and the mid-level talent is much, much better off than ever. But that raises the stakes for new businesses, as the audience pie is sliced thinner.

The role model for all the networks interested in targeting children is Viacom's Nickelodeon, which has, through a strategy built upon original programming, come to dominate the kids television market, even against competitors with access to far more households. As young viewers have flocked to Nickelodeon, so too have advertisers. Nick has become the first cable network to enter the first tier of television, which has long been the exclusive domain of the broadcast networks.

Over the last several years, Nickelodeon has crafted its own cottage industry by finding producers outside the usual realm of network-style kids shows, including Clasky Csupo, makers of *Rugrats* and John Kricfalusi, creator of *Ren & Stimpy*, hitting a motherlode of kids ages 2–11 to make the shows regulars in the top 10 cable ratings. As a result, Nick is now the biggest player in children's television.

However, Fox is not far behind. Fox Children's Network ranked No. 1 in children's programming Monday through Friday and on Saturday mornings among all viewers 2–11 and teens with its 19 hours of programming. On average, over 35 million kids and teens view at least some Fox Children's Network programming each month. Fox Children's Network is home to such shows as *The Turbo Power Rangers*, *Spiderman*, and *Where on Earth is Carmen Sandiego*? Fox Children's Network has five of the top seven children's shows, including the top two, as well as the top seven shows on Saturday mornings.

However, Fox Children's Network is under heavy attack on several fronts, with the strongest competition coming from Nickelodeon. Fox still leads on Saturday morning by 75 percent over both ABC and CBS, but its ratings are down by 27 percent against kids. Weekdays have suffered even more, with a 40 percent drop. Nickelodeon now provides about four times as many kids by audience size than does Fox.

Fox is fighting back with plans to redouble its marketing of the Fox Children's Network and with heavy sales research to show why Fox should be the best buy for those firms advertising to children. The combination of good shows and being on six days a week is a major selling point for Fox versus the broadcast nets. But Nick is on 100 hours a week. As a result, Fox runs the risk of being overpowered. A minimum 12-hour-a-day environment for kids may be the standard to meet. But Fox's children's programming is only on the air for three hours a day. That may have to change. Fox's answer could include launching of a basic kids cable net, which would significantly expand its children's audience.

Fox is also busy creating international kids offerings on cable and satellite. Fox

Children's Networks in Australia and Latin America are operational, a U.K. deal is in the works and, a Pan-Asian service through Star TV is only a matter of time. The need for a deep library to feed these global nets spurred Fox's alliance with Saban Entertainment. Although Saban received no definite commitments from Fox to air its shows, it will take over Fox Children's Network's U.S. licensing and merchandising.

## EXPANSION PLANS

Even as Fox Children's Network faces increasing competition, it is expanding its U.S. offerings. The children's market has great potential for the network, but that opportunity may not be best addressed through Fox's current more general audience focused offering. What strategy would you advise Fox to pursue in targeting the children's market? Should it continue to use its Fox network as the platform or is the idea of a children's network a better way to go? What specific price, distribution, promotion, and product elements would you propose for each alternative and why? How would you deal with the growing competition from such channels as Nickelodeon and Disney?

## Sources

Burgi, Michael. "Cable's Promised Land." *Mediaweek,* 5, 13 (March 27, 1995): 26–37.

Burgi, Michael. "Let Us Entertain You." *Mediaweek,* 6, 13 (March 25, 1996): 14–25.

Dupree, Scotty. "Back to the Future at CBS." *Mediaweek,* 6, 12 (March 18, 1996): 5.

Grover, Ronald. "Are Paramount and Warner Looney Tunes." *Business Week* (January 9, 1995): 46.

Grover, Ronald. "Rupert Runs For Daylight." *Business Week* (October 3, 1994): 56.

Grover, Ronald, Julia Flynn, and Mark Landler. "How Rupert Keeps Doing These Deals." *Business Week* (June 13, 1994): 34–37.

Grover, Ronald, and Mark Landler. "How FOX Outfoxed Itself." *Business Week* (December 20, 1993): 48.

Klemm, Alisa. "Pumping Up Sales." *Sporting Goods Business,* 28, 3 (March 1995): 38–40.

Koselka, Rita. " 'He Was an Octopus. . .' " *Forbes* (October 26, 1992): 192–194.

Landler, Mark, and Ronald Grover. "At CBS, A Steady Feed of Bad News." *Business Week* (October 24, 1994): 40.

Lesly, Elizabeth, Mark Landler, and Gail DeGeorge. "Musical Chairs May Be the Hot New TV Game." *Business Week* (June 6, 1994): 28–29.

Macnow, Glen. "The Real Fall TV Favorite." *Mediaweek,* 5, 24 (June 12, 1995): MQ26–MQ29.

*News Corporation 1995 Annual Report*

Perry, Nancy J. "The Future Is Glued to the Tube." *Fortune,* 126, 6 (September 21, 1992): 99–100.

Schmuckler, Eric. "A Youth Movement at CBS." *Mediaweek,* 5, 12 (March 20, 1995): 5.

# *Avon Products, Inc.* 9

During the 1980s, many acquisitions occurred in the cosmetics, fragrances, and toiletries industries. This rapid consolidation has important long-term marketing strategy implications because large conglomerates have thrown their hats into this consumer products ring. Their deep pockets and traditionally heavy advertising support for personal care products suggest that competitors will have to increase their advertising and R&D budgets to protect market share. Given the huge marketing and distribution systems at the disposal of these competitors, smaller companies with poorly defined market niches have tough fights ahead. Recent restructuring moves among the large players will have an effect too. Avon, and such companies as Tambrands and Gillette, have shed operations unrelated to their basic business. They entered the 1990s with a renewed focus on restoring vigor to their core product lines.

In the meantime, consumer demand is shifting, with today's shopper becoming increasingly price/value-oriented (as the prices of high-end lipsticks and eyeshadows continue to escalate), and a greater percentage of the women who buy cosmetics (many of whom are working) insist on convenience. That is good news for supermarkets and drugstores, which are making sales of makeup and skin treatments at an unprecedented pace. Therein also lie opportunities for offerings in the middle- and lower-price ranges, which have proliferated in recent years. Manufacturers are also catering to the customer's taste for quality.

## AVON PRODUCTS

Avon Products, Inc. is the world's largest manufacturer and direct marketer of cosmetics, fragrances, and toiletries. It also offers costume jewelry and other product lines. Selling in the United States is done mostly direct through door-to-door and workplace representatives who, armed with a new brochure of products (80 to 100 pages) every two weeks, make money from an approximately 40 percent commission on what they sell. These representatives are independent business people, not employees of Avon Products. After taking orders from their customers, these representatives buy products on credit from a regional distribution center, from which Avon ships each representative order within 72 hours.

In 1946, Avon's sales were only $17 million. But all that changed with the economic and sociological trends of the late 1940s, 1950s, and 1960s. Avon's major business expansion took place after World War II with the growth of disposable income, the spread of suburbanization, and the increase in the proportion of large families with women at home. Avon reached a peak in the 1970s when its stock value soared to over $125 million. After that, Avon's fortunes began to decline as its market, customers, and competitors all changed in fundamental ways. Changes in how people live their lives, the emergence of the career-oriented woman, consumerism, and competitive threats now all posed challenges to Avon's vitality and growth potential.

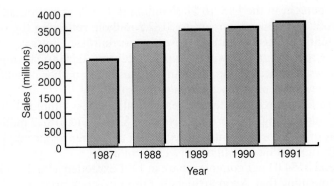

**FIGURE 6.9–1** Avon Products Worldwide Net Sales

*Source: Avon 1991 Annual Report.*

Historically, Avon's marketing costs have been lower than competitors because of its use of direct sales representatives and modest advertising. As a result, Avon has been able to obtain high gross margins. But, with changing times and costs, Avon realizes that it must consider alternatives courses of action if it is to prosper in the future.

After its peak in the 1970s, Avon experienced a series of major setbacks. The 1980s was a very turbulent decade for the firm. Avon's net sales from all operations declined from 1981 to 1985, then increased again due to several success marketing initiatives, including product mix changes and sales force reorganizations (Fig. 6.9–1). Net income from all operations bottomed in 1988, when the firm lost nearly half of its stock holder's equity (Fig. 6.9–2). Draconian cost cutting and the sell-off of several investments in unrelated businesses improved Avon's financial position. However, some argue that no amount of cost cutting will help Avon because it needs to significantly increase sales.

In 1991, Avon had 1,120,000 active sales representatives, operating in its four geographic divisions, which include Europe, the Pacific, the Americas, and the United States. International operations (not including the United States) showed a sales gain of 9 percent to $2.08 billion and a rise in pre-tax profits of 5 percent to $326.7 million. Unit sales rose 6 percent and active representatives increased by 3 percent. Particularly significant for Avon's future was its success in the emerging markets of the former Eastern Bloc of Europe and continued sales growth in China.

**FIGURE 6.9–2** Avon Products Worldwide Net Income

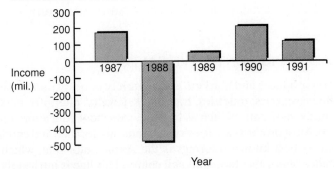

*Source: Avon 1991 Annual Report.*

A sales decline of 2 percent in the U.S. to $1.36 billion in 1991 was attributed to the recession. Pre-tax profit was down 3 percent to $182.2 million, reflecting the soft sales results and investments directed at future growth opportunities. Unit sales declined 5 percent and active representatives were down 4 percent to 425,000. The number of active representatives is critical to the company because the number of sellers times the average size of the orders each places equals total sales.

However, Avon's pre-tax figures for international operations (less United States) and the United States are misleading. The pre-tax profits of $326.7 and $182.2 million above do not include corporate expenses, interest expenses, and other losses and expenses that lead to a 1991 total net income figure of $135.7 million.

Also, Avon's dividend of $4.04 per common share in 1991 exceeded actual net income per share of $1.89, meaning that Avon artificially raised its stock price by guaranteeing a dividend greater than what was justified by its net income. Net income per share actually declined from 1990 to 1991, going from $2.60 per share to $1.89 per share mainly due to a discontinued healthcare business.

## AVON'S STRATEGY

In 1991, Avon continued to implement basic operating strategies that guided the company over the previous three years:

1. Building on or "leveraging" the direct selling system in developing countries.
2. Adapting and contemporizing direct selling in developed countries.
3. Expanding into new geographic markets.
4. Making use of global synergies in sourcing, facilities, and human skills.
5. Making prudent investments for growth while managing with a close eye on the balance sheet.

During 1991, Avon U.S. began implementation of its twin sets of strategies to establish Avon as the "best place" for consumers to buy and the "best place" for representatives to sell. Consumers were offered alternative ways to buy and a variety of new products. Representatives had the benefit of increased training, enhanced materials, and the opportunity to earn more by participating in a tiered sales system. These programs, available to approximately 20 percent of the United States in the latter half of 1991, rolled out nationally during 1992. Supporting both sets of strategies were image enhancement programs, including a redesigned product brochure and a return to mass-media advertising.

## PRODUCT LINE AND REPRESENTATIVE SALES

In the United States, Avon produces and markets a wide variety of beauty and beauty-related products, including cosmetics, toiletries, fragrances, jewelry, plus gifts, decorative items, and more recently, new entries such as lingerie, preschool educational toys, and videotapes (Fig. 6.9–3). Most products are for women, some are for men and children.

Among the company's best-known offerings is the Avon Color line, which includes more than 350 shades of lip, eye, face, and nail colors. This line is intricately or-

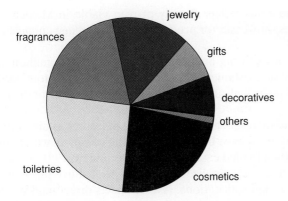

**FIGURE 6.9–3** Avon U.S. Category Sales Distribution (1991 estimated)

*Source:* Estimated from various sources.

ganized to present exactly the right shades for each customer so that a total "look" is coordinated.

Shortly after Avon Color was introduced in 1988, the company provided sales representatives with a new high-technology tool known as the Avon Beauty Vision Personal color computer. In less than five minutes, it analyzed a customer's skin tone, categorized it in one of four color groups, and printed out a variety of recommended shades for each application.

In terms of sales representatives, Avon is well known for its sales force of "Avon ladies" who ring doorbells. But, these sales representatives are no longer just calling on suburban homes. Only about one-third of the firm's worldwide sales comes from traditional door-to-door selling, which is a reduced but still substantial market. Another one-third is produced by selling in the workplace. The Avon sales occur only during lunch or coffee breaks. In the past, Avon discouraged representatives from selling where they were employed or for making calls on offices and plants. But the firm now claims that studies show managers and owners of businesses often encourage such selling because it keeps employees on the premises rather than running out to do shopping, which might delay their return to work. The final one-third of Avon's sales comes from sales representative telemarketing and other sales channels that might be more accurately called "direct marketing" rather than "direct selling."

## BEYOND DIRECT SALES

Avon is becoming a fundamentally different company because it has chosen to move beyond the direct selling approach to distribution. Avon is adding retail outlets, testing ads, and considering infomercials with 800-numbers in an attempt to increase U.S. sales. By using 800-numbers in its advertising and exploring retail opportunities, Avon is looking for new ways to give consumers greater access to its products. Avon estimates there are 10 million customers who do not have an Avon representative and would use an 800-number.

Additionally, Avon is also considering increasing the number of sales distribution centers now serving Avon sales representative in the United States. With this expansion, representatives can pick up products at these new centers, but consumers can also buy products directly there. The concept has already proven viable in Mexico and Tokyo, where the centers serve as showcases for products and as an image enhancer to consumers.

Avon is increasing its U.S. advertising budget by 50 percent to $11 million and running 15-second network television commercials and national print ads touting the options of ordering from its catalog through an 800-number, via fax, by mail, or through a traditional sales representative.

Avon is also working hard to increase sales through such measures as direct mail. Since 1990, some Avon representatives have been supplying the company with names of potential customers, who are then mailed catalogs. As of December, 1991, about 11 percent of customers responded to the personalized campaign, well above the average 3 percent response rate for direct-mail solicitations. Avon expects direct mail will account for $300 million to $500 million in sales within three to five years.

## AVON'S CUSTOMERS AND SALES REPRESENTATIVES

To illustrate Avon's consumer franchise, six product lines are profiled, perfume and cologne, face creams and lotions, foundation make-up, mascara, eyeshadow, and eye liner. Avon's product line appears among the top five competitors in each of the product categories (Table 6.9–1).

Avon sells primarily to women, and secondary to their families. Its product line appeals to both young and middle-aged consumers (Table 6.9–2) contains profiles of Avon's product-line users for some selected products). These customers are also more likely to have upper-lower and lower-middle class incomes.

The best way to understand the demographics of those customers is to compare the Avon's profiles with the profiles of selected competitors (Table 6.9–3) and with those of heavy category users (Table 6.9–4). Such comparisons show that some of Avon's competitors appeal much more to young consumers than does Avon. For example, "Obsession" attracts mostly young customers, while Avon's line of perfumes and colognes appeals to all ages (Table 6.9–2 versus Table 6.9–3). For mascara, Avon appeals more to those 25–54, while Max Factor's product line is more likely to attract those under 35 (Table 6.9–2 versus Table 6.9–3).

**TABLE 6.9–1  Top Five Brand Market Share Rankings**

| Rank | Perfume and Cologne | Face Creams and Lotions | Foundation Make-Up | Mascara | Eye Shadow | Eye Liner |
|------|---------------------|-------------------------|--------------------|---------|------------|-----------|
| 1 | Avon | Oil of Olay | Cover Girl | Maybelline | Maybelline | Maybelline |
| 2 | Estee Lauder | Avon | Mary Kay | Cover Girl | Cover Girl | Cover Girl |
| 3 | Charlie | Mary Kay | Avon | Avon | Avon | Avon |
| 4 | Giorgio | Pond's | Clinique | Mary Kay | Mary Kay | Mary Kay |
| 5 | Chanel | Clinque | Estee Lauder | Estee Lauder | Estee Lauder | Revlon |

*Source:* Simmons Market Research Bureau, Inc., 1991.

TABLE 6.9–2   Avon Products, Inc. Selected User Demographics (women)

| | Perfume and Cologne | Face Creams and Lotions | Foundation Make-Up | Mascara | Eye Shadow | Eye Liner |
|---|---|---|---|---|---|---|
| *Age* | | | | | | |
| 18–24 | 81 | 61 | 60 | 81 | 92 | 129 |
| 25–34 | 108 | 67 | 92 | 129 | 124 | 121 |
| 35–44 | 105 | 105 | 104 | 136 | 144 | 136 |
| 45–54 | 108 | 145 | 131 | 133 | 119 | 115 |
| 55–64 | 92 | 129 | 121 | 86 | 79 | 69 |
| 65 and over | 101 | 115 | 101 | 24 | 30 | 22 |
| | | | | | | |
| *Employed* | | | | | | |
| Full-time | 102 | 100 | 100 | 116 | 127 | 124 |
| Part-time | 91 | 75 | 104 | 136 | 104 | 95 |
| Not employed | 100 | 105 | 99 | 77 | 73 | 78 |
| | | | | | | |
| *HH income* | | | | | | |
| $60,000+ | 57 | 85 | 57 | 85 | 70 | 57 |
| $50,000–$59,999 | 67 | 64 | 62 | 93 | 107 | 82 |
| $35,000–$49,999 | 76 | 86 | 97 | 113 | 113 | 122 |
| $25,000–$34,999 | 116 | 135 | 122 | 112 | 118 | 101 |
| $15,000–$24,999 | 121 | 112 | 121 | 112 | 107 | 111 |
| Less than $15,000 | 126 | 98 | 107 | 80 | 84 | 100 |
| Single | 84 | 56 | 54 | 85 | 89 | 99 |
| Married | 102 | 117 | 122 | 120 | 113 | 108 |

Note: Index values above are computed by dividing the proportion of women in a particular grouping by their proportion of the population. For example, if an age group has 20.2% of the products users and represents 18.3% of the population, the index value for the grouping is 110. Index values over 100 signify above average usage and index values below 100 signify below average usage. However, values over 110 or under 90 are the most significant.

*Source:* Simmons Market Research Bureau, Inc., 1991.

Consistent with who buys Avon's products, those who sell for the firm are a more middle-aged than younger group. Avon representatives are not very glamorous; they are your typical middle-American, working-class crowd, who are short on skills and money.

Avon's attraction to blue-collar, working-class consumers (and potential sales representatives) is probably based on the company's image (lower middle to downscale fashion connotations combined with low-end prices and quality). Realistically, the firm's image among consumers is a lot less fashionable than the models in its sales brochure would suggest; it is more suburban, working-class frumpy than high fashion and glamorous. If you go to a regional sales meeting for Avon representatives, you will find a collection of women in their late 30s and 40s, almost all of whom are not high fashion or glamorous (in a "Madison Avenue" sense).

TABLE 6.9–3 **Competitor Profiles Selected User Demographics (women)**

|  | Perfume and Cologne "Obsession" | Face Creams and Lotions "Clinique" | Foundation Make-Up "Cover Girl" | Mascara "Max Factor" | Eye Shadow "Cover Girl" | Eye Liner "Maybelline" |
|---|---|---|---|---|---|---|
| *Age* | | | | | | |
| 18–24 | 173 | 140 | 162 | 155 | 197 | 144 |
| 25–34 | 131 | 124 | 125 | 120 | 144 | 135 |
| 35–44 | 117 | 106 | 92 | 111 | 106 | 115 |
| 45–54 | 73 | 104 | 80 | 82 | 62 | 88 |
| 55–64 | 67 | 67 | 87 | 93 | 51 | 70 |
| 65 and over | 26 | 52 | 49 | 37 | 22 | 33 |
| *Employed* | | | | | | |
| Full-time | 120 | 127 | 87 | 117 | 120 | 132 |
| Part-time | 103 | 121 | 106 | 94 | 114 | 82 |
| Not employed | 80 | 69 | 111 | 85 | 78 | 73 |
| *HH income* | | | | | | |
| $60,000+ | 130 | 233 | 86 | 136 | 89 | 103 |
| $50,000–$59,999 | 88 | 146 | 92 | 95 | 105 | 85 |
| $35,000–$49,999 | 109 | 101 | 110 | 111 | 131 | 85 |
| $25,000–$34,999 | 110 | 93 | 109 | 96 | 96 | 131 |
| $15,000–$24,999 | 111 | 79 | 107 | 103 | 103 | 139 |
| Less than $15,000 | 66 | 36 | 90 | 75 | 77 | 64 |
| Single | 188 | 148 | 120 | 122 | 133 | 125 |
| Married | 87 | 97 | 96 | 104 | 99 | 93 |

*Source:* Simmons Market Research Bureau, Inc., 1991.

## THE CHANGING ENVIRONMENT

Changing economic conditions, orientations toward work, and traditional roles in the American family have challenged the creativity of Avon and others in the direct selling industry. The sensitivity of Avon's sales revenue to business cycle fluctuations, some speculate, is amplified by its popularity with blue-collar families. And, it is this group that suffered real declines in their incomes during the 1980s and 1990s. Some economists believe that members of that group are becoming permanently unemployed in large numbers because they compete with unskilled and semi-skilled workers in third world countries, as well as highly automated and better trained workers in Japan and Germany.

Avon's ability to recruit sales representatives is also related to the economic situation. Typically, women become Avon representatives to earn some money for Christmas or some other special event. However, the income potential is very low; the average representative earns about $3,300 per year (1991 dollars). Very few sales representatives are long-term sellers for Avon, which is only about 20 percent of the to-

TABLE 6.9–4   Heavy User Profiles Selected User Demographics (women)

| | Perfume and Cologne | Face Creams and Lotions | Foundation Make-Up | Mascara | Eye Shadow | Eye Liner |
|---|---|---|---|---|---|---|
| *Age* | | | | | | |
| 18–24 | 103 | 95 | 148 | 160 | 150 | 203 |
| 25–34 | 91 | 49 | 83 | 109 | 123 | 101 |
| 35–44 | 104 | 122 | 107 | 141 | 128 | 115 |
| 45–54 | 105 | 132 | 112 | 94 | 97 | 100 |
| 55–64 | 113 | 102 | 97 | 76 | 62 | 69 |
| 65 and over | 91 | 124 | 70 | 20 | 29 | 24 |
| | | | | | | |
| *Employed* | | | | | | |
| Full-time | 116 | 90 | 125 | 147 | 141 | 139 |
| Part-time | 86 | 81 | 99 | 94 | 124 | 99 |
| Not employed | 87 | 113 | 76 | 55 | 55 | 61 |
| | | | | | | |
| *HH income* | | | | | | |
| $60,000+ | 102 | 110 | 105 | 139 | 159 | 135 |
| $50,000–$59,999 | 104 | 87 | 99 | 132 | 130 | 96 |
| $35,000–$49,999 | 98 | 95 | 106 | 125 | 126 | 113 |
| $25,000–$34,999 | 104 | 112 | 95 | 102 | 95 | 107 |
| $15,000–$24,999 | 106 | 111 | 101 | 77 | 75 | 97 |
| Less than $15,000 | 91 | 87 | 95 | 63 | 60 | 70 |
| Single | 113 | 88 | 120 | 136 | 128 | 168 |
| Married | 93 | 100 | 94 | 97 | 93 | 88 |

P & C = more than 7 times per week.

F C & L = more than 14 times per week.

F M = more than 7 times per week.

M = more than 7 times per week.

E S = more than 7 times per week.

E L = more than 7 times per week.

*Source:* Simmons Market Research Bureau, Inc., 1991.

tal sales force. Some representatives depend on their Avon incomes for regular living expenses increases during poor economic times. However, this group leaves Avon when better, higher paying, jobs become available.

The consumers most affected economically by recent changes in the U.S. economy and workforce tend to be those in Avon's prime market. The squeeze on the middle class is taking its toll by making it more difficult to purchase a single family home, to afford an education for one's family, and to purchase discretionary, nondurable items such as those offered by Avon. The prolonged recession and unemployment period of the late 1980s and early 1990s caused uncertainty in the minds of all but the most secure individuals. A more prolonged period of such uncertainty and insecurity could have an unpredictable long-term effects on purchasing patterns and attitudes toward nondurable goods.

More women are working and more are also single. In a sense, this is good news because both working women and single women purchase and use more cosmetics, fragrances, and toiletries. It is bad news because working women are harder to reach because workplace sales are more difficult to make than door-to-door sales. Avon also benefits by more women seeking work, but not if they need incomes greater than those offered by Avon's representative selling system.

As if these pressures were not enough, Avon faces a challenge from a growing number of powerful and sophisticated marketers, including other direct sellers such as Mary Kay Cosmetics and discount and department store brands manufactured and marketed by such firms as Revlon and Max Factor.

## WHERE IS AVON GOING?

The U.S. domestic door-to-door business is weak, and Avon is having trouble keeping turnover rates among its sales representatives down to reasonable levels. Avon's Giorgio and Red lines of luxury fragrances sold in department stores are also in trouble.

More troubling still is the slowdown in Avon's international operations, which represent 55 percent of total sales. Avon now operates in over 100 countries, and its far-flung activities have been a buffer against gloomy times at home. But results in key markets such as Brazil and Japan were off in 1991, and overall growth is sluggish.

With an eye to returning the company to its traditional emphasis on cosmetics, fragrances, and toiletries, Avon sold off the company's holdings in health care and retirement homes. But Avon still has plenty more work to do to improve its position. The firm's U.S. beauty business, which accounts for 40 percent of sales, has been flat since 1989, compared with the 5 to 7 percent annual growth for the industry as a whole. In response, prices on such items as nail enamel and shampoo have been discounted by up to 75 percent.

Avon is also taking its Giorgio and Red scents to new foreign markets to offset the downturn in the United States. But, the price cuts and push into new markets is pinching margins, which fell to 14.1 percent in 1991, pretax, from 15.4 percent in 1990. It is also trying to do more to retain Avon's sales representatives, who now have a 250 percent annual turnover rate. Under a new program tried in California and 25 other states, representatives can earn up to 21 percent in bonuses on the sales of new sellers they recruit.

Not all of the sales force is happy with these changes, and the representatives are an all-important constituency at Avon. Realistically, they are the backbone of the company, and, if they are dissatisfied, Avon's sales can suffer a serious decline. Avon says it is committed to its sales force and has no intention of supplanting them with other forms of selling such as direct mail. But the firms's actions seem to indicate just such a strategy, if only on a limited basis.

What marketing strategy would you recommend for Avon? What specific price, distribution, promotion, and product elements would you propose and why? How would you deal with competition from other direct marketers? How would you handle the representative sales force? What roles would direct selling other forms of direct marketing, and retailing play in your plans?

## Sources

"Avon Products," *Contemporary Cases in Consumer Behavior*, eds. Roger D., Blackwell, W. Wayne Talarzyk, and James F. Engel (Chicago, IL: Dryden Press, 1990) pp. 39–49.

*Avon Products, Inc. 1991 Annual Report.*

"Avon Rings Millions of New Bells." *Sales & Marketing Management* (October 1992): 35.

Hager, Bruce. "Despite the Face-Lift, Avon is Sagging." *Business Week* (December 2, 1991):101–102.

Healy, Denis F., "Avon Products, Inc.: For Whom the Bell Tolls," in *Consumer Behavior Dynamics: A Casebook* ed. M. Wayne DeLozier (Colombus, OH: Charles E. Merrill, 1977) pp. 94–103.

*Simmons Market Research Bureau, Inc., 1991.*

Zellner, Wendy. "Mary Kay is Singing 'I Feel Pretty'." *Business Week* (December 2, 1991): 102.

Zellner, Wendy and Bruce Hager. "Dumpster Raids? That's Not Very Ladylike, Avon." *Business Week* (April 1, 1991): 32.

# CASE 10
## *CompUSA*

In 1995, sales of personal computers (PCs) and related products from retail stores rose about 50 percent, driven largely by interest in CD-ROM multimedia software and on-line services. However, this consumer buying boom had a surprising element. Although computer superstores like CompUSA and Computer City generated their highest revenue ever for 1995, with estimated sales of $6.5 billion, their overall market share in the category was down.

The market share gainers were electronics superstores such as Circuit City and Best Buy, which promoted heavily and more than doubled their sales in the computer-related category. Their market share grew from 11 percent in 1993 to 16.3 percent in 1994 to 17.1 percent in 1995, with total sales of about $3 billion. Office superstores such as Office Depot and Staples also saw gains, with sales of $1.7 billion. Warehouse clubs nearly doubled their sales of computers and related products, while mass merchants such as Target and Sears saw large percentage gains.

Why were alternative channels able to take market share from the computer superstores? Some suggest that to the first-time, nontechnical buyers, computer superstores are unfamiliar and intimidating. Ever since IBM introduced its PC Jr. in the early 1980s with a consumer advertising campaign built around a Charlie Chaplin look-alike, computer manufacturers have sought to make their products appealing to a mass audience. However, it has only been in the last few years that consumers in large numbers have taken an active interest in PCs and have shown a willingness to pay the money to purchase hardware and software in volumes which justify those items being carried by stores not specializing in computer related items. When consumers go to these stores, they have frequently already come in to shop for other things. They feel comfortable, and they know the prices are competitive.

Shrinking margins are an issue for all stores selling PCs. With both computer manufacturers and retailers battling each other for market share, profits in the category are becoming increasingly difficult to achieve. The average gross margin on computers is now down to about 13 percent, from 40 percent only five years ago. Shrinking margins and over-expansion have led to financial problems at CompUSA and other outlets focusing on the PC category.

Baby boomers (the fastest growing segment of software sales) buy more of their day-to-day goods at mass market stores, so they are now looking for mass market stores to provide their software choices too. The shift of software sales from technically sophisticated buyers at Software Etc. and CompUSA to family, and particularly female, buyers at mass market stores is led by Wal-Mart, with a 100 percent increase in software sales in 1995. Target and Sears are each also experiencing big sales increases. Women account for the majority of mass market purchases in general, so this shift to mass market PC software sales to women is a logical result. However, men still out-buy women by 55 to 45 percent.

In 1995, PC market household penetration was about 33 percent, still well below popular consumer electronics products such as televisions and VCRs. In that year, some 44 percent of consumer PC owners had a 486 or better chip and 79 percent ran Windows. About 41 percent of installed PCs contained CD-ROM drives, while 67 percent had a modem, but only 25 percent of consumers with computers used an on-line service. All those with PCs were using more applications, more categories of software and they spent more hours in front of their PCs each week.

## CompUSA

CompUSA Computer Superstores is America's largest computer superstore retailer. Its stores carry all major brands of computers, including Apple, AST, Compaq, Compudyne, Epson, Hewlett-Packard, IBM, and Packard Bell, and it carries more than 2,000 software titles.

In 1994, CompUSA celebrated its 10th anniversary, marking a decade of rapid growth in which the Dallas-based company mushroomed from nothing to more than $2 billion in sales nationwide. The chain started in 1985 as Soft Warehouse. It followed that Dallas store in 1988 with its first Computer Superstore in Atlanta. In 1991, Soft Warehouse changed its name to CompUSA Computer Superstores and began an expansion period leading to its national position today. While checking expansion recently, CompUSA has focused upon enhancing and improving in-store services, amenities, and operations.

CompUSA's mission is to remain the dominant retailer of PC hardware, software, accessories, and services by being the low-cost computer superstore operator and by providing its customers with the lowest prices, the widest product assortment, and full customer service.

At of the end of 1994, CompUSA operated 85 superstores in 41 metropolitan areas. CompUSA Superstores enjoy the highest annual sales per square foot of any major U.S. retailer, with an average of 25,000 square feet per location. The superstores offer discount prices on more than 5,000 computers and computer-related products for retail, business, government, and institutional customers. The company employs nearly 9,000 persons.

Before CompUSA, computer retailers typically were small boutiques with limited selections and space. By contrast, CompUSA Superstores carry many brands of computers and software. Before CompUSA, no computer retailer handled the chain's volume, so none could price products as competitively. Until CompUSA, there were two options when consumers purchased a PC: pay more at a small store or call a mail order house. CompUSA recognized what computer buyers wanted more options so it designed a superstore for computer hardware, software, training, personal service, technical support, and networking all under one roof.

Specifically for corporate customers, CompUSA's Direct Sales group has a team of salespeople at each computer superstore who undertake telemarketing sales activities to service their accounts. These customers receive a number of special services that include telephone ordering, same-day shipping, flexible business leasing plans, a corporate pick-up and service counter, evaluation programs, and national account coordination.

CompUSA customers can take advantage of service after the sale through a variety of maintenance agreements, and it offers in-store, authorized service and repair of any computer model it sells, during store hours seven days a week. To help ensure the prompt repair of equipment, each CompUSA Computer Superstore service department maintains an extensive inventory of parts.

## CompUSA PERFORMANCE

Financially, 1995 was a good year for CompUSA (Figure 6.10–1 and 6.10–2). It reported record net sales of $2.8 billion, up 31 percent compared with $2.1 billion in 1994. Net income was at a record level of $23 million, compared with a loss of $17 million in 1994.

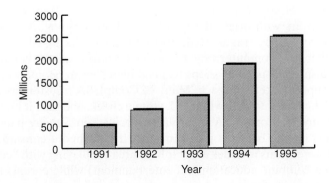

**FIGURE** 6.10–1 CompUSA Total Sales

*Source: CompUSA 1995 Annual Report.*

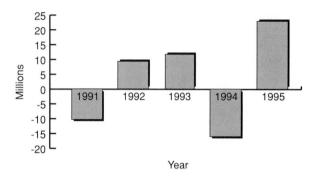

**FIGURE 6.10–2** CompUSA Net Income

*Source: CompUSA 1995 Annual Report.*

However, CompUSA was a different organization in 1995 than it was in 1994. The firm had decided to focus on controlled, profitable growth through improved store execution, expense control, and inventory management. Its store prototype was redesigned to make the stores more exciting, interactive, and easier to shop for first-time buyers, particularly families. CompUSA slowed its store expansion rate and plans to increase its store unit count by approximately 20 to 25 percent each year.

Prior to 1995, CompUSA had been rapidly expanding its store base, opening 20 computer superstores in 1993 and 28 computer superstores in 1994, which represented 71 percent and 58 percent unit growth, respectively. However, after several changes in senior management, beginning in 1994, the firm adjusted its strategy from a high-growth, decentralized approach to a more controlled growth, centralized approach. In addition, the firm developed a business plan that redirected its focus from rapid store growth to improving operations, controlling and reducing expenses, and reorienting the firm's corporate culture to emphasize profitability. To enable it to apply its resources toward implementation of the plan, CompUSA reduced its store expansion to nine superstores in 1995.

CompUSA maintains no distribution centers. Its' volumes are so large that suppliers truck large shipments directly to each store. Low costs translate into bargain prices for customers. CompUSA adds a 13 percent margin onto the wholesale price, which is half the markup at electronics retailers. The firm uses local surveys to match or beat the prices for competing products.

## NEW DIRECTION

Toys "Я" Us captivated kids, Home Depot hooked the tinkerers, and CompUSA is now attracting computer buyers with bright flashy stores and, in so doing, it is now bringing mass marketing to a once fragmented, elitist business. As PCs become friendlier and more familiar, the computer buyer is evolving into a more everyday shopper. CompUSA has displaced specialty shops manned by technical people with a high-service, low-priced, supermarket approach. Many of CompUSA's customers no longer need a lot of help. They want to play with a PC, write a check, and take it home.

To reach first-time buyers, CompUSA now places circulars in Sunday papers rather than advertisements on the business page. In 1995, it launched a consumer-friendly format in several stores. This includes a CompKids area for playing with "edutainment" titles (those that combine education and entertainment) while parents try any of 400 programs or watch technology demos. CompUSA wants it to be a place people come every weekend to see what is new in computer hardware and software.

## CompUSA AND THE MASS MARKET

With a wider audience of computer hardware and software buyers, CompUSA and the other large store mass marketers of PC-related items are revising their respective business strategies to appeal to more consumers. In the process, CompUSA is competing more directly with mass marketers such as Wal-Mart, which sell more than just computer items. This has necessitated rapid changes in the internal culture of CompUSA. However, some question the wisdom of this move because not attempting to appeal to first-time buyers and rather continuing to focus on more sophisticated computer owners who know more about what they want is also a viable strategy. Consumers who are buying a computer for the first time now will, in four years, be more computer savvy, and may prefer and computer superstore format for their second purchase.

What marketing strategy would you advise CompUSA pursue in the selling to the home and business markets? What specific price, distribution, promotion, and product elements would you propose and why? How would you deal with the growth of competition from large non-computer retailers? What do you think about CompUSA's new focus on less experienced computer users versus those with more savvy about computers?

## Sources

"10-Q report: Channels-CompUSA." *Computer Reseller News* (May 9, 1994): 68.

Burrows, Peter, "It's All Starting To Compute Now." *Business Week* (March 13, 1995): 94.

*CompUSA 1995 Annual Report.*

"Filling the power space." *Chain Store Age*, 71, 11 (November 1995) 111–112.

Flynn, Mary Kathleen. "Taking A Byte Out of The Bottom Line." *U.S. New & World Report* (November 14, 1994): 106–107.

Fox, Bruce. "Can the Computer Superstore Survive?" *Chain Store Age Executive,* 71, 2 (February 1995): 35–36.

Gold, Howard R. "CompUSA Flies High Again; Credit PC Boom, Management." *Barrron's*, 75, 28 (July 10, 1995): 10.

Greco, Susan. "Selling the Superstores." *Inc.*, 17, 10 (July 1995): 54–61.

Johnson, Jay L. "CompUSA: The Computer Superstore." *Discount Merchandiser*, 34, (January 1994): 24–33.

Johnson, Jay L. "Computer City: A Three-Year-Old Billionaire," *Discount Merchandiser*, (January 1995): 46–56.

Johnson, Jay L. "In this Corner." *Discount Merchandiser*, 35, 1 (January 1995): 8.

Lorenzo, Benny. "No Pricing Slowdown." *Computer Reseller News*, 593 (August 29, 1994): 33–34.

Mullich, Joe. "CompUSA Seeks Profit Boost." *Business Marketing*, 79, 1 (January 1994): 3, 36.

Roach, Loretta. "Accentuate the Positive." *Direct Marketing* (August 1994) 48, 50.

Roach, Loretta. "Accentuate the Positive." *Discount Merchandiser*, 34, 8 (August 1994): 48–50.

Sherwin, Richard. "Shift in Software Sales: Good News for Mass Marketers." *Dealerscope Merchandising*, 37, 4 (April 1995): 1, 60+.

Stewart, Doug. "Comparison Shopper." *Inc.*, 15, 12 (Winter 1994): 22–28.

Tetzeli, Rick. "Computer Category Killer." *Fortune* (Autumn/Winter 1993): 21.

---

# *Deal-A-Meal USA* *

Success in the weight loss and dieting industry is becoming increasingly difficult as the number of competitors grows and the intensity of competition becomes more ferocious. Fueling demand is a tremendous interest in losing weight by many segments of the population. Every year, more and more Americans join the ranks of the obese, or just cross into that zone between being plump and fat. However, the vast majority who make the attempt to lose weight eventually put back on all that they lose and more. Millions of consumers are searching for the next great weight loss scheme, but, for most, this search represents stopping points on a fruitless journey replete with failures and reduced self-esteem.

Periodically, a dieting plan emerges from the pack and becomes widely popular or even institutionalized, names such as Jenny Craig and Nutri/System come quickly to mind. However, if these plans really worked, they would quickly put themselves out of business. In reality, weight loss is a lifestyle issue and not a one time effort to shed a few pounds. The plans that appears to work best encourages regular exercise and an eating regiment that includes a significant reduction in the consumption of fatty foods. One of the most successful such programs is offered by Deal-A-Meal USA.

## DEAL-A-MEAL USA

Deal-A-Meal USA is a privately held firm that relies heavily on infomercials to market its products. Its main spokesperson, and owner, is Richard Simmons, the perky exercise guru. The Deal-A-Meal diet and exercise plan, which includes exercise tapes and dieting system has sold millions of copies.

---

*Although Deal-A-Meal USA is an actual competitor in the dieting and weight loss industry, the scenario and conversations in this case are fictional.

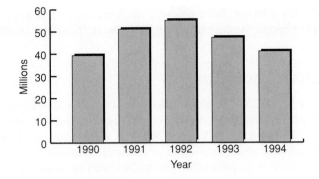

**FIGURE 6.11–1** Deal-A-Meal Revenues

*Source:* Estimated from various sources.

## Product Description

The Deal-A-Meal Life Plan has four parts:

1. The Deal-A-Meal Card System consists of a relatively small folder with diet cards that are moved from one side of a card holder to the other depending on what the dieter eats. At the point when the requisite number of daily calories on the cards is transferred, the dieter stops eating. An audio tape and instruction manual for the Deal-A-Meal weight loss plan comes with the diet cardholder.

2. The *Golden Edition Cookbook* contains low-cal, low-fat, low-sodium recipes that the dieter can prepare.

3. The *Sweating to the Oldies 3* and *Stretching to the Classics* exercise video tapes instructs the dieter on how to perform regular, exercise routines that tone the body and reduce weight.

4. The *Project Me* motivational tapes are designed to encourage dieters to think positively and to feel good about themselves.

The entire system is sold via direct response television. It is usually priced at three payments of $29.95, for a total of $89.85. There is no lengthy commitment involved because it is a one-time purchase. Purchase incentives are offered, such as free audio tapes.

## Performance

Because Deal-A-Meal USA is privately held, the firm's sales and income can only be estimated. Industry sources believe that the company has steadily increased its revenues over the last several years. Income in 1994 was expected to reach 6 million on sales of 65 million (see Figures 6.11–1 and 6.11–2).

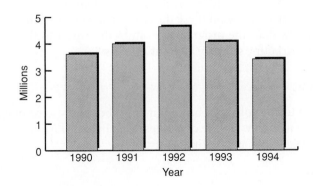

**FIGURE 6.11–2** Deal-A-Meal Net Income

*Source:* Estimated from various sources.

While Deal-A-Meal USA's offerings have enjoyed much success, it has not produced any really new concepts beyond the core diet plan that started the whole venture in the early 1990s.

## YOUR NEW JOB AT DEAL-A-MEAL USA

As a new employee at Deal-A-Meal USA, you are looking forward to your first meeting with company president Richard Simmons. You have seen him many times on television in half-hour infomercials and on the talk shows, but this will be your first face-to-face encounter. Richard is clearly a genius; he is a potentially intimidating person who is not only smart but rich and very popular. Because he has been so successful with his Deal-A-Meal program, you are wondering what he might want from you in the way of a better understanding of the weight loss and dieting market.

In preparation for the meeting, you have been reading the files of your predecessor, David Robinson. His memos to Richard are of particular interest because they provide you with an indication of the types of issues that Richard discussed with David. In your search, you have found several relevant memos. After reading all the memos, you conclude that David's memos to Richard dated June 23, 1994, August 12, 1994, and August 24, 1994, plus Richard's memo to David on August 21, 1994 (memos follow) provide a good indication of the business issues that concern Richard.

## THE MEETING WITH RICHARD

During your meeting with Richard, it becomes clear that he expects you to know a lot about marketing dieting and weight loss products. He also keeps asking you questions about how consumers think and behave with respect to weight loss and dieting and about how friends and family influence a consumers dieting and weight loss goals. Richard's theories about why people are successful with the Deal-A-Meal USA program touch on everything from needs satisfaction to attitude change and the role of American culture in establishing standards of beauty.

Evidently, Richard wants you to produce a thoughtful understanding of the dieting and weight loss business and its consumers. You agree with him that certain specific areas need more consideration: (1) What consumer needs are being or not being satisfied by dieting and weight loss? How do these needs differ for men versus women? (2) What are the attitude and belief aspects of consumers' behavior in relation to dieting and weight loss? (3) What are the social and cultural influences that operate on consumer weight and dieting standards? How do these differ for men versus women? and (4) For Deal-A-Meal USA, how does the program operate with respect to the aforementioned factors and what marketing strategy alternatives exist?

## BACK IN YOUR OFFICE

After the meeting, you return to your office to begin thinking about how to respond to Richard's request. You decide to review the file of memos again before starting to write your own memo about the weight loss and dieting industry.

*Memo*

*TO: Richard Simmons*

*FROM: David Robinson*

*SUBJECT: Weight Loss and Dieting Industry Trends and Competition*

*DATE: June 23, 1994*

As requested, this memo covers the competition and competitive structure of the weight loss and dieting industry. Little published information exists on many companies, but there are highlights that should prove helpful.

One of every four Americans is dieting at any given time. Of those people, 97 percent cut down on high-calorie foods, 88 percent exercise, 29 percent skip meals, 12 percent crash diet, and 4 percent use diet pills. How may of these dieters reach and maintain their weight loss? Unfortunately, not many. Otherwise, the number of Americans on diets would steadily dwindle to nothing.

Approximately 34 million adults, one-quarter of the population, are significantly overweight. Only one in five clients of commercial weight loss centers stays with the program long enough to lose an appreciable amount of weight. It is estimated that up to 90 percent of all dieters who lose 25 or more pounds on a diet regain the weight they have lost over a two-year period, and only one in 50 manages to keep the weight off for seven years.

Nonetheless, dieting industry revenues have soared. Meanwhile, weight loss methods that do not promise a quick fix languish. Health and fitness centers are having revenue declines and closings. Americans crave quick results and are ripe for exploitation by companies promising rapid weight loss.

The revenues of commercial dieting centers grew by 18 percent in the 1980s, reaching $2 billion in 1990. In 1991, however, revenues fell. The recession hurt as many dieters turned to cheaper, do-it-yourself liquid diets, books, and video plans.

Many weight loss centers are launching ambitious marketing and advertising campaigns. Some of the programs have raised questions in the medical community, including those about the use of celebrities in weight loss center advertisements. Weight Watchers International creates a new food plan each year, making the program faster or easier to follow and giving the company yet another selling point. Weight Watchers targets its advertising to group-oriented women between the ages of 20 to 54 who have tried to lose weight in the past year. The fact that weight loss centers make statements about health and fitness, yet do not provide information on their track records is troubling to some people. Nutri/Systems targets overweight adults and relies primarily on radio and newspaper advertisements. In place of the traditional celebrity endorsement, the company has built a force of 1,000 disc jockeys that it supplies with Nutri/System food and services in exchange for daily on-air progress reports.

Some 2,600 hospitals have entered the medical end of the weight loss business, which grew 15 percent annually in the 1980s. When talk show hostess Oprah Winfrey revealed a 67 pound weight loss through the use of liquid-diet Optifast in November 1988, the market experienced a boost. However, a hospital's ability to profit on a weight loss center is not as simple as it has been in the past; because of this and a downturn in the market, many are limiting their expansion plans. To increase revenues, Optifast is creating a program for patients who need to lose as little as 25 pounds, and Health Management Resources has created a program for those trying to lose 30 to 60 pounds. Manufacturers stress that the powder product is only a small part of the entire process and that training and support from hospitals is necessary.

Dieting books and videos are enjoying a boom in sales. Millions of dollars are being spent on such diverse offerings as motivational tapes, fasting cookbooks, and comprehensive plans detailed in long and sometimes tedious books.

Table 6.11–1 contains a listing of the major business segments and competitors in the weight loss and dieting industry. The industry is divided into four segments: organized programs, enrollment programs, medically supervised programs, and weight loss and dieting books and videos.

**Organized programs.**    These are organizations that help people with eating disorders and/or weight problems to overcome their destructive behavior and to lose weight through the strength of fellowship with people who have similar problems. These are not diet programs per se because they view overeating and being overweight as problems more complex than simply choosing what foods you eat. Through strength in numbers, in group support and compassion, members strive to achieve control over their eating, weight, and lives in general. Members may use any effective eating plan in tandem with group affiliation.

**Enrollment programs.**    Enrollment plans are fee-for-service businesses designed to help people lose and maintain weight. While most enrollment programs offer support and counseling, they are limited by the realities of business because the counselors are paid employees and their time has a cost associated with it. Those counselors may be genuinely concerned about the dieter's plight, or they might just be doing their job, reciting from a memorized script without much feeling or interest. On the other hand, enrollment programs are comprehensive, offering a support system, nutritional counseling, a diet plan, and, in some cases, diet food that works in conjunction with the plan.

**Medically supervised diet programs.**    Medically supervised diet programs are designed primarily for those whose obesity puts them at medical risk, such as diabetics and individuals with heart disease. A number of programs require that participants be at least 20 percent above their ideal body weight before enrolling and going on a very low-calorie diet. These programs operate under the supervision of a medical doctor, and for good reason, because rapid weight loss is highly stressful on the body and can produce severe side effects.

**TABLE 6.11–1   The Weight Control Diets Business Segments**

*Organized Programs*
Overeaters Anonymous
Take Off Pounds Sensibly (TOPS)

*Enrollment Programs*
Diet Center
Jenny Craig
Nutri/System
Shapedown
Weight Watchers

*Medically Supervised Diet Programs*
Health Management Resources
MediBase
Medifast
Optifast
Optitrim
United Weight Control Corporation
Weigh to Live

*Weight Loss and Diet Books and Videos*
The Choose to Lose Diet (book)
The Executive Success Diet (book)
The Feel Full Diet (book)
The New American Diet (book)
Not Another Diet Book (book)
Deal-A-Meal USA (videos and books)
The Amazing Micro Diet (video and book)

**Weight loss and dieting books and videos.**   Of all the available weight loss approaches, diet books and videos are by far the most popular and numerous. The selection is staggering, with a wide range of books and videos. Some programs are complete plans addressing food, behavior, and exercise. Others only address one or two of those components but do so in an effective way and can thus become a successful part of a successful weight control program. These plans require a great amount of self-imposed structure, discipline, and motivation.

---

*Memo*

*TO: Richard Simmons*

*FROM: David Robinson*

*SUBJECT: Weight Loss and Dieting Industry Customers*

*DATE: August 12, 1994*

In response to your recent questions about consumers, I am writing this memo to summarize what we know about weight loss and dieting. I feel that it is clear we, and the weight loss and diet industry in general, know very little about our customers. As you noted in our meeting, the current economic situation represents a big potential opportunity for Deal-A-Meal USA. Because we are low priced compared with our competitors, the organized programs, the enrollment programs, and medically supervised diet programs, consumers should be gravitating to us in large numbers. I know you want Deal-A-Meal USA's customers to succeed. One sure way to insure that the purchasers of the Deal-A-Meal USA program lose weight is to understand why they tend to succeed or fail with their dieting.

Some recent research on dieting suggests that people with lower weight loss expectations go into a dieting program with a better chance of keeping with that program. These people also receive greater support from family and friends, and they have a more positive attitude about their chances for permanent weight loss. Program dropouts, on the other hand, seem to expect to fail. In other words, getting started is easy; staying motivated is not.

Most obesity experts agree that quick-fix diets promote a pattern of fasting and bingeing. They suspect that the so-called yo-yo syndrome may disturb the body's metabolism. There is also some speculation that this could explain why chronic dieters find it ever more difficult to lose weight. Some experts believe that when dieters attempt to resume a normal eating pattern, not only are they bedeviled by all their old compulsive habits, but their body has lowered its metabolism in an attempt to conserve those precious calories. No sooner do people lose significant weight than they begin to overproduce an enzyme called lipoprotein lipase, which helps restore fat cells shrunk by dieting. The heavier the person, the more enzymes produced; this may be why people often regain lost weight quickly. This may also explain why chronic dieters have to struggle to not only lose weight but to maintain the loss.

---

### Memo

TO: *David Robinson*

FROM: *Richard Simmons*

SUBJECT: *Your Memo on Weight Loss and Dieting Industry Customers*

DATE: *August 21, 1994*

I read your memo on what we know about the weight loss and dieting industry customers with great interest. However, I was disappointed. Based on what you wrote, it appears that we have a limited understanding of the marketing issues in the weight loss and dieting industry. This is a serious weakness because I believe that a better grasp of what motivates people to lose weight or diet and why they succeed or fail is fundamental to Deal-A-Meal becoming the number one program in the country.

I would suggest that you write me a memo on what you think are the marketing issues in the weight loss and diet business. I want you to use your accumulated knowledge and experience, including any marketing and consumer behavior courses you had in college, to provide me with a thoughtful representation of your understanding as to what the marketing dynamics are in our industry.

---

### Memo

TO: *Richard Simmons*

FROM: *David Robinson*

SUBJECT: *Deal-A-Meal Infomercial Analysis*

DATE: *August 29, 1994*

I conducted an analysis of one of our 30-minute infomercials for the Deal-A-Meal USA program. In doing the work, I applied a communications and offer analyses. It helps summarize our creative strategy and offer. I was able to define the benefits and reasons why in the infomercial. Please see the summary below (Table 6.11–2).

---

**TABLE 6.11–2  Deal-A-Meal USA 30-Minute Commercial Summary**

*Creative Strategy*

Key selling concept (USP) . . . Be in control of your weight
Desired action . . . Purchase/order Deal-A-Meal package through 800#.
Message strategy . . .
   Primary target market . . . women 25–49, larger bodies
   Secondary target market . . . men 25–49, larger bodies

| Benefits | Reasons why |
|---|---|
| being in control | do-it-yourself plan |
| self-esteem | testimonials |
| confidence | simple, safe, easy, fun |
| good feelings | |
| ''a new you'' | |

*Offer Proposition*

Product description
   The 4-step Deal-A-Meal Life Plan
      1. The Deal-A-Meal Card System.
         The audio tape and instruction manual (describing the Deal-A-Meal weight loss plan).
      2. The *Golden Edition Cookbook* (low cal, low fat, low sodium recipes).
      3. *Sweating to the Oldies 3* and *Stretching to the Classics* video tapes.
      4. *Project Me* motivational tapes.
         Price . . . 3 payments of $29.95 (total = $89.85)
         Length of commitment . . . none
         Incentives . . . free with order, 2 free audio tapes *Take a Walk* and *Take a Hike,* plus $50 savings.

---

When consumers buy products to satisfy needs, they are really buying the benefits they believe the products provide rather than the products per se. For example, consumers buy headache relief, not aspirin. Reasons why establish credibility. They can be linked to tangible attributes of the product such as materials, design, or the manufacturing process. In other words, product descriptions tend to be reasons why. Also, associations with a company or brand name are reasons why. Testimonials are also powerful reasons why.

## DEAL-A-MEAL'S FUTURE

In proposing any changes to Deal-A-Meal's current marketing approach, you have three main concerns: (1) make maximum use of the available information on the weight loss and dieting industry to appeal to the largest potential audience, (2) find the right mix of Deal-A-Meal program elements and themes so as to appeal to those who have failed with other diets, and (3) keep the program interesting to those who started with Deal-A-Meal but are still working on their weight problems. The right product mix and distribution are critical. Recent Deal-A-Meal offerings have included bigger packages of video tapes, books, and other items. There may also be an opportunity to mix in some higher ticket items with these more traditional items. One idea is a line of home exercise equipment that could be promoted in the same infomercial as the regular line of products. These items would be targeted toward more affluent consumers who might own other home exercise equipment, which seldom gets used.

The real questions for firms in this category revolve around marketing issues: how to develop and keep a differential advantage in a highly competitive and dynamic market, while maintaining sales growth and, above all, profitability. What marketing strategy would you recommend for Deal-A-Meal USA? What specific distribution, price, promotion, and product elements would you propose and why? How would you deal with the growth competition in the dieting and weight loss industry?

## Sources

"The Allure Diet Survey." *Allure* (November 1991): 146–149, 178–180.

Blodget, Bonnie. "The Diet Biz." *Glamour* (January 1991): 136–139, 175–176.

"Losing Weight." *Consumer Reports* (June 1993): 347–357.

Scanlon, Deralee. *Diets That Work.* Chicago: Contemporary Books, 1991.

Schroeder, Michael. "The Diet Business is Getting a Lot Skinnier." *Business Week* (June 24, 1991): 132–134.

# CASE *TV GUIDE* 12

When *TV Guide* magazine first appeared in 1955, many people thought a publication based on something available for free from newspapers as television program listings was a dumb idea. Yet, 40 years later, *TV Guide* has a circulation of 14.5 million, making it the largest magazine in the United States. This weekly bible of television posted double-digit increases in both ad pages and revenue in each of 1993 and 1994, while facing increased competition from Sunday-newspaper television supplements and on-screen television program listings. However, circulation dipped slightly over the same period. *TV Guide* took in $391 million in advertising revenue in 1994, and, even after a 10-cent cover-price hike, it was selling 5 million newsstand copies each week, at 99 cents each. In 1994, *TV Guide* became the first magazine to gross more than $1 billion (Fig. 6.12–1 and 6.12–2)

Each week, *TV Guide's* staff produces 119 editions that will be read by about 21 million television viewers. Developing each edition requires 100 steps from preparation to print. To improve the management of this array of details, *TV Guide* retired its outdated cut-and-paste process in favor of speedy electronic publishing tools. Technology is also allowing publishers such as *TV Guide* to target editions of their magazine at specific audiences.

For a magazine like Radnor, Pennsylvania-based *TV Guide*, targeted editions are more than a marketing tactic, they are essential to the publication's existence. With its multimillion circulation, *TV Guide* must use sophisticated database technologies to set up a customized, database-driven workflow system to produce the magazine's editions.

*TV Guide* editions generally share a common four-color cover and features, but the black-and-white features and listing sections are specific to each individual market. The program listings include scheduling information (show name, time, channel), explanatory listings (what episode), and features, such as the kids' section, close-ups, and the crossword. Because much of this information is unique to each version, this section is in a constant state of flux.

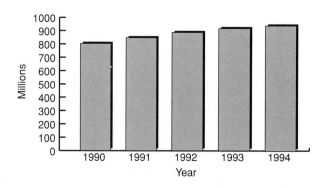

FIGURE 6.12–1 TV Guide Revenue

*Source:* Estimated from various sources.

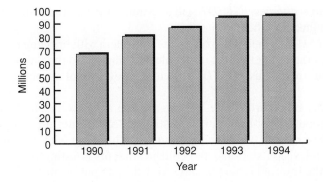

**FIGURE 6.12–2** TV Guide Net Income

*Source:* Estimated from various sources.

With its powerful publishing technology, *TV Guide* can create final, digitally imposed pages ready for output. The process begins in the editorial department, where powerful databases and personal computers (PCs) capture the two major types of editorial content: scheduling information and listing information. Advertisements, which also change from region to region, are managed separately by an advertising production system.

*TV Guide's* strength has always been in its easily accessible listings. However, it plans to also continue to take the editorial high ground, which is another source of consumer interest in the magazine. Advertisers are interested in *TV Guide* readers because of their demographics. However, some wonder if *TV Guide* magazine can continue to grow in a magazine format, which is a dated, digest-sized one at that.

### iGUIDE

In 1996, *TV Guide* launched an interactive online version of the weekly television listings magazine. This offering is called *iGUIDE*. Ultimately, the service will offer from a rotating headline home page with some 17 editorial categories, including books, computing, games, Internet, kids, government, science, movies, music, news, politics, shopping, sports, travel, TV, work/money, and the world. Most of the content will be original, although owner News Corp.'s Fox Broadcasting and movie properties will be represented. The service will have forums organized around soaps, sports, movies, kid shows, and other programming categories that allows users to communicate with one another, and even interact with stars. The architecture will be similar to that of *TV Guide* magazine, and that includes advertising. However, television listings will be less prominent in *iGUIDE* than in the magazine, avoiding potential conflicts with *TV Guide* magazine and *TV Guide's* new onscreen offering, which is accessible as part of a cable system.

The completed version of *iGUIDE* will allow users to create "personalized TV grids" for organizing the television viewing hours that their World Wide Web use is displacing. In the *Movies* section, a search feature called *CineBooks* will allow users to access detailed information on about 30,000 films. *Political Pulse* will compete with every other media outlet in North America to offer the definitive online coverage of the 1996 elections. *Your Work, Your Money* will help users analyze personal financial data and recommend investment strategies. *iGUIDE* will also integrate with the wider Web by offering reviews of and links to other Web sites.

*TV Guide*, just as most established magazines, has a problem with bringing in new younger readers who are perhaps just the sort of people who might find the online version while browsing the Internet. Thus, *iGUIDE* provides a new way of attracting this hard to reach audience.

It is easy to forget that the World Wide Web went from a relatively small audience to mass-market acceptance in a brief period. Estimates of Internet usage in the United States vary from fewer than 10 million to about 25 million. But with consumer product companies, local television stations, and college students boasting their own Web pages, it is clear that the Internet is here to stay. And, despite public protestations, that fact is understood in the executive suites of the major commercial online services. Prodigy has begun relocating to the Web; the Microsoft Network (MSN) is making a total shift to the Web; AOL debuted a separate Internet access service; and CompuServe began offering its customers an Internet-only service, called Sprynet.

The commercial on-line networks are, in part, victims of their own success. By stimulating the consumer appetite for easy access to information and other computer users, services like AOL, Prodigy, and CompuServe helped seed the market for the Web's growth. But increasingly, consumers refuse to limit themselves to a single, closed network when they can have access to the vastly greater riches of the Internet, including such free services as *iGUIDE*.

## THE ALTERNATIVE OF ON-SCREEN GUIDES

The television program listings field is going to get even more crowded as improved on-screen listings appear, including *TV Guide's* own joint venture with Tele-Communications Inc., which will potentially cut into *TV Guide* magazine's customer base.

One major potential threat to *TV Guide* is Prevue Networks, whose onscreen listings reach more than 40 million subscribers in the U.S. and Canada. Television viewers will generally use the channel listing service offered free with their cable service. However, viewers need to go to that channel and wait for the program listing they are interested in to scroll by to view it. This listing lacks program content description, except for brief movie summaries. Prevue Networks is positioned as an alternate source that coexists with other listing sources in the marketplace.

StarSight Telecast Inc. was the first company to offer television viewers an interactive electronic program guide alternative to using *TV Guide*, or other publications, to locate television programs. At the touch of a few buttons, this guide leads a viewer directly to a desired program. Users of the service pay an additional $4 a month for an extra data feed that goes into their set-top electronic box. That box or in some coming versions, the television includes StarSight-designed circuitry that translates the signal into data about all of the shows accessible on the cable system or on broadcast television.

When a user turns on the television set, a notice appears indicating the name of the show tuned into, what it is all about, and the time remaining. If the viewer wants to see what else is on, he or she can use a remote to flip to a grid guide, similar in appearance to a newspaper television listing. Or, if the viewer knows what type of show he or she wants, the remote can be used to pull up a theme menu with categories to choose from. To record a show, the viewer just presses "record." As interactive devices go, it is pretty passive; it makes it easier to sit on a couch and do nothing.

Each converter box or television with a StarSight chip has a serial number. Star-Sight is able to activate or deactivate the service over the air by matching the serial number with a code that is transmitted in the data stream. StarSight is promoting the system not just to cable operators but to television, VCR, and satellite dish manufacturers. Zenith Electronics, Goldstar, and Mitsubishi have already agreed to include the StarSight chip in some of their television sets. (In Zenith's case, it will add $50 to the price of the set.)

Not long after StarSight Telecast appeared, other television industry players decided to create similar services. News Corp. and Tele-Communications, Inc. share ownership of *TV Guide On Screen*. Not only does the product have significant name-brand recognition, but thanks to the popular magazine, it also has the backing of an industry giant which reaches 40 percent of all cable viewers.

## BALANCING NEW AND OLD OUTLETS

Media coverage of the content of other media, from *TV Guide* to *Entertainment Tonight*, has become a huge information category of its own. It will explode on the World Wide Web, which not only allows individuals to be publishers themselves, but also provides a venue where text, sound, and images are hyperlinked to other Web sites. This convergence may create a new audience of occasional or one-time readers willing to pay for content that fits a particular need or interest.

The interactive nature of the Web has attracted millions of consumers and these people are potential visitors to the *iGUIDE* site. However, some wonder if a chance to read about what is going on in television and entertainment from many sources plus the wide availability of television listing might not discourage people from buying *TV Guide* magazine. With so much free information available, will people be willing to pay for the magazine for access to *iGUIDE* Web content?

Even with all of the success *TV Guide* magazine has enjoyed over the years, it cannot become complacent. Now, it is being squeezed by other sources of television listing and by the many sources of news about entertainment. And, there is the threat that technology will move beyond what *TV Guide* is able to do with a combination of its *TV Guide* magazine and its *iGUIDE* while still making a profit. Then there is the problem of attracting younger readers and how *TV Guide* should handle that issue. This needs to be done while holding onto the magazine's existing large customer base. What marketing strategy would you advise *TV Guide* to pursue? What specific distribution, promotion, product, and pricing elements would you propose and why? How would you balance the new *iGUIDE* offering with the existing *TV Guide* magazine? How would you deal with the growth competition from other sources of information about television?

## Sources

Adams, Mark, "Growing *TV Guide*." *Mediaweek,* 5, 27 (July 10, 1995): 5.

Asbrand, Deborah. "*TV Guide* Stays on Schedule With Workflow App." *InfoWorld*, 17, 37 (September 11, 1995): 56.

Asbury, Eve. "Give Your Readers What They Want." *Folio: The Magazine for Magazine Management,* 24, 21 (December 15, 1995): 57–59+.

"The Battle of On-Screen Guides," *Dealerscope Merchandising,* 37, 6 (June 1995): 1, 21+.

Berniker, Mark. "*TV Guide* Going Online," *Broadcasting & Cable,* 124, 24 (June 13, 1994): 49.

Brady, James. "The Little Magazine That Could . . ." *Advertising Age,* 64, 14 (April 5, 1993): 26.

Endicott, R. Craig."Ad Age 300: Ad Age Ranks the Nation's Largest Magazines." *Advertising Age,* 63, 24 (June 15, 1992): S1–S14.

Hutheesing, Nikhil. "Interactivity for the Passive." *Forbes,* 152, 13 (December 6, 1993): 244–245.

Krantz, Michael. "Murdoch Eyes Another Empire." *Mediaweek,* 5, 27 (July 10, 1995): 4.

Krantz, Michael. "News Corp. Lays Off 189." *Mediaweek,* 6, 7 (February 12, 1996): 6.

Lynch, David J. "End of the Line for On-line Services?" *Upside,* 8, 5 (May 1996): 24–34.

Manly, Lorne. "*TV Guide* Tunes in to Online Service." *Folio: The Magazine for Magazine Management,* 23, 11 (June 15, 1994): 62.

Montague, Claudia. "How Viewers Feel About TV." *American Demographics,* 15, 3 (March 1993): 18–23.

*News Corporation 1995 Annual Report.*

---

# CASE 13
## *Nu Skin International*

Multilevel marketing (MLM), also known as network marketing, is booming. Some experts predict that 50 to 60 percent of all goods and services in the United States will be sold through MLM methods during the 1990s. MLM uses people, rather than retail outlets and advertising, to sell and promote its goods and services. In addition to benefiting the companies that use it, MLM provides an opportunity for individuals to earn incomes as independent distributors because start-up costs are low and the potential for earnings is high.

A major player in MLM is Nu Skin International. This privately owned company sells high-priced skin-care, hair-care, and nutritional products to the public through 100,000 active independent distributors. Nu Skin has devised a complex MLM that spans the United States and many other parts of the world, including Canada, Hong Kong, Japan, Taiwan, New Zealand, and Australia.

## WHAT IS MLM?

MLM is a method of personal selling in which customers have the option of becoming product or service distributors, who in turn develop "downlines," or levels of distributors beneath them, all levels sharing in the profits of the level(s) below them. MLM companies bypass traditional wholesaler-retailer arrangements and rely on networks of independent distributors to reach potential customers.

Although the MLM approach has been used by MLM giants such as Amway and Shaklee since the late 1950s, the industry itself is still in its early stages. MLM was once restricted to personal care and household products, but has since expanded to such items as computer programs, financial advice, travel packages, books, and many other products and services.

### How MLM Works

MLM is essentially the personal selling of products and services through a tiered structure of independent distributors. Companies that chose MLM as a distribution channel make their offering available to people willing to work on 100 percent commission. In exchange for selling merchandise and signing up new distributors, these entrepreneurs receive commission income and the opportunity to build their own sales networks. New distributors who are recruited by existing distributors also have the opportunity to recruit others. The result is an expanding MLM distribution system.

Ideally, the relationship between a MLM company and its distributors benefits both parties. From the company's point of view, the costs of supporting the distribution network, providing brochures, audio and video tapes, holding presentation meetings, warehousing, and transporting merchandise are less than that of using retail outlets. From the individual distributor's perspective, the time and minimal start-up costs, and other expenditures, should be outweighed by the profit opportunity.

MLM has both advantages and disadvantages that companies seeking to use it, and prospective entrepreneurs seeking to become involved in it, must evaluate carefully. Advantages include: a high earnings potential, a relatively small capital investment, being your own boss, and operating a business from home. The disadvantages include: long hours, potential difficulty in selling, the constant need to stay motivated, and the need to stay active or loose MLM network benefits.

### The Multiplier Effect

From the participant distributor's perspective, the key to making money in MLM is the multiplier effect. With that effect, the amount of money earned is directly related to the distributor's ability to sell the product or service and the recruiting of others to sell for him. Most descriptions of how money is made in MLM place the burden for ultimate success on the individual seller, although it really also depends on which MLM company is involved.

Initially, the distributor (A) makes money at the personal use and customer (Customers) contact level by selling products or services to friends and others (see Fig. 6.13–1). This income is computed by multiplying the sales commission rate by the total sales volume. Thus, if the commission rate is 50 percent of the product's retail price, on sales of $1,000, the seller (A) would receive $500.

FIGURE 6.13–1

With the multiplier effect, or the ability to make money from the sales of others, those people (B) brought into the seller's (A) MLM structure, and those that they, in turn, bring in themselves also contribute to the income of seller (A) (Fig. 6.13–2).

If seller (A) brings in three other people (B), who, in turn, bring in three additional people (C), the business would look like Figure 6.13–3. In this structure, seller (A) would continue to earn a 50 percent commission on all the merchandise that (A) personally sells to customers plus a percentage of the sales generated by each of the 12 network members. Depending on the terms of the agreement with the MLM company, the average amount of that percentage is usually from 5 to 20 percent. With 12 distributors selling a total of $12,000 worth of merchandise, at a 10 percent commission rate, seller (A) would receive $1,200 in income. Over time, the 12 person downline would hopefully grow into a huge structure as others (D) are added (see Fig. 6.13–4).

Each MLM organization has its own marketing plan describing how many levels seller (A) can get credit for and the percentage payout at each of the levels. The Nu Skin International marketing plan is very clear on this point. The maximum number of levels is six. In general, some MLM organizations allow a seller or distributor to have five levels, while others allow seven or more. And, the commissions received from the levels in the downline also vary by MLM firm. Usually, the more levels below seller (A), the more money he or she makes in commissions, although some MLM firms such as Nu Skin do not pay commissions beyond a fixed number.

## Ways to Generate Income

Although there are a number of different types of compensation plans utilized by MLM companies, Nu Skin International offers two main earnings opportunities:

- *Commissions and personal sales.* This is income from goods sold directly to consumers. It is the difference between the wholesale price, what is paid by seller (A), and the selling price seller (A) receives from his customers.

- *Group bonus.* This is the percentage seller (A) receives from sales volume generated by the members of his downline.

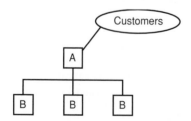

FIGURE 6.13–2

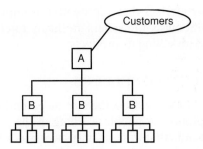

FIGURE 6.13–3

## UNDERSTANDING MLM FIRMS AND THE INDUSTRY

The strength of a MLM company can be measured in many ways: the number of years it has been in business, demonstrated financial success, position within its industry, the quality of its management team, its marketing plan, and so on. In examining these factors, along with any others, you can get a sense of the direction in which the company is headed, its ability to consistently deliver the quality products, and the leadership advice necessary for building a profitable network.

These factors, years in business, financial success, and industry position, are all historical in nature. They show what the company has done, but not necessarily what it is capable of doing. To stay successful, a company must know how to make the best use of its resources and be able to anticipate and react to change. This is why it is important to pay close attention to a company's management team and overall marketing strategy. Frequent issues involve the professional and educational backgrounds of the top managers in the company, how long have they been involved in MLM, the new products or services the company is planning to offer, pricing or promotion changes being developed, and the consumer groups identified as target markets.

Another major issue is whether the MLM company operates in an industry that is growing or shrinking. For example, during the 1970s, when the nation's birth rate was low, companies that sold baby-related goods, infant clothes, toys, furniture, and personal-care products fared badly. During the 1980s, though, when the "baby boom" generation started having children, the baby products industry took off.

In addition to reflecting the times, the industry should be one that is viewed favorably by the public and the press. Because network marketing is built around

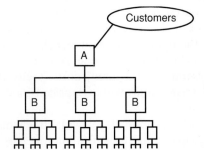

FIGURE 6.13–4

"friends telling friends" about the products or services they represent, it is important for the industry to have a positive image. Otherwise, the sellers are likely to end up spending more time defending the company than selling its products.

## WHAT MLMs DO NOT TELL PROSPECTIVE SELLERS

Advertisements and recruiters promoting MLM always stress the income potential and the multiplication of sales due to the proliferation of people working in the seller's downline. They tend to ignore the following factors that work against success as a MLM participant:

1. There are costs associated with recruiting and sponsoring new members.
2. Frequently people who join stop buying the company's products shortly thereafter.
3. Many distributors make little or no effort to sponsor others or to distribute the company's products. They may be good customers because they still buy products.
4. It costs distributors dearly to get dropped for insufficient sales because they lose their place in the pyramid.
5. The companies sometimes fail to make a profit and go out of business leaving the distributorships worthless.
6. The MLM company, if it fails to provide a genuine product or service or if its advertising is overzealous, may face costly regulatory actions that affect distributors.

## AVOIDING PYRAMID SCHEMES

Some MLM companies operate genuine marketing networks while others operate illegal pyramid schemes. Because both have the same organizational structure, it is easy to confuse them. Legitimate MLM companies generate income from sales of a product to consumers; pyramids generate income simply from bringing in a new member and charging them fees.

Pyramid schemes (also known as "Ponzi schemes" after the man who originated the concept) operate much like a chain letter with newcomers to the group (or chain) paying money to those already in the group. Once in the pyramid, the only way for a pyramid member to make money is to bring in new people who, in turn, pay a fee. The problem with pyramid schemes, and the reason that they are illegal, is that only the first people who join have a chance of making any money. Eventually the pyramid collapses when the people on the bottom discover that there is no one left to bring into the group.

Some of the more devious pyramid schemes actually do offer a product for sale, but the "product" is nothing more than window dressing. Rather than selling it to customers at a profit, distributors at one level in the pyramid sell it at a profit to the distributors on the level beneath them. Those distributors do the same. And so the product goes, passing from one level in the pyramid to the next, until finally those distributors on the bottom are left "holding the bag," stuck with overpriced goods that cannot be sold.

Two of the most common tip-offs that a company is an illegal pyramid scheme are headhunting fees and inventory loading. A company that uses headhunting fees pays members for bringing in new recruits who are charged an entry fee to join the organization. A company that engages in inventory loading requires new distributors to purchase large amounts of nonreturnable merchandise. Part of the company's proceeds from each distributor's order then goes to that person's sponsor.

Companies operating illegal pyramid schemes generally do the following:

- Promise extremely high earnings.
- Downplay the importance of hard work and personal sacrifice in achieving success.
- Are more interested in recruiting new members than in making sales to consumers.
- Pay headhunting fees for new recruits.
- Charge a high entry fee to become a distributor.
- Do not have a product or service to sell.
- Have a product with a low repeatability quotient—people may buy once, but not on a regular basis.
- Are structured so that only the distributors at the bottom of the organization actually sell to customers.
- Require new distributors to purchase large amounts of inventory.
- Have an inadequate "buy back" policy for unsold inventory.

## Nu SKIN INTERNATIONAL

Nu Skin International is located in a sparkling new 10-story headquarters building in downtown Provo, Utah. In the seven brief years since its founding, Nu Skin has grown into a major enterprise with 1991 projected revenues of $500 million (Figure 6.13–5) and about $55 million in income (Figure 6.13–6).

If Nu Skin is not a household name, it is because it concentrates most of its sales messages toward its distributors, relying on them to get the Nu Skin message to consumers. Nu Skin aggressively recruits sellers and distributors with powerful messages about earnings, independence, and economic freedom (see Table 6.13–1).

Nu Skin distributors tell prospective sellers that top distributors can earn commissions of up to $400,000 a month. This pitch is delivered at thousands of recruiting meetings and in sophisticated recruitment videotapes, including one narrated by the late Bill Bixby, the star of television's *The Incredible Hulk*. That tape shows average people telling Nu Skin success stories.

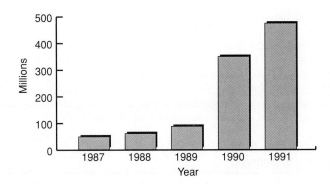

FIGURE 6.13–5 Nu Skin International Estimated Revenues

*Source:* Estimated from various sources.

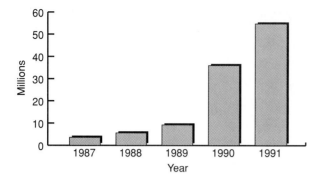

**FIGURE 6.13–6** Nu Skin International Estimated Income

*Source:* Estimated from various sources.

Most Nu Skin recruiting occurs at meetings that are attended by Nu Skin distributors and the prospects they bring. At these sessions, the emphasis is not on what the product can do for the customers but rather on what selling the product can do for sellers (see Table 6.13–2 for a description of the line). These are not sales meetings so much as inspirational gatherings aiming to get prospects to become Nu Skin sellers by becoming part of their sponsor's downline.

At these meetings, a great deal of emphasis is placed on how building a downline and receiving commissions can result in huge incomes and other benefits. Some say that this emphasis on recruiting as opposed to selling products makes Nu Skin a pyramid scheme. However, whether Nu Skin is a pyramid is unclear and currently the subject of judicial deliberations. Generally, a MLM operation crosses the line of legality when its primary purpose is to make money from recruiting instead of from selling products to consumers. It is perfectly legal to share commissions when the commissions are earned from selling products to consumers, but it is not legal in most states to operate a MLM firm that encourages commission money derived primarily from product sales to the recruits themselves.

To become a Nu Skin distributor, there is a $35 registration. Recruits are also encouraged to buy a $200 kit of skin care products from the new recruits sponsor. And, those kits do involve commissions that are distributed up the downline.

Nu Skin buys nearly all of its products from outside manufacturers and, after mark ups of as much as 300 percent, makes those products available to members of its

**TABLE 6.13–1   A Nu Skin International Meeting**

Objective: Create an environment where your "friend" can recruit you to be on his downline members.

Meetings emphasize reaching your goals, dreams, desired life style—not by selling products—but by getting others to sell for you.

Benefits: be your own boss, achieve economic freedom, anyone can do it, make money in your free time, make so much money you can quit your regular job, the products sell themselves, no capital required.

Much of the meeting involves hearing testimonial of individual successes.

They keep saying "don't listen to doubters."

---

**TABLE 6.13–2   Nu Skin International Product Line**

- Facial system (13 items): Intensive Eye Complex, Cleansing Lotion, Facial Scrub, Enhancer, Face Lift, Nutriol Mascara, Nutriol Eyelash, etc.
- Body care system (11 items): Body Bar, Liquid Body Lufra, Body Smoother, Hand Lotion, Glacial Marine Mud, Sunright 4, 8, 15, 24, etc.
- Hair care system (7 items): Total Performance Shampoo A and B; Gentle Conditioning Shampoo; etc.
- Interior design (5 nutritional and vitamin supplements).
- Subliminal tapes (27 motivational tapes).

---

MLM sales force. The company claims it paid out about 45 percent of its revenues in commissions. At the top of the Nu Skin hierarchy are about 60 distributors known as blue diamond executives. They collect 5 percent commissions on sales from executive distributor groups as much as six levels below them. If an executive distributor fails to meet monthly quotas, that person can lose future executive commissions from his or her downline.

Becoming a blue diamond is a long journey, and the odds are long too. The first step is to become an executive distributor by meeting monthly sales quotas. Next, the seller needs to two distributors he or she recruits to become executives. The seller is promoted to the next executive level and collects 5 percent commissions on executive group sales as far as two levels down. Recruiting four executives leads to another promotion and the ability to collect commissions three levels down, and so on, up to six levels deep.

To qualify as an executive the seller must personally order $2,000 of product from Provo over four months. People the seller recruits have to order $7,500 more. After that seller's personal quota is $100 a month. Failure to meet the quotas results in loss of position on the pyramid and the commissions that come with it. There is no doubt that some of the Nu Skin stuff ends up in the garages or attics, put there by executives desperate to meet quotas and hold their rung on the ladder. Few executives focus on retailing the product to customers.

## MLM IS A NUMBERS GAME

We can form a realistic idea of the profit potential of any MLM marketing plan only by considering both the positive (income) and negative (expense) forces operating. Profit, after all, is income minus expenses. MLM company promotions imply that huge amounts of money can be made. And, the company may imply that it is expanding rapidly and you must join right away before everyone in the world signs up and there is no one left to recruit. The objective is to create excitement and the sense of urgency needed to close the sale (getting you to join). These messages have been given so often that the people giving them have become believers.

In truth, however, having too many members has never been either a real problem or a real determinate of the size of the seller's eventual downline. The downline reaches its maximum size when the recruitment rate and dropout rate exactly balance each other. Customers only have a limited lifespan. As a purely mathematical problem, and for purposes of discussion, assume that a seller wants to maintain 1,000 people in his or her downline. Assume the only limit to how long they stay is the human lifespan and that after 45 years the seller will still have 50 of the originals. The seller would have to recruit five or six new members each month to keep up with the rate at which he or she loses them. If the seller loses members because they become tired of the products or bored because they are not making money, he could be down to 50 members after just three years. Then, he would have to recruit 80 new members each month to maintain 1,000. If it costs more to recruit 80 members than there are profits from the 1,000, the whole scheme is not profitable.

Would others in the seller's downline help with some of this recruiting? Certainly. And, they may also share in the profits, depending on how the program is structured. The seller's recruitment rate will depend mostly on the attractiveness of his or her offer and efficiency in spreading the message.

## THE FUTURE OF MLM

Overall, MLM has a bright future. Rapid growth is being fed by individuals looking for new income opportunities and by innovative MLM companies offering products and services consumers want to buy. Many companies are also looking to MLM distribution channel opportunities as technology changes the nature of communications and marketing. MLM has great value in part because it is personal selling, basically face-to-face marketing in a world that is increasingly impersonal.

Nu Skin International is emerging as a major player in this new way to sell products and services. While Nu Skin has growth phenomenally in the last few years, there are indications that it still has significant potential. With that opportunity comes challenges. Of particular interest to those concerned is the potential impact of competitors, especially major manufactures such as Clinique and Revlon, that are adding MLM to their retailing activities; other new alternative distribution channels, such as televised home shopping; and the procedural and legal issues associated with operating a MLM firm.

What marketing strategy changes would you recommend to Nu Skin? What specific price, promotion, and product elements would you propose and why? How would you deal with the growth competition from other MLMs?

## Sources

Kishel, Gregory and Patricia Kishel. *Build Your Own Network Sales Business.* New York: John Wiley & Sons, 1992.

Nadler, Beverly. "Multilevel Marketing." *Business Connections* (January 1984): 19–22.

Nu Skin. The Company marketing plan, sales meetings, brochures, and other promotional materials.

Por, Richard. "Network Marketing." *Success* (May 1990) 74.

Provini, Charles R. "Become a Millionaire Without Ever Leaving Your Home." *Money World* (October 1989): 12–16.

Roha, Ronaleen R. "The Ups and Downs of Downlines." *Kiplinger's Personal Finance Magazine* (November 1991): 63–70.

Stern, Richard and Mary Beth Grover. "Pyramid Power?" *Forbes* (November 11, 1991): 136–148.

# CASE *L.A. Gear* 14

The athletic footwear industry has grown rapidly over the past two decades. Retail growth averaged roughly 20 percent per year between 1985 and 1993 to about $6 billion in sales. The forces responsible for that growth include the popularity of running in the late 1970s, with that sport eventually reaching non-runners, and the purchase of running shoes for casual use piggybacking the trend toward more casual lifestyles.

The emergence of aerobics in the early 1980s created a new fashion and fitness trend for women who wanted fashionable apparel and footwear. They preferred stylish items that were comfortable and colorful, with more variety than traditional exercise outfits. The early 1980s also produced shoes designed for individual sports and technological innovations in material and design. From those 1980s trends emerged two seemingly distinct athletic shoe market segments, that is, consumers who wanted performance versus those who were primarily interested in fashion.

In the 1990s, athletic footwear is worn to make a statement. The shoes are not only for serious athletes but also for casual athletes and fashion wearers looking for comfortable, attractive shoes that represent the wearer's personality and life style. Athletic footwear has evolved from being an accessory to an essential clothing item.

From high-tops to high-tech, the sneaker has made it to the high style of fashion's runways. In the recent designer collections, sneakers took front stage as footwear's must-have accessory. The sneaker also received another honor, a special award from the Council of Fashion Designers of America for its uniquely American influence on world fashion. The sneaker is the most universal item in everyone's wardrobe. It is now also becoming integrated into different aspects of every consumer's life, from the office to the home. The sneaker represents everyone's sense of fitness and health; everyone feels young and healthy wearing sneakers.

When it comes to serious footwear, Nike is the market leader. Its modern track shoes energized an industry and produced a $3.5 billion footwear superpower with superstar advertising. Celebrity athletes such as Michael Jordan and Bo Jackson have convinced lots of fans on and off the playing field to "Just Do It." Nike is best at enhancing an athlete's ability with a shoe that has the latest technology.

Other major contenders in the athletic footwear business are Reebok and L.A.

Gear. They, along with Nike, are in a marketing war with stakes that include dominance of the U.S. and international athletic shoe markets and image leadership in a product category where performance and fashion become blurred in an avalanche of new technologies and styles.

## ATHLETIC SHOE BUYERS

Although the shoes sold by Nike, Reebok, and L.A. Gear appeal to consumers of all ages, incomes, and both genders, there are significant differences between the customer profiles for the brands.

Tables 6.14–1 and 6.14–2 separately profile women and men on key demographics for purchase behavior in the last 12 months and by leading competitor (L.A. Gear versus Nike versus Reebok). According to Table 6.14–1, some 59 percent of women purchased a pair of shoes in the last 12 months, with Reebok the most likely brand of choice. Similarly, some 52 percent of men purchased at least one pair of sneaker/athletic shoes in the last 12 months and, among men, the most likely brand is also Reebok. The tables also show that L.A. Gear's shoes are most popular with young women, while Nike's shoes do well with young men. What these numbers do not show is the fact that women purchase significantly more shoes than men, as much as 20 to 30 percent more.

The pie charts in Figures 6.14–1 and 6.14–2 reinforce the information on gender differences in the tables by showing that major brand market shares differ by gender. Reebok and L.A. Gear are more popular with women than with men, probably due to their historical emphasis on fashion over performance. Nike does slightly better with men than with women, presumably due to its reputation for innovation and technology in support of its performance positioning.

However, in reality, the market for performance shoes overlaps with the fashion shoe market. The two positioning dimensions, fashion and performance, are frequently difficult to separate because performance (or appearing as though you could perform) is a form of fashion. Realistically, those who purchase performance shoes are more likely to be found wearing them on a walk in the mall than playing at competitive sports. Only one pair of athletic shoes out of seven ever sees any real sweat. However, to be the market leader, a shoe firm needs to sell to both the performance and fashion

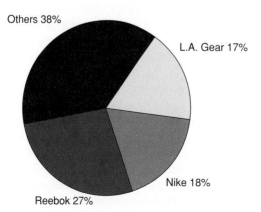

FIGURE 6.14–1 1991 Athletic Shoe Shares for Women Consumers

*Source:* Simmons Market Research, 1991.

**TABLE 6.14–1   Sneakers/Athletic Shoes Purchase Behavior in Last 12 Months (women)**

| | Brought in last 12 Months (%) | Index | L.A. Gear (%) | Index | Nike (%) | Index | Reebok (%) | Index |
|---|---|---|---|---|---|---|---|---|
| All women | 59.4 | 100 | 17.0 | 100 | 17.6 | 100 | 27.1 | 100 |
| Mothers | 71.4 | 120 | 24.9 | 144 | 26.5 | 151 | 35.7 | 132 |
| Employed mothers | 29.2 | 119 | 26.0 | 153 | 27.5 | 156 | 34.1 | 139 |
| | | | | | | | | |
| *Age* | | | | | | | | |
| 18–24 | 59.9 | 101 | 22.6 | 133 | 17.2 | 98 | 24.8 | 92 |
| 25–34 | 77.9 | 113 | 21.9 | 129 | 18.7 | 106 | 31.0 | 114 |
| 35–44 | 70.1 | 118 | 22.6 | 133 | 27.7 | 157 | 37.1 | 137 |
| 45–54 | 64.3 | 108 | 16.0 | 94 | 20.5 | 116 | 32.9 | 121 |
| 55–64 | 57.0 | 96 | 10.8 | 64 | 12.9 | 73 | 22.3 | 82 |
| 65 and older | 36.4 | 58 | 4.6 | 27 | 5.9 | 34 | 10.9 | 40 |
| | | | | | | | | |
| *Marital status* | | | | | | | | |
| Single | 57.6 | 97 | 20.9 | 123 | 17.7 | 101 | 21.5 | 79 |
| Married | 65.1 | 110 | 17.6 | 104 | 19.9 | 113 | 31.8 | 118 |
| Divorced, etc. | 47.5 | 80 | 12.6 | 74 | 12.3 | 70 | 20.3 | 75 |
| Parents | 71.4 | 120 | 24.9 | 146 | 26.5 | 151 | 35.7 | 132 |
| | | | | | | | | |
| *Region* | | | | | | | | |
| Northeast | 59.6 | 100 | 15.8 | 93 | 15.8 | 90 | 28.1 | 104 |
| Midwest | 56.8 | 96 | 16.2 | 95 | 20.7 | 118 | 27.7 | 102 |
| South | 59.8 | 101 | 17.5 | 103 | 15.9 | 90 | 27.1 | 100 |
| West | 61.5 | 104 | 18.2 | 107 | 18.7 | 106 | 25.2 | 93 |
| | | | | | | | | |
| *Income* | | | | | | | | |
| $75 + | 64.1 | 108 | 18.3 | 108 | 25.8 | 146 | 33.8 | 125 |
| $60 + | 65.3 | 110 | 17.8 | 105 | 23.0 | 131 | 33.6 | 124 |
| $50 + | 65.2 | 110 | 17.6 | 104 | 21.8 | 124 | 34.2 | 126 |
| $40 + | 65.3 | 110 | 18.2 | 107 | 21.5 | 122 | 33.7 | 125 |
| $30 + | 65.4 | 110 | 18.2 | 107 | 21.6 | 122 | 32.8 | 121 |
| $30–$39 | 65.6 | 110 | 18.2 | 107 | 21.7 | 123 | 30.1 | 111 |
| $20–$29 | 59.1 | 100 | 17.4 | 102 | 14.7 | 84 | 27.2 | 101 |
| $10–$19 | 54.7 | 93 | 17.6 | 104 | 11.6 | 66 | 20.8 | 77 |
| Less than $10 | 42.8 | 72 | 11.3 | 67 | 13.7 | 78 | 13.2 | 49 |
| | | | | | | | | |
| *Presence of children* | | | | | | | | |
| Under 2 years | 66.2 | 112 | 20.6 | 121 | 19.1 | 108 | 33.4 | 123 |
| 2–5 | 68.6 | 116 | 22.1 | 130 | 20.3 | 115 | 30.7 | 114 |
| 6–11 | 73.4 | 124 | 29.7 | 175 | 28.2 | 160 | 33.3 | 123 |
| 12–17 | 70.7 | 119 | 27.3 | 161 | 32.9 | 187 | 36.2 | 134 |

Note: Index values above are computed by dividing the proportion in a particular grouping by their proportion of the population. For example, if an age group has 20.2% of the products users and represents 18.3% of the population, the index value for the grouping is 110. Index values over 100 signify above average usage and index values below 100 signify below average usage. However, values over 110 or under 90 are the most significant.

*Source:* Simmons Market Research Bureau, Inc., 1991.

**TABLE 6.14–2** Sneakers/Athletic Shoes Purchase Behavior in Last 12 Months (men)

| | Bought in last 12 Months (%) | Index | L.A. Gear (%) | Index | Nike (%) | Index | Reebok (%) | Index |
|---|---|---|---|---|---|---|---|---|
| All men | 51.7 | 100 | 10.5 | 100 | 19.1 | 100 | 22.8 | 100 |
| *Age* | | | | | | | | |
| 18–24 | 54.1 | 105 | 10.1 | 96 | 25.9 | 136 | 27.4 | 120 |
| 25–34 | 55.5 | 107 | 11.9 | 113 | 19.9 | 104 | 24.0 | 105 |
| 35–44 | 58.0 | 112 | 15.3 | 145 | 23.4 | 122 | 26.4 | 116 |
| 45–54 | 54.8 | 106 | 11.3 | 107 | 21.5 | 113 | 25.3 | 111 |
| 55–64 | 44.8 | 87 | 6.0 | 57 | 13.5 | 70 | 20.2 | 89 |
| 65 and older | 35.2 | 68 | 4.2 | 40 | 6.2 | 33 | 10.2 | 45 |
| *Marital status* | | | | | | | | |
| Single | 50.6 | 98 | 8.8 | 84 | 20.6 | 108 | 21.9 | 96 |
| Married | 53.6 | 104 | 11.6 | 110 | 19.5 | 102 | 24.7 | 108 |
| Divorced, etc. | 43.5 | 84 | 8.7 | 83 | 13.6 | 71 | 14.9 | 65 |
| Parents | 61.9 | 120 | 16.8 | 160 | 27.3 | 143 | 29.0 | 127 |
| *Region* | | | | | | | | |
| Northeast | 53.1 | 103 | 9.6 | 91 | 15.4 | 81 | 18.9 | 83 |
| Midwest | 56.9 | 110 | 9.1 | 87 | 20.0 | 104 | 22.1 | 97 |
| South | 48.8 | 94 | 11.0 | 105 | 18.3 | 96 | 24.4 | 107 |
| West | 48.8 | 95 | 12.3 | 117 | 23.3 | 122 | 25.2 | 110 |
| *Income* | | | | | | | | |
| $75 + | 58.3 | 113 | 10.2 | 97 | 21.8 | 114 | 25.1 | 110 |
| $60 + | 57.5 | 111 | 9.6 | 91 | 23.3 | 122 | 24.7 | 108 |
| $50 + | 56.8 | 110 | 9.4 | 90 | 22.0 | 115 | 26.7 | 117 |
| $40 + | 56.0 | 108 | 10.1 | 96 | 22.0 | 115 | 27.1 | 119 |
| $30 + | 55.7 | 108 | 10.5 | 100 | 21.2 | 111 | 26.4 | 116 |
| $30–$39 | 54.9 | 106 | 11.7 | 111 | 19.1 | 100 | 24.5 | 107 |
| $20–$29 | 52.6 | 102 | 10.7 | 102 | 18.2 | 95 | 21.5 | 94 |
| $10–$19 | 43.9 | 85 | 9.9 | 94 | 15.5 | 81 | 16.5 | 72 |
| Less than $10 | 33.6 | 65 | 11.5 | 109 | 11.7 | 61 | 10.3 | 45 |
| *Presence of children* | | | | | | | | |
| Under 2 years | 58.9 | 114 | 15.5 | 148 | 23.5 | 123 | 28.8 | 126 |
| 2–5 | 56.2 | 109 | 14.3 | 136 | 20.9 | 110 | 23.2 | 101 |
| 6–11 | 62.2 | 120 | 19.5 | 185 | 27.6 | 145 | 28.3 | 124 |
| 12–17 | 62.8 | 122 | 19.5 | 185 | 31.5 | 165 | 31.8 | 139 |

Note: Index values above are computed by dividing the proportion in a particular grouping by their proportion of the population. For example, if an age group has 20.2% of the products users and represents 18.3% of the population, the index value for the grouping is 110. Index values over 100 signify above average usage and index values below 100 signify below average usage. However, values over 110 or under 90 are the most significant.

*Source:* Simmons Market Research Bureau, Inc., 1991.

markets. And, in the 1990s, firms must also have a strong product design and marketing position (based primarily on advertising) in more than one athletic shoe market gender segment. While technological innovations produce better made and better fitting high-performance shoes, an emphasis on advertising and sales promotion activities drives consumer demand and supports a unique brand image.

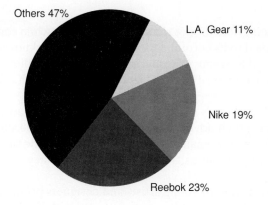

**FIGURE 6.14–2** 1991 Athletic Shoe Shares for Men Consumers

*Source:* Simmons Market Research, 1991.

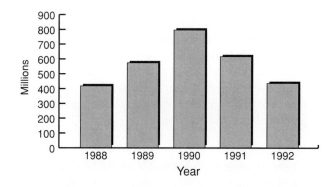

**FIGURE 6.14–3** L.A. Gear Revenues

*Source: L.A. Gear 1992 Annual Report.*

## L.A. GEAR, INC.

Since 1979, L.A. Gear has specialized in sneakers that symbolize the southern California lifestyle. After a slow start, success came quickly. From sales of $11 million in 1985, a peak was reached in 1990 at $820 million, and declined to $430 million by the end of 1992 (Fig. 6.14–3). Previously considered only a trendy shoe company, L.A. Gear found a niche in the fashion segment of the athletic footwear industry and exploited it. With its unusual use of colors and shapes, L.A. Gear established a strong niche.

L.A. Gear initially designed and sold roller skate shoes and owned roller palaces. In 1983, it introduced a canvas tie-on shoe with a flat rubber bottom called *The Street Walker*. As athletic shoes ceased to be worn only for running and jumping, the firm provided shoes for wearers who chose athletic shoes for casual wear. L.A. Gear now has an extensive product line for all styles and occasions.

## A Fashion Leader

L.A. Gear prides itself on being able to spot trends in the market, while continuing to introduce products that appeal to its current customers. It readily acknowledges that designing for trends that appeal to young women can be risky, but it believes that by staying in close touch with its customers, it can prosper even in such a high risk and volatile market segment.

Industry analysts attribute L.A. Gear's success to a combination of good advertising and merchandising. By placing their advertisements on MTV and cable stations, L.A. Gear reached its target—the young woman who wear skirts and athletic shoes. Its shoes are not technically sophisticated, but as trendy fashion shoes, they have few equals.

In L.A. Gear's design studio, dozens of young artists and designers produce prototypes that are both stylist and faddish. Those shoes are designed with bright colors, multiple laces, inlaid rhinestones, stylish trims, leather accessories, and buckles, making L.A. Gear the favorite of trend-seeking women from coast to coast.

L.A. Gear has been hugely successful with women, selling some 65 percent of its volume to that group in 1992 (about 30 percent went to men, with the remaining volume in children's shoes). The firm still has much room to grow in the men's segment of the market. If L.A. Gear is to become number one in the overall athletic shoe market, it must be able to spot trends and market products to men as well as it does for women. As the growth in the overall athletic shoe market eventually levels off, L.A. Gear must obtained new market share from the traditional men's athletic shoe segment. Although L.A. Gear has limited experience with that market, it must achieve significant successes there if it's to aggressively go after Nike and Reebok.

## Recent Problems

On December 1, 1992, L.A. Gear announced that it would lose about $80 million for the fiscal year that ended November 30, 1992, including $30 million in the fourth quarter (Fig. 6.14–4). As suddenly as it went hot, L.A. Gear went cold. As its quality slipped and its image became passé, buyers turned to Nike and Reebok. The result was a decrease in sales. During that year, the firm had overflowing inventories, with too many low-quality shoes to sell. However, in focusing on clearing out the warehouses and revamping shoddy manufacturing, the company failed to produce enough new

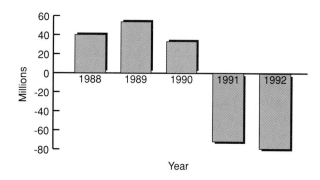

FIGURE 6.14–4 L.A. Gear Net Income

*Source: L.A. Gear 1992 Annual Report.*

products for 1993's first half. And, reluctant retailers who were burned by L.A. Gear's discounting did not rush back to commit themselves further.

L.A. Gear counted millions of pairs of shoes in warehouses and only a few million in cash. Investors took control of the company and kicked out the founders. The first step was to stop inventory from piling up by shutting down production at contract factories overseas. The firm stopped marketing apparel, a multimillion dollar money loser. It then began a sale of excess inventory, which further hurt the firm's brand image, however, but gave the company tens in millions of much-needed cash. It also stopped selling shoes in discount outlets, swap meets, and 7-Eleven's, in favor of full-price department stores and shoe stores. That move helped to restore its quality image and, more important, boosted gross profit margins.

## STRATEGIES

The main battle for sales and market share in the athletic shoe market is primarily between Nike and Reebok, with L.A. Gear a distant third (Figs. 16.14–5, 16.14–6 and 6.14–7). By the end of 1992, Nike and Reebok were the number one and two U.S. market share holders, respectively. They achieved those market positions by investing millions of dollars in highly produced, superstar media campaigns and new product introductions that included many innovations and new materials. However, historically, Nike has had a performance focus based on technological attributes, while Reebok has emphasized the fashion aspects of its line. More recently, both have struggled for product differentiation in the performance market by highlighting technological innovations in shoe design. L.A. Gear, third in retail sales in the U.S. market, grew with the fashion segment. As the market expands to new users, however, old competitors (Keds, Converse, and Adidas) are also trying capitalizing on the industry's growth to recapture market share.

Nike, Reebok, and L.A. Gear all have essentially the same objective, to increase market share, but their strategy executions are quite different. Each firm must effectively target its customers and develop a solid brand preference. However, the market-

**FIGURE 6.14–5** Sales by Athletic Shoe Brand

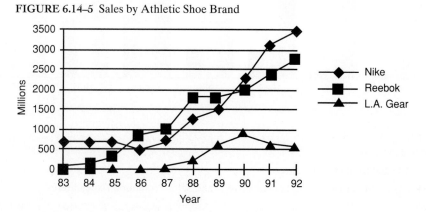

*Source:* Estimated from various sources.

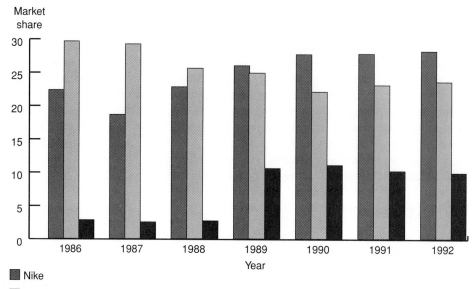

Source: Estimated from various sources.

FIGURE 6.14–6 Major Athletic Shoe Brand Market Shares

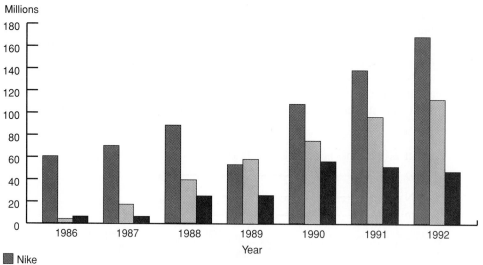

Source: Estimated from various sources.

FIGURE 6.14–7 Major Brand Market Advertising and Sales Promotion Expenditures

ing complexities in this highly competitive industry are numerous and multifaceted, requiring well-managed manipulations of price, product designs, distribution, and promotion.

The athletic footwear battles are a war, with R&D and marketing skills, plus financial resources, critical to having an edge. However, the firm that is innovative and moves first in both the performance and fashion markets by implementing major new strategies has a significant advantage. Each of the top three firms in this industry achieved its successes with extraordinary marketing skills and each of those shoe marketers will defend its market share with those same skills.

In the past, the entire athletic shoe industry enjoyed terrific growth, so each firm could report favorable results. Now, the firm's specific strategies will have more relevance because industry growth is now more difficult. And, with the cost of shoes increasing yearly, buyers may rebel significantly reducing sales, especially if they decide to wear the shoes they now have for longer periods of time rather than buy new shoes with each technological or fashion innovation.

## L.A. Gear

With L.A. Gear well established as a fashion expert, it now needs a strategy for capturing a greater share of the men's shoe market. It has the potential to overtake Reebok, if it can continue to have success in its marketing efforts directed toward expanding beyond the women's segment.

L.A. Gear has not promoted the performance aspects of its shoes in the past, focusing instead on fashion for different occasions. However, in an effort to attract more men buyers, it is placing a greater emphasis on athletics, while not adopting a completely performance driven image.

L.A. Gear's strategy to gain share in the performance segment of the market raises some risks that such campaigns could blur the firm's image, including that consumers may become confused about whether L.A. Gear represents fashion or athletic performance. This repositioning effort has more than a few skeptics because it requires the firm to have different images by major market segment. Both Nike and Reebok have claimed some achievements in obtaining that same dual image goals. While L.A. Gear is trying to develop this athletic image, it could alienate fashion conscience buyers, confusing its product offerings with other performance promoted shoes and by blurring its distinctive fashion positioning with women.

## Reebok

Reebok has also been trying to reposition itself from a fashion firm to a performance shoe firm with aggressive advertising that targets Nike and emphasizes Reebok's new performance image. Reebok's strategy assumes it is in direct competition with Nike, and thus must beat Nike on its own distinctive attributes, innovation and performance, if it is to capture a significant part of the men's market.

## Nike

At this point, Nike appears to be well positioned to defend its leadership position. Creative advertising with Bo Jackson and a host of other athletic stars portray a professional athlete and their shoe of choice. Nike's positioning emphasizes technological innovation and athletic performance, with the testimonials to prove it.

## MORE SHARE BATTLES

The marketing strategies of Nike, Reebok, and L.A. Gear are converging to gain market share by simultaneously straddling both the performance and fashion segments of the market because those firms cannot afford to remain uniquely performance or fashion oriented. Although Reebok and Nike have the financial resources to outspend L.A. Gear, in the past L.A. Gear has effectively targeted its market segment with a fashion message and built product image and brand awareness with impressive sales growth. Now that it is a solid player in the fashion segment, getting 70 to 75 percent of its (non-children) sales from 15- to 25-year-old women, the firm believes that it needs to aggressively and effectively pursue the men's market, symbolized by performance shoes. Success in that market apparently requires both the image and reality of technological innovation and solid athletic performance attributes.

So far, L.A. Gear has successfully produced highly fashionable, rhinestone studded, pink and white shoes for the 12- to 25-year-old women's market, representing L.A. Gear's continuing competence at making various styles, but what does it need to do to be successful in the men's market? And, how does its image as a fashion shoe firm conflict with or support its attempt to gain a stronger position in the men's segment of the market? If L.A. Gear intends to grow sales, it needs to become a major player in that market without sacrificing its position in the women's market. Advise L.A. Gear about its marketing strategy options for gaining a larger share of the men's market (while still holding onto a major part of the women's market). What specific recommendations would you make and why? What are the potential benefits? How serious are the risks associated with this major change in marketing strategy? What is wrong with remaining a niche marketer? Can you make an argument for L.A. Gear continuing to focus on the fashion needs of women exclusively?

## Sources

Barr, Stephen. "Adidas on the Rebound." *CFO* (September 1991): 48–56.

Barrett, Amy. "L.A. Gear Still Looks Like An Also Ran." *Business Week* (December 21, 1992): 37.

Darlin, Damon. "Getting Beyond A Market Niche," *Forbes* (November 22, 1993): 106–107.

Hammonds, Keith H. "The 'Blacktop' is Paving Reebok's Road to Recovery." Business Week (August 12, 1991): 27.

Impoco, Jim and Warren Cohen. "Nike Goes To The Full-Court Press." *U.S. News & World Report* (April 19, 1993): 48–50.

Jereski, Laura. "Can Paul Fireman Put The Bounce Back In Reebok?" *Business Week* (June 18, 1990): 181–182.

Kerwin, Kathleen. "L.A. Gear Calls in a Cobbler." *Business Week* (September 16, 1991): 78, 82.

Kerwin, Kathleen and Mark Landler. "L.A. Gear Is Tripping Over Its Shoelaces." *Business Week* (August 20, 1990): 39.

*L.A. Gear 1992 Annual Report.*

"L.A. Gear," in *Strategic Marketing*, 3rd ed., David W. Cravens (Homewood, IL: Irwin, 1991), pp. 245–251.

"L.A. Gear," in *Strategic Marketing Management Cases*, 4th ed., eds. David W. Cravens and Charles W. Lamb (Homewood, IL: Irwin, 1993), pp. 443–449.

Magiera, Marcy. "Small Rivals Leap As L.A. Gear Stumbles." *Advertising Age* (June 8, 1992): 12.

Meeks, Fleming. "Be Ferocious." *Forbes* (August 2, 1993): 40–41.

Meeks, Fleming. "The Sneaker Game." *Forbes* (October 22, 1990): 114–115.

"Nike, Inc." in *Cases in Consumer Behavior*, 2nd ed., ed. Hale N. Tongren. (Englewood Cliffs, NJ: Prentice Hall, 1992), pp. 26–40.

Novak, Joanne E. "L.A. Gear," in *Cases in Marketing Management*, 5th. ed., eds. Kenneth L. Bernhardt, and Thomas C. Kinnear (Homewood, IL: Richard D. Irwin, 1991), pp. 411–453.

Quelch, John A. and Tammy Bunn Hiller. "Reebok International," in *Cases in Advertising and Promotion Management*, 3rd ed., eds. John A. Quelch, and Paul W. Farris (Homewood, IL: Richard D. Irwin, 1991), pp. 484–508.

Reichlin, Igor, *et al.* "Where Nike and Reebok Have Plenty of Running Room." *Business Week* (March 11, 1991): 56–57.

Smith, Geoffrey and Mark Maremount. "Can Reebok Regain Its Balance?" *Business Week* (December 20, 1993): 108–109.

Yang, Dori Jones and Robert Buderi. "Step By Step With Nike." *Business Week* (August 13, 1990): 110–111.

# CASE *Kmart Stores** 15

In the summer of 1993, Kmart convened a senior management team to assess the impacts that emerging social, economic, and political changes in the United States would have on the future of the firm. This team of Kmart's best planners and operations managers, dubbed the "F-Team," was instructed to pay particular attention to building sce-

---

*Although Kmart is an actual competitor in the American retailing industry, the scenario in this case is fictionalized to dramatize the marketing issues facing the firm.

narios about the nature of American society in the next 10 to 20 years and strategies for reacting to those scenarios.

The F-Team worked for several months and produced a list of scenarios that top Kmart management reviewed and ranked based on their interest in further work and on the likelihood of that trend posing a major threat to Kmart's future.

High on the list of visions about the future of the United States was a scenario where the America's middle class significantly declines in size due primarily to the influences of international competition and the globalization of country economies. The term "middle class" is a colloquial term, the more precise description is the 72 percent of the U.S. population included in the groups labeled "lower middle class" and "upper lower class." The first group (about 28 percent of the population) includes non-managerial white-collar workers and high paid blue-collar workers. The second group (about 44 percent of the population) is composed of blue-collar workers.

The middle class decline scenario details how competition between countries changes the income and social class structure of the United States by diminishing, if not removing the "American labor premium," which is the difference between what low-skilled (and a larger number of skilled) American workers get paid for their work for tasks that third-world workers are willing to do for a fraction of the cost.

Accordingly, some economists characterize the top one-third of all U.S. workers as "world class," but they describe the other two-thirds as "third world." The argument is that two-thirds of the U.S. labor force does not warrant a wage rate higher than that paid to comparable workers in Korea or Mexico and that those U.S. worker wages will systematically fall in the future.

As the American labor premium disappears, significant downward mobility will occur in the United States, accompanied by a diminution in living standards and purchasing power. Some workers will become permanently unemployed or underemployed as they take low-wage services jobs. And, the less skilled will not be alone. Workers with strong technical backgrounds who live in India, Russia, and Korea, among many other countries, will siphon off jobs from North America and Europe. These changes are already occurring in such occupations as computer programming and commercial design.

As the scenario unfolds, these declining incomes and lower living standards will lead to a material change in the social class structure of the United States. As American middle class is significantly reduced in number, the class structure of the United States becomes third world, with the highly educated, world-class workers at the top, a small number in the middle, and the majority of the population at the bottom (employed at low-wage service jobs or not working at all). Those who subscribe to this scenario say that the top group in the new social class structure will represent about 25 percent of households, while the bottom will represent close to 65 percent, with the remainder in the middle. Thus, the scenario describes an American middle class where the majority is downwardly, not upwardly, mobile.

As a result of the downward mobility, firms selling products or services to the shrinking American middle class will need to move down or up the social-class spectrum to maintain their sales. Those firms will have to change their positioning, including targeting and merchandise mix, to more upscale consumers or lower their sights to target the increasing number of less affluent shoppers.

This scenario is of particular concern to Kmart because these changing demographics will have a major influence on all aspects of retailing in America. They will directly affect the nature of consumer demand at the store level and the ability of retailers such as Kmart to survive. The consumer lifestyles serviced by retailers represent product and service consumption patterns, and as standards of living change, so too do consumer purchasing patterns in stores.

## THE REPORT

After receiving the approved list of scenarios from Kmart's top management, the F-Team set about expanding on each one by developing a indepth analysis of the threat, its current manifestations, and a description of attempts by Kmart and competitors to deal with similar events as portrayed in each of the scenarios. This stage of the F-Team's effort represented an interim phase because Kmart management wanted to see the details about each scenario before the F-Team began formulating specific marketing strategies.

To follow are highlights of what the F-Team wrote about the scenario involving the decline of the American middle class. It stops short of making specific marketing recommendations, focusing instead on characterizing recent trends in retailing, the role of consumer demand in shaping the strategies of Kmart and its competitors, and Kmart's strategies over the last several years.

### Another Perspective on Mass Marketing

As consumer buying power increased in the 1960s and 1970s, stores serving the American middle class prospered and expanded. However, some argue that the 1980s and 1990s were decades of decline for those same retailers. The 1980s were particularly hard on such mass marketers as Sears & Roebuck, J.C. Penney, Montgomery Ward, and Kmart (see Figure 6.15–1 for 1991 market share estimates). An exception was Wal-Mart, which serves the lowest end of the social-class spectrum. It prospered, becoming the largest retailer in the United States (bigger than Sears and Kmart combined).

Each of Sears & Roebuck, J.C. Penney, Montgomery Ward, and Kmart engaged in "upscaling" during the last two decades, and, in the process, left behind significant numbers of customers. While this upscaling involved improved ambiance, comfort, and

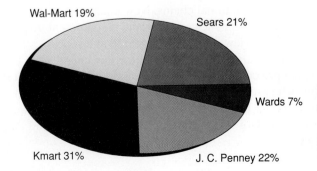

**FIGURE** 6.15–1 Top Five Stores Estimated 1991 Market Shares

*Source:* Simmons Market Research Bureau, 1991.

convenience for shoppers, it mainly meant providing a more expensive product mix, including a trend toward offering branded products that on average cost more than house brands. Upscaling also increased costs for the discount retailers and reduced margins. Overall, the goal of upscaling had been to enhance the discounter's position and attract a broader customer base. However, in doing this, discount stores usually alienated their traditional customer.

Upscaling was not meant to alienate those who already shopped at the discount stores, but instead it was supposed to make the stores more appealing to those with slightly higher incomes. With this strategy, apparel departments in discount stores began carrying an upgraded fashion mix that included designer and brand name merchandise as well as improved private brands. In hardgoods areas, more branded goods were stocked to provide higher product quality and more customer satisfaction.

In turn, this trend led to stores resembling each other and marketing wars over essentially the same customers. Their similarities, their desire to attract the same customers, and an excess retailing space led to price cutting. This encouraged the consumer to look for the lowest price merchandise; however, they still wanted quality goods for their money. By significantly lowering prices, the major retailers minimized their own profits.

**The Retailing Industry**

The retailing industry can be divided into several general segments that contain somewhat overlapping types: full-line department stores, discount department stores, discount drug stores, specialty stores, supermarkets, and convenience stores. However, merchandise scrabbling, which occurs when retailers add goods and services that are unrelated to each other and the retailer's original business, and the trend toward one-stop shopping, has blurred these distinctions between store types. Shoppers can purchase cosmetics in supermarkets, department stores, discount drugs stores, and even convenience stores. Clothing is sold in discount drug stores, specialty stores, and many other places. Food items are in drugstores and discount stores as well as in supermarkets.

At that same time, consumer loyalty to particular stores and store locations diminished as buyers shopped around for the lowest prices at the highest quality. This stimulated competition among retailers and increased options for consumers. The retailers cut their prices to increase store traffic and to build store loyalty, but, in the process, they also further conditioned consumers to shop for the lowest price with good quality. Regional discounters with more attractive stores and more fashionable products took market share away from the national chains. New kinds of discounters specialized in particular merchandise areas for such areas as sports equipment, toys, drugs and beauty products, small appliances, jewelry, books, apparel, and shoes.

Historically, the biggest mass-market retail competitor has been Sears. During the 1970s, Sears moved to higher priced, more stylish merchandise. However, that strategy confused many customers who preferred discounters for their lower prices and specialty shops for their greater product line depth. Many Sear's clothing labels were replaced by fashion labels associated with such popular personalities as Arnold Palmer, Joe Namath, and Cheryl Tiegs.

# KMART

S.S. Kresge Company opened its first Kmart in 1962. Since then hundreds of stores have appeared throughout the United States. Kmart's initial strategy was to provide consumers with general merchandise at a discount price, stressing value over fashion. By offering a full line of merchandise, from clothing to toothpaste to sporting goods, Kmart was able to successfully expand nationwide. Its stores sold low- to medium-quality merchandise that was priced less than its competitors. The firm's approach was very successful, especially among price conscious shoppers who left full service department stores to shop at Kmart and the other discounters. As a trade off for lower prices, the consumers had to accustom themselves to low overhead conditions and self services. Overall, the firm's margins were lower than regular retailers due to a reliance on high-volume sales and inventory turns.

Kmart focused on satisfying families with limited budgets, particularly those unwilling to pay higher prices for similar products. These customers began to recognize Kmart as the place to go for discount prices on merchandise. Kmart did not concern itself with the most effective store layout or effective merchandising because it let its price discounting image fuel growth.

However, Kmart's success lulled it into a false sense of security, and as the firm entered the 1980s, both net income and sales leveled off. Sales per square foot compared unfavorably with similar discounters, but inventory turns were down significantly, which was a bad sign for a company that depended on high-volume sales. Even in that situation, over 50 percent of the population still shopped at a Kmart at least once a month. The problem was that the customers were not buying as much per store visit as in the past; the new competition offered more appealing alternatives in clothing and children's items, to name a few.

## The 1980s

By the late 1970s, competitor discount chains began drawing significant numbers of Kmart shoppers away. While other discounters upgraded their stores and began emphasizing brand name merchandise, Kmart continued to sell its private label and generic goods in its same less fashionable and out-of-date stores. As a result, the firm started to fall behind; it entered the 1980s in a weaker competitive position in an increasingly cut-throat industry.

During this period, shoppers wanted higher quality merchandise and were willing to pay for it. While Kmart stuck with its traditional approach, other retailers moved to satisfy this need. In that process, a very competitive retailing environment developed. During its initial expansion period, Kmart primarily faced competition from national and regional chains, but the successful market penetration of warehouse clubs and specialty stores into the retailing industry meant even more trouble for the firm.

## The 1990s

Today's Kmart differs significantly from its forerunner of the 1960s, 1970s, and 1980s. Now, Kmart emphasizes national brand goods, but also still has a mix of private-label products for value-conscious customers. Some new introductions to the merchandise lines include designer sportswear and jeans, name brand athletic shoes, prestige cosmetics and fragrances, and brand name health and beauty aids. Kmart offers everything from clothing to housewares, from delicatessen foods to hardware, from sporting goods to stationery and toys. The product line also includes such products as tires, batteries, building materials, and garden supplies not commonly carried by conventional department stores. Major competitors include J.C. Penney and Sears (Figure 6.15–1).

By mid-1993, Kmart spent $3 billion on its renewal program, but still did not operate as well as other stores in such critical areas as sales, profits, and inventory management. The refurbished and new Kmarts had an updated interior design with innovations such as a fresh color scheme and contemporary hanging displays in the clothing departments. New departments featured expanded assortments of goods in areas of special interest, including Home Care Centers, Kitchen Korners, Domestic Centers, and Home Electronics Centers.

Kmart also acquired specialty chains, which enhanced its competitive position. By the early 1990s, Kmart's specialty retail group included seven divisions: PACE Membership Warehouse, Builders Square, Payless Drug Stores, Walden Book Company, The Sports Authority, Office Max, and Borders Inc.

## KMART'S RECENT PERFORMANCE

Kmart achieved record sales and earnings in fiscal 1992 despite the weak U.S. economy (Figs. 6.15–2 and 6.15–3). Consolidated sales in 1992 were $34.6 billion, a 7.8 percent increase over 1991 sales of $32.1 billion. Consolidated sales in comparable stores increased 3.7 percent over 1991. Net income in 1992 was $859 million, compared with $756 million in 1991, an increase of 13.6 percent. The increase in 1992 net income resulted from improved profitability in domestic Kmart stores, particularly the fashion departments, and strong sales and earnings gains in the specialty retail group.

## KMART'S CONSUMERS

Kmart's target customer is the budget-conscious mother, ages 25 to 55, who accounts for 60 percent of spending in the United States. The firm's fashions division is trying to move toward a shop concept that presents coordinates in a way that makes it easier for these women to pick something out.

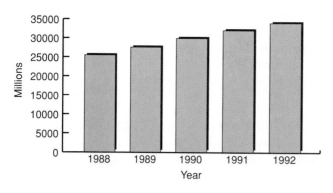

**FIGURE 6.15–2** Kmart Revenues

*Source: Kmart 1992 Annual report.*

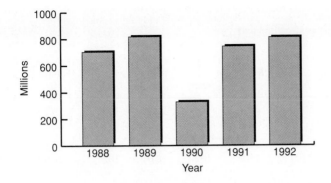

**FIGURE 6.15–3** Kmart Net Income

*Source: Kmart 1992 Annual Report.*

A profile of who shops at Kmart, broken down by gender, age, marital status, region, income, and presence of children can be found in Table 6.15–1. The first profile is of all adults who shopped at a department, discount, and clothing store in the last three months. That profile is quite similar to the Kmart shopper profile, except that Kmart shoppers have lower incomes and are more likely to be parents with children. Sears attracts a higher income group than Kmart, while Wal-Mart attracts a lower income group. Regional differences between the chains reflect the distribution of store locations.

## KMART'S CURRENT STRATEGY

Kmart has also been working to make its name synonymous with fashion. Everything its stores carry has to be considered fashionable and on-trend, whether it is hardgoods or softgoods. Current Kmart CEO Joseph E. Antonini believes that regardless of their income level, people want nice things. According to Antonini, Kmart's customers are looking for value, low prices, and fashion, whether it is apparel, jewelry, cosmetics, housewares, or stationery. And, customer feedback about the new focus on fashion has been favorable.

To stay at the forefront, Kmart selects products that are fashionable today, and to make sure that the selection is on target, buyers travel the country and the world to determine future trends. Kmart features such labels as Gitano, Wrangler, and Hanes, but has also developed a following for its private label collections, such as that of Jaclyn Smith in ladies apparel and Martha Stewart in domestics. However, as a general merchandiser, Kmart cannot get various brand names, so it ends up with a mix of promotional, middle-, and higher-priced name brands and private labels.

While coordination has always been an important issue in apparel, it now has become important in the home fashion area as well. Kmart's new program of bed and bath ensembles offer consumers the opportunity to match window treatments with bedding, or the shower curtain with the bath mat. As part of the program, buying procedures for the window treatment department underwent a turnover, with the bedding buyer choosing treatments for bedroom ensembles and the bath buyer picking patterns appropriate for the bath. In addition to flexibility and color coordination, presentation figures prominently in securing sales. Programs are supported with in-store signage that gives customers ideas as to how they can decorate.

**TABLE 6.15–1   Department, Discount & Clothing Store Shopped in Last 3 Months (respondents are all adults)**

| | Shopped at any (%) | Index | Kmart (%) | Index | Sears (%) | Index | Wal-Mart (%) | Index |
|---|---|---|---|---|---|---|---|---|
| Total | 81.5 | 100 | 42.3 | 100 | 29.5 | 100 | 26.2 | 100 |
| *Gender* | | | | | | | | |
| Male | 78.0 | 96 | 41.5 | 98 | 29.0 | 98 | 25.5 | 97 |
| Female | 84.8 | 104 | 43.1 | 102 | 30.0 | 102 | 26.8 | 102 |
| *Age* | | | | | | | | |
| 18–24 | 79.7 | 98 | 37.9 | 89 | 24.0 | 81 | 25.4 | 97 |
| 25–34 | 84.9 | 104 | 45.6 | 108 | 29.5 | 100 | 29.1 | 111 |
| 35–44 | 85.5 | 105 | 43.7 | 103 | 34.8 | 118 | 27.4 | 105 |
| 45–54 | 82.8 | 102 | 44.4 | 105 | 31.4 | 106 | 24.7 | 94 |
| 55–64 | 79.9 | 98 | 42.3 | 100 | 30.7 | 104 | 25.2 | 96 |
| 65 and older | 72.9 | 89 | 37.6 | 89 | 25.3 | 86 | 22.9 | 87 |
| *Marital status* | | | | | | | | |
| Single | 79.7 | 98 | 35.3 | 84 | 24.6 | 83 | 22.2 | 85 |
| Married | 83.3 | 102 | 45.9 | 108 | 32.8 | 111 | 28.1 | 107 |
| Divorced, etc. | 78.1 | 96 | 39.1 | 92 | 25.0 | 85 | 24.9 | 95 |
| Parents | 85.7 | 105 | 37.5 | 112 | 32.1 | 109 | 29.8 | 114 |
| *Region* | | | | | | | | |
| Northeast | 78.9 | 97 | 34.1 | 81 | 34.8 | 118 | 1.4 | 5 |
| Midwest | 85.3 | 105 | 54.5 | 129 | 31.7 | 107 | 27.9 | 106 |
| South | 81.5 | 100 | 41.4 | 98 | 27.4 | 93 | 50.1 | 191 |
| West | 79.9 | 98 | 37.9 | 90 | 25.3 | 85 | 9.6 | 37 |
| *Income* | | | | | | | | |
| $75 + | 83.2 | 102 | 36.1 | 85 | 32.7 | 111 | 16.2 | 62 |
| $60 + | 83.1 | 102 | 39.6 | 94 | 34.6 | 117 | 18.9 | 72 |
| $50 + | 83.2 | 102 | 40.6 | 96 | 35.3 | 119 | 20.4 | 78 |
| $40 + | 83.9 | 103 | 41.9 | 99 | 35.3 | 115 | 21.6 | 83 |
| $30 + | 84.1 | 103 | 42.7 | 101 | 34.5 | 117 | 23.1 | 88 |
| $30–$39 | 84.7 | 104 | 45.0 | 106 | 32.4 | 110 | 27.3 | 104 |
| $20–$29 | 83.0 | 102 | 44.3 | 105 | 29.1 | 99 | 30.2 | 115 |
| $10–$19 | 79.3 | 97 | 42.5 | 100 | 21.7 | 73 | 32.1 | 122 |
| Less than $10 | 69.3 | 85 | 37.1 | 88 | 16.4 | 55 | 27.1 | 103 |
| *Presence of children* | | | | | | | | |
| Under 2 years | 85.4 | 105 | 51.7 | 122 | 27.4 | 93 | 29.1 | 111 |
| 2–5 | 84.3 | 103 | 48.8 | 115 | 30.3 | 102 | 27.7 | 106 |
| 6–11 | 84.5 | 104 | 47.1 | 111 | 31.4 | 106 | 32.4 | 124 |
| 12–17 | 83.6 | 103 | 46.3 | 109 | 32.0 | 108 | 28.8 | 110 |

Note: Index values above are computed by dividing the proportion in a particular grouping by their proportion of the population. For example, if an age group has 20.2% of the products users and represents 18.3% of the population, the index value for the grouping is 110. Index values over 100 signify above average usage and index values below 100 signify below average usage. However, values over 110 or under 90 are the most significant.

*Source:* Simmons Market Research Bureau, Inc., 1991.

## OPTIONS FOR THE FUTURE

After reading the F-Team' report, senior Kmart management wanted specific marketing strategies to address each scenario, particularly the one about America's changing social class and income structure. They instructed the F-Team to develop strategies that were consistent with the firm's need to deliver a solid return on investment to its shareholders, while at the same time investing in Kmart's future growth.

In providing direction to the F-Team, Kmart's upper management had several concerns that the strategies should specifically address: What should Kmart's target customer be? What is the right product mix for that customer? Can Kmart appeal to new customers without losing its traditional customer base? What are the potential customer confusions over what Kmart represents? and What changes are needed in Kmart's store and merchandise to address existing and new customer targets?

Also Kmart upper management had a series of more specific concerns under the middle class decline scenario: What should Kmart's product mix look like? Should Kmart be trying to mix some higher ticket items and/or lower ticket items with the traditional products? What kind of repositioning program would be necessary to appeal to a new target market, and can the changes be made without alienating traditional customers?

Upper management also wanted to know about the differences between the marketing strategy recommended by the team and the path Sears chose in the 1970s, when it lost a large portion of its customer base to Kmart due to its efforts at upscaling? What exactly will Kmart's image be at the end of the implementation of the new strategy? Will the firm be another Wal-Mart or more like a Bloomingdales or a Marshall Fields with an upscale customer based? If Kmart attempts to become more trendy, what obstacles does it face and what marketing efforts will be necessary to convince consumers that Kmart is the place to shop?

Develop marketing strategies for the middle class decline scenario. Be sure to address the specific questions and concerns of Kmart upper management.

## Sources

Caminiti, Susan. "The Pretty Payoff in Cheap Chic." *Fortune* (February 24, 1992). 71–73.

Cortez, John P. "Kmart Studies Boomers." *Advertising Age* (October 12, 1992): 21.

Cortez, John P. "Shaping Kmart's New Style." *Advertising Age* (December 7, 1992): 20–21.

Cortez, John P. "Kmart Unleashes Its 'Category Killer' Chains." *Advertising Age* (February 1, 1993): S-4.

Cortez, John P. "Kmart Profits Soar on So-So Sales." *Advertising Age* (March 8, 1993): 6.

Forest, Stephanie Anderson. "Trapped Between the Up and Down Escalators." *Business Week* (August 26, 1991): 49–50.

Garfield, Bob. "Kmart Fashion Trades Up, And the Effort Pays Off." *Advertising Age* (November 2, 1992): 39.

Kinnear, Constance M. "Kmart Corporation," in *Cases in Marketing Management*, 5th ed., eds. Kenneth L. Bernhardt and Thomas C. Kinnear (Homewood, IL: Irwin), pp. 263–275.

*Kmart 1992 Annual Report.*

"Kmart Stores," in *Strategic Marketing Management,* 4th ed. eds. David W. Cravens and Charles W. Lamb (Homewood, IL: Irwin, 1993), pp. 174–197.

Kotler, Philip. *Marketing Management.* 7th ed. Upper Saddle River, NJ: Prentice Hall, 1991.

Morgenson, Gretchen. "Back to Basics." *Forbes* (May 10, 1993): 56–58.

Simmons Market Research Bureau, Inc., 1991.

Staples, Kate. "Attention Kmart Shoppers." *Glamour* (May 1992): 140–147.

Woodruff, David and Christopher Power. "Attention Kmart Shop. . . Hey, Where is Everybody?" *Business Week* (January 18, 1993): p 38.

Zinn, Laura. "Can Gould Put the Bloom Back on Bloomie's?" *Business Week* (June 10, 1991): 38–39.

Zinn, Laura and David Woodruff. "Attention, Shoppers: Kmart is Fighting Back." *Business Week* (October 7, 1991): 18–20.

# *Austin & Associates Marketing Services**

## CASE 16

Austin and Associates Marketing Services (AAMS) is a consulting firm that specializes in consumer goods marketing problems. This year is expected to be a major turning point for the firm because AAMS will be handling all the party and candidate level marketing for the Libertarian Party (LP). David Austin, the owner of AAMS, decided to accept the LP account because the party was willing to sign an exclusive contract for all of its 1992 campaign-related work. This signing will add significantly to AAMS's current revenues and income (Figs. 6.16–1 and 6.16–2).

### PARTY PREFERENCES AND VOTING

Deciding which political party you prefer and what candidates to vote for is a form of consumer behavior. In that sense, people use the same decision-making processes to make choices in voting as they use when they buy a car or a new television set. And, the forces that influence people to vote for a candidate are the same kinds of forces that influence them to make product or service choices.

Political parties and candidates are marketed using the same theories and techniques that sell toothpaste and detergent. Campaign marketing consultants apply segmentation studies to target voters with specific interests and needs, position their can-

---

*Although the Libertarian Party is a real political party with the all the characteristics described in this case, Austin and Associates Marketing Services is a fictional entity. To this author's knowledge, the Libertarian Party does not use a marketing consulting firm or any other similar service.

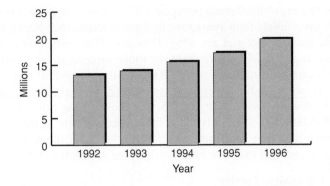

**FIGURE 6.16–1** Austin and Associates Net Sales

*Source:* Austin and Associates Marketing Services.

didates as the means to fulfill those needs, and promote those candidates through the same media that carry ads for goods and services. Both Democrat and Republican campaign consultants conduct these demographic and psychographic studies to focus their campaigns.

## AMERICANS AND POLITICS

Non-voters in the United States represent a trend toward political apathy among Americans. Many are contemptuous of politicians and cynical about the motives of government and business. The United States now ranks 23rd in voter participation among Western democracies, and the share of adults who vote in presidential elections has dropped 20 percent since 1960. Only 50 percent of adults voted in 1988. And the figure for off-year congressional elections is even lower: 36 percent of all adults voted in 1990, versus 46 percent in 1962.

### The Public is Alienated

More than six out of ten American adults feel a sense of powerlessness and disenchantment with those running the nation's major institutions. In 1966, 29 percent of all adults felt alienated. It reached an all-time high of 62 percent in 1983, then headed downward during the economic expansion. It is now rising rapidly, from 54 percent in 1988 to 58 percent in 1989 and 61 percent by 1990.

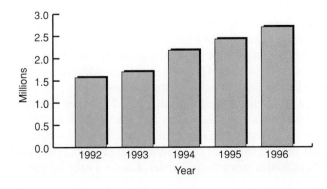

**FIGURE 6.16–2** Austin and Associates Net Income

*Source:* Austin and Associates Marketing Services.

Pollsters agree that the most disaffected groups are the young, the poor, and the poorly educated. Groups more likely than average to feel alienated include high school dropouts, those whose household incomes are $25,000 or less, Hispanics, and blacks. Groups less likely than average to feel alienated are the more successful: adults with a postgraduate education, those with incomes of $50,000 or more, suburban residents, and adults aged 40 to 49. However, adults over 55 years of age are about twice as likely to vote in presidential elections as those under age 55, and those whose household incomes are greater than $35,000 vote at slightly more than twice the rate of those with less than $35,000 in household income. High school graduates with no college are three times more likely to be unregistered than are four-year college graduates.

**The Impact of Modern Campaign Tactics**

Apathy also may be aggravated by modern campaign tactics. Evidence is building that negative television advertising damages the democratic process. Generic negative campaign messages about opponents discourage voting in general. Advertising in the 1989 race for Governor of New Jersey was so negative that by the end of the campaign at least 60 percent of the voters had an unfavorable opinion of each candidate. The people were guaranteed a governor that a majority did not like.

Declining voter turnout makes campaign managers ignore hard-core nonvoters and loyal party voters. More and more, campaigns are designed to persuade people whose past voting records make their future voting behavior unclear. This declining pool is most fought over. As a result, nonvoters just are not being reached; campaign managers just do not care about them.

## LIBERAL AND CONSERVATIVE TRENDS IN THE UNITED STATES

Overall, the post-World War II period has been a time of liberal advances. Liberal trends outnumbered conservative trends by over two-to-one. Liberal gains were strongest on such topics as race relations, abortion, civil liberties, and sexual morality, which dealt with individual choice. Topics dealing with material concerns and government regulation have shown mixed trends. Responses to calls for more government action have also been mixed, with the number of trends for more government edging out trends in favor of less government.

## THE VOTING PUBLIC'S PARTISAN EVALUATIONS

The Democrats lost a sizable share of self-identified partisans (those expressing a particular party preference) in recent years. In 1980, for instance, Democrats held a 20 percentage point lead over the Republicans. By 1988, that lead shrunk to about 6 percentage points. In addition, there are indications of a pro-Republican tide among the young, suggesting that further gains by the GOP may be on the horizon.

While the GOP made some gains in the 1980s, that trend may not continue. The fortunes of the parties have had peaks and valleys over the last 50 years. In 1964, for instance, the GOP appeared to be retreating on nearly all fronts. Yet by 1968, it had won the White House. Such shifts suggest that caution should be used when interpreting recent changes in the public's attitudes toward the parties. Caution may be particularly appropriate given that the Democrats retain a plurality of self-identified partisans, control of both houses of Congress, and hold a majority of governorships and legislatures in the 50 states.

Despite recent defeats in presidential elections, the Democratic party remains the favored party. Its edge in the public's overall partisan evaluations was about the same in the 1980s as it was in the 1950s. In addition, the electorate's relative evaluation of the Democrats and Republicans on issues has not changed greatly over the last 20 years. The Democrats continue to benefit from concerns associated with business and labor and also remain ahead on social-welfare issues. The only significant change is on economic issues, with the GOP having a lead over the Democrats in recent years. The young people of voting age do not appear to be highly pro-Republican in their evaluations of the parties, suggesting that generational change may not lead to a GOP majority.

The idea that only major issues pull and tug on citizens' overall evaluations of the major parties highlights the biggest obstacle facing a minority party's climb to the top. Permanent, large-scale shifts in the overall partisan evaluations of the public may be impossible without a highly salient issue that dominates the concerns of most citizens and is perceived by the public as heavily favoring one party. The Great Depression and FDR's response to it apparently brought such a shift. Without a shock of similar magnitude, partisan evaluations only change slowly and modestly. Accordingly, pro-Democrat evaluations may well continue. And, Reagan's legacy, although important, does not appear to be strong enough to significantly altered the overall partisan evaluations of the U.S. public.

## THE LIBERTARIAN PARTY

The Libertarian Party (LP) is the third largest political party in the United States and the fastest growing. It claims to have over 100 elected or appointed office holders in 22 states and more than 200,000 voters have registered as Libertarians (only 15 states allow voters to register as Libertarians) (Fig. 6.16–3). The LP believes that the answer to America's political problems is the same commitment to freedom that earned America its greatness: economic freedom and the abundance and prosperity it brings; a dedication to the preservation of civil liberties and personal freedom; and a foreign policy marked by nonintervention, peace, and free trade. The LP professes pride in the progress it has made during its short history against what is described as insurmountable odds.

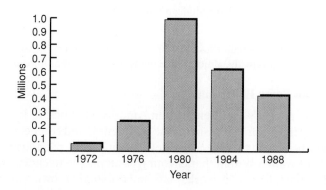

**FIGURE** 6.16–3 Libertarian Party Presidential Votes

*Source:* Estimated from various sources.

A chronology of the party's history includes:

**1971**

LP is founded by disillusioned Republicans and Democrats, as well as political newcomers who hoped to create an alternative to the old parties.

**1972**

First national convention nominates John Hospers, a California university professor as presidential candidate. Ticket wins one electoral vote making vice-presidential candidate Tonie Nathan the first woman in U.S. history to receive an electoral vote.

**1976**

Roger MacBride runs as party's presidential candidate, getting on the ballot in 32 states.

**1978**

Ed Clark receives over 5 percent of the vote for governor of California. Dick Randolph, of Alaska, becomes the first elected Libertarian legislator.

**1980**

Presidential candidate Ed Clark receives almost one million votes and appears on the ballot in all 50 states, the District of Columbia, and Guam. His campaign, with its extensive national television ads, offers many Americans their first look at what the LP has to offer and results in the media recognizing the LP as a political force. Dick Randolph is re-elected to Alaska State Legislature. Ken Fanning is elected to the Alaska State Legislature.

**1982**

Louisiana congressional candidate receives 23 percent of the vote; Alaska gubernatorial candidate receives 15 percent of the vote; Arizona gubernatorial candidate receives 5 percent of the vote; seven statewide candidates receive 15 to 33 percent of the vote.

**1984**

Andre Marrou becomes the third Libertarian to be elected to the Alaska State Legislature. Libertarians are elected to 11 more local offices. David Bergland runs for president.

**1986**

More than 200 statewide candidates across the United States receive 2.9 million votes. Candidate for California state treasurer receives 570,000 votes, largest ever for non-Democrat or non-Republican candidate in that state.

**1987**

Doug Anderson is elected Supervisor of Elections in Denver, Colorado. Libertarians are elected to every seat on the City Council and Mayor's office in Big Water, Utah. Former Congressman Ron Paul resigns from the Republican Party and joins the LP.

**1988**

Ron Paul runs for President, gaining ballot status in 46 states and the District of Columbia, receiving over 430,000 votes nationwide, almost twice the total of any other third party.

### Summary of the Libertarian Party Philosophy

The LP claims to be the people's representative in American politics. It describes itself as the only political organization that respects the uniqueness and competency of the individual. Libertarians believe in the American heritage of liberty, patriotism, and personal responsibility. They want a system that encourages all people to choose what they want from life and lets them live, love, work, play, and dream their own way. Libertarians believe that each individual is unique. They want a system that respects individuals and encourages them to discover the best within themselves and to develop their full potential.

The Libertarian way is an approach to politics based on the principle of self-ownership. Each individual has the right to control his or her own body, actions, speech, and property. They see government's only role in helping individuals to defend themselves from force and fraud.

The LP was created by people who believed that the politicians had strayed from America's original libertarian foundation. Their vision is the same as that of America's founders: a world where individuals are free to follow their own dreams in their own ways, a world of peace, harmony, opportunity, and abundance.

According to the Libertarians, the politicians in Washington and the state capitols have led the United States away from the principles of individual liberty and personal responsibility. They believe that government at all levels is too large, too expensive, inefficient, arrogant, intrusive, and dangerous. They believe that the Democrat and Republican politicians have created the status quo and do not intend to change it.

The LP poses the Libertarian option as: (1) substantially reduce the size and intrusiveness of government and cut all taxes; (2) let people offer their goods and services to willing consumers without a hassle from government; (3) let people decide for themselves what to eat, drink, read, or smoke and how to dress, medicate themselves or make love, without fear of criminal penalties; and (4) the U.S. government should defend Americans and their property in America and let the taxpayers off the hook for the defense bill of the wealthy countries such as Germany and Japan.

Included here is the first page of the LP 1992 Program (Figure 6.16–4), which summarizes the party's positions on all the major issues (as of early 1992).

## A Profile of Libertarian Supporters

Libertarianism is an upper-middle class phenomenon (based on the use of three measures of class: self-identification, income, and education). Those identifying themselves as middle class among the libertarians outnumbers working-class self-identifiers two-to-one. In contrast, the percentages for each class are roughly equal among both liberals and conservatives. The distribution of ideologies across income levels offers an even more striking contrast. The proportion of libertarian supporters increases dramatically along with annual income, with almost none at the lower income levels. Libertarianism claims the support of significant minorities (8 to 14 percent) in the middle-income brackets, about 20 percent of those with upper-middle incomes, and the lion's share (36 percent) of those with upper-middle class incomes. Conservatives claimed only 15 percent of the highest income bracket, and Liberals, who draw support evenly from all income levels, receive roughly one-quarter of the top bracket.

Libertarianism is most popular among the highly educated. In 1980, 34 percent of those believing in libertarianism claimed an advanced degree, while 32 percent had a college degree. Only liberals displayed a similar pattern, while conservatives received under one-fifth of the college-educated respondents. Libertarians and liberals are younger than conservatives. More than half of all libertarians and over two-thirds of liberals are under 41 years of age. The libertarian constituency is primarily composed of young professionals. It is almost entirely white (96 percent).

FIGURE 6.16–4A  Libertarian Party sample 1992 print advertisements.

# Who defends your right
### to keep 100% of what you earn?

Libertarians believe that you have the right to keep what you earn—that taking people's earnings from them forcibly through taxation is wrong and counter-productive. Public services are best provided by the free market and voluntary charitable organizations.

## The Libertarian Party
### DEFENDERS OF LIBERTY
**1-800-682-1776**

1528 Pennsylvania Avenue, SE · Washington, DC 20003

# Who defends your right
### to choose your own way of life?

Libertarians believe that you have the right to pursue happiness as you choose, so long as you do not use force or fraud in your dealings with others. The law should protect the liberties of all people—married and single, straight and gay, conventional and unorthodox—and should treat all individuals equally.

## The Libertarian Party
### DEFENDERS OF LIBERTY
**1-800-682-1776**

1528 Pennsylvania Avenue, SE · Washington. DC 20003

# Who defends your right
### to read or view what you choose?

Libertarians believe that you, and you alone, should decide what words or images your mind is exposed to. When one group of people has the power to control what others see and hear, new ideas get suppressed and the process of thought control has begun.

## The Libertarian Party
### DEFENDERS OF LIBERTY
**1-800-682-1776**

# Who defends your right
### to make your own decisions about drugs?

Drug abuse is a personal and social problem, and making drug use a crime doesn't solve it. By outlawing drugs the government has created a huge criminal empire, and has responded with police state tactics which threaten the liberty and safety of all Americans. The solution: re-legalize drugs, and treat drug abusers humanely.

## The Libertarian Party
### DEFENDERS OF LIBERTY
**1-800-682-1776**

# LIBERTARIAN PARTY
# *1992 PROGRAM*

## *Adopted by the Libertarian National Committee, 28 August 1991*

### PREAMBLE

The Libertarian Party wants all Americans to be able to plan their own futures. Libertarians believe that individuals, families, associations, and businesses have the right and the ability to deal with their own problems by working with other people in a peaceful and honest way. We reject the idea that the aggressive use of force, whether by criminals or government, is either a moral or practical means for achieving positive ends. Libertarians seek a world in which voluntary cooperation replaces force in human relationships. Toward that end, we offer the following ten point Program.

### DEFENDING AMERICANS IN AMERICA

An important reason for having the federal government is national defense. Its job is to defend Americans in America from foreign attack. The federal government should work to provide security for us at the lowest possible cost, in a way which does not undermine our domestic economic productivity or violate our civil liberties.

U. S. military spending is over $300 billion per year. Rather than defending America, the bulk of this pays for defending other countries. People in many of those countries pay less for their own defense than American taxpayers pay to defend them.

The United States has many thousands of nuclear weapons more than needed to deter a Soviet first strike, yet we spend billions every year building more.

U. S. military intervention in Central America, Southeast Asia, and the Middle East has not made Americans more secure. In fact, Americans are less secure, because U. S. military policy has made us more enemies than friends, making all Americans targets of terrorism. American military adventurism routinely results in unnecessary bloodshed without producing positive results. The United States should rely less on military force and threats and more on negotiation and trade to establish harmonious international relationships.

The Libertarian Party proposes the following initial steps to improve the security of Americans and reduce the costs of defense:

1. Notify our allies that they must plan for their own defense needs and take responsibility for paying for them. Provide allies with a timetable for the return of American military personnel to America in order to defend America.

2. Negotiate arms reduction treaties which do not compromise our national defense.

3. Adopt a policy that Americans who travel abroad and companies which invest abroad do so at their own risk and are subject to the laws and customs of other countries while abroad. The United States will no longer use gunboat diplomacy on their behalf at taxpayers' expense.

4. Reject the "Reagan Doctrine", which engages the United States around the globe and risks the security of all Americans by increasing the possibility that the U. S. will become embroiled in a foreign civil war.

### FEDERAL SPENDING MUST BE CUT

Federal spending and federal taxation are connected. We must reduce spending to reduce taxes.

Unfortunately, the United States government has expanded its operations and spending far beyond the original constitutional plan. No matter what the subject, there is some group which wants government to regulate or subsidize it, and there are always those in Congress eager to take over more power and control. But it is impossible to get something for nothing. The government produces no goods, so it can hand out favors to some people only by taking the earnings and property of others first.

In recent years the government has attempted to hide its expensive meddling by forcing private organizations and businesses to adopt certain expensive programs, rather than have the government implement them directly. These programs are no less costly nor less intrusive than if they were adopted directly by the government.

Libertarians join with the vast majority of Americans in calling for a smaller, less expensive, less meddlesome government. The following are some first steps in the process of bringing federal government spending under control:

1. Place the federal budget under a "cap" at current levels. Any increase in spending on any project must be accompanied by an equal or greater reduction in other spending.

2. Phase out spending on aid to foreign governments and international organizations such as the World Bank and the International Monetary Fund.

3. Phase out federal subsidies to all businesses such as the tobacco industry, the maritime industry, agriculture, or the military-industrial complex.

4. End federal subsidy programs to state and local governments. These programs merely take taxes out of the community and then send the money back, minus the amounts consumed by the government bureaucrats who administer them.

5. End all federally mandated programs forced on individuals, organizations, and businesses.

### CHOICE IN EDUCATION

Government-run public schools have failed our children. Their cost keeps rising while student performance drops. Today one out of five teenagers can't even read at a grade school level, and colleges must teach many students how to read and write.

Poor children suffer most because they attend the worst schools. Few families can afford tuition for private schools while paying taxes for public schools. Private schools provide better education at a much lower cost.

Most families have no choice but to send their children to the neighborhood public school, regardless of its quality. This makes public schools a pro-

**FIGURE 6.16–4B** Libertarian Party 1992 program.

## The New Right and Libertarianism

Ronald Reagan's conservative crusade against big government cut heavily into the libertarian vote. His economic policies and antistatist rhetoric played to the same constituency. Moreover, his own ideological affinity for libertarianism was reflected in the appointment of libertarian activists to White House posts.

However, one should not overestimate libertarian influences on the Reagan White House or to confuse what has been called the "Reagan Revolution" with the libertarian agenda. Reaganism is better understood as a blend of laissez-faire, anti-Communism, and traditionalism. The success of the "New Right" testifies that the popular revolt against the modern state is not born of a simple passion for the free market or a desire to be left alone to do one's own thing. Its preoccupation with secular humanism and evolution is symptomatic of deep-seated cultural anxieties and the resentment felt by local communities toward distant, imperious bureaucrats and their alien values.

Reagan sided with estranged Americans against the cosmopolitan elite in control of the country's power structure. Reaganism and the New Right amounted less to a rejection of statism per se than to a repudiation of modern American government. It was less a conflict of economic or political interests than a competition over values.

New Right politics and libertarianism reveal their differences even where they appear to have the most in common in economic policy. While they agree on the superiority of capitalism as an economic system, they have very different attitudes regarding its virtue. Libertarians deny the free market any special moral content—the market accommodates all moralities equally well, as long as they observe the procedural constraints governing market transactions. It is precisely this tolerance of a wide variety of moral preferences, and their associated life styles, that makes the libertarian defense of the market attractive. New Right champions of the market, on the other hand, invest capitalism with a specific moral content that reflects the teachings of fundamentalist Christianity.

Libertarian themes represent the complaints of a wealthy, well-educated, middle-class constituency who are unhappy over the cost and paternalistic inclinations of the modern state. Libertarians are radically individualistic and unabashedly hedonistic. They rebel against the tradition of authority in politics. In contrast, the New Right articulates the anger and frustration of a less well-educated, lower-middle class constituency. The New Right has no sympathy for the social anarchy, which is at the heart of the libertarian vision. The New Right attacks the modern state for its role in the dissolution of customary social norms and seeks to control it to reverse the damage done to traditional values.

## CONSULTING WITH THE LIBERTARIAN PARTY

The current political environment may represents a big potential opportunity for the LP. Because voters are eager for fundamental change in government and the political process, Austin is in a good position to help the LP make major gains in the 1992 election.

Provide insights about the drivers of political party preferences and voting from your accumulated knowledge and experience, including any marketing and consumer behavior courses, to produce a thoughtful representation of the dynamics involved in politics. Consider how voters think and behave. Think about friends and family and how media influences them to have particular political preferences. What are the dynamics of political marketing and the related aspects of party preferences and voting: What needs are satisfied by party preferences and voting? What macroenvironmental influences operate? How does the individual's decision-making process relate to the act of voting for a particular candidate? For the LP, what is the current marketing strategy and what are the alternatives for 1992?

## Sources

Geer, John G. "The Electorate's Partisan Evaluations: Evidence of A Continuing Democratic Edge." *Public Opinion Quarterly* 55 (1991):218–231.

Libertarian Party publications.

Newman, Stephen L. "The Chimeras of 'Libertarianism': What's Behind the Political Movement?" *Dissent* 34 (1987):308–316.

Smith, Tom W. "Liberal and Conservative Trends in the United States Since World War II." *Public Opinion Quarterly* 54 (1990):479–507.

Uebling, Mark D. "All-American Apathy." *American Demographics* (November 1991):30–35.

# *National Rifle Association*

CASE 17

As many as one in four United States households have handguns, and while there are no firm statistics on how many are owned by women, officials from the National Rifle Association (NRA) estimate that between 12 million and 20 million American women have handguns and, according to handgun manufacturers, more women are also carrying guns. Why do these women own guns? Guns are the great equalizer, and, according to the NRA, learning how to shoot can empower women. Historically, guns have been symbolic of men's culture, but now women want the protection they offer, too. Personal safety is the driving force behind most gun purchases by both men and women. According to the NRA, over 58 percent of its responding 2.8 million members said their last handgun purchase was for self-protection.

Gun sales traditionally have been driven by men, but as the male market became increasingly saturated, firearm marketers set their sights on women. Thus, young, single women concerned about personal protection and home defense have become an attractive target market for the firearms industry. In adopting marketing images of strong, sexy, gun-toting women, handgun manufacturers are trying to make guns more acceptable to women in general.

After its gun sales declined sharply in the mid-1980s, Smith & Wesson targeted the women's market by introducing three LadySmith handguns, these "feminine" revolvers ranged in price from $399 to $450. The LadySmith is basically a daintier version of the .357 magnum, with special features designed specifically for the ladies, such as a smaller handle and more rounded edges on the trigger and hammer. The trigger is also much easier to pull.

A 1988 Smith & Wesson campaign played up personal safety and encouraged women to call an 800 number for more information. But because guns were not actually mentioned in the advertisements, Smith & Wesson was criticized for misleading the reader. This was an attempt to soft-sell guns. A 1992 advertisement was more gun oriented. It depicted an attractive, serious-looking, thirtyish woman poised at a shooting range, with the headline "What Would Mom Think Now?" Personal safety was the emphasis of the advertisement, with such statements as: "The world is different today than when you grew up," "Personal security is a very real issue," and "It fits your lifestyle as well as your hand." With its 1992 LadySmith campaign the company was not shy about saying, "It's OK today for a professional woman to own a gun." Smith & Wesson also began offering to pay the average $50 fee for an NRA-certified handgun-training course for any woman who bought a LadySmith.

In 1992, *Ladies Home Journal* carried an advertisement for Colt Manufacturing Co. Inc. It was the first time the general interest women's magazine had accepted an ad from a firearms maker. Colt's ad pictured a younger mother tucking her child into bed. Under this blissful domestic scene were two models of Colt semiautomatic pistols with the headline: "Self-protection is more than your right...it's your responsibility," and "You always have a right to protect yourself in your home. Even more important, you have a responsibility to be there for those who depend on you," the ad's copy asserted.

*Women & Guns* magazine started in 1989 and has doubled its circulation each year since. Personal safety and self-defense are the focus of the gun ads geared toward women, which has antigun critics upset. They say that the ads are creating fear in women in order to persuade them to buy guns. The firearms industry claims the advertisements are only a response to a genuine market need. The fear is already there and it is not being created. Open up any newspaper and it will show why there is fear. As the number of single women rises and as more women join the workforce, they are also more likely to find themselves in potentially dangerous situations. Some say that the firearm industry does not prey on women but rather gives them a solution about how to be self-sufficient with self-protection.

The resulting jump in female gun shoppers is real. Women-only weapons classes, given across the country, have quadrupled in enrollment over the last several years. Feminine Protection, a Dallas store that carries holster alternatives, sold 3,000 handbags with James Bond-like secret compartments in 1992, up from 60 in 1986. Smith & Wesson indicates that sales for its dainty guns have doubled in just the last two years. Other manufacturers have begun cashing in as well. New England Firearms introduced its own $149.95 Lady Ultra gun. Lorcin does not bother advertising the feminine version of its $79 L-25 handgun, which has a pink grip, because it has done so well since its 1989 introduction, with sales jumping 20 percent annually to $500,000 in 1993. But, it does advertise its $130 sleek, black .380 handgun, showing it on a desktop with a Vogue and a photograph of three children.

In the meantime, the number of firearms has grown to well over 200 million, vastly increasing the number of stakeholders. In addition, the market has shifted from one dominated by sporting firearms to one dominated by self-protection firearms. This presents policy makers with a much more different environment than what existed in earlier years. One impact of existing policies and related debates has been an acceleration of the market, as buyers become convinced that they must act before the rules change.

The opposing camps in the gun control controversy have attempted to define the debate by controlling its language. In doing so, they have operated at various times within three main orientations, including that of crime control ("control guns and you can control gun-related crime") push by those advocating gun control. The sovereignty argument comes from those opposing gun control. It involves mistrust and the fear of government and collective security, with freedom resting with armed individual citizens. And, most recently, control advocates in the medical and public health community have begun to apply the language of public health to gun control.

## THE NATIONAL RIFLE ASSOCIATION

The NRA is a membership organization with millions of Americans representing a diversity of age, sex, race, and religion. Americans have joined the NRA from every state in the union, from every economic background, and from every political affiliation. What members share with every other member is an appreciation of the shooting sports, a belief in their constitutional right to keep and bear arms, and a commitment to safety, responsibility, and freedom. Estimated revenues for the organization are substantial (Fig. 6.17–1).

The NRA was incorporated in 1871 to provide firearms training and encourage interest in the shooting sports. This organization has grown steadily, and now is directed by a 76 member board of directors elected by its voting members. The NRA membership's broad range of interests and activities is represented by 36 standing and special committees. Service to its membership requires a dedicated staff. Over 300 men and women work in the NRA's Fairfax, Virginia main offices. In addition, the NRA membership is served by a staff of field representatives located across the United

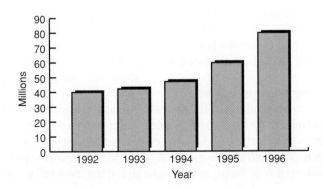

FIGURE 6.17–1 NRA Revenues

*Source:* Estimated from various sources.

States. The scope of this operation requires an annual budget of approximately $80 million.

The NRA's organizational structure includes divisions representing its firearm safety effort, firearms training, law enforcement programs, junior shooting activities, women's issues, hunter services, recreational shooting, competitions, gun collecting, and defense of the Second Amendment. The NRA staff works with such diverse groups as the Boy Scouts of America, 4-H clubs, The American Legion, VFW, hunting and shooting clubs, schools, and law enforcement organizations.

Of special interest is its Women's Issues & Personal Safety Division, founded in 1994 to support the growing number of women involved in gun-related activities. The objective of the NRA is to give women all the information they need on personal safety, hunting, firearms safety, and a wide range of other topics. The Women's Personal Safety Department helps women evaluate their personal safety options through the "Refuse To Be A Victim" personal safety program and other offerings.

The NRA warns American woman that three out of four of their number will fall victim to violent crime at some time in their lives. They are admonished to fight back and not be a statistic. The single most important factor in surviving a criminal attack is to have an overall strategy before it is needed. The NRA offers a three-hour confidential seminar taught by women for women to provide the personal safety tips and techniques needed to avoid dangerous situations and ways to avoid becoming a victim. Women learn about the psychology of criminal predators, home security, phone security, automobile security, physical security, physical training options, personal protection devices, and much more.

## GUN CONTROL

Gun control has lingered at the margins of the American political agenda without resolution for many years. During that time, a political environment favoring individualism, incrementalism, and pluralism had produced a stalemate, which has only resulted in some gun control measures for the more lethal weapons such as machine guns and other such items.

However, with passage of the Brady Bill, and the subsequent focus on assault weapons, the issue of gun control has returned to the public spotlight. Both opponents and advocates of gun control have used the heightened interest and increased media attention to advance their cases. For those familiar with the history of gun control in the United States, the current process invokes a certain sense of déjà vu. In addition to having the most lenient, but complex, firearms laws in the industrialized world, the United States has been unique in the level and duration of controversy over gun policy. Some have viewed this as resulting from the role that guns played in American history. An examination of gun policy over the years reveals more about the American political process than about the country's romance with guns.

Gun control, as a policy applicable to the general population, began in 1909 with the New York State Sullivan Law, which mandated permits for the possession of handguns. Passed in an era when the prohibition of drugs and alcoholic beverages was being widely advocated, the law was a result of these influences, as well as fear of crime. New York police have used the law to deny handgun access to all but the most influential citizens, particularly in New York City. This highly restrictive approach has provided a model for control advocates and a rallying point for opponents.

With the passage of Brady, the political dynamics of gun control appear to have again shifted by creating a national gun ownership waiting period. However, the majority of the population already lived in states with waiting periods. Brady fell short of most existing state laws, even prohibiting the retention of the sale information by police. It failed to address private transactions, in which most prohibited persons obtain their firearms. The decision to use local police to check sales, rather than to require state or federal checks resulted in some local sheriffs and chiefs filing suit to prevent implementation. The federal agency known as the Bureau of Alcohol, Tobacco and Firearms (ATF) has been faced with implementing a statute complicated by state and local variations using numerous agents with whom they have little leverage.

In response, some began advancing more comprehensive policy options such as owner licensing and registration, but the congressional response was lukewarm. Focus then shifted to the prohibition of certain assault weapons, defined more by form than function. Conceptually, such approaches face a significant problem. Assault weapons are functionally identical to semi-automatic pistols, which are also concealable. There is little practical justification for controlling the assault rifles while avoiding the politically riskier action of controlling pistols. The U.S. Congress has attempted to circumvent this through controls on the magazines for the pistols.

Some believe that gun control policy in the United States is overly influenced by the NRA, which is described as a well-financed special interest lobby by the press. According to that popular press, the NRA thwarts the desires of the majority of the U.S. population by manipulating key legislators. While the NRA has played a key opposition role since 1934, the majority of Americans appear to favor more regulatory controls than now exist. However, that portrayal falls short of describing the real dynamics of this issue. The elements that have molded the history of gun control policy, and most likely other policies, are more complex than a mere special interest manipulation of Congress.

The NRA is more than simply a well-financed special interest lobby. It is a grass roots organization with widespread and intense constituent support extending beyond even its membership. The NRA and its allies have exercised as much control over public policy by molding public attitudes as they have by directly influencing Congress.

## LOBBYING

In its efforts to influence laws about gun control, the NRA engages in lobbying. Lobbying is increasingly being recognized by many as essential to the modern, complex process of government. Lobbyists put a human face on legislation by communicating a perspective to legislators on how a proposed law would impact specific industries or people. There is a widespread perception that lobbying is bad and that anyone who lobbies belongs to a "special interest group."

Some would define a "special interest group" as one that seeks to place its own selfish interests above those of society as a whole and profit at the expense of others. But that is not an accurate description of most lobbyists. The fact is that organizations that maintain lobbyists in Washington, D.C. and state capitals, include foreign governments, large business corporations, and citizens' groups ranging from the American Civil Liberties Union and Common Cause to the NRA.

Lobbying is protected by the U.S. Constitution, especially by the First Amendment's guarantees against interference with freedom of speech and the right to petition. Lobbying is a respectable, legitimate, and essential part of a democratic form of government. Lobbying protects the public interest, and it can be both effective and ethical.

In a democratic society, where government is designed to represent and protect the interests of all citizens and all parties, talking with legislators is exactly what people should do in order to ensure that decisions and legislation reflect a consensus and take into consideration the interests of all parties affected.

Lobbyists provide busy legislators with a flow of practical information that helps in the drafting of technical legislation, and they work with administrative agencies to obtain clarifications and rulings on regulations.

The targeting for lobbyists in the legislative or regulatory arena includes:

- 7,600 state legislators.
- 535 members of Congress.
- 50 governors.
- One president of the United States.
- Hundreds of regulatory officials with Alcohol Beverage Control boards, environmental agencies, consumer agencies, and others at all levels of government.
- Thousands of mayors and city councils across the United States.

At each biennium, there are more than 200,000 bills introduced in the state legislatures and 12,000 bills introduced in Congress. Any one of these bills could have a limiting effect on an industry.

## GAINING WOMEN MEMBERS

With the NRA gaining new women members, the influence of this lobbying organization is also growing. However, it needs to do more in targeting women as potential and current owners to greatly increase its membership. This new and increasingly important group of gun enthusiasts should help the NRA exert even greater influence over the legislative process. What marketing strategy would you advise the NRA to pursue in targeting new women members? What specific marketing techniques would you propose and why? What would you do to leverage the NRA's increasingly strong position with women in its lobbying activities?

## Sources

Farnham, Alan. "A Bang That's Worth Ten Billion Bucks." *Fortune* 125, 5 (March 9, 1992): 80–86.

Goerne, Carrie. "Gun Companies Target Women Foes Call It 'Marketing to Fear' " *Marketing News* 26, 18 (August 31, 1992): 1–2.

Klemp, Richard. "Lobbying: Can it Be Both Effective and Ethical?" *Executive Speeches*, 9, 1 (August/September 1994): 42–46.

Kopel, David B. "The Violence of Gun Control." *Policy Review* 63 (Winter 1993): 1–8.

Jones, Maggie. "Gunmakers Target Women." *Working Woman* 18, 7 (July 1993): 10.

National Rifle Association promotional materials.

Vizzard, William J. "The Impact of Agenda Conflict On Policy Formulation and Implementation: The Case of Gun Control," *Public Administration Review* 55, 4 (July/August 1995): 341–347.

# *National Football League*

In 1995, the National Football League (NFL) and maverick Dallas Cowboys owner Jerry Jones continued their public feud over marketing matters, with the league slapping Jones with a $300 million lawsuit for signing sponsorship pacts with NFL non-sponsors Nike and Pepsi. In response, Jones sued the NFL for $750 million over the rights to market and sell the Cowboys' trademarks and logos. The move by the NFL was designed to deter Jones from breaking with NFL control over team marketing agreements.

In his suit, Jones asked the courts to declare that the NFL teams have the right to license their trademarks and logos as they see fit and that the teams have the right to determine the apparel and marks worn by the players, coaches, and other personnel during games. Jones also wants to insure that transactions entered into by Texas Stadium (the Cowboys' home field) and Jones with Dr. Pepper, Pepsi, Nike, and American Express are legal. A courtroom victory by Jones, which would likely add millions to the Cowboys' coffers, and he would not have to share that income with other member teams of the NFL.

For Jones, this is a simple money issue. He argues that independent team marketing efforts can be grown into a lot more money if the NFL would let the individual clubs go out and do it on their own. Under the current system, NFL Properties, the NFL's marketing organization with substantial and estimated income (Fig. 6.18–1 and 6.18–2), provides each NFL team with about 5 percent ($3.5 million) of its gross revenues obtained from marketing the NFL. However, that pales in comparison with the $40 million owners get from television contracts and the $20 million a team earns from its 60–40 split from gate receipts. The Cowboys, who have led the league in sales of licensed goods (hats, t-shirts, mugs, etc.) the past five years, feel they deserve more of the revenue from those sales.

Jones claims that a double-standard is being used. The Cowboys' suit says that a number of NFL teams, including Chicago and Detroit, have sponsorship agreements authorizing the use of their trademarks in product categories covered by national exclusive sponsorship agreements with the NFL.

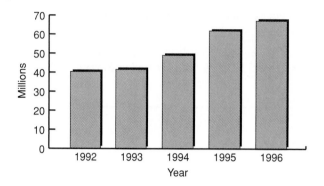

**FIGURE 6.18–1** NFL Properties Revenue

*Source:* Estimated from various sources.

Just weeks after Nike publicly undercut NFL Properties by making its deal with Jones and Texas Stadium, the league and the sporting goods giant came to an agreement, which they jointly termed the "largest deal in the history of team sports licensing." With this deal, Nike became a Pro Line licensee and outfitter to several NFL teams with jerseys and sideline apparel starting with the next season, and sponsor of some of the league's youth initiatives. It is widely speculated that Nike will be assigned the much-coveted Dallas Cowboys, who continued to wear brandless and logoless sideline apparel even after the Nike-NFL agreement was announced.

The issues involved in this dispute are about marketing philosophies and innovative ways to do business in the next century. Dallas claims it is trying to improve the league and develop marketing strategies that are best suited for the future.

## NFL PROPERTIES LICENSING

In the past, NFL Properties was able to license out to a large number of firms because the business was so strong. But licensing has changed forever, and both NFL Properties and its licensees need to have a more strategic and focused approach. NFL Properties has embarked upon a "lean-and-mean" strategy, paring down the number of companies licensed by the league. The initiative started by cutting between 70 to 100

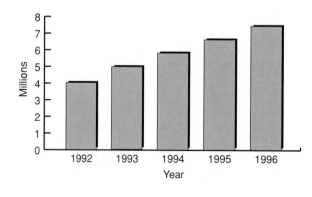

**FIGURE 6.18–2** NFL Properties Net Income

*Source:* Estimated from various sources.

manufacturers from the roster of approximately 400, with additional licensees let go later.

Apparel is the major area of consolidation, with niche programs such as NFL Golf, Beach, Rock and Western eliminated from the league's program of offerings. In addition, NFL Properties will cut back significantly on the number of companies licensed for the Super Bowl, which now includes approximately 60 manufacturers. NFL Properties' new philosophy means it will be working with increasingly larger vendors. It will also be providing its licensees with a greater opportunity to gain market share. In return, it will expect more from its licensees in terms of product development, on-time shipping, and marketing.

NFL Properties also plans to provide licensees with proprietary opportunities to develop products that tap into the deep rooted heritage of each team. Different color blocking schemes for its 30 teams does not set one apart from the other. The NFL wants to energize the sidelines and develop products that screams the Pittsburgh Steelers or Chicago Bears. All this also includes a uniform evolution program.

In charting a new course in the flat licensing business, NFL Properties will pay closer attention to its three-tiered merchandising plan and the programs each tier umbrellas. The big three are: Performance (Pro Line), Lifestyle (Throwbacks), and Family (NFL Kids, NFL At Home, Back To School, and Game Day). The plan is to place greater emphasis on key licensing programs that address a changing marketplace in which sales of licensed products are increasing at a slower rate than in years past. This will work to strengthen the NFL brands within that three-tiered structure by backing them with stronger personnel support and corporate realignment by brand.

NFL Properties is also looking at programs aimed at a younger market to drive future growth. Films such as *Little Giants,* a movie about two youth football teams, have emerged as important marketing venues for the sport. While the movie may not have been a huge success at the box office, the video release is expected to be very popular. Five million copies, each featuring an NFL Pro Line commercial at the beginning, will be supported by a gift-with-purchase promotion. The movie specifically targets children who are also football fans and, hopefully, future fans of the NFL.

The "Hollywood" factor of promoting the league is only part of the NFL Properties' effort to increase business. Its merchandising and marketing arm is also committed to supporting sales at the retail level. The league plans to maintain its lead by expanding the integrated marketing and promotional programs that have proven successful in the past. The Landing Zone promotion helped stores in the Los Angeles area sell Raiders' tickets; J.C. Penney stores sell its Starter product; and it promoted Air It Out, a four-on-four football tournament, which will be expanded into additional cities. Another successful initiative to hit additional markets is the painted bus promotion, where fans win a trip to an NFL game on that bus and receive a Starter goodie bag and a tailgate party catered by McDonald's.

For retailers, the plan is to offer varying levels of support to those that carry officially licensed NFL products. The NFL plans to work in tandem with retailers such as Foot Locker, J.C. Penney, Macy's, and The Sports Authority to design individual in-store merchandising support that provides them with a point of difference. Rather than having 40 stores in one market offering the same discounts and ticket promotions, NFL

Properties aims to differentiate them in the way they look and present their NFL merchandise.

The NFL Properties' in-store merchandising support effort also includes a more enhanced basic point-of-sale program. The program is available at no charge to all of the NFL Properties' retail partners, from a multistore chain to a retailer just getting into the business. Available through co-op dollars are more fixtures such as goal post four-ways, yard-marker T-stands and lockers, as well as decorative displays such as helmets, footballs, and framed autographed jerseys.

Even during this transition, NFL Properties reported record licensed product sales, attendance, and television ratings. The fact that more than 1.5 million NFL jerseys were sold in 1994 is just one indication that what is happening on the NFL playing field is impacting what is happening at retail. NFL Properties continues to promote sales of NFL jerseys by creating more interesting interpretations of its uniform such as NFL Throwbacks jerseys, the Dallas Cowboys' special events jerseys, and the 1995 Pro Bowl uniforms.

NFL Kids is yet another success story, which NFL Properties plans to extend beyond apparel. Home products, back-to-school merchandise, and video games are untapped and growing areas that would make nice fits for NFL Kids. Extending sales into these areas will depend on raising the childrens' interest level in the game of football itself.

Reaching that end is going to take more concerted team level efforts, for example appearances at footbal camps by San Diego Charger Junior Seau, the NFL Kids spokesperson, and corporate promotions directly targeted at kids.

A Back-To-School program already allows retailers to display everything from backpacks and lunch boxes to pens and zippered day runners. Retailers who have taken advantage of the display unit, and the obvious synergy of back-to-school and the start of the football season, have reaped the rewards.

NFL At Home has also witnessed exponential growth due to the creation of more comprehensive shop concepts. J.C. Penney doubled its yearly sales of At Home products. There are approximately 40 companies involved in the At Home program. They include domestic products, electronics, home furnishings, tailgate and bathroom accessories, as well as items ranging from plastic silverware and little lockers for kids, to computer mouse pads and screen savers.

The NFL believes that there is a strong future for At Home, with 94 percent of Americans watching football at home, and 74 percent watching with friends and family. At Home business is exploding; people are staying home more because it is more expensive to go out. And there is a rebirth of family values, with parents spending more time with their kids. As a result, people are spending more money on home products in general. At Home merchandise can easily translate into life style-oriented products that are fun for casual living in an entertainment atmosphere.

## NFL COMPETITION

Other sports just cannot compete well with football. Baseball is feeling the poststrike apathy of its fans. Viewer interest in basketball rises and falls with the fortunes of its handful of superstars. The National Hockey League struggles to make a dent with a national U.S. audience. But the NFL practically sells itself. The product is so good and the demographics are so strong that the best way to broadcast the NFL is just to turn on the cameras and stay out of the way.

That is a lesson Fox learned quickly after it took the National Football Conference (NFC) from CBS with a four-year, $1.58-billion deal. The games on Fox closely resembled what had been on CBS for decades, which is not surprising because most of the network's talent and production staff came over from CBS. However, Fox did bring a new energy to showing the games, including an on the screen clock and an hour-long pregame show.

This new enthusiasm for the sport has apparently extended to advertisers as well. Weeks before the 1995 NFL advertising time selling season opened, sources from the networks carrying the NFL forecast advertising rates 15 to 25 percent above the year before. They cited several factors, including increased competition among advertisers, many with new products to promote; the year before high football ratings; Fox's strengthening in many markets; and the residual effects of the baseball strike.

Advertising agency media buyers agreed that the cost for NFL spots should rise at least 10 percent, and could go much higher. Early trends indicated a seller's market. TNT (the cable channel), which began sales earlier than the others because its abbreviated NFL schedule concludes in October, had raised rates about 20 percent. That put the cost of a 30-second commercial at around $75,000 on the smallest channel carrying the NFL.

Fox typically charged about $110,000 for 30-second spots in 1994, and got up to $500,000 for commercials on the NFC championship game between the San Francisco 49ers and Dallas Cowboys. Fox billed slightly more than $300 million for the 1994 football season.

The NFL has positioned itself as one of Fox's largest marketing partners, and this link between television drama and sports may be growing stronger. The Hollywood factor of promoting the league is only part of NFL Properties' effort to increase business.

## THE FUTURE OF NFL PROPERTIES

The future is both dark and bright for NFL Properties. On the one hand, it must deal with rebellions such as that of Jerry Jones and, on the other hand, it can celebrate its successes with Fox and its robust marketing programs, which put the NFL's offerings in many locations and in front of large numbers of consumers. However, there are still some questions about the viability of the NFL as a marketing organization, even though there is no equal in sports competition, and there is no prospect of any other sport displacing football as the favorite of millions in the United States.

The problems of the NFL revolve around maximizing the returns from its football and team marketing efforts to a point where the chances of team owners going out on their own are minimized. This involves capitalizing on all of the NFL's assets, including television rights, merchandise licensing, and other promotional opportunities. What marketing efforts and strategy would you advise NFL Properties to pursue in promoting the NFL and its member teams? How would you deal with the owner rebellions such as that of Jerry Jones? What would you do to create more interest and involvement by younger people in football and the NFL teams?

## Sources

Bernstein, Andrew. "Nike and NFL Join Forces for Pro Line License Deal." *Sporting Goods Business* 28, 11 (November 1995): 10.

Collingwood, Harris. "Did the NFL Owners Gain Yardage." *Business Week* (February 8, 1993): 118.

Coxeter, Ruth and Chris Roush. "Meet the NFL's Newest Quarterback." *Business Week* (November 7, 1994): 143–144.

"Duracell Taps NFL for 4Q Promotions." *Dealerscope Merchandising* 37, 8 (August 1995): 34.

Jensen, Jeff. "Jones Fails to Snare More NFL Renegades." *Advertising Age* 66, 38 (September 25, 1995): 3, 8.

Klemm, Alisa. "The Big Squeeze," *Sporting Goods Business* 28, 3 (March 1995): 35–36.

Klemm, Alisa. "Pumping Up Sales." *Sporting Goods Business* 28, 3 (March 1995): 38–40.

Lane, Randall. "The Market Clears." *Forbes* (October 24, 1994): 228–230.

Lans, Maxine S. "Sports Team Logos Are Big Business." *Marketing News* 29, 12 (June 5, 1995): 6.

Macnow, Glen. "The Real Fall TV Favorite." *Mediaweek* 5, 24 (June 12, 1995): MQ26–MQ29.

NFL Promotional materials.

"NFLP Scouts the 'Home' Team." *Discount Store News* 34, 20 (October 16, 1995): A38.

Pesky, Greg. "NFLP Implements 'lean & mean' Strategy for Licensing Program." *Sporting Goods Business* 28, 1 (January 1995): 28.

Stanley, T.L. "NFL Drafts Women, Kids." *Mediaweek* 6, 1 (January 1, 1996): 8.

Symonds, William C. "Is the NFL Hearing Footsteps?" *Business Week* (February 14, 1995): 91

Taylor, Jean Jacques. "Can the NFL Keep Up With the Joneses?" *Sales & Marketing Management* 148, 1 (January 1996): 15.

# *American Airlines* CASE 19

After 1994, it was clear that airline profits were increasing, but so was turmoil in the industry. The price of fuel was down, fares had stabilized, international markets were rebounding, and the U.S. economy, the key factor in whether people travel, had improved. Airline industry earnings were $750 million in 1994, while profits were mainly the result of cost cutting and an 8 percent increase in passenger traffic. However, there were few celebrations by United, American, and Delta because the airline business normally experiences one storm after another. Ultimately, 1994 will be better remembered for changes in the industry than for its profits because employee ownership of United Airlines and pressures from low-cost rivals such as Southwest Airlines forced the major carriers to change how they did business.

Some argue that the airline industry is programmed for self-destruction because no matter how many employees are laid off or how many labor concessions are gained, the costs of planes, fuel, and facilities, remain relatively high. The costs of adding passengers on a partly filled flight are negligible because the extra costs of food, fuel, and ticket process are small. So airlines need not charge much to make that seat worth selling. The result is that about 90 percent of airline passengers buy their tickets at a discount and pay on average just 35 percent of full fare.

## AIRLINE INDUSTRY COMPETITIVE DYNAMICS

The years of rising full-fare traffic and falling or stable costs began in the 1960s with the introduction of the first jets, but ended sometime in the mid-1980s. Now, in the 1990s, the airline business has clearly matured and costs in real, inflation-adjusted terms are no longer falling. What is worse for the high-cost scheduled jet carriers is that the passenger mix had changed in a way that hurts revenues. The proportion of business travelers, which includes those who pay full-economy or first-class airfares, is down from 52 percent in 1982 to around 40 percent in 1995 and continues to decline. This reflects the reduction of management ranks by corporations and the impact of new telecommunications technologies on how business is conducted. That leaves leisure passengers as the principal customers for the airlines. But, leisure fliers above all want the cheapest fares because they prefer to spend their money on the ground, regarding the trip itself as a commodity.

As a result, the airlines are having to make fundamental changes, requiring entirely new ways of doing business, including different corporate organizations. What is under way is the "Wal-Martization" of the airline business. In this environment, the high-cost carriers must reduce their unit costs to match those of their low-cost competitors. The next few years will produce radically different national airlines because the surviving carriers will be those that define their function and market more narrowly and tailor their costs accordingly.

Market stratification is already a fact of life on short-haul routes, up to about 150 miles, versus long-haul routed, those over 150 miles. Most jet carriers' costs are uneconomically high for the former market, so they are increasingly conceding that business to regional carriers. These carriers account for only a tiny fraction of total air travel, 10.4 billion revenue passenger miles, or just 2.8 percent, but their market share is growing fast. The carriers are economically efficient, but flying them is even less attractive than flying a no-frills jet carrier because they pilot small, cramped planes and they fly low, where the air is often bumpy.

What other market segments might there be? One, obviously, is the full-service, high-cost national airline business lead by United and American. There is also the low-cost, point-to-point market, which Southwest Airlines has served well over the past 20 years. However, given its low costs, it is hard to see any of the full-service carriers displacing Southwest from any of its markets.

Another segment involves purely leisure vacation markets, who are the most price-sensitive of all travelers. Serving this market could involve increased charter service. Charter requires very high density, and, in the United States, that is limited to such markets as New York-Orlando or Los Angeles-Newark. But there is no reason why Southwest, American, or United, could not launch charter services between other major population centers and destination resorts.

In the future, passengers insisting on a specific seat assignment, baggage check through, liqueur, food, and a movie will pay more, and there will probably be fewer flights offering those services. For price-sensitive travelers, fares will remain at bargain levels but amenities will shrink, with fewer meals, movies, and other frills, and more tightly squashed seats. Southwest, for instance, serves no meals and few snacks. Frequent-flier miles, which account for around 7 percent of the scheduled jet carriers' total reported revenue miles, will disappear. There will be fewer convenient hubs for travelers even though they typically generate 20 percent more revenue per plane than a comparable point-to-point flight. This advantage is being eliminate by high labor costs and low productivity.

## COMPETING WITH CUSTOMER SERVICE

Mass marketing is incompatible with knowing customers personally and satisfying their needs through personalized service. However, mass marketing is a cost-effective and efficient system, where customers obtain greater variety and lower prices. In an effort to offer customers the benefits of mass marketing and more personalized service. American is practicing a new approach that depends on a clear understanding of individual customers' economic potential and on marketing efforts that use continuously refined information about current and potential customers to anticipate and respond to their needs. This "continuous relationship marketing" allows marketers to obtain all kinds of new information about their customers and use that information to provide more personalized customer service. For example, American's gate agents know who is a valuable customer and can upgrade that person to first class in preference to a once-a-year holiday traveler.

Many airlines are investing heavily in relationship marketing, yet they are failing to address the key elements needed to create value for customers, and they are thus missing the opportunity to have a true impact on their business. Many create "most valuable customer" programs, but neglect to change the behavior of their front-line service employees. Others succeed in making individual marketing campaigns more effective, but fail to convert responses into long-term customer relationships. A few never even get around to properly running continuous relationship marketing programs.

Many companies attempting to practice relationship marketing fail to treat some customers better than others despite differences in value to their business in the 10 to 100 times range. Some in the full-service airline industry have done well in this area by creating multilevel frequent-flyer programs, dedicated ticket reservation lines, priority upgrades, and so on. For example, American gives its flight crew a list of every platinum or gold customer on the plane, along with their seat numbers.

## AMERICAN AIRLINE'S STRATEGY

American Airlines (which is owned by AMR) provides airline passenger and cargo carrier services. American's strategy throughout the 1980s emphasized "value pricing," with a simplified fare structure and a refusal to allow anyone to underprice it. From 1983 to 1988, American invested about $7 billion into new planes doubling the size of its fleet to 468 aircraft, and it increased workforce to 78,000 employees. What made that possible was its two-tier wage structure where new hires were paid significantly less than old employees. Thus, as the airline grew, it became cheaper to operate.

During the recession in the early 1990s, American was able to take over the routes and assets of troubled carriers such as TWA and Eastern Air Lines. American had no choice but to take these growth opportunities. The same was true for United and Delta, which were buying aircraft and foreign routes as fast as American. However, in the end, American felt that it had to reconsider this approach. In the process, it cut its capital-spending plans and decided to model itself after its non-traditional rival Southwest Airlines, which had been consistently profitable over the past decade.

Southwest flies point-to-point, short trips at very low prices, as opposed to a hub system. Southwest offers customers a cheap ticket, no advance boarding passes, no meals, and no automatic baggage transfers. The absence of those services and an extremely productive workforce, gave Southwest a major cost advantage over American. Some worry, however, that American's emphasis on a no-frills product, even under a separate brand name, could tarnish the image of its regular service because American has built a reputation for excellent full-line service. Yet, even if American does well in emulating Southwest, it may not be enough. American may need to leave some markets and close some of its hubs.

## AMERICAN AIRLINES PERFORMANCE

In 1994, American's operating revenues increased 0.7 percent to $14.8 billion, compared with $14.7 billion in 1993 (Fig. 6.19–1), but passenger revenues decreased. In that year, American derived 71.5 percent of its passenger revenues from domestic operations and 28.5 percent from international operations. Its net income in 1994 was $268 million and, in 1993, it was $23 million (Fig. 6.19–2). During 1994, American's domes-

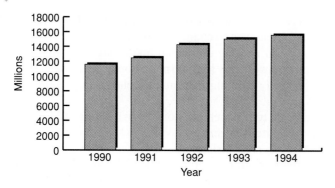

**FIGURE 6.19–1** AMR Corporation Total Sales

*Source: AMR Corporation 1994 Annual Report.*

tic traffic increased 0.4 percent, to 70.0 billion revenue passenger miles, while domestic capacity decreased 6.0 percent. International traffic grew 5.2 percent, to 28.9 billion revenue passenger miles on a capacity reduction of 2.7 percent.

These improved results reflect American's new strategic framework, as well as strong economies in most of the markets it serves, stringent cost controls, and relatively low fuel prices. In light of the changing competitive environment toward lower costs and lower fares, in 1993 American began implementing a new strategic framework, known as the Transition Plan. This plan has three parts, including making the core airline business bigger and stronger where economically justified; shrinking the airline where it cannot compete profitably; and reallocating resources and effort to American's growing information and management services businesses, which are more profitable than the airline.

In the low-fare environment of recent years, American's efforts to increase unit revenues have focused on its share of the premium fare market. American added flights at its major hubs; increased service between major business markets such as Dallas/Fort Worth, Chicago, and New York; added more first-class seating on narrow-body aircraft; expanded its successful transcontinental three-class service; and continued to increase international service.

During the same period, American continued to downsize, primarily in domestic markets. Older, less efficient jet aircraft were removed from service as American trimmed about 30 cities and over 100 routes. In addition, American closed several hub

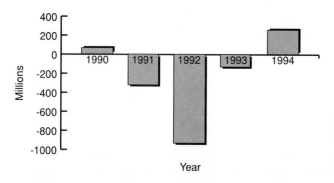

**FIGURE 6.19–2** AMR Corporation Net Income

*Source: AMR Corporation 1994 Annual Report.*

operations and eliminated thousands of service, flights, and administrative employee positions.

## THE FUTURE OF AMERICAN AIRLINES

American Airlines has determined that it needs to significantly change its revenue and earnings prospects. This is due to the increasing competition from low-cost, low-fare carriers. Over the long-term, parent company AMR wants to continue to reduce airline costs and to bring the airline operations to acceptable levels of profitability. Based upon the success or failure of those efforts, AMR will make ongoing judgments about the appropriate level of investment in its airline operations, which may result in termination if the airline cannot be run profitably over the long-term.

Despite the challenges faced by American, the airline has historically had many basic strengths. These include a hub-and-spoke route network that allows it to efficiently serve thousands of domestic and international markets; a modern, quiet, fuel-efficient fleet; the AAdvantage frequent flyer program; and leading-edge computer technology. In the past, these strengths and American's continued focus on premium-fare traffic have helped to lessen the impact of an adverse pricing environment. While competitive pressures continue to weaken per passenger value, stronger economic conditions and revenue management have led to better passenger revenue.

What marketing strategy would you advise American Airlines to pursue with the consumer and business markets? What specific price, distribution, promotion, and product elements would you propose and why? How would you deal with the growth competition from other airlines? What do you think about American's strategy for appealing to a variety of market segments? How would you handle the competition from Southwest Airlines?

## Sources

*American Airlines 1994 Annual Report.*

*AMR 1994 Annual Report.*

Banks, Howard. "A Sixties Industry in A Nineties Economy." *Forbes* (May 9, 1994): 107–112.

Barker, Robert. "Ten Things Your Airline Won't Tell You." *Medical Economics* 72, 20 (October 23, 1995): 184–191.

Butler, Charles. "The American Way." *Successful Meetings* 41, 7 (Part 1) (June 1992): 44–49.

Churchill, David. "The Airlines' First Priorities." *Management Today* (October 1995): 90–94.

Ellis, James. "Not-So-Friendly Skies For Frequent Fliers." *Business Week* (September 5, 1995): 88–89.

Kelly, Kevin. "Keep those Seatbelts On." *Business Week* (January 10, 1994): 98.

Kelly, Kevin, Wendy Zelner, Andrea Rothman, and Michael Mandel. "Ready To Soar Again?" *Business Week* (April 26, 1993): 26–28.

Smith, Timothy K. "Why Air Travel Doesn't Work." *Fortune* (April 3, 1995): 42–56.

Zellner, Wendy. "American Airlines May Be Too Healthy." *Business Week* (October 31, 1994): 114.

Zeller, Wendy, Andrea Rothman, and Eric Schine. "The Airline Mess." *Business Week* (July 6, 1992): 50–55.

# CASE 20 *Microsoft Home*

The CD-ROM, once a rarity, is now ubiquitous in the personal computer (PC) market. The home segment is the fastest growing part of the PC market. Millions of individual CD-ROM players have been sold in the past few years. Multimedia PCs are rapidly becoming the standard for the home and office. The number of home-based CD-ROM players increased by 241 percent in 1994, and unit sales of CD-ROM titles in all categories rose 178 percent from the first half of 1994 to the same period in 1995. This rapid increase in CD-ROM sales is a result of more consumer-oriented computer programs being made available on those discs. About 20.1 million CD-ROM discs were sold in the United States in 1994. For 1995, the forecast is an increase to 33.2 million discs, and for 1996, 48.7 million, and there is an expectation of continued growth as computer hardware prices come down and as there is more competition based on price for CD-ROM sales.

Given that consumers like the convenience and versatility of CD-ROM software, the task of CD-ROM marketers is to figure out how to promote their sales in stores. One example of a successful vendor is Softkey International Inc., which sells $12.95 titles in supermarkets, convenience stores, Kmarts, and office superstores such as Staples. Softkey specializes in this low-end, low-priced software with distribution in conventional mass-market retailers as well as specialty outlets. Its aim is to keep prices low, display items as if they were any other kind of packaged-good product, and achieve high volume while still making good margins.

Encyclopedia publishing is an area in which the dramatic changes in CD-ROM software are clearly evident. The newest generation of CD-ROM encyclopedias are far more sophisticated and easier to use than earlier models. The speed of searching, the ease of interaction with the program, the clarity of sound and video, and the range of special features make these items essential CD-ROMs for any professional or personal collection. With encyclopedia publishing reaching a level of maturity, developers are using advanced features and extra content to differentiate their products from those of the competition. For users this means more information, better access, price cuts, and

**FIGURE 6.20–1** Microsoft Home Products Ad

a better selection of alternatives. Today, consumers can chose from Microsoft Encarta, Compton's, the Grolier product, or the Britannica version.

One of the most common types of CD-ROM application has been the translation of works from print to this electronic format. Especially in the children's and reference categories, this application has been very popular with publishers and generally quite inexpensive to produce, especially if no multimedia features are added. Producing even a multivolume reference set does not necessarily mean much more than taking the text version and using some form of indexing and hypertext to enhance access. This is very popular with some low-end publishers of literary texts (e.g., the works of Shakespeare or Dickens) and with distributors of government information.

Games are by far the largest segment of CD-ROM consumer sales. The types of products mirror those of software games in general, including games that simulate activities such as flying; adventure games that take players to new places; action games that frequently involve violence; role-playing games in which the player sees the world through the eyes of a fantasy character; board games such as the classic monopoly game; sports games about golf and football; and many others.

As more and more multimedia titles flood the market, the quality of these products will be of paramount importance to consumers. They want to be assured that the product is built on accurate and authoritative content, that it will be easy to use, and will provide hours of enjoyment. Many will expect to be able to increment those hours with new information delivered to their desktop through a modem.

## PERSONAL COMPUTER CD-ROM MARKET TRENDS

CD-ROM publishing has reached new levels of sophistication and maturity in product design. Developers are using CD-ROM to meet target audience needs and the requirements of their content offerings. All major publishers of professional and informational electronic products are looking carefully at this marketplace for ideas about how to better design and market their products. A huge potential market share is at stake in both the professional and home computer user markets. The latter also wants to access professional or business information and services at home via CD-ROM discs and/or online.

Today, there is much software, databases, reference texts, and clip art on CD-ROMs, and the market for these products continues to grow as more publishers create electronic versions of their new and existing products. For these publishers, CD-ROMs also mean more buyers for little additional work if they are already publishing in an electronic format. Bibliographic databases and other standard reference works are good examples of this source of additional revenue.

Some say that the World Wide Web posses a potential threat to CD-ROM publishing, but until Internet standards better protect intellectual property and until such issues as payment mechanisms, security, and bandwidth are resolved, CD-ROMs will continue to hold a strong share of the publishing market. The increasing availability of CD-ROM drives as standard equipment on microcomputers is also guaranteeing that CD-ROMs will remain a publishing staple in the foreseeable future.

One problem is that this computer medium increasingly requires the sophisticated use of media other than text and the adoption of powerful retrieval and search techniques to be successful in today's marketplace. CD-ROM's strength, in fact, is not with text-intensive material. Few users are impressed today with the quantity of information available because they want selective quality. Whether it is an interactive children's book, a medical text, or a how-to manual, in order to sell in today's increasingly competitive marketplace, developers cannot just reproduce text on a screen.

The key to success is understanding both the audience and the content well enough to know how the information/content will be used and which aspect of what is to be delivered will most benefit from enhancement. The utility and value to users revolves around the content, which is a point missed by many CD-ROM developers. Information professionals may yet be willing to tolerate electronic books and databases with no real enhancements, but few others will.

Increasingly, the CD-ROM market is being driven by a few hit titles, rather than seeing a widening range of diverse products. For example, in 1994, the top ten game titles represented 29 percent of retail dollar sales for that category. Price cutting at the retail level is also common, further limiting the risk dealers are willing to take on new, untested products or games with a more limited audience.

## MICROSOFT HOME AND CD-ROMS

Overall, Microsoft develops, manufactures, licenses, sells, and supports a wide range of software products, including operating systems for PCs, workstations, and servers; business and consumer applications for productivity, reference, education, and enter-

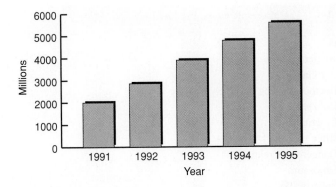

**FIGURE 6.20–2** Microsoft Corporation Total Sales

*Source: Microsoft Corporation 1995 Annual Report.*

tainment; and software development tools. Microsoft also sells PC books and input devices, and is engaged in the research and development of online and advanced technology software products.

Microsoft's net revenues grew 24 percent in 1994 and 28 percent in 1995 (Figs. 6.20–2 and 6.20–3). Software license volume increases were the principal reason for this revenue growth. However, the average selling price per license decreased, primarily because of general shifts in the sales mix from retail packaged products to licensing programs, from new products to product upgrades, and from stand-alone desktop applications to integrated product suites.

Just a few years ago, Microsoft Corporation's CD-ROM sales were negligible. However, the firm now predicts that by the year 2000, home- or consumer-based CD-ROM products will constitute over 50 percent of its revenues. Microsoft's Consumer Division offers five categories of CD-ROMs under brand name "Microsoft Home," including: (1) Reference & Entertainment, (2) Kids' Creativity, (3) Entertainment, (4) Personal Productivity, and (5) Accessories. These categories include many individual titles (Table 6.20–1). Many of the Microsoft Home titles, such as those about the classical composers, ancient lands, or dinosaurs, deal with past worlds. Under the Microsoft Home brand, the firm's goal is to create useful, enjoyable products for individuals in the home environment.

Microsoft Home showed continued growth as it expanded its offerings in the areas of CD-ROM multimedia reference titles and software products for home and small

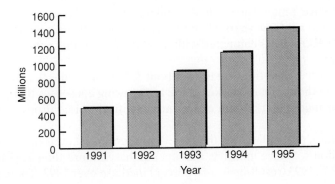

**FIGURE 6.20–3** Microsoft Corporation Total Net Income

*Source: Microsoft Corporation 1995 Annual Report.*

| TABLE 6.20–1. The Microsoft Home Product Line |
| --- |
| 500 Nations |
| Microsoft Ancient Lands |
| Microsoft Art Gallery |
| Microsoft Beethoven: The Ninth Symphony |
| Microsoft Bookshelf '95 |
| Microsoft Cinemania |
| Creative Writer |
| Microsoft Dangerous Creatures |
| Microsoft Dinosaurs |
| Microsoft Encarta '96 |
| Microsoft Explorapedia: The World of Nature |
| Microsoft Explorapedia: The World of People |
| Fine Artist |
| How the Leopard Got His Spots |
| Isaac Asimov's The Ultimate Robot |
| Scholastic's The Magic School Bus: Explores the Human Body |
| Scholastic's The Magic School Bus: Explores the Ocean |
| Scholastic's The Magic School Bus: Explores the Solar System |
| Microsoft Mozart |
| Microsoft Musical Instruments |
| Microsoft Oceans |
| Microsoft Publisher |
| Microsoft Schubert |
| Microsoft Space Simulator |
| Microsoft Strauss |
| Microsoft Stravinsky |
| The Ultimate Frank Lloyd Wright |
| Microsoft Works |

office productivity, children's creativity, and entertainment. Microsoft's CD-ROM consumer business expanded 70 percent in 1994 to about $100 million. That represented 7 to 8 percent of Microsoft's revenues. Microsoft has a sizable portion of the entire market, which has been estimated at about $400 million. This market may reach the multibillion level within the next few years when the typical home PC user is expected to own more than 20 CD-ROM titles compared with the three or four that are the norm for productivity software.

Most of the Microsoft Home titles retail for about $50 each. While this price is considered competitive in the software market, there is a growing consensus that price points for the consumer media market will experience significant price drops as this market expands.

Educational software, particularly for the larger children's market, is the hottest segment of the $6.8 billion software industry. Parents purchased more than $243 million worth of "kidware" in 1993, resulting in a 66 percent increase over 1992. There are more than 15 million U.S. homes with PCs and school-age children, and that figure is expected to double by 1998. More and more parents see computers as something essential for their children's education. Microsoft is involved mainly through partnerships with companies that have a strong history in the children's market.

## CD-ROM DISTRIBUTION

The key to successful retail sales for CD-ROM publishers is to have products on the shelves that customers want to buy and to display them attractively so customers can identify the product and the need it addresses. But, retailing is generally a very low-margin business. The retailer is the last member of the sales chain and at the front line with customers. Retailers want products that already have their own customers who will come to a store or to work with producers who will spend enough on promotions to create customers. Retailers want products that are popular, that either sell very quickly to a lot of people or create repeat business.

Retailers offer CD-ROM developers and publishers exposure and access to potential customers. This exposure provided by the retail environment is critical because the package on the shelf is always working to sell shoppers. While mail order can be cheaper, there is a certain security in buying a product in a store and the immediate gratification associated with taking the product home and using it that day. CD-ROM publishers need to insure that their products are being displayed on retail shelves in stores around the country. However, one big problem is that 1,500 titles are contending for only about 200 to 300 retail shelf slots in each store, with new products being introduced daily.

Bookstores have been slow to carry CD-ROM for reasons ranging from a fear of having to support complicated computer installation and operation issues to the relatively high price per unit of the product, although more robust software and lower prices, combined with more interesting mass-market titles, has begun to change this attitude. The overall feeling after the 1994 American Booksellers Association convention was that bookstores are going to sell CD-ROMs in larger numbers. Borders, the superstore arm of Ann Arbor, Michigan-based Waldenbooks, is planning six to eight new stores with space built for 750 to 1,000 CD-ROM titles. However, Microsoft cautions bookstores that CD-ROMs are not just another ancillary product, as are books-on-tape with a one-to-one relationship to the printed version. Rather, the CD-ROM is a major event all by itself because it will find its way into the market in a different way as a fundamentally unique way of communicating.

Other traditional entertainment and media-oriented outlets are also taking their time in carrying significant numbers of CD-ROM titles. Although music and video stores seem to be natural outlets for consumer CD-ROM titles, there is, however, no major movement toward product adoption. In contrast, mass merchandisers such as Wal-Mart, Kmart, and other major chains are investing heavily in multimedia computers and CD-ROMs.

Distributors provide valuable service to publishers, especially smaller ones, because they buy an inventory of the product and have established relationships with retailers. Most distributors like to see well-formed marketing and product development plans, which will create demand from their retail customers at high minimum order volumes. Sometimes the distributor is not enough, leading a publishers to want partnerships with an "affiliate label" program. This involves joining with a vendor who already has a great deal of strength in the marketplace. Electronic Arts, Sony, Compton's New-Media, and Maxis are established vendors who create alliances with smaller publishers. In this type of relationship, the smaller publisher gets carried in the marketplace alongside a well-known vendor and adopts the prestige of a larger product line. These affiliate labels are typically not distributors, but work with traditional distributors to obtain favorable treatment on discounts, promotion to retailers, and special offers.

The use of sales representatives involves the publisher contracting with a representative firm to handle its products. These representatives visit retail outlets and buyers, and sell the product, passing orders directly through to the publisher for fulfillment. The representatives' commission is relatively small, 10 to 15 percent, but the publisher must handle all the warehousing, shipping, and inventory management as well as all marketing and promotion costs.

In a publisher/copublisher relationship, a larger publisher takes the work of another publisher and operates as if the original publisher were an author, who receives an author's royalty. The copublisher handles all manufacturing of discs and packaging, all marketing, all distribution, and so on. The Microsoft Home label is an example of a copublisher.

## GROWING MICROSOFT HOME'S CD-ROM BUSINESS

More and more companies or business units within large companies, are developing, publishing and/or marketing CD-ROM titles. Microsoft is the most obvious example with its consumer publishing division employing 700 people and its long list of "edutainment" (combining education and entertainment) titles. Only a few years ago, Microsoft focused solely on system and business productivity software. Microsoft's move into CD-ROMs is associated with rapid change in the internal culture of the firm. Previously, when the company developed a product such as its spreadsheet, Excel, it was an entirely in-house product, with all of the developers communicating only with each other and protected their technology from the outside world until they were ready to sell it. Products such as Excel are entirely form and function, where the user fills in the content and operates the product as a tool. In contrast, CD-ROM titles are very rich in content. Products like Encarta are very content rich, containing pictures, video clips, and sound, but traditional text takes up only about 10 percent of what is there.

What marketing strategy would you advise Microsoft Home to pursue in the consumer CD-ROM market? What specific price, distribution, promotion, and product elements would you propose and why? How would you deal with the growth in competition in the CD-ROM-based edutainment market, particularly from firms that mass market CD-ROMs at relatively low-price points? What do you think about Microsoft's current plans to market CD-ROMs as a copublisher?

## Sources

Beiser, Karl. "CD-ROM—Understanding A Newly Mature Technology." *Online* 18, 2 (March 1994): 92–95.

Brandi, Richard and Amy Cortese. "Bill Gates's Vision." *Business Week* (June 27, 1994): 57–62.

Bowers, Richard A. "Distributing the Wealth—Sliding CD-ROM Into the Consumer Channel." *CD-ROM Professional* 7, 6 (November/December 1994): 16–32.

Deutschman, Alan. "Bill Gates' Next Challenge." *Fortune* 126, 14 (December 28, 1992): 30–41.

Goh, Calvin. "MPC2 Enables CD-ROM Multimedia." *Computer Technology Review* 14, 4 (April 1994): 45–46.

Gussin, Lawrence. "CD-ROM Publishing, Education, and Boom Years Ahead." *CD-ROM Professional* 8, 6 (June 1995): 58–70.

Herther, Nancy K. "CD-ROM Publishing Today: What's Hot & What's Not." *Database* 18, 4 (August/September 1995): 27–41.

Herther, Nancy. "Microsoft's Tom Corddry on Multimedia, The Information Superhighway and the Future of Online." *Online* (September/October, 1994): 27–29.

Jacso, Peter. "Intermedia '94—We Got the Picture." *Information Today* 11, 4 (April 1994): 41–43.

Major, Michael J. "Microsoft, CD-ROM, and Home, Sweet Home." *CD-ROM Professional* 8, (January 1995): 36–44.

*Microsoft Corporation 1994 Annual Report.*

Pitta, Julie. "New Hope for Computer Illiterates?" *Forbes* 155, 2 (January 16, 1995): 88–89.

Pinkerton, Janet E. "Bringing Consumers to 'Microsoft Home'." *Dealerscope Merchandising* 36, 11 (November 1994): 1, 22+.

---

# *White Castle System, Inc.*

CASE 21

White Castle System, Inc. is an unusual competitor in the world of fast-food restaurants. Established in 1921, White Castle is generally considered the original fast-food hamburger chain. The name White Castle was chosen to connote more than a mere physical description of the restaurants. According to company history, "White" signifies purity and cleanliness, while "Castle" stands for strength, permanence, and stability.

White Castle invented a limited menu, fast-food service, and developed and perfected methods that have become standard in the industry. Its 24-hours-a-day concept was an innovation and remains almost unique in fast-food operations. The company literally created the take-out food industry by developing packaging to keep its burgers warm.

While most fast-food chains have come into prominence through franchising, White Castle has refused the franchise route domestically, preferring to retain complete ownership and control of its own units. White Castle stock is not publicly traded. The company is entirely held by the founding family, which takes an active interest in operations.

White Castle was founded by the late E.W. "Billy" Ingram, E.W. "Edgar" Ingram, Jr., is retired but functions in the post of chairman of the board, and E.W. Ingram III is currently the president and chief executive officer.

In an industry notorious for high personnel turnover, approximately 10 percent of White Castles, over 9,000 employees, have from 10 to 45 years of unbroken service. The company has the broadest benefits package of any fast-food organization, and the basic benefits are provided to every employee, regardless of station.

Early growth was rapid. There were 100 units open as soon as 1930, but the number fell to below 70 when World War II brought meat rationing. After the Korean War, the company grew again, establishing itself principally in urban areas in the Northeast. Gross sales in 1989 were less than 1 percent of the nation's fast-food revenue.

Over the years, White Castle has concentrated on its menu of burgers, fries, and beverages. Although, just because White Castle has not introduced salad bars does not mean it lacks an innovative marketing strategy. Its ability to change has been demonstrated throughout its history and continues to be reflected in its recent telemarketing and frozen product efforts. A carefully considered promotional strategy, including aggressive public relations, contributes to White Castle's continued success and helps differentiate it from other fast-food/quick service operations. However, as competitive pressures mount and as consumer preferences change, White Castle needs to continually reassess its marketing strategy, particularly its pricing and promotional activities, to determine what approach will be most effective in the future.

## FAST-FOOD INDUSTRY TRENDS

The restaurant business in general, and the fast-food industry in particular, is experiencing sluggish growth and diminished profits due to increased competition and fickle consumers (Table 6.21–1). Industry revenue only grew by about 6 percent in 1990 and future estimates make that figure sound bullish. During the boom times of the 1980s, revenue growth was a high as 12 percent per year.

The entire $147-billion eating place industry, from haute cuisine to the corner diner, is in a state of turmoil. Operating margins for several large publicly traded restaurant chains were squeezed sharply in 1988–1989. The malaise is partly the result of technology and changing eating patterns. On the technology front, the biggest threats to restaurants have been from microwave ovens and videocassette recorders.

Consumer eating habits and preferences are evolving. Baby boomers find eating at home more economical and more convenient. Many millions of Americans are tired of eating out or cannot fit it into their schedules. Consumer lifestyles are changing and that is effecting what, how, and when they eat; they also appear to want more types of

TABLE 6.21–1.  Major Market and Industry Trends

More competition
Healthier items
Menu expansion
Slow market growth
More emphasis on customer service
Expanding hours of service
More items at lower price points
Higher operating expenses
Changing labor force
Changing population demographics

food to select from. If restaurants are the losers, then the winners are the purveyors of take-out and take-home food. For most restaurants, adaptability is the key to survival, including a willingness to change what is on the menu and how it is served.

The $70-billion-a-year U.S. fast-food market, dominated by McDonald's, has suffered as customers have defected to other chains for discounts, stayed at home for meals, and began shunning red meat and fried food. McDonald's, which had revenues of about $6.5 billion in 1992, still reports healthy profits, but sales are increasing much faster overseas than domestically. In an effort to attract and keep customers, the average McDonald's serves salad, chicken, and decaffeinated coffee as well as providing a more comfortable atmosphere. The next addition to the menu will be a McDonald's pizza. McDonald's hopes to lure people who stay at home into its restaurants with its new products.

To address these issues many other fast-food companies are also making changes in how they operate and what they offer. Many outlets are moving to expanded menus, operate longer hours, and sell more items at lower price points. Burger King has even introduced a mini-burger similar to White Castle's in size but with a different product design. Pillsbury Company's restaurant group, which includes Burger King, Godfather's Pizza, Quik Wok, Steak and Ale, and Bennigan's, is attempting to apply more organizational discipline to help its bottom line. Wendy's International revised its marketing approach after its first-ever loss in the first quarter of 1987. It developed a new advertising campaign in an attempt to re-establish the strength of its burger and spent more on training and store operations.

## AN INDUSTRY LEADER

White Castle has a reputation as an industry leader in sales per store, often surpassing all other major fast-food restaurant chains. Comparing menu item unit sales for all menu prices at White Castle with similar figures from other fast-food restaurants also reveals that traffic at White Castle restaurants is higher than that of the competition. Average store location sales were over $1.5 million in 1992 for its 257 restaurants (surpassed only by McDonald's sales per store) for total sales of $338 million. White Castle System revenue and income remained strong (Figs. 6.21–1 and 6.21–2). Gross sales

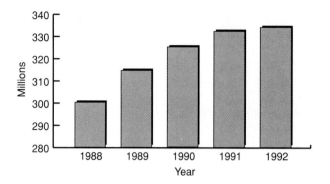

**FIGURE 6.21–1** White Castle System Revenues.

*Source:* Estimated from various sources.

in 1992 were more than $92 million. That is something of a surprise, given the overall slump in which the fast-food industry remains.

## Company Expansion

White Castle is projecting growth of as many as 10 to 15 new stores per year in new and existing markets nationwide. Money for White Castle expansion comes for the most part from available funds, so growth has been controlled and steady.

## International Franchising

In late 1988, the company entered into an Asian franchise agreement with a group of Malaysian investors. The first White Castle restaurants opened there in the second quarter of 1989. In the first quarter of 1992, White Castle opened a restaurant in the Bahamas.

## New Products

The new Castle Meal "A Meal Fit For A Kid," is being offered in all White Castle restaurants. It includes a White Castle hamburger or cheeseburger, fries, soft drink, and a free surprise for children. Breakfast and chicken sandwiches are offered at nearly all locations and are developing a loyal following of their own. Clam strips, grilled chicken, and bacon cheeseburger sandwiches are available at a few stores. The introduction of products such as these is a decision made by area managers in response to local demand.

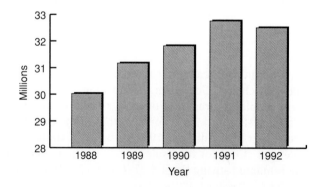

**FIGURE 6.21–2** White Castle System Income.

*Source:* Estimated from various sources.

## Expanding Distribution

In the past, some people who have moved from a White Castle market to one with only White Castle competitors, telephoned the company to order dozens of the hamburgers for delivery by air express. White Castle observed that customers were "Buying 'Em By The Sack" to take home, freeze, and reheat later in a microwave. This is possible because of the way White Castle prepares its hamburgers: they are steam-grilled, helping them to retain moisture essential to the freezing/reheating process. The company realized the potential in moving into a new area where there were no existing White Castle restaurants, and introducing its product. The resulting frozen White Castle hamburgers are marketed in most of the country on a constantly expanding basis. This decision to offer the product in grocery stores was thus based on intense consumer demand.

## A Quality Product

White Castle started with a superior product. The chopped beef cooked in the White Castle hamburger sandwich is all beef from American grown beef inspected and U.S. graded. It is shaped and compressed into squares with five evenly spaced holes on White Castle equipment to cook quickly and uniformly. Equally unique is White Castle's method of steam cooking. Others debate the merits of broiling, frying, grilling, etc. (some of which is just semantics).

Below is a nutritional breakdown for an individual White Castle burger:

| | |
|---|---|
| Weight | 2.06 oz. |
| Fat | 7.94 g |
| Fiber | 2.13 g |
| Protein | 5.88 g |
| Ash | 35 g |
| Nitrogen-free extract | 13.25 g |
| Carbohydrates | 15.38 g |
| Salt | 70 g |
| Sodium | 266 mg |
| Calories | 161.27 |

White Castle operates three bakeries and a meat-processing plant to supply its own stores.

## Promotional Efforts

Historically, While Castle has focused its promotional efforts on local radio and television advertisements and coupon premiums. Today, a centralized marketing program directs messages to specific target markets, particularly the children of their current customer base. Television advertising includes:

1. Castle Meal commercials that air on weekdays and Saturday mornings to introduce the kid's meal to 2 to 11 years olds.
2. Specific promotion and event advertising campaigns.

Radio advertising promotions attract the attention of 18 to 49 year olds. The White Castle advertisements are perceived to be:

1. Highly credible.
2. Markedly different from the competition.
3. Straightforward and humorous.
4. A continuation of what consumers perceive to be the White Castle "story" or phenomenon.
5. Informational rather than hard-sell.

White Castle has one of the most successful promotional strategies in the fast-food industry, predicated on the fact that White Castle is just plain different from the others. Word-of-mouth is an important facet of the campaign and this appears as strong as ever with no reason to feel it cannot continue.

Because the company services a limited geographic area and limited number of outlets, regional advertising is important. Demand appears to be at an acceptable level, so increasing promotional efforts may be wasteful in terms of cost and detrimental in terms of ability to handle additional demand. In fact, if White Castle's cult grows too large, it may lose this differentiating feature. Also, if it does too many special events activities, the enormous publicly generated may start to diminish as the act becomes "common place."

White Castle may want to feature some of its employees in advertising campaigns and space, given their longevity, they probably have definite stories to tell. Even this, however, would probably not have the impact of its slice-of-life commercials or the Don Adams spots.

## WHITE CASTLE'S COMPETITORS

White Castle has many competitors; Table 6.21–2 lists most of them. But, there are many more, including the nonchain fast-food operations and the less well-known regional operators, plus less direct competition with supermarkets, convenience stores, diners, and regular restaurants.

McDonald's and Burger King are the closest rivals. While White Castle started in business before they did, they have grown rapidly in the last 20 years. These competitor's marketing strategies are closely followed by White Castle, partly because they appear ready to copy some of its menu items and operating procedures.

Also, new rivals in the fast-food market are segmenting the business in ways that impact McDonald's and Burger King as well as White Castle's operations. Given the menu segmentation that is occurring, McDonald's may soon become the Sears of fast food, a lumbering giant surrounded by much nimbler rivals.

Currently, McDonald's is rethinking its traditional approach to standardizing its decor and offerings across all locations. They are beginning to foster flexibility, meaning that franchisees can now launch experiments in their food and decor. They can test new formats, ranging from self-service to small cage-style outlets to serving McDonald's fare on airplanes. This is a big gamble because the success of McDonald's is based on mass production and absolute uniformity.

| TABLE 6.21–2. White Castle System Competitors |
| --- |

*Burgers*
McDonald's
Burger King
Roy Rogers
Wendy's International
Burger Chef

*Chicken*
KFC

*Mexican*
Taco Bell

*Pizza*
Domino's
Little Caesar's
Godfathers

Over the last decade, Burger King and McDonald's engaged in the infamous advertising "Battle of the Burgers." Wendy's entered the fray in 1983 by declaring itself the winner. The battle continues today. White Castle, on the other hand, never had to enter the battle and might be declared a winner of the ultimate war in terms of sales volume and profitability.

## CONSUMER NEEDS SATISFIED BY WHITE CASTLE

White Castle is satisfying consumer's needs (Table 6.21–3) by enabling its customers to address those needs for food through an inexpensive meal with a unique taste that they have grown to love. Having been exposed to this unique tasting burger in childhood, as customers get older, they learn to associate the "white building" with small square burgers that taste delicious. This taste is a reminder of youthful days when they contemplated what to eat during late hours of the morning. White Castle's convenient 24-

| TABLE 6.21–3. Consumer Needs Being Satisfied by White Castle |
| --- |

Inexpensive meal
Unique taste
Twenty-four hour service
Quality products (all beef burgers, etc.)
Youthful nostalgia
Limited menu
Fast service
Fellowship

hour service enables consumers to avoid the task of a high involvement decision, and many fast-food establishments do not offer this convenience. The limit menu offered by White Castle simplifies the decision-making process and contributes to fast service that customers are looking for.

And, when parents dine with their children at White Castle, there may also be a limited amount of time. Thus, being able to place an order and leave lessens the frustration encountered by the parents on family outings. And, because parents are often concerned with the quality of food their children consume, White Castle's offering of pure beef steamed burgers exactly fits the bill. Parents also relive their youthful White Castle dining experiences.

The limited amount of bun and meat included with the burger and its relatively low price at 29 cents per unit allows customers to enjoy not just one but several of the miniature burgers. Customers can also buy them by the bag and obtain volume discounts. The light, airy bun is an added unique characteristic of a White Castle hamburger that also gets imbedded in the taste preferences of the loyalists.

## WHITE CASTLE'S TARGET MARKET

White Castle's customers are pre-dominantly upper-lower class individuals who look for an inexpensive, quality meal (Table 6.21–4). White Castle might not succeed in targeting a more lower-middle class market because it does not conform to what members of that social class desire in price points, ambiance, and perceived food quality. The location of most White Castles is also an issue because they tend to be built in more upper-lower class than lower-middle class neighborhoods.

It is often said that White Castle invented the hamburger addict. As the saying goes, "once customers are hooked, they are hooked for life." The chain's continuing success is attributed to customer loyalty to products and service they can count on, supported by dedicated employees who are happy in their work.

---

**TABLE 6.21–4. White Castle Target Market**

Demographic segmentation:
  Age: 15–60
  Gender: male and female
  Marital status: single, married
  Income: lower-lower to upper lower
  Occupational: blue-collar, unskilled laborers
  Education: high school, some college
Psychological segmentation:
  Lifestyle: family-oriented
Sociocultural segmentation:
  Social class: lower to upper-lower
  Family lifecycle: bachelors, parenthood
User behavior segmentation:
  Usage rate: medium to heavy
  User status: aware
  Brand loyalty: strong
Benefit segmentation: convenience, economy

---

Loyal followers of White Castle are sometimes referred to as a "fanatic cult." For example, as part of its 1980 anniversary celebration, Fountain Hills, Arizona, with a population of 2,700, imported 10,000 White Castle hamburgers. They sold out within an hour and a half. The next summer they ordered 100,000 and had Clayton Moore, who portrayed the "Lone Ranger," ride shotgun on the truck making the delivery in case White Castle rustlers showed up. It was an annual event for several years. Then frozen White Castles became available in local supermarkets.

Customers develop this high degree of brand loyalty from positive experiences in early life and from the reinforcing value of obtaining a valued good on a regular basis. Such attitudes are developed early in the individual's family life through socialized eating habits and positive associations with White Castle experiences. Thus, many of the restaurant's current customers were exposed to the unique taste of White Castle's products as children, later patronizing with peers during their teens and young adulthood.

The following concepts are frequently used to explain the "fanatic cult" of White Castle loyalists:

1. ***Attitude development.***  Initial favorable experience with the product reinforced by subsequent purchases strengthened. Favorable attitudes, leading to repeat purchases and hard-core brand loyalty.

2. ***Benefits perceived to be important.***  Customers rate White Castle hamburgers high on attributes they value. This confidence and conviction is so intensive that customers are willing to go to extraordinary lengths to purchase the product.

3. ***Lifestyle.***  White Castle hamburgers invoke a lifestyle that is memorable or pleasant to the customers (i.e., first date, family trips). Buying at White Castle is a way to relive those times.

4. ***Learning.***  If the customer grew up conditioned by White Castle hamburgers and was satisfied by them, other alternatives may seem less attractive.

5. ***Family.***  Families play an important role in White Castle loyalty because they introduce family members to its menu. Those experiences also create strong associations with positive experiences that remain into adulthood.

6. ***Peer group.***  Among many, White Castle is the only hamburger worth eating, and buying them makes those customers part of a group.

## THE FUTURE

The secrets to White Castle's success lie in its devoted customers, its unique product design (including product quality), and value pricing. White Castle's customers have acquired a passionate devotion to its good tasting little square burgers, which are uniquely prepared by steam, not fire.

The White Castle story illustrates that a fast-food organization can be very successful without following a "me-too" strategy. And, it shows the importance of an innovative and focused promotional effort. Ultimately, the White Castle experience highlights the importance of brand loyalty and the factors leading to that loyalty, while pointing to the need to adapt to a changing environment and continuing to emphasize a firm's basic strengths.

However, White Castle's past may be brighter than its future. Some argue that the firm has failed to capitalize on the uniqueness of its product offering and the loyalty of its customers. Now that the heavyweights in the fast-food industry are penetrating every niche in search of sales and profits, White Castle is in danger of losing its competitive advantage to rivals willing to imitate some of its menu, particularly its low-price points and its 24-hour operating policy. What marketing strategy would you recommend to White Castle to counter the threats to its business? What specific price, distribution, promotion, and product elements would you propose and why? How would you deal with the growth in competition in the fast-food market?

## Sources

Oliphant, Jim. "White Castle: 70 Years of Sliders." *Columbus Monthly* (February 1991): 26–32.

"Best-Run Companies." *Restaurants & Institutions* (May 29, 1989): 48–49, 62.

Therrien, Lois. "McRisky." *Business Week* (October 21, 1991): 114–122.

White Castle public relations materials.

"White Castle," in *Contemporary Cases in Consumer Behavior* Roger D. Blackwell, W. Wayne Talarzyk, and James F. Engel eds. (Chicago, IL: Dryden Press, 1990), pp. 255–270.

*Charles Schwab Investments*

Since January 1, 1990, the proportion of U.S. households that own stocks either directly or through mutual funds has grown from 32.0 percent to 37.5 percent, the highest level in history. Fabulous returns are not the only reason for the investing boom. With Certificates of Deposit (CD)-interest rates low and retirement benefits shrinking, people are being driven by need as well as an interest in financial benefits.

Buoyed by first-timers, a record $136 billion went into stock, mutual funds in 1993, up from a previous high of $82 billion in 1992 and more than the total invested in stock mutual funds during the entire 1980s. From 1990 through 1993, domestic equities returned nearly 16 percent annually, with some global mutual funds growing 40 percent a year. With CD returns low and retirement benefits shrinking, people are being driven by needs as well as an interest in higher returns. Participation in company 401(k) plans has given many of them a measure of market experience, and the growth of the mutual fund industry has made stocks more accessible to them on their own than ever before.

There are four predominant groups of new investors: the Young Bloods in their 20s and early 30s; the Bank Dropouts who are bank customers fed up with small CD returns; the Lump-Sum Crowd, those laid-off retired workers with sizable lump-sum payouts; and the Ethnic Entrants, minorities who have typically shunned the market.

Financially speaking, the Young Bloods are earning incomes 20 percent less on average than those their age a generation ago. They are faced with a slow-growth economy. And they are aware that with changing priorities in national politics and business, they cannot rely on traditional safety nets such as Social Security and corporate pension plans for their financial security. As a result, they are trying to avoid debt and to invest for the future. Their goal is self-sufficiency and financial independence. Historically, stocks have returned an average of 10 percent a year. If a person is 24 earning $25,000 a year starts saving 10 percent of gross income in the market, he or she could have saved $1.8 million by age 65.

## CHARLES SCHWAB

Not so long ago, most brokerage firms wanted to be global, full-service players in financial services. Now it is clear that more firms have prospered mainly by sticking to their niche. One such firm is Charles Schwab, a San Francisco-based discount-stock-broking firm founded by Charles Schwab. Schwab the firm is now valued at $1.45 billion, of which Charles Schwab owns 25 percent. During the past five years, the company's quarterly trading volume has increased at an average annual rate of 28 percent. Revenues and net income have increased substantially (Fig. 6.22–1 and 6.22–2).

In 1993, Charles Schwab had a dominant 44 percent share of the discount-stock-broking market in America. This clearly limited the potential for domestic expansion, but there are many ways to grow. One growth area for the firm is money management.

Schwab has become an aggressive force in America's booming mutual fund business. It has hit on a novel marketing strategy, which seems to be working. Known as "OneSource," the idea is to bring one-stop shopping to the mutual fund business. Schwab offers its customers a choice of up to 200 no-commission mutual funds and charges no transaction fees, nor is a redemption fee charged on sales. A Schwab stock-broking client also has the convenience of his or her mutual-fund holdings being in the

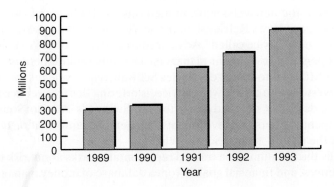

**FIGURE 6.22–1** Charles Schwab Revenue.

*Source: Charles Schwab 1993 Annual Report.*

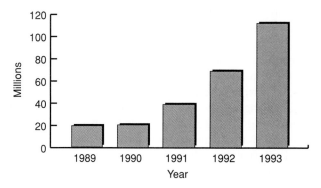

FIGURE **6.22–2** Charles Schwab Net Income.

*Source: Charles Schwab 1993 Annual Report.*

same account as his or her shares, because Schwab acts as a custodian. Schwab takes an annual fee of 0.25 percent of the assets managed by the mutual fund companies.

This one-stop shopping allows clients to buy into a mutual fund for free, and they can also move between families of funds without paying penalties. The mutual fund company enjoys the benefit of having its funds sold through Schwab's 180-odd branch network, and Schwab earns an annual fee based on the funds under management, as well as having a stake in the mutual fund business.

Schwab can offer OneSource because it does not work like a conventional stock-broker. Its staff are on salary rather than commissions, and, therefore, no-commission funds do not upset them. The firm also uses state-of-the-art technology to provide its brokerage services. However, there is one snag. This structure does not give the firm much flexibility to cut costs when it needs to.

Schwab is also turning its technological prowess to serve active stock traders who make 48 or more transactions a year, some at the rate of 10 a day. Schwab has rolled out "Custom Broker," a program that makes use of a variety of financial newswires and other information services to get data to customers fast by phone, fax, computer, or pager.

Some 20 to 25 percent of Schwab's trades are made through its TeleBroker service, which puts the investor in touch with a Schwab computer via the keypad on the phone and offers a 10 percent discount off Schwab's regular commission. Schwab is also reaching out to non-English-speaking traders with its Spanish TeleBroker and its Tele-Broker in Mandarin and Cantonese. For technotraders, it is updating its StreetSmart for Windows software, which already has sold 160,000 units since its introduction in 1993. Among the features in the new version: simplified options trading and tools to make navigating the Dow Jones News Retrieval online service faster and easier.

Charles Schwab has a new service called "AdvisorSource," which offers to match clients with independent personal investment managers. The only requirement is that customers pledge at least $100,000 to manage. Charles Schwab, who made his fortune selling stocks cheap to investors who do not want advice, is offering this free service for customers who have decided they need advice after all. Schwab's AdvisorSource matches clients with independent personal investment managers. The information does not cost a penny, even if the person is not a Schwab client.

When someone calls the 800 number, a trained representative asks about risk tolerance, investment objectives, and financial goals. From a database of money managers in 50 states, the representative reads the names of two or three suitable managers in that person's area and offers to send information on each, including a form that the SEC requires all money managers to file disclosing, among other things, whether there have been any complaints against a manager.

In addition to meeting basic professional standards, such as creditworthiness, a Schwab-recommended investment manager must supervise at least $10 million, have at least five years' experience managing money as a primary occupation, be registered with the SEC, and have all federal and state licenses. He or she must also be fee-only, meaning that the price is a percentage of the assets given to manage (generally about 1 percent), rather than commission-based. Contracts typically also include a termination-without-penalty clause.

One criterion that AdvisorSource does not screen for is performance. That is because each customer has different goals and expectations. So customers should carefully check out each money manager by asking about performance in both up and down markets and by getting references from other customers.

Schwab is not offering this service to be charitable. Advisers on the list are chosen from the 5,000 or so money-management firms that do business with the firm. The more money they handle, the more stocks and mutual funds they will trade through Schwab. The brokerage also gets a share of the adviser's fee for three years after the referral.

## THE SCHWAB REVOLUTION

Billions are pouring into this discount brokerage thanks to a radically new approach that is high-tech, low-cost, no-pressure. But the Schwab story is much more than just taking in assets. Schwab is a radically new kind of brokerage firm that is revolutionizing how financial products and services are delivered to the public. The firm sells nothing and proffers no advice. Instead, through shrewd marketing and innovative technology, Schwab lays out a large choice of low-cost and imaginative investment programs, such as no-fee mutual funds, computerized stock trading, and specialized banking services through liberal use of advertising, which often features Charles Schwab himself.

The Schwab method is diametrically opposed to that of the huge Wall Street brokerage firms, such as Merrill Lynch, Smith Barney, and PaineWebber, which are gathering assets by relying on commisioned sales personnel who court customers and provide them with advice, research, and other services.

Schwab's no-pressure, low-cost, high-tech approach to investment brokerage appeals to disgruntled clients of full-service firms and to baby boomers who are only now entering their financial prime. These people make their own investment decisions and turn to Schwab to put them into action. They can enter their orders on a telephone keypad, saving time and getting a 10 percent discount from Schwab's standard rates. They do not need a broker; they do not want to talk to a real person; and they do not have the time.

No wonder investors are beating a path to Schwab. The pace at which customer assets have been pouring into Schwab, currently at about $25 billion a year, has been quickening. Just since 1991, assets have grown 150 percent. In 1993, Schwab still opened about 700,000 new accounts. About half the new accounts were those of customers who were new to the world of brokerage. The average age of a Schwab customer is 47, 10 years younger than the industry average. Schwab still derives an estimated 75 percent of profits from stock-trading activity.

## COMPETITIVE PRESSURES

The full-service brokerages believe that even a bull market, in which stock prices are increasing, poses risks for Schwab. Higher-end investors who do well in the markets, they insist, will want a seasoned broker's advice on what to do with their money and will leave Schwab behind. Boomers are on the verge of a huge transfer of wealth through inheritance as their parents pass on. This occurrence is significant because as people become more affluent, they trade up. According to the full-service brokerages, the affluent do not want to do business through a telephone-response system. Also, in a world that is growing more and more complicated, the advice and counsel of a broker will be more important, not less important. For that reason Merrill Lynch does not even consider Schwab a direct competitor. Merrill Lynch defines itself as being in the advice and guidance business, and it considers Schwab to be in the transaction business.

Schwab doubts that customers will trade up to full-service firms. It sees no compelling force that will cause America to shift back to that system because people dislike it. But, even if investors decide they need some help, Schwab can make money on that, too, because of its independent financial advisers service.

Perhaps more worrisome for Schwab than the full-service firms are the other discounters. It faces a strong competitive threat from Fidelity Brokerage Services, which is the No. 2 discounter. Fidelity Investments, parent of Fidelity Brokerage Services, has deep pockets, and its brokerage unit has been spending heavily to gain ground in stock trading, mutual funds, and cash-management accounts to provide transaction and back-office services to financial advisers. Fidelity is also way ahead in the 401(k) business, an area in which Schwab is now starting to expand. Then there is the threat from deep-discounters attracting some of Schwab's best customers, those frequent traders. Some deep-discounters are undercutting Schwab stock trading prices by 35 percent or more. One of the most aggressive, National Discount, is charging a minimum of $25 for low-volume stock trades in over-the-counter stocks, versus Schwab's $39. Schwab thinks it can avoid a price war with those discounters by offering high-tech services that others do not offer.

To keep the money coming in, Schwab will continue to count on the increasing independence and sophistication of the individual investor. Business information is proliferating and is more easily accessible to the would-be investor. The print and electronic media are covering business and financial markets more thoroughly than ever. And online services, such as CompuServe and America Online are increasingly compiling data about companies and markets available to average individuals and not just to brokers and big investors. Because Schwab customers know what they want to trade, Schwab technology makes it easier for them to do so, and it is far ahead of rivals in adopting these new technologies.

All this high technology is softened by a marketing image that takes advantage of Chuck Schwab's friendly, trusty face. In the 1970s, when Schwab began appearing in the firm's ads, new business increased some 300 percent in cities where the ads ran. Another soft-touch marketing tool is Schwab's extensive branch network. There really is no practical need for a discount brokerage to invest heavily in branches; customers can do business with a discount broker over the phone. Indeed, Schwab's discount competitors get by with far fewer branches than its 208. Even aggressive Fidelity has limited itself to 70-branches.

## RESPONDING TO THE COMPETITION

Even with all of the success Schwab has enjoyed over the last several years, it cannot afford to become complacent. It is being pressured by the full-services broker on one side and the deep discounters on the other. It needs to ensure that its market niche is viable and strong into the future. This means that it must attract and hold new market investors while keeping its existing large customer base. What marketing strategy would you advise Schwab to pursue in selling its mutual funds? What specific commission, distribution, promotion, and product elements would you propose and why? How would you deal with the growth competition from the full-service and deep discount firms? What do you think about Schwab's current emphasis on technology and its efforts at providing more than bare bone levels of service in the form of advice referrals?

## Sources

"American Stockbroking: One-Stop Merchant." *Economist* 329, 7832 (October 9, 1993): 89 (UK 119).

Branch, Shelly. "Today's New Investors." *Money* 23, 5 (May 1994): 80–90.

Charles Schwab promotional materials.

Charles Schwab 1993 Annual Report.

Del Prete, Dom. "New Mutual Funds Offered to Lure Investors." *Marketing News* 28, 11 (May 23, 1994): 8.

Govoni, Stephen J. "Finding the Right Mutual Fund." *Working Woman* 17, 10 (October 1992): 39–40.

Jacob, Rahul. "Beyond Quality & Value." *Fortune* (Autumn/Winter 1993): 8–11.

Pare', Terence P. "How Schwab Wins Investors." *Fortune* (June 1, 1992): 52–64.

Schifrin, Matthew. "Fund Malls." *Forbes* (June 20, 1994): 234–235.

Zweig, Jason. "A Touch of Class." *Forbes* (February 3, 1992): 82–84.

Zweig, Jason, and Mary Beth Grover. "Fee Madness." *Forbes* 151, 4 (February 15, 1993): 160–164.

# *Wal-Mart Stores* CASE 23

Successful retail management in Asia requires many of the same strategies as those that have been successful in North America or Europe. While some Asian retail markets have matured into competitions over market share because of slow-growing economies, there are many others that are distinctive by their less sophisticated local operators, rapid economic growth, and new found consumer wealth, which allows large, sophisticated retailers to gain sales from both economic growth and from capturing market share. Retailers tired of competitive battles for share in the United States and Europe are wisely looking toward Asia.

Asia, including China, is home to billions of people from different cultures and countries in varying stages of development. The more mature economies in the region, such as Hong Kong, Taiwan, and Singapore, already have well-established retail industries similar to those in the United States, Canada, and Western Europe. Therefore, international retailers are now focusing their attention on newly industrialized countries such as Indonesia, Thailand, Malaysia, and the Philippines, and emerging economies such as China.

Despite the strong economic growth potential and large consumer market in Asia, the retailing industry faces a challenging environment because of shifts in demographics, lifestyles, and culturally influenced purchasing preferences. Globally successful retail strategies in the industrialized nations offer extreme selection, good service, good quality, and reasonable value (e.g., Barnes and Noble media stores, Circuit City, Micro Center); extreme value, reasonable service, reasonable quality, and reasonable selections (e.g., Wal-Mart, Makro); or entertainment, both active and passive, as part of the shopping experience (e.g., Nike Town, Oshman Sporting Goods, Planet Hollywood, Hard Rock Cafe, Disney Stores).

There appear to be three global trends that are common among industrialized nations and Asia: (1) surviving retail stores are getting bigger and are better capitalized, (2) electronic technology is creating opportunities for parallel marketing (using electronics to enhance traditional advertising, as well as using it to divert sales to cheaper warehouse space, while using expensive retail fronts to increase the mailing or contact lists), and (3) entertainment through theme development or through pleasant environmental experiences, which is an important strategy for attracting all but the most price-sensitive shoppers.

## RETAILING IN CHINA

Although China only introduced its open-door policy in 1979, it is experiencing strong demand for good retail investments. Many U.S. retailers are interested in doing business in China. However, they have reservations about establishing themselves in the country. Primarily because of licensing regulations, foreign companies are operating in joint ventures with local partners and most retailers agree that entering China generally requires a joint venture partner. A partner can help retailers understand local markets, customs and laws, and will have credibility and leverage with local banks, trading companies, and manufacturers.

Wal-Mart Stores is moving ahead with its partner in China. It sees China as a tremendous opportunity for low-cost, highly efficient formats. Consumers there have high expectations about quality and value, which Wal-Mart believes it can provide. And despite restrictions, including regulatory compliance, intellectual property rights problems, labor laws, hidden costs, the need to be "regionally correct" in merchandise assortments, and the requirement that only 30 percent of the merchandise assortment may be imported, Wal-Mart believes its efficiencies of operation, its technology, and its strong financial management will work to its advantage.

For its partner in Hong Kong and in China, Wal-Mart picked the Tai retail conglomerate CP Pokphand, a subsidiary of CP Group, which operates a supermarket chain and more than 400 7-Eleven convenience stores, and which also partners with Dutch retailer Makro. In Hong Kong, Wal-Mart and CP opened three Value Clubs that, with their 20,000-square-foot prototype, are tiny by Wal-Mart American standards. In China, the partners have only a 70 percent interest in the stores, with the remaining 30 percent held by the Chinese partner, Shenzhen.

China still remains vastly underdeveloped both in terms of retailing formats and consumer spending power. Few if any foreign entrants are operating in the black. So why enter now? Because it takes time to experiment, adapt, and learn, and because Chinese consumers are loyal, rewards accrue to those who test now and refine their formats early on. Furthermore, there are a limited number of local partners to help overcome the operational challenges.

However, some believe that no foreign retailer can compete price-wise with a Chinese store. Some of these price disadvantages may be attributed to quality or value additions appropriate to the positioning of the store, but the major reason for low Chinese prices is that accounting methods used in Chinese state-owned stores do not add up the entire cost of goods sold, and prices often reflect variable costs and not fixed ones. State-owned stores also do not pay rent; accordingly, prices need not be marked up as much as on items sold by nonstate-owned competitors.

China's retailing industry experienced an increase in volume of nearly 30 percent in 1995, and it is expected to double or triple by the year 2000. China undoubtedly is destined to become a major retailing market, but merchants will realize this potential gradually, rather than rapidly. In preparing to enter the market, the key issues to consider include: (1) Where is the consumer potential? (2) What is the existing retailing environment? (3) How can firms source product, manage the supply chain, and oversee distribution?

## TARGETED MARKETING IN CHINA

China has many large population centers. In fact, it has 78 cities with populations of one to two million, and another 17 with two million or more residents. These are all high-potential retailing markets. Higher-income consumers, however, are concentrated along the coast, so the point of entry is usually one of five major coastal cities with a collective population of about 43 million, including Shenzhen, Guangzhou, Shanghai,

Tianjin, and Beijing. Income profiles for these locales differ slightly, but they have more in common with each other than with cities in the noncoastal hinterland.

Generational differences in China are striking. People in the 35 and above age group were raised during a period of chronic instability and economic hardship; families typically had five or six children. By contrast, virtually every person in China under the age of 25 is an only child, accustomed to having most of the family budget dedicated to his or her needs. China also has its "empty nest" group, ages 50 and over.

The spending priorities of these groups are very different, as are their needs, habits, and attitudes. Understanding where the interest in a retailer's offering may come from is important, especially as some segments, such as children's clothing, become increasingly crowded. In general, there are opportunities to target moderate apparel and value grocery stores toward all age groups; specialty apparel shops toward younger consumers; price-value appliance and electronics stores toward established households; and hard- and soft-goods shops toward both empty nesters and the status- and comfort-conscious young aspirants.

Apart from getting the timing right, retailers who succeed in Asia must be oriented toward woman, who dominate shopping decisions. Any basic retail format needs to be adapted and modified to satisfy local requirements and conditions. Consumers' purchasing decisions are no longer based solely on price, product, quality, or product range. To differentiate themselves, retailers need to train their staff to provide quality service. With so many stores selling the same products, the decision to buy from a particular outlet can often be motivated by the level of service consumers experience alone.

A degree of sophistication in direct import, particularly in Asia, will probably be an advantage to retailers entering China. The planning, information exchange, logistics, and quality control models retailers develop in direct importing are useful in the transition to doing business in the country. Of course, forging vendor relationships in China and nearby economies is an added bonus. China's sourcing environment may never come to resemble the one in the United States, where domestic vendors drop-ship small, just-in-time quantities, and offer liberal return policies. Retailers seriously considering entering China should first begin a program to develop sourcing expertise. One way to achieve such a goal might be to establish a springboard first in a smaller-scale Asian country. J.C. Penney, Kmart, and Wal-Mart started by opening in smaller Asian markets.

## WAL-MART

For 1996, Wal-Mart Stores achieved record sales of $93.6 billion and record earnings of $2.7 billion (Figs. 6.23–1 and 6.23–2). That made it the fourth largest company in the United States, and the 12th largest in the world. Its earnings led all retailers and made it the 13th most profitable company in America.

The retail environment Wal-Mart faced in the United States during 1995 and 1996 was the most difficult in recent memory. High consumer debt levels caused many shoppers to reduce or defer spending on anything other than essentials. Lack of exciting new products or apparel trends reduced discretionary spending. Fierce competition resulted in lower margins and there was a lack of productivity increases.

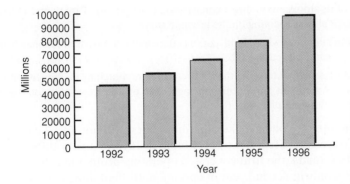

**FIGURE** 6.23–1 Wal-Mart Net Sales.

*Source: Wal-Mart 1996 Annual Report.*

As of 1996, Wal-Mart had more than 2,400 Wal-Mart Stores and 470 SAM's Clubs, with a total of 675,000 associates. Wal-Mart has a public image of being a bunch of good, old boys from Arkansas, who expanded their network primarily to the regions that the so-called "bigger" general merchandise retailers avoided or did not bother with. Wal-Mart and low prices have become synonymous, but the mega-retailer's power merchandising involves more than numbers on tags. The company's power merchandising is made up of a panoply of ancillary endeavors that have enabled it to continually reduce expenses, drive down margins, and maintain the low prices that suction off sales from competitors and swell its market share.

Applying its unique power merchandising formula across different marketing formats exemplifies how Wal-Mart's corporate culture encourages and empowers employees to contribute and execute ideas to improve operations. In effect, Wal-Mart continually renews itself, something no other competitor does as a deliberate, ongoing endeavor. Despite Wal-Mart's successful development as the premier low-priced retailer, price comparisons have not always borne its reputation as the lowest-priced retailer. When checking that claim, the selection of items that are compared is often the key to whether Wal-Mart or another discounter can be considered to offer the lowest-priced merchandise.

In the United States, Wal-Mart faces a number of critical challenges:

- Growth gets tougher the bigger firms get, which means slower share growth and more management challenges.

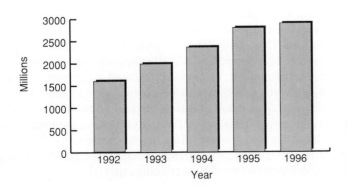

**FIGURE 6.23–2** Wal-Mart Net Income.

*Source: Wal-Mart 1996 Annual Report.*

- Some 75 percent of its stores are in direct competition from Kmart, Target, and Dillards, among others, which also are gaining on the learning curve.

- Wal-Mart is moving into areas where land, construction, and labor costs are higher than in the rural areas to which it is accustomed.

- Recent retail weakness suggest to some that U.S. consumers soon may be tapped out. Demographically, most Americans are reaching the age when personal consumption is giving way to savings and retirement planning.

Wal-Mart is committed to being a global retailer, but it will not invest more capital than justified by its results. Mexico was profitable in 1996 in a very difficult economic environment. In Canada, the firm generated operating profit and achieved a 40 percent market share in only its second year of operation. Both of these countries generated sufficient cash to support current operations and plans for growth. In addition, Wal-Mart's initial results in Argentina and Brazil were encouraging.

## INDUSTRY CONSOLIDATION AND GLOBALIZATION

Retailing in Canada, the United States, and other parts of the world has been consolidating, leaving the industry everywhere with a smaller number of larger, stronger players. Further, consolidation is expected throughout the 1990s as retailers fight more aggressively for market share and growth. The strongest players, with diversified operations in many locations, are expected to be the ones who survive and prosper in the next century. International expansion works best when firms conduct a careful analysis and do detailed initial planning. For this they gain a thorough understanding of the customers' needs, wants, and preferences in the new markets. This results in well-conceived sourcing and distribution strategies that meet local needs for products and services.

Global opportunities for growth exist for retailers for a number of reasons. The world market has tremendous growth potential in population and, even more importantly, potential growth in per capita spending. Japan, Argentina, the United States, Canada, and Italy all have high per capital retail expenditures. As the current recessions end worldwide, there is room for significant market growth through spending increases in the remainder of Europe, Australia, and Eastern Europe. In addition, areas such as South and Central America, the Middle East, Africa, and China have opportunities fueled by both population growth and expansion in retail per capita expenditures as their economies stabilize and income levels rise.

Other factors speeding retail globalization include the ease and speed of transportation and communication, a new generation of business leaders, and the decline of communism as a world market system. Most experts believe that some customization of marketing strategies is needed. Even if the retailer's products have universal appeal, sizing may need to be altered to accommodate local populations. For example, when Ralph Lauren opened a department store in Japan, he created a separate size scale, even though most of the styles were consistent with his existing product line. Although his original message was clear, this modification was needed to sell to the local population. It is likely that every retailer following a global strategy will have to adapt, at least in some small way, to the local market's culture. How much adaptation will be necessary and to what extent (if any) the company's original message needs to be changed, depend on the country of origin and the local market being entered.

Wal-Mart and its competitors are bringing something unheard of to markets such as Mexico: choice. The best local discounters stock 50,000 items per store, and in Asia, where they do exist, even fewer. Wal-Mart and Kmart routinely carry 80,000 items per store. As a result, these stores have universal appeal. The pace of building has been so furious that retailers are getting ahead of market growth.

## OVERSEAS GROWTH

The 21st century will bring unprecedented challenge for retailers. The United States is substantially overstored. American consumers, by and large, are extremely cost-conscious and do not spend as freely as they did in the high-growth 1970s and 1980s. In this environment, retailers only grow by stealing market share from their competitors. Success requires an intense focus on the customer and breakthrough tools and techniques for maximizing customer relationships. However, even with such an emphasis, U.S. sales and profits show little prospect of moving dramatically.

Because of these domestic market conditions, many believe that Wal-Mart's future is outside the United States. Although Wal-Mart believes there is still enormous domestic opportunity, it has decided to expand into the international area in a big way. In three years, it wants a third of its growth to come from outside the United States. Mexico and Canada are the two best candidates, because of the proximity of the two countries. Dominating the overall North American consumer market is Wal-Mart's first priority. The second best opportunity is in South America, because Wal-Mart believes that area will, just as Mexico and Canada, become part of a free trade agreement. Wal-Mart plans to move into Brazil, Argentina, and Chile with nine stores, including a supercenter and a wholesale club. The other great opportunity is in Asia, mostly China. Wal-Mart ranks Europe way down on the list of opportunities because of too much bureaucracy, meaning that it takes a long time to get permits or zoning, and there is rigid resistance to revolutionizing retailing with low prices and greater values.

What marketing strategy would you advise Wal-Mart to pursue in China? What specific price, distribution, promotion, and product elements would you propose and why? How would you deal with competition from local merchants and the growing number of non-Chinese firms entering China?

## Sources

"After Retrenchment, Retail Rebirth." *Chain Store Age* (Section 3) Consumer Enhancement & Development Supplement (January 1996): 6–10.

Ahmed, Munshi. "Retailers Go Global." *Fortune* (February 20, 1995): 102–108.

Allen, Randy L. "The Why and How of Global Retailing." *Business Quarterly* 57, 4 (Summer 1993): 117–122.

Andreoli, Teresa. "Value Retailers Take the Low-Income Road to New Heights." *Discount Store News* 35, 4 (February 19, 1996): 1, 19+.

Arien, Jeffrey. "New-Tier Retailers: Survival of the Fittest? *Discount Store News* 35, 5 (March 4, 1996): 38A.

Barth, Karen J., Kathleen McLaughlin, Christiana Smith Shi, and Nancy J. Karch. "Global Retailing: Tempting Trouble?" *McKinsey Quarterly* 1 (1996): 116–125.

Bergmann, Joan. "China Reassessed." *Discount Merchandiser* 35, 5 (May 1995): 94–97+.

Brookman, Faye. "Time for A Change." *Discount Store News* 34, 16 (August 21, 1995): A11–A12.

Donlon, J.P. "A Glass Act." *Chief Executive* 105 (July/August 1995): 40–49.

Green, Jeffrey S. "Retail for the Year 2000." *Discount Merchandiser* 33, 8 (August 1993): 28–30.

Herndon, Neil. "Wal-Mart Goes to Hong Kong, Looks at China." *Marketing News* 28, 24 (November 21, 1994): 2.

Kingdon, Mark D., and Janet Zhang. "Retailing in China: Poised for an Explosion." *Asian Executive Reports* 17, 1 (January 15, 1995): 9–15.

Longo, Don. "Taking the Road Not Yet Traveled." *Discount Store News* 34, 10 (May 15, 1995): 39–40.

Lyle, Ian. "Retailing and Distribution in the New Europe." *British Food Journal* 97, 6 (1995): 25–31.

Markowitz, Arthur. "State-of-the-Art Power Merchandising Propels Wal-Mart Into the Future." *Discount Store News* 33, 12 (June 20, 1994): 45–46.

Mary Beth Grover. "Tornado Watch." *Forbes* (June 22, 1992): 66–72.

Miller, Cyndee. "Retailers Do What They Must Do To Ring Up Sales." *Marketing News* 29, 11 (May 22, 1995): 1, 10+.

Minkoff, Jerry. "Short Takes." *Discount Merchandiser* 36, 2 (February 1996): 20.

Saporito, Bill. "And the Winner is Still Wal-Mart." *Fortune* (May 2, 1994): 62–70.

Sellers, Patricia. "Can Wal-Mart Get Back the Magic?" *Fortune* 133, 8 (April 29, 1996): 130–136.

Symonds, William C. "Invasion of the Retail Snatchers." *Business Week* (May 9, 1994): 12–14.

*Wal-Mart 1996 Annual Report.*

Yuan, Lim Lan. "Successful Retail Management in Asia." *Real Estate Finance* 12, 4 (Winter 1996): 59–64.

# *The NPD Group* CASE 24

The U.S. marketing research industry is becoming more worldly and cosmopolitan. Recently, two of the top 50 firms changed their names to include the word "worldwide." Others have made acquisitions of non-U.S. research firms or opened branch office operations in foreign countries. Still others have joined global networks of affiliated research firms. More global expansion is expected during the 1990s.

Now, more than ever, marketers need marketing research. The thrust of U.S. product and service companies into global markets will prove this. These firms are expanding into emerging markets in Eastern Europe, China, Africa, and Asia. They need data fast if they hope to be in the first wave of consumerism. Continental Europe is closer to home but just as inaccessible for marketers with solid brands and an interest in international markets, unless they know what to look for, and as more companies focus on cross-border marketing, they put new demands on marketing research firms.

The opportunities for research industry expansion overseas appear to be greater than those in the United States. Companies with a global presence are better positioned to meet the demand for identifying the optimal ways of marketing in foreign countries. For example, Gallup, a survey research company, has subsidiaries in 23 nations throughout the Americas, Europe, and Asia. While some are as established as Gallup U.K. (1938) and Gallup Canada (1942), others are as recent as Gallup China (1992), Gallup India (1993), Gallup Venezuela (1994), and Gallup Singapore (1996). This gives the firm a direct presence in countries that collectively account for over half (55 percent) of the world's population and over 70 percent of all global economic activity. Gallup first rose to prominence as a public opinion research firm through political polling and election forecasting. Although opinion research now accounts for only a small proportion of the company's annual sales, Gallup maintains a leadership position in this field, conducting more political and social research than any other firm in the world. Today, Gallup is a full-service market research firm whose survey research capabilities are used by the world's leading multinational corporations.

## THE NPD GROUP

The NPD Group is a privately held marketing research firm founded in 1953. In 1993, The NPD Group ranked seventh among the top 50 marketing/advertising/opinion research firms. Revenues in that year were $66 million, up 15.6 percent over 1992. In 1993, 23.8 percent of those revenues were from outside the United States.

The NPD Group is organized into four business units:

1. The U.S. Syndicated Services provides tracking databases covering store movement, consumer purchasing, and consumer attitude/awareness to industries such as toys, apparel, textiles, sporting goods, athletic footwear, petroleum products, home electronics, cameras,

restaurants, food service, and in-home food consumption. A variety of data collection methodologies is used in combination to produce these data bases.

2. U.S. Custom Services provides information based on a 300,000 household consumer panel of data (accessed by mail and/or telephone) and a number of proprietary analytical models used to forecast test market simulations, determine market structure, and optimize concept and product development. In 1993, several new products were introduced, including: BrandBuilder, a brand equity/loyalty model and tracking service, which joins behavioral and attitudinal data; E-Vol-ution, an early concept testing forecasting model; Concept Management System, a database system to facilitate cataloging and analyzing concept test results; and ESP Volumedics, a model to forecast sales volume potential.

3. ISL, a Canadian subsidiary with offices in Toronto and Montreal, was founded in 1946 and acquired by NPD in 1990. It is Canada's sixth largest research company. The services are very similar to those offered by NPD in the United States, including: the Consumer Panel of Canada, a purchase diary panel; a mail panel; and syndicated panel tracking of apparel, restaurants, auto parts, and sporting goods.

4. Worldwide was established in 1992 to facilitate expansion of NPD services, some through joint-venture agreements with foreign research firms. NPD has established four European offices (London, Paris, Nuremberg, and Milan) to operate its European Toy databases and mathematical modeling. In early 1993, NPD acquired a minority interest in ADR, a Hong Kong-based research firm that provides audits on durable goods similar to NPD's U.S. services. In mid-1993, NPD joined two firms in Mexico to develop a purchase diary panel service for that country. NPD also acquired a minority in a Brazilian purchase diary panel service and licensed its proprietary software, PowerView, to the Europanel group of companies.

In the United States, the NPD Group has 425 full-time employees in Port Washington, N.Y. Chicago, Cincinnati, Houston, and Hyattsville, MD. In 1993, new offices were opened in Greensboro, NC, and Los Angeles. Outside the United States, there are about 180 employees in Europe and Canada.

Over the years, the NPD Group has learned more than a few things about how to give its clients what they need, and on more than a few occasions it has broken new ground on its clients' behalf. It has even won patents for some of those breakthroughs, including in-home electronic data capture, bar-coded questionnaire techniques, and expert systems for computer coding responses to open-ended questions. The firm places a high value on innovation, but while technology has played an important role in moving its business forward, it is not the driving force behind NPD's success. Rather its success is the result of being able to help its clients.

Because the NPD Group is privately held, it does not have to pay out significant profits as dividends or to fund leverage-buyout debt; it can pick and choose its investment opportunities as it identifies them. NPD employees benefit from this arrangement too because of the way NPD shares its success. A group of 45 company officers impart both critical knowledge and a sense of stability. Today, 95 percent of its 1990 officers remain at NPD.

## THE COMPETITIVE TOP TEN

The NPD Group competes with such firms as the top-rated D&B Marketing Information Services' with substantial revenues and net incomes (Figs. 6.24–1 and 6.24–2) in 1993 of $1.9 billion, down 1.2 percent from 1992. This firm has independently operated

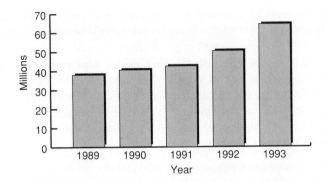

**FIGURE 6.24–1** The NPD Group Sales Revenue.

*Source:* Estimated from various sources.

marketing/advertising research subsidiaries, including Nielsen Marketing Research, IMS International, and Nielsen Media Research. Nielsen Marketing Research measures retail consumer purchases and related marketing factors for manufacturers and retailers of grocery, health and beauty aids, and other packaged and durable goods. It also measures and evaluates promotions; markets household panel-based information services; offers retail space management software; and provides geodemographic information services. The flagship service in the United States is ScanTrack, which offers weekly data on packaged goods sales, market shares, and retail prices from 3,000 UPC scanner-equipped supermarkets. About 3,700 drug and mass merchandiser stores were added to create a service, Procision, for marketers of health and beauty aid products. A companion service, ScanTrack Electronic Household Panel (based on 40,000 households), provides packaged goods purchase data via in-home UPC scanning. In other countries around the world, Nielsen offers a variety of services, including services similar to ScanTrack and Electronic Household Panel, diary-type purchase panels, ad hoc survey research, and television audience measurement services.

The NPD Group also competes with second ranked Information Resources Inc., (IRI) Chicago, IL, which is a public company founded in 1978. In 1993, this firm had revenues of $334.5 million, up 21.1 percent over 1992. About 15 percent of 1993 revenues were from outside the United States. IRI provides marketing research services in 28 countries. Its business breaks down into four areas:

**1.** Syndicated Services Division includes InfoScan, a syndicated market tracking service, is based on a sample of 3,450 grocery, drug, and mass merchandiser stores, where product

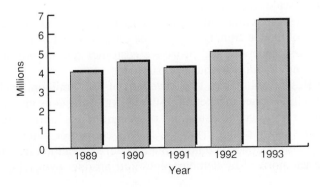

**FIGURE 6.24–2** The NPD Group Net Income.

*Source:* Estimated from various sources.

movement data are captured via UPC scanning. The Infoscan service also includes a sample of 67,000 households whose purchases are collected at store checkout scanners. This division accounts for 54 percent of total revenues.

In 1993, IRI started a roll-out of QScan/InfoScan Census, which provides data from all stores in a chain, rather than from a sample. The conversion of the service started in 1994. Census data allows for the use of store-by-store information for micro-marketing applications, especially the grocery industry's Efficient Consumer Response initiative, where IRI has developed a number of services, including LogiCNet, Catalina Information Resources, and Customer Marketing Resources.

2. The Testing Services Division includes BehaviorScan and related marketing plan testing services, which is a group of eight electronic (single-source) test minimarkets, where, in addition to measuring product movement via checkout scanners, IRI has the ability to target television commercials to specific households in a controlled environment across six markets. This division accounts for 6.6 percent of total revenues.

3. IRI Software provides decision support software, which includes the EXPRESS-based software line, with products such as DataServer, SalesPartner, BrandPartner, Executive Information Services, Sales Management System, and Financial Management System; and retailer products such as Apollo Space Management software. Software accounts for 31.8 percent of total revenues.

4. All other information services accounted for 7.6 percent of revenues in 1993.

Internationally in 1993, IRI completed a joint venture with SECODIP and GfX in France, expanded its U.K. staff, and made two acquisitions: Panel Pazar in Turkey and Market Trends Inc. in Puerto Rico.

Worldwide, IRI has about 3,600 full-time employees and 2,200 part-time employees in 11 U.S. client service offices, plus offices in the United Kingdom, France, Germany, and the Netherlands.

Another NPD Group competitor is sixth ranked Maritz Marketing Research Inc. (MMRI) with research-only revenues in 1993 of $74.4 million, up 6.7 percent over 1992. MMRI provides customer satisfaction measurement and custom research to consumer and business-to-business marketers. There are full-service offices in Chicago, Los Angeles, Minneapolis, St. Louis, and Clark, NJ. Additional client service offices are in Atlanta and New York. St. Louis also headquarters the firm's agricultural/industrial research divisions and telecommunications division, which operates client-dedicated telephone centers in five locations. MMRI's Automotive Research Group provides syndicated, custom, and large-scale customer satisfaction studies for the auto industry. Services include product clinics, consumer and dealer research, and QF/VOC (Quality Function Deployment/Voice of the Customer) studies. The group also offers proactive identification of customer dissatisfaction, and proactive customer relationship management through outbound and inbound telebusiness support.

Eighth ranked NFO Research Inc. had 1993 revenues of $51.9 million, up 10.2 percent from 1992. NFO is a full-service marketing research firm using consumer panels for conducting product testing, concept testing, tracking studies, and attitude, awareness, and usage studies using custom surveys. NFO's consumer panel is the largest in the United States with over 450,000 households (over one million individuals). Panel households are categorized by demographics and product ownership, allowing for mail and/or phone surveys of target groups. The company maintains two telephone interviewing centers with a total of 150 equipped stations.

Ninth ranked Elrick & Lavidge Inc. (E&L) of Atlanta, GA, had 1993 revenues of $47.1 million, up 0.6 percent over 1992. Revenues are divided: 59 percent from Elrick & Lavidge, a custom full-service marketing research firm, and 41 percent from Quick Test Opinion Centers, an independently operated and managed field service company, which runs a national network of 40 data collection (mall sites and focus group) facilities. The firm operates six central telephone interviewing facilities and one dedicated TELSAM facility with a total of about 300 equipped interviewing stations. Elrick & Lavidge specializes in survey research for the consumer products, telecommunications, and financial services industries through full-service offices in Atlanta, Chicago, New York, San Francisco, Dallas, and Kansas City. In addition to a full range of qualitative and quantitative services, E&L has several proprietary marketing research services.

Market Facts, Inc., the tenth largest marketing research firm, had revenues of $45.6 million in 1993, up 12 percent over 1992, not including Canadian operations. Market Facts is a custom-marketing research company. One of its principal businesses is Consumer Mail Panel, a facility that includes over 400,000 U.S. households. A number of syndicated or packaged products have been developed from the panel to serve the needs of niche markets such as health care and financial services. The company markets the Conversion Model, Marketest 2000 (a volume forecasting model), and in 1993 it launched Brand Vision, a brand tracking system. The National Showcase was also launched in 1993. It provides weekly omnibus studies in a network of national mall interviewing facilities.

## THE NPD GROUP INTERNATIONAL EXPANSION

Recently, the NPD Group announced that it and two leading European research companies would offer a new multinational research panel for North America and Europe. This offers international marketers access to data from more than a half million households throughout Europe and North America. The product is a joint venture of three marketing research companies: SOFRES of France, GfK of Germany, and the NPD Group of the United States, SOFRES, GfK, and NPD have already worked together successfully for many years on retail panels, modeling and data delivery systems. Together they have a wealth of experience in managing large-scale databases and in servicing clients in all major countries. NPD and its partners are taking on one of the biggest challenges facing any business that markets products or services in more than one country: collecting reliable information on international markets.

SOFRES is the fifth largest market and opinion research group in the world. Founded in France in 1963, the group specializes in providing all types of information necessary for marketing and communication decisions. Currently established in 18 countries (Europe and Asia-Pacific), the group mainly focuses on four business: ad hoc studies, consumer panels, advertising expenditure measurement/news monitoring, and media audience measurement.

GfK is headquartered in Nurnburg, Germany, and has offices and associates in 25 countries. Europe's second largest market research company, and third worldwide, GfK is the world leader in the consumer durables area. For the new panel, GfK has built up Consumer Mail Panel databases, has developed CATI survey techniques, and has undertaken a number of multinational research surveys.

The NPD Group's local European office is in Paris. As with the overall firm, the office specializes in providing custom and syndicated market research, and associated computer software-based information management systems, for understanding and analyzing consumer behavior, and predicting and tracking product success.

Different from other panels being assembled to meet global research needs, the new panel utilizes current consumer panels, giving marketers immediate access to participating households across Europe and North America. The panel is currently comprised of over 200,000 households in Europe, as well as 350,000 households in the United States and Canada.

This is a breakthrough for business that need to look at consumer behavior across countries. In total, this massive resource of more than 500,000 households can be tapped into with consistent methodologies to provide consumer responses to virtually all marketing questions that require multicountry information.

This venture provides all the special benefits of consumer panels, including: large sample sizes for tracking of slow-moving, low-penetration markets; screening for narrow targets; product and concept tests in home environments, without interviewer intrusions; and the ability to carry out repetitive studies for tracking changes. In addition, the service supplements its panel data with most data capture methods such as mail, telephone, and new electronic media. This provides clients with the opportunity to benefit from the most cost-effective approach. Marketers can initiate complex multicountry studies with a single phone call to any one of the local client service offices.

## NEED FOR A GLOBAL CAPABILITY

There is an increasing expectation from clients that a marketing research company will have global capabilities. International research is growing at 10 percent a year. This is due to the rise in the number of international products and brands. Clients want data that is standard across Europe. American interest in Europe has resulted in some overseas marketing research firms being acquired by U.S. companies. By the end of the century, the demand will be for worldwide data, which is why many research firms are moving into Eastern Europe and creating partnerships that take them into the Far East.

To maintain its leadership in the marketing research industry, the NPD Group needs an aggressive international expansion strategy. This may require new products and services, and perhaps, whole new ways of approaching its business solicitation activities. What marketing strategy would you advise the NPD Group to pursue in creating and marketing its products and services? What specific price, distribution, promotion, and product elements would you propose for international expansion and why? How would you deal with the growth competition from such firms as IRI and all the others in the research industry top ten?

## Sources

"1995 Directory of International Research Firms." *Marketing News* 29, 16 (July 31, 1995): 15–25.

Bond, Cathy. "Going for the Global Goal." *Marketing* (February 23, 1995): 33–34.

Caminiti, Susan. "What The Scanner Knows About You." *Fortune* (December 3, 1990): 51–52.

Drew, Jo. "Business Information in Western Europe and the EU." *Library Management* 16, 5 (1995): 52–58.

Fletcher, Karen. "Asking the Right Questions." *Marketing* (May 11, 1995): III–VII.

Honomichl, Jack. "Top 50 U.S. Marketing/Ad/Opinion Research Firms Profiled." *Marketing News* 28, 12 (June 6, 1994): H2–H16+.

Honomichl, Jack. "The Honomichl 50: Three Factors Drive Growth of Top 50 Research Firms Top 50 U.S. Marketing/Ad/Opinion Research Firms Profiled." *Marketing News* 27, 12 (June 7, 1993): H2–H18+.

Honomichl, Jack. "The Honomichl 50: Spending for Research Shows 3.5% Real Growth Top 50 Research Firms Profiled." *Marketing News* 25, 11 (May 27, 1991): H2–H34.

"Market research: Data wars." *Economist* 336, 7924 (July 22, 1995): 60–62.

The NPD Group promotional materials.

"Top 50 U.S. Marketing/Ad/Opinion Research Firms Profiled." *Marketing News* 29, 12 (June 5, 1995): H2–H16+.

---

# *Apple Computer Japan* CASE 25

By 1992, the personal computer (PC) had produced a worldwide revolution in information technology that created a $55 billion hardware business and another $34 billion in software and peripherals. In that year, the four largest PC manufacturers were IBM, Apple, Compaq, and NEC, accounting for about 38 percent of worldwide unit sales. PCs had become a global business, with more than 200 players from a dozen countries. While U.S. firms had more than 61 percent of global revenues, small Taiwanese companies, such as Acer, were gaining share in the very low end of the market and Japanese firms were the biggest players in portable computers, the fastest growing PC segment.

In the United States, IBM-compatible computers, with which Apple's machines are incompatible, accounted for over 80 percent of PCs sold. Increasingly, Apple was having to match its rivals' prices just to survive in the United States. However, Apple's overseas prospects were much brighter, particularly in Japan.

## PC MARKETING IN JAPAN

Though American companies invented the industry, continue to drive its innovation, and dominate everywhere else in the world, they had just 15 percent of Japan's $6 billion market by the end of 1992, with Japanese electronics giants having the rest. Apple Computer had done the best over the years, with its Macintosh accounting for 8.3 percent of the 2.2 million PCs sold in Japan in 1992, which was good for third place. NEC was dominant, with 53.4 percent, followed by Fujitsu, with just 9.8 percent. Toshiba was in fourth place, with 7.6 percent (see Figure 6.25–1). Still, Apple's share in Japan was only slightly greater than half of what it had in the United States. IBM and two of America's leading makers of IBM-compatibles, Compaq Computer and Dell Computer, were also struggling in the Japanese market. Together they delivered a little more than 6 percent of the PCs sold in 1992. IBM accounted for 6.1 percent of the market.

Although faced with this unusual competitive situation, America's biggest PC makers thought the Japanese firms were suddenly vulnerable in the new graphics technology areas and in hardware and software innovations. The Americans began the attack with new more powerful machines, a new Japanese-language version of Microsoft's hot-selling Windows interface, and sharply lower prices.

Compaq and Dell, which both only entered the market in 1992, forced the Japanese to slash prices. IBM Japan became more aggressive too, lowering prices on a family of machines designed and made in Japan to suit local tastes. Apple publicly set the ambitious goal of doubling annual sales in Japan to $1 billion by 1995. However, that would not be easy. The Japanese PC market is unusual, especially compared with the rest of the world. The most obvious differences stem from the unique nature of the Japanese language, which requires that PCs display and manipulate *kanji* pictograms rather than the Roman alphabet. In the early days of the PC industry, the IBM-compatible PCs so prevalent in the United States and Europe could not handle kanji. So each of the major Japanese computer manufactures, including NEC, Fujitsu, and Toshiba, among others, "Japanized" the standard PC hardware and operating system software for themselves in different and often incompatible ways.

As a result, software developers had to tailor slightly different versions of their word processors, spreadsheets, and the like to fit each manufacturer's machine. Moreover, even if users of the different Japanese PCs loaded them with the appropriate version of the same software application, say *Ichitaro* (the biggest-selling Japanese word processor) or Lotus 1-2-3, they still could not share documents or spreadsheets by swapping floppy disks. That was because NEC, Fujitsu, and Toshiba stored data in fundamentally different ways. The upshot of all this incompatibility: higher prices for both

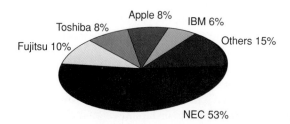

**FIGURE 6.25–1** Japan's PC Market 1992 Units.

*Source:* Estimated from various sources.

hardware and software, sluggish development of PC networks, lackluster innovation, and much less choice and flexibility for customers.

Language differences created another anomaly. Japan is not a typing culture (versus the West). Many Japanese are unaccustomed to using a keyboard. Again, that is because the Japanese language draws upon thousands of pictograms rather than on a limited number of phonetic characters to represent words. Typewriters are not practical, because they would require a keyboard as big as a desk.

Computers made typing in Japanese possible but still daunting. To produce a kanji, a user must hit several keystrokes to enter the sound of the desired character and then choose from a menu that appeared on the screen displaying various kanji that sound the same but have different meanings. The Japanese word *kisha*, for example, could mean newspaper reporter, train, one's company, or come back to the office. Each meaning is represented by a different kanji. To type the right one takes four keystrokes.

Then there is the *wahpuro* phenomenon. Many Japanese office workers who can get past keyboard phobia make do with machines that can process words but are incapable of other computing chores such as analyzing financial models, making charts, or searching databases. Indeed, the word wahpuro derives from "word processor" and describes portable devices that are more akin to electric typewriters than PCs. Because producing wahpuros, which sell for about half as much as regular PCs, is a good business for computer makers, they are reluctant to drop the prices of their more powerful machines lest they cut into that existing market.

There are also profound differences in how PCs are distributed in Japan. Most are sold in retail stores, many of which are financed or owned outright by manufacturers. One reason NEC is so successful is that it has by far the largest number of dealers, some 7,000 of them. Many stores carry competing brands, but unlike their counterparts in the United States and Europe, they rarely discount. Mail-order distribution has not caught on either, nor do many manufacturers sell directly to corporate customers.

While Japan has the world's second-largest economy and a well-educated population, the number of PCs per capita is less than half that of the U.S. (see Figure 6.25–2). Prices are roughly 50 percent higher than in the rest of the world, averaging $2,900 for a typical machine with color screen and hard-disk drive. The combination of high prices and the lack of compatibility has created the most distinctive attribute of Japan's PC market, which is stagnation. While worldwide PC sales rose at double-digit rates in recent years, the market in Japan has been more or less flat. In 1992, it actually shrank 6 percent.

U.S. hardware and software manufacturers, and even a few of their Japanese competitors, think something is wrong with this decline. The problem is incompatibility, and they have been working on ways to solve it. In 1991, IBM perfected a bilingual version of Microsoft's DOS, the standard operating system that controls about 80 percent of PCs elsewhere in the world. DOS/V, as the Japanese version is called, enables any standard PC to prepare or search documents with kanji characters, the Western alphabet, or both. IBM licensed the software to other PC manufacturers, including Dell and Toshiba, but so far only about 6 percent of PCs sold in Japan use it, mainly because it only replicates features that proprietary Japanese PCs have offered all along. Apple has sold bilingual Macintoshes for several years, hence its relative success.

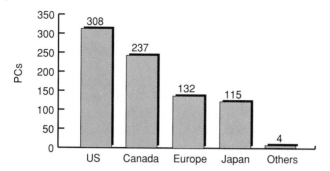

FIGURE 6.25–2 Who Has PCs Worldwide (PCs per 1,000 persons).

*Source:* Estimated from various sources.

Microsoft began a much more ambitious assault on incompatibility in 1993. The centerpiece of the strategy was a new Japanese-language version of Windows, the easy-to-use, add-on operating system software for IBM-compatible machines. Windows is highly popular in the rest of the world, where is has sold as many as one million copies a month. In Japan, however, only 440,000 copies of Windows were sold by mid-1993, largely because these earlier versions did not handle kanji well.

Microsoft decided to go all out to promote Windows in Japan because the software offered a big chance to collect more revenues per machine. In 1993, Microsoft unveiled its new product, called Windows 3.1J. It was fully bilingual and could run on just about any manufacturer's hardware, including NECs proprietary 9800 line, as well as IBM-compatible PCs. Windows 3.1J looked like a hit, judging from early reports that Microsoft took orders for 65,000 copies in two days and estimated that it would sell a million units in 1993.

American hardware vendors also hoped to ride the Windows' boom. In comparative advertisements, Compaq critiqued NEC's market-leading 9800 family of PCs. NEC responded with ads warning customers not to buy a PC "with the steering wheel on the wrong side," a reference to Compaq's reliance on American software technology.

While IBM's parent in the United States has had differences with Microsoft in the past, IBM Japan embraced Windows 3.1J with a passion. IBM wanted to use its impressive array of portable and desktop computers, plus Windows and rock-bottom prices to wean customers away both from NEC and from wahpuros. The result was IBM's sales surge in 1993 from 133,000 units to 200,000, despite competition from other U.S. PC makers.

Overlooked in all the excitement over Windows is Apple, which has methodically built a business that many American PC companies admit they would like to emulate. Early on, Apple hired its management team in Japan, sensing that Japanese would better know how to tackle the market than would expatriate managers. These executives cultivated a strong network of dealers and burnished Apple's image as an innovator.

Apple is skeptical that the new IBM-compatible PC offerings will be runaway successes right away, despite all the enthusiasm for Windows. According to Apple, the key to success in Japan is distribution. But to attract good dealers and distributors the product must be unique. To be successful, the American PCs with Windows must differentiate themselves, especially if the Japanese manufacturers start selling them.

NEC seems to be hedging its bets by promising to support Windows 3.1J on some of the machines in its 9800 series of PCs. They would not be fully compatible, however, although these machines will run the same applications as other Windows machines, floppy disks created on them will still be unreadable by PCs from other makers.

NEC executives do not think Windows will catch on quickly. It would be surprised if Windows captured 40 percent of the Japanese market by 1995. According to NEC, the problem is twofold: first, Windows machines, which require a hard-disk drive and a lot of memory, are much more expensive than the stripped-down models most Japanese by and second, NEC 9800 users can choose from more than 15,000 Japanese-language application programs, versus 450 for Windows.

Other Japanese manufacturers, however, seem to recognize that Windows offers their last, best chance to cut into NECs enormous lead. Fujitsu will continue to support its proprietary models but will emphasize other PCs that are fully compatible with Windows. To better compete on price, Fujitsu also plans to import low-cost machines made by independent manufacturers in Taiwan. Toshiba, the other big Japanese PC maker, will try to leverage its success in the United States and Europe, where its IBM-compatible portable and laptop machines are the biggest sellers. Less than one month after Windows 3.1J arrived, Toshiba unveiled a new family of desktop models tailored to that operating system.

For now, though, American PC vendors are confident. Not only is the software finally available to help them attack the Japanese market with a coherent strategy, but, in addition, the strengthening yen lets them further undercut the prices of their Japanese counterparts. The Americans can be sure, however, that the Japanese PC makers will not let market share slip away easily.

## APPLE'S JAPANESE HISTORY

Apple's worldwide sales have been good (Fig. 6.25–3 and 6.25–4). Apple's sales in Japan have been very good. From a few thousand units in 1988, Apple Macintosh sales exploded to 56,000 in 1990, 120,000 in 1991, 180,000 in 1992, and 220,000 were expected in 1993. Market share was expected to leap accordingly from less than 1 percent of the Japanese market in 1988 to about 9 percent in 1993. And, Mac sales are soaring despite a slumping market overall.

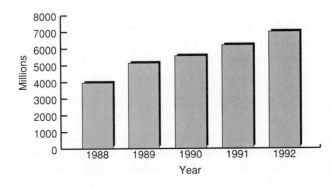

**FIGURE 6.25–3** Apple Computer Revenues.

*Source: Apple Computer 1992 Annual Report.*

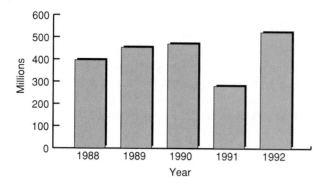

**FIGURE 6.25–4** Apple Computer Net Income.

*Source: Apple Computer 1992 Annual Report.*

Apple just may achieve a high level of growth thanks to distribution deals that could move it into Japan's lucrative corporate market. By mid-1993, five major Japanese companies had signed up to sell Macs, including business-equipment giant Brother Industries, stationery leader Kokuyo, Mitsubishi, Sharp, and Minolta.

But Japan represents much more than a new batch of customers for Apple. The company's Japanese connection is part of its core strategy to become a player in the world's gigantic consumer-electronics market and to pull away from the United States, where PC makers are fighting for modest profits and tiny gains in market share. The strategy: working with Japan's manufacturing giants, Apple will put its distinctive software into a new generation of consumer-electronics products. To execute this strategy, Apple executives have spent a good part of their time on Asian trips building blue-chip alliances. The result, Sony Corp. manufactures Apple's smallest laptop, the Power-Book 100; Sharp Electronics Corp. makes Newton, Apple's electronic organizer; and, Toshiba Corp. manufactures a new, portable, color multimedia Mac that combines video, text, and sound.

With the deals, Apple gains a competitive leg up on two of the computer industry's megatrends: the move toward ever smaller computers and, separately, toward computer-cum-consumer-electronics machines. Indeed, while Compaq, Dell, IBM, and AST fight another vicious price war, Apple marches toward whole new markets.

However, Apple's strategy has big risks. With all its business activities, the firm could find itself overloaded and distracted. And, by making its distinctive software so widely available, Apple could dilute its appeal. There is also the worry that Apple, which is manufacturing fewer of its own computers, may lose control of its destiny even as it is trying to make headway in the consumer electronics field. But taking risks is better than failure, which until recently was Apple's experience in Japan. Apple was there for almost 10 years without success other than novelty sales. It was doing everything wrong. Indeed, Apple did not hit its stride until 1990, thanks mostly to the new Japanese-language software for the Mac, and some new Japanese executives who were put in charge.

## PC BUYERS IN JAPAN

Apple, Compaq, IBM, NEC, and several other major computer manufacturers still think there is an untapped market with enormous potential in Japan. And they may be right. At the end of 1992, there were 80 million households in Japan that did not own

PCs. Despite previous failures to penetrate the home market, PC manufacturers began enlisting the help of the Japanese mass-merchandisers, promising plug-and-play capability and generous software bundles. And, while the average household income of families who own PCs in 1992 was much higher than the average, vendors hoped to start selling into homes with incomes in the less affluent range.

Buyers of PCs can be divided into four broad categories: business, government, education, and individual/home. Each customer group has somewhat different PC selection criteria and different means for purchasing computers. The largest segment is business, with roughly 60 percent of the units and 70 percent of the total revenue. Individual business PC buyers are usually unsophisticated about the technology, and worried most about service, support, and compatibility. Brand name is especially important as are full-service computer dealers.

The education and individual/home markets are driven by different channels and somewhat different criteria. While most schools have limited budgets for computers, the primary concern for most educators is the availability of appropriate software. The individual home market is a complicated mixture of people who buy computers for business work at home, and those who buy the computer for nonwork, home uses.

## APPLE'S FUTURE IN JAPAN

Worldwide, the future may be one in which people in the industrialized countries such as Japan have access to all forms of information, such as news, television, business data, wherever and whenever they want, regardless of whether they use a hand-held personal digital assistant, a kind of computerized mobile telephone, or a PC. By 2000, the consumer-electronics, television, telecommunication, entertainment, and news industries could merge into a single worldwide market, with sales of $35 trillion a year.

During the next decade, most information, including television, is expected to assume the same digital form as computer data. The spread of mobile telephones is already bringing the idea of anywhere computing in its wake. Some of the latest laptop computers can already communicate over the airwaves. More powerful chips seem certain to put enormous computing power into machines small enough to fit into the palm of the hand. More powerful software will make computers of any size and shape easier to use. The cost of storing, transmitting, manipulating, and analyzing data will drop sharply.

One thing seems certain, the new computer industry will never return to the stability or high profits of the old one. Too many companies now have access to the technology, and to the customer. As the PC industry collides with the telecommunications, publishing, and consumer-electronics industries, there will be many battles over standards. The search for alliances, such as the recent one between Apple and IBM, will become more popular. Launching new products will involve even greater risks. Nobody really knows how many people will want so much information at their fingertips, what price they will pay for it, or what they will want to do with it.

Much of the battle in the PC industry will be fought over software. Future operating systems, which provide PCs with their basic instructions, must be able to manage handwriting, video, graphics, voice, and text, all of which will be flowing over computer networks. What is not clear is which company will provide that operating system and all the associated applications programs. Also, a huge variety of applications software, the programs people use to do their work, will be needed. Sophisticated word processing, presentation development, and spreadsheet programs will merge into integrated work tools with graphical and user interfaces that include voice recognition and artificial intelligence functions.

For such a dynamic and volatile market, Apple needs a marketing strategy that builds on its historical strengths in user-friendly software and hardware combinations, but at the same time avoiding competition based on price. While Apple's plans to move into platforms that do not look like traditional computers may be a good idea in concept, to date the firm has not had any real successes to brag about. In the United States, Apple's harsh reality is that it is selling machines based mostly on price in direct competition with IBM-compatibles that run nearly all the software an Apple machine uses. While overseas, Apple is better able to capitalize on its user-friendly strength and all-American image, particularly in countries as Japan.

What marketing strategy would you advise Apple to pursue in Japan? What specific price, distribution, promotion, and product elements would you propose and why? How do those suggestions relate to what you know about the competitive environment in Japan? How do your recommendations deal with the growth competition in the Japanese market and Apple's unique place in that market?

## Sources

*Apple Computer Company 1992 Annual Report.*

"The Computer Industry." *The Economist* (February 27, 1993) a special insert survey.

Depke, Deidre A., and Richard Brandt. "PCs: What the Future Holds." *Business Week* (August 12, 1991): 58–64.

Gross, Neil, and Kathy Rebello. "Apple? Japan Can't Say No." *Business Week* (June 29, 1992): 32–33.

Holyoke, Larry. "Apple's Man in Japan Steps Up the Mac Attack." *Business Week* (October, 1994): 117–118.

Kuper, Andrew. "Apple's Plan to Survive and Grow." *Fortune* (May 4, 1992): 68–72.

Rebello, Kathy. "You've Got Company Mac." *Business Week* (March 22, 1993): 34.

Schlender, Breton R. "The Future of the PC." *Fortune* (August 26, 1991): 40–48.

# Winston Management Services

Executives succeed in a highly competitive marketplace by nourishing their organization's capacity to adapt to external and internal pressures. Sometimes this involves calling on the advice and help of management consultants. Ideally, these business advisors are objective, independent, and trustworthy, experts in their area, analytically sophisticated, and focused on problem solving rather than on organizational politics. During the consulting engagement, executives and consultants interact to define problems, analyze situations, and make recommendations about the solutions to organizational ills. Thus, consultants engage in a series of phases, including entry, contracting, diagnosis, feedback, planning, implementation, and evaluation.

When critical experience in a particular area is not available in-house, firms many times look to outside services to help them with their business operations. These companies consider hiring a consultant when they identify a need for experience, objectivity, analytical skills, full-time attention, or innovation. Certain steps need to be taken in order to select a qualified consultant. A preliminary screening investigates the types of clients served and the kinds of projects handled. Face-to-face discussions are held with prospective consulting firms to determine whether a positive client-consultant relationship is possible. Consulting firms are normally required to submit written proposals that detail experience, programs, and estimated fees. Once the contract is signed, management at the client firm monitors and measures the consultant's performance so that projects do not stray from their course.

Businesses use consultants not only for their innovative brainpower but also because it makes economic sense. Consultants are a cost-efficient source of new ideas. Any firm can avoid the cost and time involved in learning a new facet of the industry. There is also a growing trend of subcontracting work when an organization does not want to incur the overhead of hiring more full-time people. Instead, they hire consultants on a part-time basis to get greater flexibility. In this way, the business can staff-up quickly in times of fast growth and cut back if activity recedes without the regulatory burdens of laying off full-time employees. For this flexibility, companies are willing to pay consultants a premium.

## THE CONSULTING INDUSTRY

More and more people are entering the consulting field as a means to utilize their valuable brainpower, expertise, and experience. Consulting is now an acceptable career path for individuals at any point in their careers. Between 20 to 25 percent of MBA graduates from the leading schools choose consulting for their first job. At the other end of the spectrum, retirees are adding to the consulting ranks. After successful industry careers, these consultants contribute their experience and wisdom to the benefit of clients. They also extend their productive working lives via consulting rather than choosing the route of total retirement. In between these two extremes are those in mid-career who choose consulting after obtaining some job and industry experience. They enter the field as a next step in their career development. Consulting offers them an opportunity to gain experience working in other industries while tackling a wide range of problem situations. These full-time consultants are joined by hundreds of thousands of part-timers who are looking for an alternative outlet for their skills. They work full-time jobs but want the satisfaction and compensation that come from consulting work.

The size of this industry is diffult to determine because consulting is now part of every field. Estimates of the size of the business exceeded $60 billion in 1995. However, that definition of consulting only includes management and administrative services, public relations, management consulting, economic and sociological research, and unnamed "other" consulting services. It does not encompass the billions of dollars in management consulting provided by accounting firms; nor does it include engineering consulting, technical computer consulting, architectural consulting, or any of the consulting done in all of the other occupations. Nor do these numbers include the enormous amount of part-time consulting that occurs but is not reported to government agencies. It is probably safe to assume that total consulting revenues are nearly double that reported for business consulting or approximately $100 billion.

A broad definition of the consulting industry includes an estimated 850,000 to 1,100,000 full-time people. That total number represents a little less than 1 percent of the workforce in the United States. The number of part-time consultants is unknown, although they probably equal the number of full-time consultants. Thus, it is highly possible that about 2 percent of the working population engages in some kind of consulting activity.

Consulting is no longer dominated by a few large firms. There are many new ones and solo practitioners making significant inroads into shares of the large operations. But, with millions of businesses and non-profit organizations, a tremendous market exists for consulting firms of all sizes.

During the last 10 years, business consulting has grown between 10 and 20 percent annually. It is expected to continue to expand as more organizations from all industry sectors utilize the special expertise of consulting firms, and more professionals are expected to seek consulting positions. Consulting services that were once viewed as luxuries are now considered necessities. Public relations, market research, and human resource training are essential to the success of many firms. Services such as these enable businesses to maintain their edge in the face of rising competitive pressures. Technological advances have also spurred demand for consultants because new technology requires advice about its selection, purchase, and use.

Social and technological changes continue to ease entry into consulting. Personal computers make it more practical for consultants to work at home. With more than 50,000 computer programs and 2,000 computerized databases to choose from, consultants are better able to stay on top of the information explosion. More efficient office tools, such as computer-aided design, help make consultants more productive and less expensive, especially for smaller business. Computers also put these tools at the disposal of small consulting firms, which could previously not afford them.

## WHO USES CONSULTANTS?

Clients hire a consultant because they have neither the time nor the personnel to do the project, and when they cannot do something because they lack the necessary knowledge, they are requesting problem-solving services.

**Consultants are hired to:**

1. Provide need extra help for a period of time. In essence, they help clients do their work by supplementing skills they already possess.
2. Provide specialized expertise unavailable within the organization. This category represents the most common type of consultant: the expert hired to solve difficult problems. Small- and medium-sized clients offer the greatest opportunities for this type of consulting. Unlike large organizations, they cannot afford a full-time staff of experts and must rely on outside advice.
3. Obtain an opinion they cannot or will not get from an insider. Clients in large organizations frequently use consultants for political, organizational, and personal reasons.
4. Override the influences of large, highly structured organizations. Some clients turn to outsiders because large bureaucracies make access to needed internal expertise difficult. Reluctantly, the client finds it more efficient to work directly with outside consultants.
5. Obtain an outsider's evaluation of client company performance, plans, decisions, or internal conflicts. Consultants provide objectivity, thoroughness, and competence, which adds credibility to a client's plans and bolsters the confidence of the bosses, subordinates, and the public. However, some clients want the appearance, but not the existence, of objectivity because they seek consultants who will approve their preconceived ideas.
6. Get someone to take the political heat in sensitive areas. Some clients hire consultants to do their dirty work, such as firing a subordinate while they maintain a "nice guy" image.
7. Obtain the help of someone who will rescue them from losing their job or ruining their career. Some clients painfully experience the Peter Principle by rising to the level of their incompetence. Rather than muddle their chances for continued success, they call in consultants to help them out of their predicament.
8. Provide clients with needed stimulation or specialized training. Consultants often serve as catalysts for organizations that need an infusion of new ideas. Clients will use consultants to revitalize employee thinking, to keep them on the edge of new practices, and to develop their employees' working effectiveness.

## INDUSTRY CHANGES

The specialization of knowledge and expertise is increasing. The gap between specialist and generalist is widening. This gap is a boom for consultants because businesses need both specialist to solve specific difficult problems and skilled generalists to help executives understand the totality and complexity of the big picture.

After decades of using consultants, clients have become much more sophisticated about what those consultants can do and how to advantageously use them. Although clients with little experience with consultants still favor the generalist, experienced clients want specialists. They look for particular skills and information to solve specific company problems. Consequently, clients chose one consultant over another based on perceived expertise in an area of need. They desire consultants who know their field so well that they represent 90 percent of the solution just by walking in the door. Thus, for individual consultants or consulting firms to succeed in the 1990s, they must be recognized by clients as experts in their field.

These changed expectations have altered the traditional client and consultant relationship. Clients are moving away from a reliance on only one consulting firm. Instead, they are developing a reserve of consultants with different specialties, allowing new specialists to emerge and prosper. Understandably, the number of solo practitioners and small firms has grown more rapidly than the larger generalist firms, which have held steady or dropped in size during the last decade. As clients' needs become more specialized, as the world becomes more complex, and as clients look to more than one consultant for answers, the opportunities for consultants will continue to grow.

## WINSTON MANAGEMENT SERVICES

Winston Management Services is a management services firm specializing in innovative approaches to business management and planning. Its mission is to provide its clients with a significant competitive advantage through the use of strategies based on business building analysis tools and technologies. It claims to provide the finest in analytical and research-based business services and products designed to help its clients permanently increase their sales and profits. Its offerings are distinctive in their price/value relationship and consistent with the firm's commitment to excellence in the area of business planning and analysis. In all its client work, Winston Management Services is committed to viewing its business services and products as an extension of its own focus on the utilization of science and technology in the pursuit of competitive advantage. This continuing commitment has led to the development of a client support environment that is distinguished for its willingness to ask the right questions and provide responses and direction that are relevant to clients' needs.

Today's increasingly competitive business climate requires a high level of management expertise and sensitivity to how the superior use of business planning and strategy services can boost sales and profits. Companies needing these services benefit by relying on a firm that is dedicated to quality performance and expertise in this highly complex area.

Winston Management Services' dedication and performance are recognized in the corporate community. Its commitment to quality and its consistent record of success are reflected in its list of loyal clients. Through the staff it employs, the projects it conducts, and the sales and profit results it achieves, it is a major resource for companies interested in utilizing the latest approaches, tools, and technologies for generating incremental sales and profits.

The firm mainly manages projects through ad hoc teams of professionals who are assembled to address the specific objectives of each client assignment. Clients include medium- to large-size firms in the United States and Europe.

### Services and Products

The specific Winston Management Services business lines include services in the areas of: strategy analysis and planning; sales research, analysis, and forecasting; marketing research; and strategic decision support systems.

Products include: MAXIMA, which is a proprietary sales, marketing, and financial planning and analysis system; DWMS, which is a data warehouse management system; QIAMS, which is a qualitative information analysis and modeling system.

(The appendix to this case contains more details on each of these service and product offerings.)

### Clients

Winston Management Services' clients are consumer and business-to-business firms headquartered in the United States and Europe, including American Express, BIC, First Fidelity Bank, Hilton Hotels, IBM, Kmart, Levi Strauss, Mattel, Microsoft, and dozens of others.

### Personnel

Winston Management Services is staffed by five regular staff members and an ad hoc group of professionals who are hired on a project-by-project basis depending on the client assignment. The regular company staff has extensive training and experience in business analysis and planning; decision support systems; qualitative and quantitative marketing research; and operations management with consumer and business-to-business firms. Winston Management Services utilizes a large number of temporary staff to support its permanent employees. These temporary staff members include business and marketing research freelancers, statistical and database programmers, systems design specialists, and a pool of academic professors with a variety of specialties in strategic planning, marketing, decision support systems, and business analysis and forecasting.

Winston Management Services does not maintain a series of offices. Rather, it operates as a virtual corporation in that it has only one formal location, with the remainder of the firm existing wherever its regular staff members happen to be. This one location is not even an office in an ordinary sense because it represents a place where the general manager of the firm does most of his work while coordinating the regular and ad hoc staff members. This general manager is responsible for most client interfaces, new business solicitations, and quality control of the project work.

### Performance

Winston Management Services is a privately held consulting business owned by its regular staff members and a small number of outside investors. Since being incorporated in 1990, the firm has grown from a few hundred thousand dollars in net sales to annual net sales of $2.8 million and net income of $250 thousand in 1996 (Figures 6.26–1 and 6.26–2). The net sales figure is the revenue used to pay for regular staff and ad hoc staff, computer and office equipment, new business solicitations, and other operational expenses. Because the regular staff members both own the firm and are paid based on profit sharing, their incomes vary directly with the firm's consulting business volume. Net income is distributed to the small number of outside investors who do not work at the company.

## INTERNATIONAL EXPANSION

Consulting has become increasingly demanding of competence and experience. With more and more firms being established every day, it is difficult for any consultancy to maintain its business let alone expand. European expansion, particularly in the newly

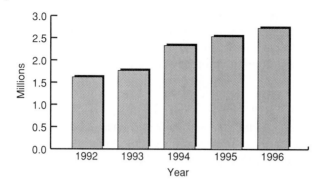

FIGURE 6.26–1 Winston Management Services Net Sales.

*Source:* Winston Management Services.

freed Eastern Bloc, represents a huge potential market. Although Winston Management Services has a number of European clients, it believes that there is much room to grow. The international market for consultants has shown a strong growth rate in recent years, providing opportunities that many other consulting firms have pursued with great success. As a result, many sole practitioners and small firms are trying to find out how to become international.

During the past decade, the management consulting market in Europe has grown significantly. However, the supply of consultants is not homogenous, with major differences in the number of consultants in different parts of Europe. While Germany has the largest number of registered consultants, there are large numbers in the United Kingdom and France also.

Consultants have been helping to develop management consultancy in India, South Africa, and the former Soviet Union. All three countries have indicated that they want to operate global capitalist economies. However, a main obstacle is their lack of know-how about modern management, especially how to design and manage change. Competent consultants are the most readily available source of this managerial know-how these countries need to become global. In India, both public and private sector performance must improve if the urgently needed economic growth and investment from abroad are to come. As in India, economic improvement must come before there can be political and social arrangements that South Africans can live with. South Africa must travel a great distance to improve management, organizational performance, and

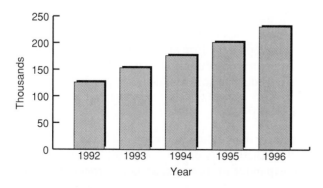

FIGURE 6.26–2 Winston Management Services Net Income.

*Source:* Winston Management Services.

its economy. Designing the former Soviet Union's future has hardly begun; domestic economies must be developed before there can be a possibility of going global.

## INTERNATIONAL GROWTH

Winston Management Services is interested in establishing a stronger European presence and in creating a new client base in Eastern Europe. While there is a great need for such services, there is also competition, particularly from large, internationally known consulting firms. What marketing strategy would you advise Winston Management Services to pursue in soliciting those new clients? What specific consulting offerings would you suggest it emphasize and how would you promote those offerings? How would you deal with the growth competition from other consulting firms?

## Sources

Blumberg, Donald F. "Strategic Examination of Marketing, Sales Costs, and Effectiveness." *Journal of Management Consulting* 8, 3 (Spring 1995): 9–20.

Blumberg, Donald F. "Marketing Consulting Services Using Public Relations Strategies," *Journal of Management Consulting* 8, 1 (Spring 1994): 42–48.

Byrne, John A. "Management's New Gurus." *Business Week* (August 31, 1992): 44–52.

Chittum, J. Marc. "How Do I Go International?" *Journal of Management Consulting* 7, 2 (Fall 1992): 30–35.

Evans, Bill, Peter Reynolds, and Peter Cockman. "Consulting and the Process of Learning." *Journal of European Industrial Training* 16, 2 (1992): 7–11.

Hassid, Joseph, and Anastasia Maggina. "Management Consulting in Greece: The Profession is Growing." *Journal of Management Consulting* 7, 4 (Fall 1993) 55–57.

Hunt, John W. "Some Observations on the European Consulting Scene." *Journal of Management Consulting* 7, 3 (Spring 1993): 2, 70.

Kelley, Robert E. *Consulting: The Complete Guide To A Profitable Career.* New York, NY: Charles Scribner's Sons, 1986.

Kendrick, John J. "Quality Consulting Services" *Quality* 31, 8 (August 1992) Q3.

Price, Charlton R., and Hari P. Johri. "Management Consulting in the Global Economy." *Journal of Management Consulting* 7, 2 (Fall 1992) 42–47.

Svatko, James E. "Working with Consultants." *Small Business Reports* 14, 2 (February 1989) 58–68.

Winston Management Services promotional materials.

APPENDIX A

## Winston Management Services and Products Summary

### SERVICES: STRATEGY ANALYSIS AND PLANNING

Winston Management Services' strategy analysis and planning offering develops and implements business strategies that effectively allocate resources, coordinate activities, and accomplish specific goals. It helps firms develop the strategies necessary to reach product or service profit and sales objectives. This includes support for how decisions are made during all phases in the planning process, how the plan is to be accomplished, and how it all will occur given a firm's strengths and weakness, problems, opportunities, and threats; and competitive advantages. Winston Management Services also shows firms how to capitalize on their competitive advantages through well-integrated marketing programs that coordinate the pricing, promotion, product, and distribution of products or services to satisfy the needs of target markets.

### SERVICES: SALES RESEARCH, ANALYSIS, AND FORECASTING

This Winston Management Services' offering involves sales research, analysis, and forecasting using client internal data and external sources and statistical models of new and existing product and service potentials and trends; sales potential models for new and existing products; and advertising and promotion elasticity studies and models. Business efforts are forecasted, measured, and evaluated through tests, experiments, and modeling. This approach provides the opportunity to estimate or forecast the probability of success with a relatively high degree of accuracy. As a result, business efforts can be allocated to programs with the highest expected value in terms of sales, profits, and/or building a customer base.

Winston Management Services applies basic and advanced statistics, research, testing, experimental design, and statistical model building to its client assignments. Research uses surveys of consumers or business to provide information on why things happen. In contrast, testing and experiments tell the direct marketer what happened in terms of sales and profit effects due to business strategies and tactics. This involves conducting comparisons between alternative ways of proceeding with a strategy or tactic by isolating exactly why a difference in performance by one or more of the alternatives may occur. Experiments are use to carefully control and manipulate conditions designed to see how one or more business alternatives may affect the behavior of the target market, and, ultimately, a sales and profit outcome. Statistical modeling involves applying forecasting methods to historical data, such as purchase rates, to predict future sales.

## SERVICES: MARKETING RESEARCH

Winston Management Services provides full-service, worldwide strategic and tactical marketing research, including a full range of custom quantitative and qualitative studies of consumer and industrial markets. This includes survey studies of attitudes, usage, preferences, and opinions; new product testing and forecasting; advertising and promotion concept and copy testing; segmentation research and target market typology definition; product attribute and product concept testing; positioning studies; and focus groups and one-on-one, in-depth interviewing.

## SERVICES: STRATEGIC DECISION SUPPORT SYSTEMS

This Winston Management Services offering involves management decision support systems designed to provide information on business trends and opportunities. These systems combined database technologies with sophisticated data modeling all with a user-friendly interface. The projects are generally ad hoc in nature because they are designed to address particular strategic and tactical issues associated with new business ventures or the need to increment existing business performance.

Winston Management Services provides the tools, training, and analytical skills necessary for sound decision making. These tools integrate rigorous business analysis with marketing plans, market responses, and financial consequences. Its business decision models use financial data and other sources in a series of up-to-date decision-support tools, allowing users to analyze individual business situations and examine relationships between strategic plan alternatives and financial results.

## PRODUCTS: MAXIMA

Through Winston Management Services' proprietary MAXIMA system, clients can organize, analyze, and forecast a company's sales, marketing, and financial information to systematically identify specific ways in which the client company can permanently increase its sales and profits.

MAXIMA is the result of years of research and innovation by some of the most successful nationally known companies. They have utilized MAXIMA's analytical and techniques to strengthen their businesses. MAXIMA is unique because these successes have been operationalized in a state-of-the-art system designed to apply the latest in computer technology and analytical techniques to potential sales and profit opportunities for your business.

MAXIMA integrates and analyzes client sales, marketing, and financial data to identify both the nature of your business opportunities and the profits to be gained as a result of following MAXIMA recommendations.

## PRODUCTS: DWMS

DWMS is a data warehouse management system designed to provide a unique way to visualize and manipulate a firm's data. This results in databases that are simple and understandable and can be easily navigated by users. The user interface is simple and easily comprehended because it has very friendly screens and clear instructions about how to operate the system.

This data warehouse approach provides access to corporate and organizational data in an immediate, on demand, high-performance environment. Responses to user queries are consistent regardless of location because all users see the same information. Data can be separated and combined by any possible measure in the business, allowing for multidimensional views. However, DWMS provides more than just data because it also has a series of tools to query, analyze, and present information. The way this system approaches data facilitates business reengineering and, thereby, helps significantly improve business performance.

In a DWMS project, Winston Management Services assembles a proper set of data warehouse requirements for an organization; creates the logical design of the warehouse data structures; plans the data extraction and transformation steps down to the individual data element; builds a user front-end tool suite; and provides instructions and training so that clients can manage the completed data warehouse internally.

## PRODUCTS: QIAMS

QIAMS is a qualitative information analysis and modeling system for conducting quantitative analyses of qualitative information from personal interviews. It provides a bridge between traditional qualitative and variable-oriented, multivariate research. This method expands the frontiers of qualitative research through sophisticated analytical approaches and it integrates features of experimental and interpretive design without departing from the general logic of case-oriented, qualitative research. This method is especially well suited to addressing questions about outcomes resulting from multiple and conjunctural causes where different conditions combine in different and sometimes contradictory ways to produce the same or similar outcomes.

While the goal of variable-oriented investigations is to produce generalizations about relationships among variables, this method seeks to understand and interpret specific outcomes in a relatively small number of individuals. It also identifies units of meaning in text by coding them. These codes not only reduce language to a less complex and ambiguous system but additionally represent interpretive and explanatory efforts designed to develop an understanding of relationships between/among meanings. The result is an explication of general ideas or themes, the quantification of categories in texts, and the development and evaluation of associations between/among codes. The process has value because interpretations are scrutinized for objectivity, reliability, and validity, corresponding to better qualitative research.

The analysis emphasizes "personal theories," which are substantive because they explain everyday situations and experiences. Although these theories are personal constructions, they are not idiosyncratic because groups of individuals often share theories about themselves and their environment. Studies analyze and describe elements of these subjective theories, with relationships constructed by discerning the nature of each individual's personal theory at the level of within-text category analyses, after which results are grouped across interviews to find types of personal theories.

This method does not require that a sample come from a particular population, and it is relatively insensitive to the frequency of different types of personal interviews. For example, if there are many instances of a phenomenon and two combinations of conditions that produce it, both combinations are considered equally valid accounts regardless of their relative frequency, with the evidence or condition either existing or not existing in those interviews.

# *American Express Travel Services* CASE 27

In 1980, James D. Robinson III, then American Express (AmEx) CEO, found AmEx's offering of financial services too constricting. He decided to transform AmEx into a far-flung financial empire. At the time, AmEx's net income was $376 million, with the biggest earnings coming from the property and casualty insurance business at Fireman's Fund.

What AmEx did well then it does well now. It spends millions a year to promote its green card as well as the more recent gold, platinum, and Optima additions. Because AmEx's green, gold, and platinum cards (collectively known as "The Card") require customers to pay their entire balance every month, the company makes money on them in only two ways: annual fees charged to cardholders, and the so-called "discounts" collected from merchants, a charge that has historically amounted to from 2.5 to 4.5 percent of each transaction. AmEx's cards are also known as charge cards because no credit is offered. Credit cards, including AmEx's Optima card, make money in three ways: annual fees, interest on balances, and collections from merchants on each transaction.

The green, gold, platinum, and Optima cards make up the biggest share of AmEx's Travel Related Services (TRS) business. AmEx officials however, acknowledge some concern over the recent successes of other card contenders, particularly credit cards, but resist any suggestion that challengers such as Citibank's MasterCard and Visa products or Sears Roebuck & Company's Discover card can match AmEx's

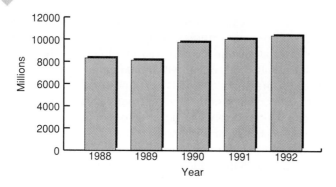

**FIGURE 6.27–1** Travel Related Services Revenues.

*Source: American Express 1992 Annual Report.*

success with upscale consumers. Nevertheless, AmEx is trying to broaden The Card's appeal to less affluent customers, stepping up marketing to college students, for example. AmEx is also trying to get more restaurant chains and movie theaters to accept The Card. Overseas, where AmEx's cards are behind the bank cards, the firm is also intensifying its marketing efforts. With AmEx now scaling down its once-grand ambitions for its travel services, it is clearer than ever how dependent AmEx is on The Card.

## AMEX PERFORMANCE TRENDS

Recent AmEx performance has been problematic. Although its card business revenues have increased (Fig. 6.27–1), net income has declined since 1990 (Fig. 6.27–2). AmEx is apologetic to its stockholders and employees about the current condition of the TRS business. However, words are of small consolation to a demoralized workforce, frustrated stockholders, and a skeptical customer and merchant base (including retailers, restaurants, airlines, etc.).

AmEx is yet another firm that once had a very successful concept that is no longer as consistent with the needs of a significant portion of its customers or the merchants who must accept The Card to make the whole system work. However, AmEx is determined to expand its volume even in the face of its shrinking customer base. In part, this is being done by increasing the number of places that accept The Card.

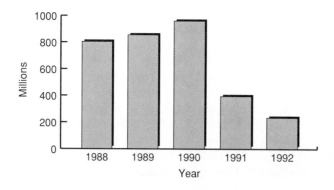

**FIGURE 6.27–2** American Express Travel Services Net Income.

*Source: American Express 1992 Annual Report.*

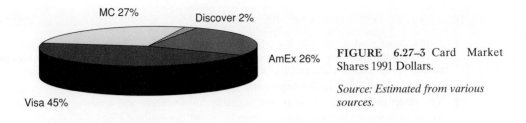

MC 27%  Discover 2%

AmEx 26%

Visa 45%

**FIGURE 6.27–3** Card Market Shares 1991 Dollars.

*Source: Estimated from various sources.*

## CARD MARKET TRENDS

Although AmEx had a 26 percent share of charge and credit card market dollars (Fig. 6.27–3), it only had a 9 percent share of cards in circulation (Fig. 6.27–4). The reason for this discrepancy has to do with the average monthly charge amounts of AmEx cardholders versus cardholders in general. AmEx generates more than twice the charge volume per card versus the credit cards.

Many argue that MasterCard and Visa International are AmEx's main competitors. These analysts are willing to assume that AmEx's charge card is competing for the same mass market as the two major credit cards. More realistically, The Card probably competes with the premium offerings of MasterCard and Visa because their gold cards are upscale products marketed to more wealthy consumers. All of AmEx's cards also compete with MasterCard and Visa for more upscale merchant accounts.

In 1990, consumers charged $158.1 billion on 135.6 million Visa cards, increases of 17.9 percent and 11.2 percent, respectively, over the previous year. MasterCard members signed for $93 billion on their 90 million cards, up 12 percent and 8.5 percent, respectively. Each company's strategy is quite different: MasterCard, being smaller, wants to grow by bringing new issuers into its plan. Visa, by contrast, has made it tougher for nonbanks to join. Table 6.27–1 summarizes some key characteristics of the card market.

Estimates are that AmEx's 1992 share of the general-purpose charge and credit card market declined 0.4 percentage points from 1991 and 5.4 percentage points from 1986. AmEx lost 4.1 percent, or 1.5 million, of its cardmembers in 1991 alone. At the same time, MasterCard International reversed a steady decline and Visa gained steadily each year.

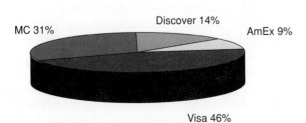

MC 31%  Discover 14%  AmEx 9%

Visa 46%

**FIGURE 6.27–4** Card Market Shares 1991 Cards.

*Source: Estimated from various sources.*

TABLE 6.27–1.    Observations About the Card Market

1. AmEx target market: affluent households (particularly upper-middle class and above) and travel-and-entertainment spenders (corporate customers), but AmEx appears to be moving toward lower-middle class and less upscale image oriented retailers.
2. AmEx constituencies: cardmembers and service establishments.
3. Visa target market: mass market (but primarily lower-middle and upper-middle classes).
4. Visa constituencies: cardmembers and service establishments and banks and other ''distributors.''
5. MasterCard target market: mass market (but primarily lower-middle and upper-middle classes).
6. MasterCard constituencies: cardmembers and service establishments and banks and other ''distributors.''
7. Status and consumption appeals are big consumer motivators.
8. Cards provide the illusion that you are not really spending money.
9. Nearly all demographic groups have cards, but employed females more so than employed males, whites more than blacks, upper income more than lower income consumers, and married more than single consumers.
10. There has been an increase in credit cardholders with outstanding balances.

## AMEX MANAGEMENT CHANGES

Harvey Golub, who succeeded Robinson as CEO, brought a new style to AmEx. To many employees, Robinson seemed remote and formal. In contrast, Golub appeared gregarious and down-to-earth.

Golub's early frank admission of an unarticulated vision suggested that he was still grappling for solutions. However, his renewed focus on service, for instance, may not be enough to differentiate AmEx's cards from its bankcard competitors. Further, AmEx's once legendary marketing skills have been unable to redefine the card's yuppie image of the 1980s for the more parsimonious 1990s. Most important, Golub's strategies tend to be aimed at putting out fires, while broader business strategy questions remain unanswered. Hanging in the balance is the future of the firm and a brand name with a history of strong consumer loyalty. If Golub fails to fix TRS, AmEx will be forced to shrink dramatically just to remain profitable.

Before Golub took charge of all of AmEx, he was only CEO of TRS with an immediate mandate to fix Optima. To differentiate Optima in a crowded market, Golub drastically cut interest rates to good customers months before the bankcard marketers lowered their rates. Then he focused on his toughest challenge: bolstering the AmEx card itself. Instead of growth at any cost, he stressed profitability and implemented new measures to determine the rate at which longtime members were dropping the card. The AmEx sales force began making more sales calls to existing AmEx merchants instead of pursuing new signings. An addition, AmEx retreated from its 1980s push to sign up as many establishments as possible.

Today, Golub's top priority is to protect the high merchant fees that generate more than half of AmEx's revenues. AmEx's argument to merchants: not taking the AmEx card will cost them business. One big reason is that the 5.1 million AmEx corporate card users traveling on business are motivated to put all their charges on their

AmEx cards, as are the 850,000 Membership Miles participants who want to use AmEx to get frequent flier miles.

Additionally, AmEx is trying to bolster its ties with cardholders, who are being bombarded with promotional offers. To enhance value, AmEx is working to add major airlines to its Membership Miles membership and is considering a similar hotel card for frequent hotel guests.

## AMEX'S MISSION

AmEx benefits from a clearly stated mission:

> To provide worldwide Corporate and individual Cardmembers with a wide range of payment options-charge, revolving credit, and debit cards–linked through a relationship-based reporting and statement system, supported by world-class global service and near universal utility, so as to earn 100 percent of their plastic spending.

This statement defines a competitive advantage: a single, worldwide, integrated service provider. It leverages AmEx's service ethic and tradition of customer focus; continues AmEx's longstanding strength in the areas of financial control, no preset spending limit, and enhanced billing; moves AmEx from a product orientation to a customer-relationship focus; challenges AmEx to expand its product offerings in response to cardmembers' needs and wants; reinforces the role of credit in AmEx's product portfolio; and requires that AmEx find ways of achieving near universal coverage.

## AMEX'S STRATEGY AND OBJECTIVES

Overall, AmEx's goal during the next two to four years for its card business is to increase coverage so that its products are accepted at establishments that account for about 95 percent of the business and household cardmembers' plastic spending. This is currently the level of coverage it provides for its corporate cardmembers.

AmEx has defined five specific strategic objectives:

1. *Improve the quality of AmEx's relationships with its service establishments.* AmEx is concentrating on bringing its value story to more service establishments—there is a significant decline in suppression (establishments suggesting to customers they would rather not accept The Card even though an acceptance sign is posted). At the same time, AmEx added high-potential new service establishments, as well as convinced a number of well-publicized cancellations to resume accepting The Card without any reduction in AmEx's discount rate.

2. *Reengineer AmEx's business processes and operating structure to achieve significant improvements in service quality, reduce cycle times, and reduce its cost structure by $1 billion or more on an annualized basis by the end of 1994, based on 1991 volumes.* So far, AmEx has identified approximately $900 million cuts and has introduced cultural changes that helped it to analyze major processes from a division wide perspective.

3. *Increase cardmember loyalty.* AmEx has done much to earn increase loyalty through such efforts as the 1.1 million members U.S. Membership Miles program with the airlines. The firm is also exploring the possibility of launching the program in a number of international markets. AmEx has put in place special programs for its highest spending, long-tenured cardmembers that was well received. It's seeing increases in the average cardmember spending.

4. ***Reposition AmEx's consumer lending products.***   As part of AmEx's "financial responsibility strategy," it has introduced a performance-based pricing structure for Optima, and improved the credit quality of its lending portfolio.

5. ***Build on AmEx's leadership position in corporate card, travel, and Travelers' Cheque.***   With the addition of LifeCo, the world's largest travel company, AmEx has added important new Travel Management Services accounts. The firm continues to add major new corporate card accounts and regain accounts lost to Visa banks in prior years. And, its business in Travelers' Cheques has won sales away from competitors around the world.

## WHO USES THE CARD AND WHY

AmEx would say that its customers are loyal to its cards because it offers a quality, long-term relationship based on service (see Table 6.27–2). If customers leave, it is due to inadequacies in that service, or at least the perception of inadequate service. However, aside from AmEx's perspective, the reasons why customers leave include at least three other issues, one based on economics, another on weaknesses in The Card's selling premise, and the last involving cultural and attitudinal shifts since the 1980s. First, The Card membership is expensive. The Card's yearly fee is far in excess of those charged by the bank cards. A second more serious issue is that an important part of AmEx's selling proposition involves saving cardholders from themselves by making them payoff the entire balance on their card at the end of each month. Given that AmEx's cardholders tend to be successful, educated people, offering customers a "father figure" who will discipline their use of credit seems to be a fallacious proposition on which to base a business. Finally, historically, the status symbol aspect of The Card's appeal has been a strong part of the brand's positioning, but the problem is that status is more a 1980s than a 1990s hot button!

---

**TABLE 6.27–2.   Customer Dynamics from Amex's Perspective**

*Why Customers Are Loyal To AmEx*
1. They have long-term, trouble-free relationships with AmEx, begun early in their adult lives. They like AmEx and are comfortable with its offerings.
2. They are financially responsible and appreciate the discipline of having to pay their bills in full every month.
3. They like having no preset spending limit, and the convenience and peace of mind this provides.
4. They like AmEx's billing systems; and its U.S. customers particularly like the copies of the charge slips and itemized summaries.
5. They like AmEx's service and the way AmEx employees solve their problems, on the phone, when they write, and in AmEx's Travel Service Offices around the world.

*Why Customers Leave AmEx*
Cardmembers who leave and people who choose not to carry AmEx's Card question the value they receive, given the fee charged. Two key reasons emerge:
1. They require better service establishment coverage.
2. They want revolving credit.

---

For non-AmEx cardholders, there are other issues limiting the growth of the business. Many consumers are not aware that charge cards exist, or, if they're aware, they do not understand them. Many merchants do not want charge programs because they say transaction fees and other charges they must pay are too high. Many consumers who are aware of charge cards do not see much reason to pay high fees for them. Some bankers are skeptical, wondering whether charge cards can ever be profitable with nonupscale customers.

## TARGETING AND THE CARD'S IMAGE

Flashing an AmEx card at a retail counter sends a message to the salesperson: I am a cut above the average Joe with a bank card. Whether the salesperson is impressed or not, it's sufficient that the cardholder thinks he is. But as AmEx pushes The Card well beyond what can technically be defined as a higher income market, The Card is in danger of loosing some of its upscale luster. AmEx is making the move because it believes that it has "mass-market" prestige (an oxymoron) that can be used to expand its customer base.

AmEx is breaking this mass market into segments, each with its own notions of prestige. Hence, the fundamental importance of those green-, gold-, and platinum-colored cards. The green card is a known trademark and status symbol. Among U.S. consumer businesses, only Coca-Cola and McDonald's are better-known brand names. The green card holder feels superior to the bank card holder; the gold card holder feels above the green card holder, and the platinum card holder feels on top. However, in its rush to woo the mass market, AmEx is putting its valuable upscale image at risk.

Thus, as AmEx moves into its fourth decade in the card business, the company is embarking on a hazardous course by tampering with its highly successful strategy of focusing strictly on upscale spenders in top-line establishments, not without reason, of course. From the 34 million cards in circulation in the United States now, The Card will peak at 37 million by the year 2000, and then will level off at 35 million. And abroad, where credit card growth will be far faster, AmEx faces even more of an uphill battle. Hence, the new strategy is to get current customers, and less affluent new ones, too, to use their cards on many more mundane occasions.

But flashing the AmEx card at Tiffany & Co. may not confer as much status as it once did when the shopper knows that someone could be using that same card to charge 10 gallons of gasoline at a grimy self-service pump. Meanwhile, banks are challenging AmEx's dominance in the upscale market by offering premium cards of their own through their Visa and MasterCard networks. And the banks are trying to draw attention to their corporate prestige, much in the same way that AmEx does.

## THE SUPPRESSION PROBLEM

AmEx is adopting a risky strategy by encouraging cardholders to fight back against retailers that encourage them to use Visa, MasterCard, or some other credit card. In an AmEx TV spot, comedian-actor Jerry Seinfeld is seen expressing mock outrage when a clothing store clerk tells a customer he prefers a different card than AmEx's green card. Seinfeld then gives the customer a nudge to resist.

In 1991, AmEx also began an extensive public relations campaign to combat this "suppression problem," including a toll-free number to let employees report those retailers who violate its policies. AmEx's central problem, industry observers say, is that it is trying to protect its flanks while increasing its customer base, and the two goals are not necessarily complementary. On the one hand, the firm's executives have said repeatedly that they will focus their marketing efforts almost exclusively on The Card's shrinking core of affluent, frequent business travelers, promising added services and the preservation of its prestigious image, but at the same time AmEx is courting mass merchants such as Wal-Mart and Kmart.

AmEx is also using advertising to aggressively woo new customers by hammering bank cards for their "up to 19 percent interest" rates and "preset spending limits," subjects analysts say mean little to most of AmEx's existing customers.

## THE FIGHT TO DISCOURAGE MERCHANT DEFECTORS

AmEx claims to not have suffered any harm from merchant defections. It says it is still signing up thousands of restaurants and other establishments and moving fast to placate some merchants, negotiating card fees, and offering marketing support. However, the merchant discount, the amount AmEx keeps from the charges submitted, averages about 3.5 percent. The banks take as little as 2.25 percent on their credit cards, and Discover gets only 2.7 percent. For a low-margin or struggling business, an extra penny or more per dollar is a significant amount, and AmEx is losing a lot of merchants as a result.

AmEx officials offer no apologies. They say their charges are higher across the board because their cards' quality is superior, supposing that customers are interested in the best product, not the cheapest product. A higher fee is worthwhile for merchants, AmEx officials argue, because people spend more money when using the AmEx card than any other. According to AmEx, the Visa and MasterCard brands also lack distinct personalities.

In 1991, a group of Boston merchants created their own version of the Boston Tea Party. The eateries threatened to boycott AmEx cards and complained that the merchant fees it collects every time a diner charges a meal were too high. AmEx responded by shaving off half a percentage point from its fee for larger restaurants that file their charge records electronically.

Although the uprising against AmEx was initially confined to restaurants, it's spreading to other merchants, including direct mail companies and retailers. AmEx denies a merchant backlash exists and downplays competitive pressures.

So far, the companies that supply the biggest portion of AmEx's business have been quiet. Airlines, which contribute about 25 percent of AmEx's merchant fees, and hotels, contributing an additional 20 percent, do not appear to be among the protesters. However, many have already negotiated lower fees.

## HEAVY COMPETITION

New competitors were drawn to the card industry at the start of the 1990s partly because of simple economics. The cost of money had fallen to about 6 percent while the major banks were charging their credit card customers an average of 16.5 percent interest on their unpaid balances.

Until recently, the conventional wisdom was that cardholders are insensitive to card interest rates because they expect to pay balances promptly: But today, only 32 percent of cardholders do so, versus over 50 percent a decade ago. The average balance of about $1,700 is double that of a decade ago.

Everyone from General Motors to the local phone company wants to get some of the credit card business away from the banks. But the real winners will be consumers. In a little more than a year, the credit card industry has reinvigorated itself. The newer entrants in the credit card wars did not simply tried to steal existing customers from established card companies by attacking head-on. Instead, most targeted market segments where credit-card use had traditionally been relatively low and designed card features and services to increase their penetration of those groups.

In Sears' case, for example, a large portion of its retail charge customers consisted of moderate-income families who were reluctant to use credit cards because of high annual fees and interest charges. Sears designed the Discover card to appeal to them by charging no annual fee and offering rebates of 1 percent of the purchase price of items charged on its card.

## FUTURE DIRECTIONS

The competition from bank cards is beginning to cut into AmEx's growth. The banks began issuing premium cards five years ago, and have now overtaken AmEx in premium cards circulating. Since then, AmEx's growth rate in charges per card has been less than half that of the bank cards.

Going forward, the brightest growth area for credit cards seems to be abroad, where AmEx now has roughly nine million cardholders. For the future, AmEx sees a target market abroad of 100 million people. But AmEx lags far behind its competitors in Europe and Japan. Eurocard, which is linked with MasterCard, claims 18.9 million cardholders in Europe, double the number five years ago. Eurocard is accepted in 1.5 million locations, and sales totaled $27 billion last year. And within three months of Eurocard's launch of its gold card in the former West Germany, it won 400,000 new customers.

However, with offices all over the world, AmEx already has an overwhelming advantage over the bank card associations with Americans traveling abroad. And with perhaps the most recognized name in the world after Coca-Cola, it should have a clear edge in other countries where the use of both charge and credit cards is just beginning to catch on.

Not surprisingly, AmEx's international growth rate is faster than its domestic rate. Volume per card is significantly higher overseas than in the United States. Even in Japan, where the local vested interests have repeatedly thrown roadblocks in front of AmEx's advance, business is booming. The company now has over 800,000 cards in circulation in Japan, and the number is growing by well over 20 percent annually.

Back in the United States, the fastest growing basic card is the corporate card, which are cards issued to company employees for corporate use, allowing companies to better monitor expenses. Also offered with the corporate card is an entire travel management service, complete with travel booking, bill paying, and data massaging to provide even more information. At a time when businesses are struggling to keep their travel and entertainment expenses under control, the service has proven extremely popular.

What marketing strategies would you recommend to AmEx for dealing with the competition and in preparing for the future in the United States? What does AmEx's travel service group need to do to ensure its differential advantage in the highly competitive and dynamic U.S. card market? What specific price, distribution, promotion, and product mix would you propose and why?

## Sources

American Express Company 1992 Annual Report.

Chakravarty, Subrata N. "A Credit Card is Not a Commodity." *Forbes* (October 16, 1989): 128–130.

Jaffe, Thomas. "Lots of Work to Do." *Forbes* (February 15, 1993): 45–46.

Levin, Gary. "MasterCard's Plan: Keep Pushing Values." *Advertising Age* (August 31, 1992): 9.

Levin, Gary. "AMEX Ads Say Fight, Don't Switch." *Advertising Age* (November 30, 1992): 28, 52.

McWilliams, Gary, and Leah Nathans. "Jumping into the Credit Gaps." *Business Week* (October 19, 1992): 94–96.

"Plastic Profits Go Pop." *The Economist* (September 12, 1992): 92.

Saporito, Bill. "Who's Winning the Credit Car War." *Fortune* (July 2, 1990): 66–71.

Saporito, Bill. "Melting Point in the Plastic War?" *Fortune* (May 20, 1991): 74–77.

Saporito, Bill. "The Coup at American Express." *Fortune* (December 28, 1992): 12.

Spiro, Leah Nathans. "What's in the Cards for Harvey Golub?" *Business Week* (June 15, 1992): 112–114.

Spiro, Leah Nathans. "Curiouser and Curiouser at AMEX." *Business Week* (February 8, 1993): 109–111.

Woolley, Suzanne. "The Dawn of the Debit Card. Well, Maybe." *Business Week* (September 19, 1992): 79.

# Bally's Health & Tennis Corporation

Bally's Health & Tennis Corporation is an indirect wholly owned subsidiary of Bally Manufacturing Corporation. That parent corporation designs, manufactures, distributes, and sells coin-operated amusement and gaming equipment; designs, produces, and distributes video lottery machines; operates casino hotels; operates a nationwide chain of family amusement centers, theme parks and wax museums, and restaurants that contain amusement game rooms; designs, assembles, and sells computerized player tracking, cash monitoring, accounting, and security data systems for gaming machines worldwide; and owns and operates the largest chain of fitness centers in the United States.

Bally's health clubs operate under such names as Bally's Chicago Health Club, Bally's Jack LaLanne, Bally's Scandinavian Health Spa, and many more. The chain has more locations than any other competitor. The individual club facilities are large, with some having as much as 100,000 square feet of space. Most locations offer aerobics, weight training, exercise machines, and cardiovascular equipment such as treadmills, stationary bicycles, and stairclimbers. Many also have swimming pools and tanning areas. Because of the size of these club locations, they attempt to attract a large clientele. They also rely extensively on first-time buyers because club membership recruiting involves a situation in which the vast majority of members pay, use the facilites for awhile, and never return.

Over the last several years, Bally's parent company Bally Manufacturing has undergone tremendous changes, including bankruptcy, a major departure at the top, and a massive reorganization. This is reflected in variations of revenues, income, net, and earnings per share (Figs. 6.28–1, 6.28–2, and 6.28–3). In the process, Arthur M. Goldberg seized control of the firm in 1990. Goldberg inherited an unsteady firm burdened with $1.9 billion in debt, an out-of-control cost structure, and an uncertain strategy. Since then, however, he has addressed some of Bally's most serious problems and has put the company in a position to capitalize on the surge in gaming and continuing consumer interest in health and fitness. Both of Bally's major operating units, its two New Jersey casinos and 313 health clubs, turned around in the first quarter of 1992 after operating losses in five of the previous six quarters. The company's stock, which bottomed at 1¾ in January 1991, trades at several times that price.

Bally's troubles are the product of an era, the 1980s, and Robert Mullane. Among Mullane's biggest acquisitions were the two Nevada casinos, for which Bally paid $440 million in 1986. Three years later, it paid $730 million for Atlantic City's Golden Nugget casino. The casinos were sound, but Bally could not handle the debt, and by 1990, it was deep in the red.

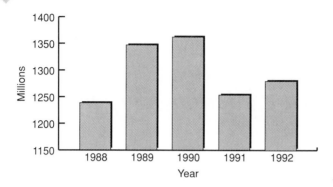

**FIGURE 6.28–1** Bally Manufacturing Corporation Revenues.

*Source: Bally Manufacturing Corporation 1992 Annual Report.*

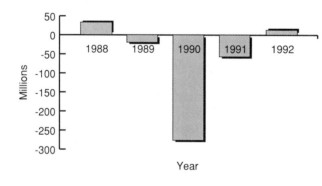

**FIGURE 6.28–2** Bally Manufacturing Corporation Net Income.

*Source: Bally Manufacturing Corporation 1992 Annual Report.*

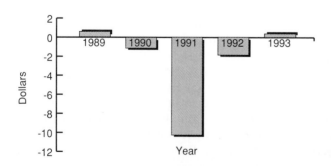

**FIGURE 6.28–3** Bally Manufacturing Corporation Earnings per Share

*Source: Bally Manufacturing Corporation 1992 Annual Report.*

Goldberg made major changes at Bally's Health & Tennis Corporation, which accounts for around half of Bally's total revenues. He closed several unprofitable clubs, cut expansion plans, and instituted a new sale commission structure based on revenues, not memberships booked.

## HEALTH CLUB INDUSTRY STRATEGY ISSUES

In a changing, competitive, and difficult-to-succeed-in health club industry, the key to success is a well-planned, long-term strategy. As the industry matures, club owners increasingly perceive the need to focus on long-term issues, trends, and market forces that impact on their business. For all clubs, of all sizes, the growing complexity of the industry requires an explicit understanding of market dynamics and strategy alternatives.

Within the movement toward fitness and activity, there is both growth and loss. Tennis grew dramatically from 1968 to 1980 but has since decreased by 40 percent. Running exploded in the early 1980s but has also declined since. A number of fitness activities are experiencing significant growth. In 1986, 6.8 million people began exercising with equipment, 6.8 million began to walk for exercise, and 4.5 million started aerobic dancing. The number of participants in exercise walking grew by almost 13 percent from 1985 to 1986, and the demographics show that activity is attracting a wider age range.

## UNDERSTANDING THE HEALTH CLUB INDUSTRY

The goal of any strategy is to find a position in the market where a firm can defend itself against competitive forces, and the key to developing that strategy is to delve below the surface and analyze the competitive dynamics.

### Capital Requirements

Costs for entry into the high end of the club industry range from approximately $50 to $125 per square foot, exclusive of land costs. In major metropolitan areas, it costs about seven to ten million dollars to build a major club.

At the same time, it is increasingly difficult to attract capital from financial institutions for a single, stand-alone club. Although sophisticated industry players use market studies and other data to support their propositions, capital remains difficult to obtain.

### Customer Loyalty

Historically, there has been little customer loyalty to specific clubs. Further, club attrition rates of 25 to 40 percent suggest that relatively few clubs serve their markets in a distinct enough fashion to create significant loyalty. And, although clubs are increasingly utilizing higher initiation fees, switching costs for members are relatively low.

### Favorable Geographic Location

A key factor in the decision to join a health club is location. And, there are very few markets in which existing clubs have such market dominance as to have locked up all favorable sites. The purchase of a club membership is also a particularly local decision.

So, while some specific high-traffic/easy access sites are clearly favorable, they are unlikely to deliver fatal blows to potential competitors.

### Regulation

Governmental regulation of membership, contracts, and sales procedures has been increasing over the past few years and is likely to grow. Internal industry regulation, codes of ethics, certification for clubs and staff, and club rating systems, are historically lacking in the industry.

### Barriers to Expansion

There are indications that future club industry expansion and the opening of additional clubs will be easier. A track record will enable expanders to attract capital more effectively, efficiently, and potentially at more favorable terms. Multiple-club operators leverage their experience and knowledge to lower their cost of capital for second clubs by as much as 15 percent. Additionally, multiple-club owners have an advantage because of their knowledge about operations, sales, marketing, and member service across a range of operations. Economies of scale also accrue to multiple club operators. Spreading marketing costs across a number of clubs in similar markets, or creating an in-house advertising agencies can reduce costs by 15 to 20 percent.

### Substitute Products

The distinction between competitors and substitutes is often somewhat arbitrary. What are the potential choices buyers have, from the buyers' perspective? Substitute products become attractive at different sensitively levels. To a nonsophisticated runner, for example, a sit-up board for home use may be a reasonable substitute for a club membership, while to a single buyer seeking social benefits, membership in a mountain climbing club may fulfill the need at a more attractive price. Realistically, however, clubs must continually contend with competitive products and services, from home gyms to diet pills to personal trainers, which can fill some or all of a person's needs.

### Competitive Rivalry

Chains such as Bally's, by virtue of their lower cost of capital and marketing/advertising economies of scale, are the low-cost competitors in their markets. They typically target a broad, price sensitive buyer segment, age 18–40, and are driven by membership sales as opposed to relation (many earning 80 percent of their revenues on first-year membership sales). They typically have more advertising and promotion savvy than other competitor groups and leverage their investment in advertising across clubs.

The chains also have the resources to hire sophisticated management talent. These typically well-capitalized, strategically sound competitors are extremely well-positioned; any single club seeking to match them on price will fail. At the same time, this segment, as structured, can only thrive as long as there exists a large base of first time buyers through which they can churn. As they exhaust that market, they will either fail or, more likely, move to other strategies such as focusing on retention and member service.

Local storefronts represent the other end of the market. They have an ability to focus on specific market segments, especially those interested in low-cost memberships. Storefronts require little to no capital investment and can take advantage of the local nature of the membership purchase decision. The limited facilities that characterize storefronts are not necessarily viewed as a disadvantage by the consumers they target.

Clubs dedicated to serving the corporate market have emerged over the last year as models of buyer-focused operations. These clubs seek a narrow range of people and serve their specific needs extremely well.

Hospitals involved in health club activities have some particular competitive advantages. However, they tend to lack the management talent, systems, flexibility and adaptability, and organizational commitment to become major players. Amenity clubs, including hotels, residential developments, and office parks, have the potential for becoming strong competitors because of their favorable locations, captive markets, and low return-on-investment (ROI) requirements.

Multipurpose clubs are in danger of becoming stuck in the middle without a distinctive competitive advantage. They target a broad market at a middle-price range, which is caught between the high value-added/high-price competitors on one hand and the low-cost entries on the other. Multipurpose clubs succeed when they offer programs and services that their members value at a price/value ratio they are willing to pay.

## THE CONSUMER MARKET

Individual competitors must determine which consumer groups they want to attract. Certain ones have more potential and attract more competition. Mass-market strategies are increasingly a losing game, as more competitors enter the market and successfully target the specific needs of the larger and more profitable market segments.

In the 1980s, 70 percent of club members were between the ages of 25 and 44 (versus a national population in which 35 percent were 25–44); simply following that group into the 1990s would suggest that 35 to 50 year olds would be the prime target group. As the industry matures and becomes more competitive, however, it is increasingly clear that age alone no longer suffices to characterize that group of buyers because they represent such a diverse segment. Rather, the 35 to 50 age group includes a number of different segments that must be identified, analyzed, and targeted.

The 55+ market is consistently identified as a major opportunity segment. Representing about 12 percent of the population, seniors will constitute 14 percent by 2000; they already control 18 percent of the nation's discretionary income. And, while not as active as 25 to 34 year olds, the 55+ market is more involved in fitness activity than previous stereotypes might suggest. People over 50 are also perceived as attractive because they use clubs in nonprimetime hours, typically take better care of facilities than others, and have networks of friends whom they can influence to use a club. To date, few clubs have targeted or experienced success targeting this group, much less integrated them into a club with younger members. It appears that the needs of the 55+ market include exercise, meeting and spending time with others, and finding constructive and purposeful ways to keep active.

The junior market, those aged 6 to 17, represents approximately 20 percent of the U.S. population and is a potential growth segment. By virtue of its large size and relative lack of competition, juniors are an attractive target market. At the same time, their apparent price sensitivity makes them a less attractive segment than others. Niche competitors appear likely to target this group as a complement to the family segment.

Singles have historically been the easiest members for clubs to attract. The singles market does not appear to be changing significantly in size, although some observers suggest that today's 18 to 24 year-old may not share the same fitness orientation of those 5 to 10 years their elder. Singles' social, recreational, and personal-appearance needs are likely to continue to drive this market. While the market is attractive by virtue of its size and discretionary income, it is also probably the most sought-after segment. Clubs seeking this market face increasingly stiff competition. Those competing for this market will also be squeezed by price wars and by the necessity of adding more services to attract and retain members.

The family market is seen by many as a particularly attractive segment. The structure of the family market in the 1980s has changed, with increasingly few families comprised of a mom, dad, and two children. Furthermore, decreases in discretionary time and other pressures suggest that meeting the needs of families is a very different proposition than serving the needs of singles.

The dual-income-no-kids (DINK) market is attracting attention in a number of industries. While these couples have high-discretionary income, it is not clear how much discretionary time they will have or how that time will be allocated. As with the singles and family markets, DINKs have distinctive needs, including the opportunity to enhance their careers and reinforce their upscale self-images.

Overall, the most relevant predictors of likelihood to join a club may be related less to age, income, and martial status than to fitness orientation and behavior. Some suggest that people move through stages of fitness behavior, from being inactive to being active in self-reliant activities that do not require club facilities, such as running, walking, or tennis, to joining a low-cost/high-awareness club alternative such as a YMCA or a fitness studio, to upgrading to a high quality, often more complete and expensive facility.

## BALLY'S HEALTH CLUB BUSINESS

Bally's fitness centers revenues for 1992 increased $39.5 million (Fig. 6.28–4), but net income was negative (Fig. 6.28–5). The 11 percent revenue increase was primarily due to more new memberships sold and, to a lesser extent, an increase in dues and renewals offset, in part, by a decline in the average selling price of new memberships. As a percent of new membership revenues, cash sales and down payments are about 25 percent.

Bally's management also believes the weakened economy will continue to have a negative effect on revenues and operating income. However, it also believes that its focus on cash sales and higher down payments, together with improvements in selling and collection policies and procedures implemented in 1991, helped to stabilize liquidity and cash flows and improved collection experience by reducing delinquency and fail-

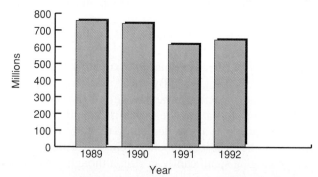

**FIGURE 6.28–4** Bally's Health & Tennis Corporation Revenues.

*Source: Bally's Health & Tennis Corporation 1992' Annual Report.*

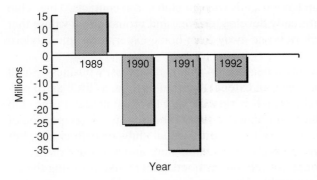

**FIGURE 6.28–5**  Bally's Health & Tennis Corporation Net Income.

*Source: Bally's Health & Tennis Corporation 1992 Annual Report.*

ure rates. Additionally, it believes that the standardization of membership types and prices, together with changes in sales and collection commission structures, as well as technical changes in its collection cycle and improvements in cost efficiencies in its customer service procedures, have all contributed to improving operating results.

## BALLY'S MARKETING EFFORTS

Bally's Health & Tennis business is well known for its high-intensity marketing efforts, particularly in high-pressure sales tactics and high-visibility television advertising. To some, Bally's sales practices are unethical and destructive to the image of the club industry. Bally's efforts reinforce its sales practices through advertising targeted at those who are price- and/or social interaction-oriented. Bally is after the young and the working class to moderately skilled white collar, which is the mass market for health clubs. In 1992, Bally's Health & Tennis Corporation spent an estimated 28.3 million on advertising concentrated in a limited number of major markets.

Bally, and many other clubs, thrive on the illusions consumers have about exercise and fitness. Most Americans say they want to exercise regularly and vigorously, but the reality is very different. Less than 1 percent of the population lifts weights (free weights and machines) at least three times per week; similarly, less than 4 percent of the population does aerobics 20 or more days a year. The point is that most consumers who join a health club (and agree to pay money) never make use of the facilities. The psychological game is that people assume that if they pay money for the membership, they will use it—wrong.

If all the people who joined did exercise regularly, there would not even be standing room available at the clubs. Bally's sales practices make good use of this aspect of consumer psychology by selling life-time memberships (among other options), requesting automatic credit card deductions for time-based membership payments, and manipulating the combinations of payments, price, and length of membership to maximize consumer confusion and acceptance.

## PLANNING OPTIONS

The fitness market will not go away because the industry addresses fundamental consumer needs. While continuing to evolve, it will remain strong well into the foreseeable future. At the same time, it is important to recognize that this is a voluntary market; the purchase of a club membership is a luxury, and not a necessity. Consumers can be fit without club equipment, and can have friends without club social contacts. Thus, club owners and managers must continually develop, deliver, and promote real values that are otherwise not available, such as home-away-from-home experiences and modern equipment.

Now and in the future, owning a health club will be a very risky business. Small changes in membership revenues over an extended period of time, as little as 10 percent of total sales, can sink a club. And, it is very difficult to make money in the club business because capital investment are high and labor expenses are a large portion of total expenses. Consumers are not very loyal to individual clubs or club chains, but small wonder, because most consumers pay for memberships and never use them.

Some argue that clubs should not rely on members joining and not using the facilities as the primary way to be profitable. However, it is not possible to accommodate all those who join and remain profitable either. Thus, the club business is based on a dubious premise, the notion that turnover and not customer service drives sales and profitability.

Large operations such as Bally's are rare. After Bally's the next group of clubs is regional or only concentrated in one metropolitan area. In fact, Bally's started as a conglomeration of regional clubs that were formed into a less than cohesive single unit. The third tier of clubs consists of the multiple location, private owner operations, with an average of three clubs, and, finally, there are the single location operators, of which there are many.

It is clear that some buyer segments, especially young singles, are aggressively pursued. Clubs such as Bally's that seek these buyers must recognize that they will face strong competition, limiting their ability to price at a premium and suggesting the need to compete with many other players.

In planning its future, Bally's faces many marketing strategy issues as it plans for the rest of the 1990s and beyond: Are larger "magnet" health clubs with their mixture of different types of people and facilities viable? Can Bally move to a service and quality orientation from a sales orientation as the pool of potential first-time club members declines, and still survive? What marketing strategy would you recommend? What specific price, distribution, promotion, and product elements would you propose and why?

## Sources

Bally Manufacturing Corporation 1992 Annual Report.

Bally's Health & Tennis Corporation 1992 Annual Report.

Greising, David. "Turning the Tables at Bally." *Business Week* (June 29, 1992): 92–93.

Leopold, Don. *Vanguard Marketing: Winning in the '90s,* Boston: IRSA Publications, 1988.

Simmons Market Research Bureau, Inc. 1991.

*Leading National Advertisers*, Arbitrion Company, 1992.

# *Apple Computer* 29

By 1992, the personal computer (PC) had produced a revolution in information technology that created a $50 billion hardware business and another $30 billion in software and peripherals. During its first 16 years, the industry evolved through three successive periods. The first five years were characterized by explosive growth, with a relatively small number of competitors vying for a share of the market. With IBM's introduction of its PC in 1981, a second stage in PC computing began. Over the next five years, PC firms battled over technical standards and retail shelf space. During that period, IBM, Apple, Compaq, and NEC emerged as leaders. The third period was characterized by increasing fragmentation, with many formerly small competitors emerging as significant players. Most notable were the mail-order firms such as Dell, Zeros, and Gateway. New manufacturers of IBM clones grabbed share from the industry leaders as new channels of distribution emerged. All this was accompanied by significant product innovation in PC performance and capabilities, even as prices fell and revenue grew.

Although by 1992, the four largest PC manufacturers were still IBM, Apple, Compaq, and NEC, they only accounted for about 37 percent of worldwide unit sales (Figure 6.29–1). PCs had become a global business, with more than 200 players from a dozen countries. While U.S. firms had more than 60 percent of global revenues, small Taiwanese companies, such as Acer, were gaining share in the very low end and Japanese firms were the biggest players in portable computers, the fastest growing PC segment.

Today, IBM-compatible computers, with which Apple's machines are incompatible, account for over 80 percent of PCs sold. Increasingly, Apple is having to match its rivals' prices just to survive. Apple's historical success is in jeopardy, and its future as a company is in the balance.

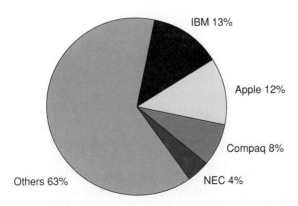

IBM 13%

Apple 12%

Compaq 8%

NEC 4%

Others 63%

**FIGURE 6.29–1** Computer Market Shares, 1992 Units.

*Source: Estimated from various sources.*

## THE EARLY DAYS: 1977–1984

When the Apple II was announced in March 1977, it began a revolution in computing that changed the scope and nature of information technology. However, when IBM entered the PC market in 1981, Apple's competitive position changed fundamentally. While Apple's revenues continued to grow rapidly, market share and margins fell. Apple responded with two new products, the Lisa and Mac. These innovative computers featured a user friendly graphical interface that allowed users to operate several applications at once. A mouse made applications easier to use. However, both computers were incompatible with the IBM standard. They were technically sophisticated, but expensive.

IBM's entry into the market ended the industry's closed or proprietary systems phase. IBM unintentionally created a whole new group of PC competitors by offering a designed that was copied or cloned. Apple's system followed the opposite path. Apple was successful in legally defeating all attempts at cloning by keeping its system closed and, thereby, rendering the computer incompatible with competitor products.

IBM never intended to create a computer that would be so easy to copy. But it was in such a hurry to get its PC to market that it left the door wide open. Rather than build all the components and software for the PC itself, as it did with its larger computers, IBM turned to outside suppliers, notably Intel and Microsoft. Intel provided microprocessors; tiny, privately held Microsoft provided DOS (disk operating system), the operating system software that controls the interaction between the PC's hardware and application programs such as spreadsheets and word processors. This open system concept has big advantages for customers because they can mix and match hardware and software from different competitors to get the best price and performance combination.

Although IBM's open system fostered many imitators during this period, few were capable of overcoming the strength of IBM's brand name and product quality. It became the market leader, particularly among the Fortune 1000 where it captured almost 70 percent of the market. Much of this initial success resulted from IBM's mainframe computer foothold in these large companies. Also, PCs were still considered new technology and those who had authority to purchase them felt comfortable with IBM's reputation for reliability, quality, and service.

## THE GO-GO DAYS: 1985–1990

Between 1986 and 1989, Apple's sales exploded; it introduced new, more powerful Macs that roughly matched the newest IBM-compatible PCs in speed. Even more important, the Mac offered superior software and a variety of peripherals (e.g., laser printers) that gave Apple a unique market niche as the easiest computer to use with unmatched capabilities at desktop publishing. Apple's strategy of being the only manufacturer of its hardware and software made the firm's profitability the envy of the industry.

As IBM-compatibles with MS-DOS/Intel became the standard, IBM faltered, losing almost half its market share. Because Intel and Microsoft provided all PC manufacturers with identical parts, it was IBM's clones that offered compatibility with the installed base of PCs. An emerging group of PC clone manufacturers such as Dell,

Gateway, and Zeros found that most customers could not distinguish between low priced and premium brands. Because these machines ran all the software written for IBM's machines, users began buying PCs based on price. Finally, the greatest differentiation in the industry had been between standards—IBM versus Apple. However, when Microsoft introduced its Windows 3.0 graphical user interface in 1990, differences in user-friendliness between Apple's Macs and the IBM-compatibles virtually disappeared overnight.

In this stage, Apple chose an encirclement strategy to attack IBM. This involved targeting the smaller untapped market segments not well served by the leader, including the nontechnical, user-friendly, desktop publishing, and low-end, engineering workstation segments. The fact that Macs were easy to use, with better graphics, and had features that appealed to middle managers established the Apple offering as a strong competitor in what was a niche market. While IBM focused on "power users," Apple appealed to "the rest of us." However, beginning in 1986, Apple came up against market resistance. As Apple raised its prices and focused on its segmentation, it alienated schools, price-conscious consumers, and small businesses.

As Apple's strategy faltered, unit sales of Macs started to slip, and Apple's worldwide market share position declined from 8.2 percent in 1988 to 8.0 percent in 1989. Revenue growth for 1990 sagged to below 6 percent due to the dramatic changes in the PC industry. As price became the main selling point among the IBM compatibles, Apple kept churning out premium Macs. By late 1989, the company seemed totally out of step: a Mac with a color monitor, large memory, and hard disk cost $5,000—the price of two comparably equipped IBM clones.

Microsoft's Windows 3.0 delivered the mortal blow, and, as a result, Apple lost its differential advantage. IBM-compatible machines now had the user-friendly, graphical of a Mac with the same icons and pull-down menus. Since 1990, Microsoft has sold some 27 million copies of Windows, considerably more then the 10 million Macs in use. And, meanwhile, other software companies have produced hundreds of Windows-compatible applications programs, which outpace Mac applications three-to-one in sales dollars.

In response, a new strategy emerged for regaining market share and reducing Apple's costs. The short-term remedy was straightforward: new Macs with lower price tags, more advanced software, and price cuts on older models. If the market responded favorably to the new line, Apple would gain the time it needed to pursue a more critical, long-term strategy: a replacement for the Mac. But if Apple did not recover, its chances of recovery thereafter would be small.

## THE TROUBLED TIMES: 1990 AND BEYOND

By 1990, it was clear that Apple had mistakenly assumed that its early graphical and user-friendly advantages insulated it from price or profit pressures. Thus, having the most easy to use and friendly computer was only temporary. Apple machines also lacked the software depth of the IBM compatible PCs and they could not run the IBM compatible software. And, as consumers became more sophisticated about computers, they became more discriminating about what they were willing to pay a premium for.

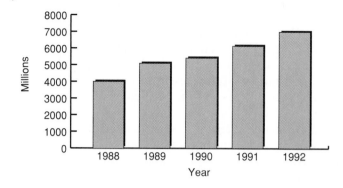

FIGURE **6.29–2** Apple Computer Revenues.

*Source: Apple Computer 1992 Annual Report.*

### Slicing the Apple

Alarmed by Apple's shrinking market share, John Sculley, then Apple's chief executive, reversed the company's direction in 1990, slashing prices, cutting costs, and pushing new versions of its computers out of the door faster. Apple realized that it did not have a survivable company.

Apple cut Mac prices 30 percent in 1991, producing a 60 percent increase in unit volume (Fig. 6.29–2). Because that put pressure on profits, Apple also reduced its staff 10 percent, mostly in sales, and reduced the salaries of top managers as much as 15 percent, which was reflected in net income (Figure 6.29–3).

In 1991, Apple revamped its popular Mac product line, rolling out three new systems priced to undercut similarly equipped IBM compatibles. One of the new machines, a budget model retailing for less than $1,000, made it from drawing board to factory in under nine months, half the usual development time. Another, outfitted with a full-color monitor, sold for under $2,500, half the price of current color Macs.

Apple began winning back market share and revenues increased (Fig. 6.29–2) as did income (Fig. 6.29–3). But there is a chance that it is too late. Windows has a very strong place in the market. That makes it far harder for Apple to switch IBM PC users to the Mac. Nobody who uses a PC will buy a Mac, and nobody who uses a Mac will buy a PC. Apple looks like the Beta of the Beta versus VHS video recorder battle in the 1980s.

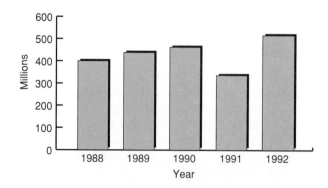

FIGURE **6.29–3** Apple Computer Net Income.

*Source: Apple Computer 1992 Annual Report.*

## A Solution?

Sixteen years after helping to pioneer the industry, Apple plans to move beyond it and become a global electronics holding company overseeing multiple business. Apple's vision for the year 2000 and beyond is of a vast market taking shape as all sorts of information is converted into digital form. Everything from high-definition pictures to local phone calls will be reduced to the zeros and ones that computers already use. Apple is betting that when that happens, several industries will converge into a $3 trillion mega-market. Apple's goal is to grab an early lead by using its ability to paint a user-friendly face on complex digital machines.

Thus, in the future, Apple plans to concentrate on building and selling consumer electronics, all sorts of software, telecommunications devices, and computers. As computer technology invades everything from television to electronic newspapers, the list of other applications may grow. The first machine to test Apple's new strategy is a gadget named "Newton." At its most basic, Newton is an electronic organizer that helps track appointments, phone numbers, and addresses. But it also recognizes hand printing, has a built-in fax and data modern, and runs faster than any other hand-held organizer.

Apple says Newton will eventually be a family of products, with the first model swiftly followed by versions that will take Newton both up- and down-market. But Apple admits it will not fix the specification of any follow-up models until it gauges reaction to its first effort. For Apple, much is at stake. Because the price wars in the PC market are hitting its profit margins, Apple hopes its unique technology will allow it to maintain a price premium over other innovative products.

Newton was on store shelves in 1993, however, significant sales are not expected until the mid-1990s. Initial reviews were very discouraging. Apple's troubles with its new product reached a frenzy as critics in all major PC magazines panned it and a Doonesbury cartoon made fun of Newton's ability to read handwriting.

Also, while the Newton is an interesting product, handwriting input computers are not unique. At the time Newton was introduced, there were already two others on the market. That points to Apple's most basic dilemma: creating another computer revolution that will equal the original, back in 1984, when Apple introduced its Mac.

As Apple undergoes a transformation from a one-product company with a simple distribution system to a multibusiness conglomerate that sells new types of products through new channels and new customers, it faces the need to fundamentally change. Firms that produce innovative consumer electronics operate with different distribution networks and price points than the PC industry. Some of these businesses also have radically different cost structures and product cycles than what Apple is accustomed to.

Apple grew to a $6 billion company by selling $2,000 machines, so electronic gadgets that bring in $250 apiece seem an odd basis for further growth. Apple would have to sell eight million of them a year to add $2 billion in revenues. However, the core business for Apple today, five years from now, and even 10 years from now, will still likely to be computers.

## PC BUYERS

Apple, Compaq, IBM, NEC, Tandy, and several other major computer manufacturers still think there's an untapped market with enormous potential out there. And they may be right. At the end of 1992, there were 70 million households in the United States that did not own PCs. Despite previous failures to penetrate the home market, PC manufacturers began enlisting the help of the mass merchandisers such as Sears, Circuit City, and Staples, promising plug-and-play capability and generous software bundles. And, while the average household income of families who own PCs in 1992 was about $54,000, vendors hoped to start selling into homes with incomes in the $30,000 to $35,000 range.

Buyers of PCs can be divided into four broad categories: business, government, education, and individual/home. Each customer group has somewhat different PC selection criteria and different means for purchasing computers. The largest segment is business, with roughly 60 percent of the units and 70 percent of the total revenue. During the 1980s, PCs were most often bought by individuals or small departments in corporations, without much input from the corporation's MIS staff. Individual business PC buyers were usually unsophisticated about the technology, and worried most about service, support, and compatibility. Brand name was especially important and full-service computer dealers, such as BusinessLand and ComputerLand, built billion dollar businesses servicing these customers.

Now, individual business consumers are becoming more knowledgeable about the PC. Full-service dealers suddenly became an expensive channel. Demand exploded, superstores such as CompUSA and Staples, as well as mail order outlets, offered computers and peripherals at 30 percent to 50 percent off list price. Even Kmart, Costco, and other mass merchandisers started to sell large volumes of PCs.

Because business organizations were increasingly demanding that their PCs be networked, another channel evolved, called value-added resellers (VARs). Most VARs are low overhead operations that buy computers in volume, package them with software or peripherals, and then configure the PCs into networks. Finally, some computer manufacturers bypassed third-party distribution entirely, selling directly through the mail, with phone support for customer service.

The education and individual/home markets are driven by different channels and somewhat different criteria. In the early 1990s, education accounted for roughly 9 percent of units and 7 percent of revenues. While most schools had limited budgets for computers, the primary concern for most educators was the availability of appropriate software. The individual/home market comprised about 31 percent of units and 23 percent of revenues; however, the market was a complicated mixture of people who bought computers for business work at home, and those who bought the computer for home use. Most of these consumers purchased PCs through mail order or other high-volume, low-priced channels.

## APPLE'S FUTURE

The future may be one in which people will have access to all forms information—news, television, business data, wherever and whenever they want, regardless of whether they use a hand-held personal digital assistant or a PC. By 2000, the consumer-electronics, television, telecommunication, entertainment, and news industries could merge into a single market, with sales of $35 trillion a year.

Over the next decade, most information, including television, is expected to assume the same digital form as computer data. The spread of mobile telephones is already bringing mobile computing in its wake. Some of the latest laptop computers can already communicate over the airwaves. More powerful chips seem certain to put enormous computing power into machines small enough to fit into the palm of a hand. More powerful software will make computers of any size and shape easier to use. The cost of storing, transmitting, manipulating, and analyzing data will drop sharply.

One thing seems certain: the new computer industry will never return to the stability or high profits of the old one. Too many companies now have access to the technology and to the customer. As the PC industry collides with the telecommunications, publishing, and consumer-electronics industries, there will be many battles over standards. The search for alliances, such as the recent one between Apple and IBM, will become more popular. Launching new products will involve even greater risks. Nobody really knows how many people will want so much information at their fingertips, what price they will pay for it, or what they will want to do with it.

Much of the battle in the PC industry will be fought over software. Future operating systems, which provide PCs with their basic instructions, must be able to manage handwriting, video, graphics, voice, and text, all of which will be flowing over computer networks. What is not clear is which companies will provide that operating system and all the associated application programs. Also, a huge variety of applications software, the programs people use to do their work, will be needed. Sophisticated word processing, presentation development, and spreadsheet programs will merge into integrated work tools with graphical and user-interfaces, which include voice recognition and artificial intelligence functions.

While Apple's movement into platforms that do not look like traditional computers may be a good idea in concept, to date the firm has not had any real successes to brag about. Today, Apple's harsh reality is that it is selling machines based mostly on price in direct competition with IBM-compatibles, which run nearly all the software an Apple machine uses.

CPUs (the instruction processor that manages the computer) that operate faster and more effectively than the Intel processor may enable Apple to regain its market position by selling a new proprietary technology at a premium price. But, many would argue that competitive advantages based on hardware are a thing of the past, and that only continual innovation in software married with new software delivery vehicles can place a firm in a sustainable, strong position.

What marketing strategy would you advise Apple to pursue? What specific price, distribution, promotion, and product elements would you propose and why? How would you deal with the growth competition in the computer hardware market? What do you think about Apple's plans to sell devices that do computer tasks but do not look like computers, including sophisticated cable converter boxes, high-tech portable phone systems, and others?

## Sources

*Apple Computer Company 1992 Annual Report.*

Buell, Barbara. "The Second Comeback of Apple." *Business Week* (January 28, 1991): 68.

"The Computer Industry." *The Economist* (February 27, 1993): a special insert survey.

Daly, James. "Spindler Likely to Prune Apple Orchard." *Computer World* (June 28, 1993): 1, 20.

Depke, Deidre A. "IBM and Apple: Can Two Loners Learn to Say 'Teamwork'." *Business Week* (July 22, 1991): 25.

Depke, Deidre A., and Richard Brandt. "PCs: What the Future Holds." *Business Week* (August 12, 1991): 58–64.

Deutschman, Alan. "Odd Man Out." *Fortune* (July 26, 1993): 42–56.

"Dreamware." *The Economist* (February 13, 1993): 68–69.

Gross, Neil, and Kathy Rebello. "Apple? Japan Can't Say No." *Business Week* (June 29, 1992): 32–33.

Kuper, Andrew. "Apple's Plan to Survive and Grow." *Fortune* (May 4, 1992): 68–72.

Rebello, Kathy, and Robert D. Hof. "Steve Jobs Has a New fix for NEXT: Software." *Business Week* (November 18, 1991): p 72.

Rebello, Kathy. "Apple's Daring Leap Into the All-Digital Future." *Business Week* (May 25, 1992): 120–122.

Rebello, Kathy. "You've Got Company Mac." *Business Week* (March 22, 1993): 34.

Schlender, Breton R. "Yet Another Strategy for Apple." *Fortune* (October 22, 1990): 81–87.

Schlender, Breton R. "The Future of the PC." *Fortune* (August 26, 1991): 40–48.

Schwartz, Evan I. "IBM-Apple Could be Fearsome." *Business Week* (October 7, 1991): 28–30.

Yoffie, David B. "Apple Computer 1992." Harvard Business School, case #9-792-081.

---

# CASE 30
# *First Fidelity Bank*

In 1994, First Fidelity Bancorp was one of the largest U.S. banks with $36 billion in assets. It also had subsidiaries that performed commercial banking operations, investment banking services, international banking services, brokerage services, and other related financial activities. Headquartered in Newark, New Jersey, First Fidelity had positioned itself as a regional player and repositioned itself for growth in a crowded marketplace. In the previous three years, it had acquired several out-of-state banks. That growth strategy came none too soon because the business that boomed in the early 1980s dropped off at the end of the decade. A credit crunch and

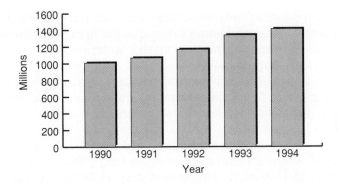

**FIGURE 6.30–1** First Fidelity Bank Corporation Total Sales.

*Source: First Fidelity Bank Corporation 1994 Annual Report.*

a recession affected the loan market and increased competition drew upon First Fidelity's customer base.

In 1994, First Fidelity achieved record earnings, improved asset quality, increased dividends, and made strategic acquisitions (Fig. 6.30–1). Net income for the year was a record $451.1 million, up 13.1 percent from a 1993 high of $398.8 million (Fig. 6.30–2). It had total assets of $36.2 billion at year-end.

A steadily improving economy accelerated demand for its customer and commercial loans in 1994, giving important support to Fidelity's revenue trend. Net interest income on a taxable-equivalent basis was $1,432.6 million in 1994, up from $1,387.4 million in 1993. Total loans averaged $21.7 billion in 1994, up 11.9 percent from the 1993 average of $19.4 billion.

Fidelity's program to expand its franchise into attractive contiguous markets continued in 1994 with the acquisition of The Bank of Baltimore and its 41 branches. It also entered into agreements to acquire several other banks. First Fidelity has made more than 20 acquisitions since 1990, and every one has been, or is expected to be, influential on earnings within 18 months of closing.

Fidelity has initiated programs designed to enhance fee-based income, especially in the areas of trust and private banking, consumer banking, and investment products. These programs include the introduction of new products such as the First Fidelity VISION Banking relationship product, which had over 130,000 relationships, representing $5.2 billion in deposits by the end of 1994.

Fidelity also did a better job of leveraging its distribution network to effectively market new and existing products. In addition, it did better at marketing all of its prod-

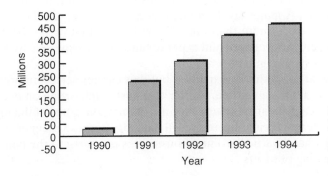

**FIGURE 6.30–2** First Fidelity Bank Corporation Net Income.

*Source: First Fidelity Bank Corporation 1994 Annual Report.*

ucts throughout the bank. Cross-selling and relationship banker referral programs in its various lines of business maximized opportunities to broaden and strengthen customer relationships. Fidelity utilized its branch offices to make a wider range of products available to consumers and small businesses.

Of course, the success of the bank's strategic program depends greatly on its quality of service initiatives. It expanded the measurement programs for customer service in all of its lines of business, and it was successful in raising customer satisfaction levels throughout First Fidelity in 1994.

With all of these initiatives, First Fidelity Bank should have been a survivor in the Darwinian evolution of America's banks. However, in June 1995, it was sold to First Union Corporation for $5.4 billion, the largest bank deal in U.S. history. The sale came from management's conclusions that the bank had fallen behind its toughest competitors and might never catch up. However, some argue that First Fidelity devoted to much attention to bank productivity and not enough attention to customer relationships and that was the major source of its relatively weak position in the banking industry.

## BANK PRODUCTIVITY

In recent years, the banking industry has been caught up in a movement toward greater efficiency and productivity, with the impact on service to and relationships with customers a sometimes casualty of this movement to stabilize profitability. However sweeping or timid their actions, most banks claim to be involved in a reengineering movement driven by the need to become more competitive with other companies offering financial services. Many banks are taking steps on both sides of the balance sheet to improve their competitive positions, mining their technology systems for increased efficiency, redesigning how work gets done, and focusing on individual business lines.

In the face of unprecedented competition, the industry is working to ensure its viability. Almost all bank chief executive officers realize that high overhead expenses are a serious competitive disadvantage that can be exploited by other banks and by nonbank competitors. In fact, most bankers believe that the key to survival is in becoming more efficient. However, reengineering to increase efficiency has wide ranging impacts throughout banking operations.

For effective reengineering and restructuring, banks must consider that indiscriminate cost cutting can actually hurt more than help in the long run. Banks that equate efficiency or reengineering with reducing employee head count, for instance, are not likely to be survivors. A major layoff of employees to cut costs is a short-term approach, which is difficult to do more than once. Some believe that banks' balance sheets are about 20 to 30 percent oversized and expense burdens are excessive by 10 to 15 percent, including the costs of regulation.

Banks must concentrate on reducing expenses, but they cannot neglect improved results on the revenue side at the same time. Rather than just emphasizing on overall efficiency, banks need to establish target returns by lines of business. Some of the highest returns come from the least efficient businesses in banking. Because reengineering includes examinations of what a particular line of business is returning to the bank, it can lead to a bank eliminating products.

Redefining the actual process of conducting a business is a key factor in bank reengineering. The interaction among employees, and between employees and customers, is the most important aspect of a bank's operation, yet even smaller banks are stifled by bureaucracy and sunk by bad customer service. Outdated procedures slow down service delivery and shift employees' time from customer service and sales to paperwork. The actual process of doing the work gets in the way of achieving goals.

Though bankers may disagree on how and what to reengineer, or even on what reengineering is, almost all agree that the time is right for change. Banks may feel more pressure now from outside competitors than ever before, but they are also in a good position to address the industry's problems. However, bankers are also aware that much of their profitability comes not from their own smart business practices, but from an interest rate environment that provides wide net interest margins, resulting in higher profits. As interest rates rise and the spread narrows between what banks are paying for funds and what they are making on investments and loans, profits will begin to evaporate.

## RELATIONSHIP MARKETING

For many years, marketers have struggled to find more effective and reliable ways to achieve an elusive goal: building and sustaining customer loyalty over an extended period of time. These efforts have often been labeled as "frequency marketing," "database marketing," or "relationship marketing." But creating and sustaining a lasting bond between a consumer and a product or service is a far more complex, interactive, and dynamic process than such reductive terms would suggest. It involves more than collecting data about customers and then selling to them. It means entering into a relationship with customers, giving them a sense of satisfaction with the purchase decision they have made, letting them know that the firm recognizes and values their business, and showing them the firm understands their needs and will respond accordingly.

The objective is to make them feel special, needed, and wanted, not just as "consumers" or "prospects," but as individuals. Many banks now sense that they may have focused too much time, effort, and marketing dollars on building bank awareness and acquiring new customers, while neglecting the investment required to maximize the profit potential of their existing customer base. These leading banks now understand how important long-term relationships are to their profitability and how much can be gained by cultivating existing relationships and focusing marketing efforts on building new ones.

Just as the implicit rules that guide personal relationships, customer relationship management principles are grounded in such old-fashioned values as respect, open communications, and trust. It is the skillful application of these values to every aspect of the customer relationship, through thoughtful strategic planning, imaginative database management, and informed creative executions, that is the heart of relationship management in banking as well as other industries.

The fundamentals of relationship management in banking include: building the framework for relationships; establishing relationships; developing an ongoing dialogue; maximizing the value of relationships; rewarding loyalty; and sustaining the relationships. To effectively manage the development of long-term relationships, a bank needs to create the basic building blocks that support all subsequent interactions. If it does not have a current customer database and an ongoing means of capturing new names, the process should begin there.

## THE FUTURE

Some predict that banks will continue to consolidate over the next few years as they scramble to increase their profitability and maximize their operational efficiencies. But cost-focused responses to competitive pressures may in the end be more harmful than helpful. It is easy to argue that no business can survive without a loyal customer base, which has some attachment to a particular firm. This means that banks need strong business building strategies to accompany their productivity and cost-management efforts, which should also emphasize customer service and customer relationships.

What marketing strategy would you advise First Fidelity's new owner, First Union Corporation, to develop in establishing strong relationships with customers? What specific price, distribution, promotion, and product elements would you propose and why? How would you deal with growing competition from other banks?

## Sources

"Bank Consolidations Shift into a Higher Gear." *Corporate Growth Report* (July 21, 1995): 7951, 7962.

Bosco, Pearl. "Little Banks, Big Bang." *Bank Systems & Technology* 31, 3 (March 1994): 52–58.

Brierley, Harold M. "The Art of Relationship Management." *Direct Marketing* (May 1994): 25–26.

Cantrell, Wanda, and Mark Borowsky. "Reinventing the Bank." *Bank Management* 69, 8 (August 1993): 26–32.

"Customer Service Can Reap Rich Rewards." *New Library World* 95, 1113 (1994): 5–6.

*First Fidelity Bank 1994 Annual Report.*

Holland, Kelley. "Leaner Isn't Always Meaner." *Business Week* (July 3, 1995): 33.

Kantrow, Yvette. "First Union Gets First Look At New Capital Markets Boss." *Investment Dealers Digest* 61, 28 (July 10, 1995): 7–8.

Kantrow, Yvette. "Wall Street's Winning Bankers in the Mega-Bank Merger Boom." *Investment Dealers Digest* 61, 30 (July 24, 1995): 4.

Lazo, Shirley A. "Speaking of Dividends: For Bank Investors, A Week to Savor." *Barron's* 75, 26 (June 26, 1995): 43.

"The Largest Bank Merger Announced." *Corporate Growth Report* (June 26, 1995): 7915–7916+.

Milligan, John W. "Bank of Boston's Merger Blues." *US Banker* 105, 9 (September 1995) 10–12.

Milligan, John W. "Why Big Banks Are Getting Bigger." *US Banker* 105, 8 (August 1995) 24–33.

Radigan, Joseph. "Shake, Rattle and Roll." *US Banker* 105, 9 (September 1995): 51–69.

Schifrin, Matthew. "The Early Bird." *Forbes* (December 7, 1992): 168–169.

Spiro, Leak Nathans, and Michele Galen. "Are Fewer Banks Better?" *Business Week* (August 17, 1992): 92–93.

Ward, Sandra. "Has the Market Lost Its Touch? Or Are Banks Just Irresistible?" *Barron's* 75, 29 (July 17, 1995): 10.

Wallenstein, Andy. "First Union Shines in Record Bank Deal." *Advertising Age* 66, 26 (June 26, 1995): 39.

Weber, Joseph, Wendy Zeller, and Zachary Schiller. "Seizing the Dark Day." *Business Week* (January 13, 1992): 26–28.

Woolley, Suzanne. "Mutual-Fund Houses Start to Hear Footsteps." *Business Week* (February 3, 1992): 68–69.

# *Foote, Cone & Belding Communications, Inc.*

CASE 31

The advertising industry is a triad of advertising agencies, the media, and the advertisers (usually agency clients). Agencies create and place most national and many retail ads in such media as television, radio, magazines, and billboards. In 1992 about $120 billion was spent in the United States by some quarter of a million national advertisers and nearly two million local advertisers. About 28 percent of the total came from the 100 top national advertisers, led by such nationally known firms as Kraft General Foods, Procter & Gamble, General Motors, and Sears & Roebuck.

Advertising agencies serve their clients with a variety of experts. Account executives act as liaisons between advertiser-client and agency, meeting with the client to determine objectives and budgets. Agency copywriters and art directors take their assignments from the account executive, who brings their work back to the client for approval or modification. When decisions on content are completed, often after research studies to determine the consumer response, the production department prepares the finished advertisements, with the aid of typographers, printers, and radio or television commercial production companies. Concurrently, the media department prepares a comprehensive media plan covering the purchase of space in newspapers or magazines or time on radio or television. After the completed printing plates, tapes, or films are shipped to the appropriate media, the media department checks for proper scheduling and adequate reproduction.

Closely related marketing activities, such as public relations and sales promotion, are handled by the advertising agency, other outside organizations, or the advertiser. Advertising must be coordinated with these other activities and with the client firm's overall objectives.

The most common advertising goal is to influence the consumer decision-making process, particularly the product or service purchased. These products and services are symbolized by brands, with successful brands having well-recognized images and strong consumer franchises. Marketing research can determine which types of consumers are most likely to buy a brand and test the features, benefits, images, or appeals to which consumers might respond, with advertising associating the brand with those appeals. Other promotional techniques focus on more immediate goals, such as a bar sign for beer seeks to produce an immediate purchase, but may not be effective without mass-media ads that cause familiarity with the name, associate appeals with the brand, and create favorable beliefs and attitudes.

Today's large agencies, except for Leo Burnett and Young & Rubicam, are primarily the result of mergers and acquisitions. Well over half the magazine ads and commercials consumers encounter are made by a large organization, with several thousand employees in offices all over the globe. However, in the process, there has been a great loss at the agencies because the work has become routinized.

## ADVERTISING AGENCY OPERATIONS

Advertising agencies differ in culture and personality, which vary substantially depending on management philosophies and organizational policies. Agencies are also know to have particular creative styles and approaches to advertising development that frequently contribute to distinctive advertising campaigns. For example, Leo Burnett often used cartoon characters such as the Kebbler Cookie Elf or the Pillsbury Dough Boy.

The agencies are classified by the types of accounts they tend to handle—consumer versus industrial, services versus products, or automobiles versus food items. Regardless, an agency never has responsibility for two competitors in the same market—that is, not two different beer companies or two different car manufactures.

Historically, agency compensation has been a 15 percent commission on the dollar value of the media placed for a client. For example, a campaign that uses $850,000 worth of television time was billed to the client as $1 million, with the agency getting revenues of $150,000. However, in the last 10 years, increasing numbers of clients have sought to negotiate agency fees, particularly large accounts with high media expenditures. They argue paying less than 15 percent is more appropriate because the total cost of developing a campaign is fixed, regardless of the media expenditure. The result is that large accounts tend to pay lower fees than a 15 percent commission rate, while smaller accounts may actually pay more because some agencies refused to take accounts below a certain size unless the client agreed to a commission rate greater than 15 percent. In addition, smaller clients tend to receive less attention in large agencies.

Large agencies have a competitive advantage in media placement because there are economies of scale in media purchasing. For example, individual agencies routinely purchase large blocks of network television time at as much as a 10 percent discount and then divide that time among clients, passing along the discount. However, those same large agencies have a competitive disadvantages in their size because the work of advertising campaigns (research, media planning, creative development, etc.) at the larger agencies frequently becomes entangled in bureaucratic mazes, with multiple levels of approval required to accomplish any task. Many of the bigger agencies have attempted to address this issue by forming smaller, independent units within the agency, which are similar to small advertising agencies.

Because the turnover of accounts already located at an agency is very low, competition among agencies occurs mostly over the new product or service introductions by large, established marketers or over small clients looking to establish their first agency relationship. In this competition for new business, clients select agencies primarily based on the work done for previous clients and on the "chemistry" between the teams at the client's firm and the agency who will work together.

## INTERNATIONAL ADVERTISING AGENCIES

The major influence on the growth of international advertising agencies has been the rise of multinational corporations. Many multinational advertisers find that only a large agency with offices in many countries can service their needs. These agencies usually employ specialists who can create and administer campaigns in several countries simultaneously. Large agencies use their international presence as a competitive advantage, drawing on their international experience in television, magazines, and newspapers.

Although U.S. agencies dominated the early growth in worldwide marketing, that position eroded significantly during the 1970s. In the 1980s, mergers of many large agencies produced mega-agencies owned by British investors, including WPP and Saatchi & Saatchi. Also important has been the rise of Japanese advertising agencies such as Dentsu. Also, many local offices of the U.S. agencies have served as training grounds for employees who later started their own agencies. At the same time, Madison Avenue's reputation for creative and marketing excellence declined, with European agencies claiming more creativity and marketing savvy. The mega-agencies are usually in the list of top 10 agencies in every country.

Worldwide advertising in the 1990s is a multibillion dollar industry with billings of nearly $200 billion expected by the end of the decade. The largest agencies are steadily increasing their share of worldwide advertising. Currently, they control about 30 percent but are expected to have 35 to 40 percent by the end of the decade. The United States is still by far the largest advertising market with about $120 billion in spending—Japan is second at about $30 billion, with the United Kingdom at about $12 billion and Germany at roughly $10 billion.

## FOOTE, CONE & BELDING COMMUNICATIONS, INC.

Foote, Cone & Belding (FCB) provides advertising, direct marketing, sales promotion, public relations, and related services through various media, such as television, radio, newspapers, and magazines they produce, merchandise and sell promotion programs, package design, trademark, and trade name development. It is a global marketing communications company that services clients worldwide. FCB's activities are conducted through an organization of 180 offices in 46 countries on six continents, including the combined Publicis FCB Communications group in Europe.

In 1992, FCB ranked as the ninth largest marketing communications company in the world and ninth largest in the United States. The U.S. client list contains many leading firms (Table 6.31–1). On a combined basis, FCB and Publicis had revenues of $884 million and billings of more than $6.1 billion.

In Bangkok, Brussels, Bogota, and more than 100 other world cities, FCB people are pursuing ideas and proposing initiatives that will move their clients' business forward. Employees are rooted in their country and culture and motivated toward achieving creative excellence in everything they do.

The FCB goal is to be the best agency in each market, providing its clients with a level of creativity they can't find elsewhere. The competition for global business advantage may be plotted in New York, London, or Tokyo, but it is won market-to-market and consumer-to-consumer. FCB has learned that global consumers do not buy its

---

**TABLE 6.31–1.    Some of FCB's 1993 Major U.S. Clients**

AT&T
Avon Products
California Raisin Advisory Board
Campbell Soup
Citicorp
Clorox
Colgate-Palmolive
Coors Brewing
Corning Glass Works
Johnson & Johnson
Kraft General Foods
Levi Strauss
Marriott
Mattel
Mazda
MGM Studios
Nabisco Foods
Northwest Airlines
Novell
Pillsbury
R. J. Reynolds
Sunkist Growers
Taco Bell
Zenith Electronics

*Source:* Various sources.

clients' products, *local* consumers do. Often consumer-based insights provoke inspired ideas that result in significant marketing success and inventive advertising.

As with all agencies, FCB's principal asset is its people, with its success depending in large part on FCB's ability to attract and retain personnel who are competent in the various aspects of the communications business. At the end of 1992, FCB employed 3,631 persons in its majority-owned offices: 2,411 were employed in the domestic offices and 1,220 were in the international offices. Of the 3,631 total employees, 1,100 were engaged in the creation and production of advertising, 1,176 in account management, 505 in media and research activities, and 850 in administrative and clerical functions.

FCB operates fully staffed offices in the United States, Canada, Latin America, Asia, and the Pacific. Together with its partner, Publicis Communication, the Publicis FCB Communication group operates fully staffed offices in Europe. These international offices handle U.S.-based and foreign-based multinational and national advertising assignments.

FCB, through its wholly owned and partially owned companies, analyzes the advertising needs of clients, plans and creates advertising for their products and services, and places that advertising for dissemination through various media such as television, radio, newspapers, and magazines. In accordance with standard agency practice, the physical preparation of finished newspaper, magazine, television, and radio advertising is performed by outside contractors under supervision by FCB. FCB also offers its clients such additional services such as design and production of merchandising and sales promotion programs, public relations, and collateral services such as market and product research, package design, and trademark and trade name development.

FCB also provides specialized communications services to its clients. These services include direct marketing, sales promotion and design, health care and yellow pages advertising. The principal sources of FCB's advertising revenues are commissions and related fees earned on advertising placed with the various media, with FCB purchasing the time and space from advertising media on behalf of its clients. The media bills FCB for the time and space, and FCB in turn bills its clients and pays the media less the agency commission, normally 15 percent.

FCB receives production commissions from its clients for services, materials, and talent furnished by independent contractors in the preparation and production of advertising. These commissions are customarily 17.65 percent of the independent contractor's charge (which is the equivalent of 15 percent of the gross billing for such charge). In addition, FCB receives from certain clients fees for various other services performed in connection with advertising, research and marketing studies, and public relations activities. FCB performs these services for national and international advertisers of consumer and industrial goods and services. During 1992, the agencies 10 largest clients accounted for approximately 45 percent of consolidated revenues (commissions and fees); only one client, Mazda, accounted for as much as 10 percent of consolidated revenues.

## 1992 Performance

FCB had an outstanding year in 1992, with significant progress against its two overall priorities: bringing creative intensity to everything it does, and ensuring that its shareholders and employees profit better from this creativity.

FCB's creativity has vastly improved, and FCB is now beginning to receive more public recognition for its work:

- *Advertising Age* and *Adweek* both chose FCB's Levi's Dockers work as the "Best Campaign of the Year."
- *Adweek* cited five of FCB's efforts as best all-around campaigns of 1992, more than any other agency.
- Two different and well-known client trade journals selected FCB as "Agency of the Year."

This focus on improving creativity has led to significant growth. FCB added more than $300 million in new business, a 22 percent increase over 1991, and FCB was a big gainer among all major U.S. agencies. These new clients included: Louis Rich, a unit of Kraft General Foods and Wesley-Jessen, maker of DuraSoft contact lenses (FCB Chicago); Tandem Computer, Zima, a brand of Coors Brewing Co., Macromedia, SunSoft, and Dockers Footwear from Johnston & Murphy (FCB San Francisco); Fila Sportswear and Colgate-Palmolive Softsoap (FCB/LKP, New York); Metro-Goldwyn-Mayer and Giorgio's "Wings" fragrance (FCB Los Angeles); and U.S. Healthcare (FCB Philadelphia).

For 1992, virtually every financial objective was met. The highlights of FCB's 1992 financial performance were (a selected list):

- **Total billings.** Total billings for FCB and their European alliance Publicis FCB increased 13 percent in 1992 to over $6.1 billion (see Figure 6.31–1 for revenues growth).
- **Net income.** Total net income after tax was $21.7 million, the highest in history and 29 percent ahead of the prior year's net income of $16.8 million, exclusive of 1991 restructuring charges (see Figure 6.31–2).
- **Return on equity.** ROE increased 33 percent in 1992 to 12.6 percent from 9.5 percent in 1991, exclusive of 1991's restructuring charges.

FCB also invested in the future by expanding FCB's global presence through the acquisitions and joint ventures.

### FCB's Creative Excellence

To enhance its sales success and reward initiatives that produce marketplace advantages for its clients, the FCB Chairman's Award was established in 1992. In that year, the award went to FCB's Levi's Dockers television campaign.

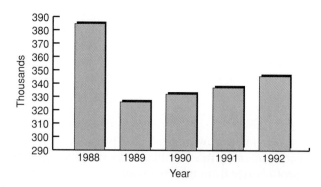

**FIGURE 6.31–1** FCB Revenues.

*Source: FCB 1992 Annual Report.*

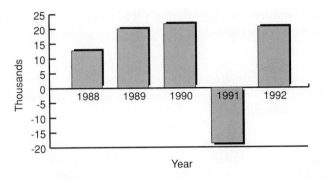

**FIGURE 6.31–2** FCB Net Income.

*Source: FCB 1992 Annual Report.*

### Television

In television commercials FCB celebrates both the tenderness and bravado of youth—Levi's 501 jeans; savors the power and precision of a unique automobile—Mazda MX-6; captures the essence of beauty—Isabella Rossellini for Lancomé; evokes a smile—Leslie Nielsen for Coors Light; reveals the innermost thoughts of real people—V8-Wherehouse; and finds joy in everyday life—Lea & Perrins.

### Print

FCB measures the contribution of a print ad by what the audience does with it, a triumphant image beckons the champion in all of us—Head Sports Equipment; a simple timepiece is transformed into a global fashion icon—Swatch; a classic rag-top becomes the road to adventure for a generation eager to create new memories—Mazda Miata; an alluring fragrance imparts an air of mystery to delight today's woman—Giorgio Armani's Gio; and a provocative headline whets the appetite for a new taste—Zima.

### Other Media

Pacific Bell Yellow Pages introduced viewers to California Olympic hopefuls through 60-second athlete profiles on a Los Angeles television station during the Olympics. The attention the show gave to the Yellow Pages was as good as gold. A star was born when Levi Strauss & Co. used the syndicated television program, "This is the NFL" to spotlight the colors of its Dockers line of casual wear, by showing the similarity between the teams' colors and Dockers. For Off! Skintastic, SC Johnson Wax staged a sampling spectacular. To reach a family audience, the product made a free appearance before fans at such venues as Disney World, outdoor concerts, and sporting events. SC Johnson Wax also made Raid Max a success in the bug season across America. They bypassed television clutter to reach urban dwellers by booking all available ads on buses, inside and out.

### Consumer Research

At FCB, research, both qualitative and quantitative, is used to stretch the imagination. FCB's researchers have a passion for consumers. They collect, search, wander, listen, and distill insights that act as levers to launch the creative mind.

FCB's famous Levi's campaign began with focus groups of women telling why they like their favorite casual outfit, and then it ended by sending them home with cameras to record their lives. This anthropological approach led to Levi's advertising that captured the essence of contemporary women.

### Sales Promotion

Marketing messages must be original, compelling, and carefully crafted to induce a consumer response. IMPACT, FCB's sales promotion company, builds brands and bottom lines with value-added marketing.

### Direct Marketing

FCB Direct helps build enduring relationships with customers. It also constantly invents ways to target customers and prospects with customized messages.

## THE FUTURE OF ADVERTISING AGENCIES

### Integrated Marketing?

FCB and the entire advertising agency business are evolving, but some would argue that much more needs to be done more rapidly. While clients and consumers are changing their behavior, many agencies still cling tenaciously to an obsolete way of doing things. This is happening in the face of mass-media fragmentation, the increasing power of retailers, and the growing skepticism of advertisers. Because of their general unwillingness to pioneer the future, many ad agencies are now threatened with extinction or obsolescence. Which brings us to what some argue may be the ad industry's only real chance for survival: a 20-year-old concept called *integrated marketing*, new jargon for getting a client to coordinate all its marketing efforts, television and radio ads, magazine placement, direct mail, special events, billboards, even public relations, preferably through one agency, which creates a single image for the product.

What everyone seems to forget, however, is that integrated marketing has not worked in the past. In the last 10 years, most agencies set up ancillary services as units that handle anything other than print, television, and radio advertising as separate profit centers, so each division was motivated to push its own expertise rather than come up with an integrated approach. Even worse, the ancillary services were treated with disdain by the agency's creative specialists, who preferred making television commercials.

The proponents of integrated marketing contend that these problems are being solved. Ancillary services at their agencies are learning to work together, and the same team of creative people is assigned to handle every aspect of a client's campaign, from direct mail to cable television, so that a consistent message is delivered. The method of advertising will vary, depending on what works best for the product. But if integrated marketing is to finally achieve its potential, agencies must become fully diversified marketing service companies. So far, only a few agencies, including FCB, are making a significant attempt to meet that challenge.

The most significant difficulty facing those agencies pushing toward integrated marketing is that there are few takers so far. Many advertisers appear to prefer to orchestrate their own coordinated packages rather than entrust everything to one agency. In a survey conducted by the American Association of Advertising Agencies, leading advertisers overwhelmingly averred that agencies cannot coordinate diversified programs any better than they can. These big marketers also said they would not limit themselves to one agency for all their communications needs. If the advertising industry is to win back its clout, it is going to have to make a serious effort at making integrated marketing work, including both within agency changes in organization and functions and without with respect to convincing clients to use their full range of services. The marketplace has migrated away from the agencies; they have to come up with compelling reason why clients should shift back to them.

What strategies and actions would you recommend for FCB? What roles should integrated marketing, international competitions, and creative strategies play in your recommendations? What will FCB's competitive advantage be as a result of those strategies and actions? If you do not favor integrated marketing and internationalization, what are your alternatives? Are there other strategies to pursue? Also, what about the issues related to agency size and the ability to service clients? What are the trade-offs between an agency organized around small, entrepreneurial miniagencies versus the large, megaorganizations so popular with the top international agencies?

## Sources

Bissell, John. "What Ails Ad Agencies." *Advertising Age* (November 16, 1992): 22.

Collins, David. "Saatchi & Saatchi Company PLC: Corporate Strategy," Boston: Harvard Business School, 1992, case no. 9–792–056.

Duncan, Tom. "Integrated Marketing? It's Synergy." *Advertising Age* (March 8, 1993): 22.

*Foote, Cone & Belding Communications Annual Report, 1992.*

Foote, Cone & Belding Communications Public Relations materials, 1992.

Landler, Mark. "A Blizzard of Pink Slips Chills Adland." *Business Week* (December 10, 1990): 210–211.

Mayer, Martin. *Whatever Happened to Madison Avenue?* Boston: Little, Brown, and Company, 1991.

Rice, Faye. "A Cure for What Ails Advertising?" *Fortune* (December 16, 1991): 119–122.

Schultz, Don E. "Why Ad Agencies Are Having So Much Trouble With IMC." *Marketing News* (April 26, 1993): 12.

Schultz, Don E. *Strategic Advertising Campaigns*. 3rd ed Lincolnwood, Illinois: NTC Business Books, 1991.

*Standard Directory of Advertising Agencies*, New Providence, New Jersey: National Register Publishing, 1993.

Wells, Melanie. "Top-shop Ranks Suffer Cutbacks as Uptick Seen," *Advertising Age* (December 7, 1993): 34–35.

# CASE *Ford Taurus* 32

In 1992, there was a marketing war between Ford Taurus and Honda Accord over the top spot in the highly competitive American car market. At stake in this struggle was the leadership position and bragging rights in a competition that pitted the marketers at Ford against those at Honda. This was a classic battle for a multibillion dollar consumer market and the prize was both tangible, as sales and profits, and intangible, as higher moral and prestige.

In 1989, Ford's subcompact Escort was toppled as the best-selling car in America by the then compact Honda Accord. Ever since, to the embarrassment of domestic car makers, Accord advertising bragged about the car's leadership position. However, Ford produced another contender with its newly restyled Taurus with which Ford nearly closed the sales gap with the Accord.

Near the end of 1992, the battle between the Taurus and Accord was too close to call (see Figure 6.32–1). The two cars were running neck and neck, with Honda ahead one month and Ford ahead the next. Indeed, Taurus' sales were so strong that Ford's total market share rose a full point during the first part of 1992, and the company turned a $338 million first quarter profit, which was its only profitable quarter since the summer of 1990 (see Figure 6.32–2 and 6.32–3).

In 1992, midsize family sedans such as the Honda Accord, Toyota Camry, Ford Taurus, and Chevrolet Lumina made up 34 percent of the total car market. They also returned an average 16 percent to 18 percent profit margin. On smaller cars such as the Ford Escort, manufacturers generally lost money. Because aging baby-boomers drive the demand for midsize cars, that demand was projected to stay strong through the 1990s and midsize sales were expected to rise 20 percent through the late 1990s.

**FIGURE 6.32–1** Taurus versus Accord Unit Sales.

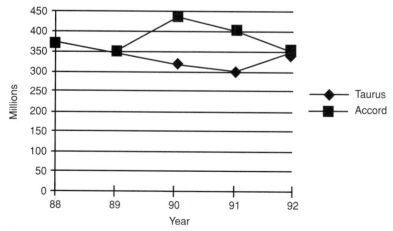

*Source: Estimated from various sources.*

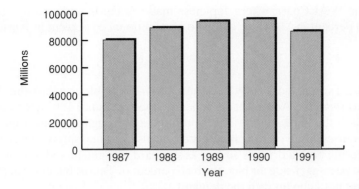

**FIGURE 6.32–2** Ford Motor Company Revenues.

*Source: Ford Motor Company 1991 Annual Report.*

By the end of 1992, nearly all of the auto companies were doing their best to grab a piece of the midsize market. Nissan Motor Company was getting the Altima ready for its debut. And Chrysler planned to launch its midsize LH sedans, including the Dodge Intrepid, Eagle Vision, and Chrysler Concorde. But the newcomers faced a tough challenge in dislodging the three leaders, which held a combined 76 percent of the category. Indeed, Ford's sales were so strong that it tended to dismiss its onetime rival, Chevrolet. Chevrolet's Lumina was in trouble and sinking fast. However, Chevy was not giving up; it had plans to come out with a revamped version of the model.

The Toyota Camry and Honda Accord have competed for years for the title of best compact sedan. In 1990, the newly redesigned Accord edged out the Camry according to automotive experts and held that edge through the 1991 model year (which was introduced in the fall of 1990). The new midsize 1992 Camry (introduced in the fall of 1991) was based on the Lexus ES300 design, but it felt more like a luxury car than a middle-class workhorse. It was Camry's larger body that moved it up from the compact to the midsize class, where it joined the Ford Taurus and Mercury Sable. At the same time, Accord grew to become a midsize competitor. Also for the 1992 model year, the Taurus and Sable were redesigned, though their basic chassis and engine lineup remained unchanged.

## HONDA'S ACCORD

The Honda Accord grew over the decades from a compact to a midsize sedan as its baby boomer customers matured. But in 1992 the Accord was showing its age, and, as a result, the new Toyota Camry and Ford Taurus were cutting into Accord's customer

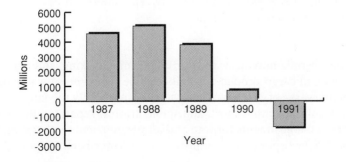

**FIGURE 6.32–3** Ford Motor Company Net Income.

*Source: Ford Motor Company 1991 Annual Report.*

base. Indeed, on the West Coast, where Japanese-made Accords were mostly sold, sales plummeted 50 percent in March of 1992 and an additional 26 percent in April of 1992.

## A Marketing Blitz

Meanwhile, the Taurus and Camry launched a marketing blitz against the Accord. Unlike its Ford rival, the Accord had not been remodeled since 1990 and would not be until 1994. Both the Ford and the Toyota offered a V-6 engine, a bigger motor than the Accord's four-cylinder power plant. Ford was also pushing safety: it was the only midsize car offering both a driver's air bag as standard equipment and, for an extra $400, an optional passenger side air bag. With 80 percent of Taurus buyers ordering dual bags, Ford could not keep up with the demand.

Honda did not seem to be panicking, but the anxiety level was growing as it had problems working down inventory. Dealer stocks of the Accord were hovering at around an 80 days' supply. That was a lot of cars waiting to be sold, especially considering that at one time in 1983 Honda had only 30 days' worth of Accords in inventory. Privately, even some Honda officials conceded that Taurus would win top-seller honors in 1993.

## The 1992 Honda Accord

The 1992 Honda Accord four-door EX listed for $18,245. Standard equipment included a 2.2 liter SOHC 16-valve FOUR, five-speed manual transmission, driver's air bag, air conditioning, antilock brakes, power windows, power door locks, power mirrors, power sunroof, power antenna, cruise control, intermittent wipers, tilt steering column, rear window defroster, alloy wheels, and stereo cassette sound system. Other styles included the two-door DX at $13,025, the LX at $16,625, the four door DX at $13,225, the LX at $15,825, the LX wagon at $17,450, and the EX wagon at $19,900.

### Performance

The 2.2-liter FOUR accelerated as well as V-6 cars, but had better mileage, at about 24 mpg. The engine in the EX developed slightly more horsepower than the one in other Accord versions, with no penalty in fuel economy. The electronically controlled automatic transmission shifted less smoothly than its midsize competitors.

The Honda handled smoothly and nimbly in routine driving. The nicely weighted power steering provided good feedback. The car responded crisply in abrupt maneuvers, with only a hint of body lean and tail wag. In hard turns, its response remained smooth and crisp. The front wheels plowed moderately. The antilock brakes stopped short and straight on both dry and wet pavement.

### Comfort and Convenience

Lightly loaded, the car rode nervously and stiffly, pitching, kicking, and jiggling. A full load of passengers and cargo produced a smooth ride. Road noise was rather high. The cars instruments were very clear and easy to read, especially the large numbers on the odometer. A console with a short, adjustable armrest separated the front seats. Both seats had manual adjustments for fore and aft position and seatback angle. The driver's seat in the EX incorporated an adjustment for lower-back support. The seat was low, and it lacked a height adjustment. Fortunately, the instrument panel and windowsills were also low, affording the driver excellent visibility. An adjustable steering column helped, too.

Passengers assumed a relaxed, reclined posture in the Honda's roomy rear seat. The center passenger sat slightly ahead of and higher than those on either side, so three people did not feel pinched. The low seats and roof made access a bit awkward. Those entering the car could tilt the steering column up or down, but it did not pop up and out of the way, as it did in many other models. The climate system furnished warm or cool air quickly and distributed it well. The rear-window defroster worked slowly but thoroughly.

Four Pullman bags and three weekend cases fit into the Honda's sizable trunk with room to spare. The trunk was expandable; the rear seatback folded down easily.

The basic warranty lasted for three years or 36,000 miles. Rust-through protection lasted for three years, with no mileage limit.

### Safety and Reliability

The height of the upper anchors for the front shoulder belts were adjustable, insuring comfort for short and tall riders. Securing a child safety seat was easy. The Accord had consistently maintained a much-better-than-average reliability record.

## FORD'S TAURUS

When the Ford Taurus first went on sale on December 26, 1986, it heralded the renaissance of Ford—a comeback for U.S. car making. The Taurus, and its twin the Mercury Sable, brought back many foreign-car buyers and led to a major shift toward more aerodynamic car designs.

Critics praised Taurus' first major redesign in 1991. The new Taurus and Sable symbolized not only Ford's strengths but also its major weakness: slow new-product development. Ford had spent six years and $600 million updating the car. Some believed that the redesign was too timid; others praised the car for its sleeker interior and added features. However, external changes were minor, including different headlights and taillights. The Taurus was not due for another revamp until 1995, and dealers feared that the design will go stale. While Ford was letting the Taurus grow old, Japanese companies were overhauling their designs every four years. But, Ford was more concerned about alienating the 1.5 million Taurus owners by changing the car too much. Ford's primary marketing objective was to get current Taurus owners into a new Taurus.

Without a snappier new Taurus, Ford could have a hard time holding on to the gains it made in the previous several years. Taurus pushed Ford's market share in midsize sedans from 14 percent in 1985 to 38 percent in 1991, mainly at the expense of GM. Taurus also added nearly $7 billion to Ford's revenues in both 1988 and 1989, and it was very profitable.

### The 1992 Ford Taurus

The 1992 Ford Taurus four-door LX listed for $17,775. Standard equipment included a 3.0 liter OVH V-6, overdrive automatic transmission, driver's air bag, air conditioning, power windows, power door locks, power mirrors, power driver's seat, intermittent wipers, "autolamp" system, rear window defroster, alloy wheels, and stereo radio. Other styles included the four-door at $14,980, the four-door GL at $15,280, the four-door SHO at $23,839, and the L wagon at $16,290, the GL wagon at $16,290, and the LX wagon at $19,464.

### Performance

Both engines available in the Ford performed well. The extra cost 3.8-liter V-6 was more responsive than the standard 3.0-liter V-6. But the smaller V-6 was thriftier: 23 mpg versus 21 mpg overall. The electronic overdrive automatic transmission shifted smoothly but sometimes felt indecisive and abrupt at low speeds. The car's normal handling was predictable, though not as crisp as the Toyota's or Honda's. The car responded fairly quickly and accurately in accident-avoidance maneuvers, and the tires griped well. There was some tail wag, but little body lean. In hard turns at steady speeds, handling felt sluggish. The car tended to plow ahead, but letting up on the accelerator tightened the turn. The steering felt numb. The optional antilock brakes stopped very short on both dry and wet track.

### Comfort and Convenience

The Taurus rode softly on good roads, but rocked on bumpy roads where the ride becomes busy, but a full load calmed things down. The individual front seats afforded good, firm support. The center console incorporated a storage bin and a comfortable armrest. Both seatbacks had a manual recliner and a power operated lower-back support. The driver's seat, with its six-way power adjustment, and the tilt steering column, suited most drivers well. The car seated six if the owner choose the split bench seat. The rear seat held three adults in comfort. The steering wheel popped up, out of the driver's way. To get into the rear, a person entering the car had to climb over tall, broad doorsills and duck under the roof pillars. Foot clearance was tight. The climate system moved lots of air and distributed it evenly. To get a bilevel setting (which provided warm air below and cooler air above), the customer had to buy an optional electronic climate control system.

The Ford's roomy trunk packed in four Pullman cases and four weekend bags, unless the buyer purchased the optional full-service spare, which raised the trunk floor a couple of inches. A high trunk sill made loading heavy items difficult.

The Taurus came with a three year or 36,000-mile basic warranty and a six-year or 100,000-mile warranty against rust-through.

### Safety and Reliability

The car's optional passenger-side air bag was designed into the dashboard without sacrificing the glove compartment. The front safety belts fit comfortably. Installing a child seat was easy. The Taurus, and similar Mercury Sable, had compiled an average repair record over the past several years.

### The Taurus' Unique History

The Taurus resulted from a consumer focus designed to produce a car that would excite market interest and begin a new era in European styling for American cars. For the first time, the *customer* came first. This meant research throughout the development process to ensure that the Taurus addressed consumer needs. Ford knew it had quality and design problems with its existing car models so it sought more information about what consumers wanted in a midprice, family-oriented car.

The Taurus' aerodynamic styling was essential to Ford's philosophy that form should follow function in design. Even though there was uneasiness about how the U.S. mid-car market buyers would accept a radical new styling, the practical benefits of the design outweighed those concerns because the design delivered better gas mileage, improved handling, and reduced wind noise, resulting in a quieter ride.

Ford studied every interaction between driver and car to produce the best match between automobile and owner. This meant designing a front-seat area that brought all the instruments and control systems within quick and easy reach, and it included a focus on *safety* as well as comfort.

## CUSTOMER PROFILES FOR THE TAURUS AND ACCORD

The demographic profiles of Taurus and Accord owners are quite different (Table 6.32–1). Ford Taurus buyers were more likely to be men, ages 35 to 44, married with children, living in the northeast, and with household incomes over $30,000 per year. Honda Accord owners were better balanced by gender, between the ages of 18 and 54, married with young children or single, living in the west, and with incomes over $30,000 per year.

The reasons that the customer profiles for the Taurus and Accord were dissimilar may be due to a combination of factors, including differences in image. The Taurus was a family car and the Accord was a slightly more sporty car. Accord had a two door model and Taurus did not, although both offered sedans and station wagons; and, obviously, Taurus was an American car and Accord was Japanese (regardless of where they were actually made).

## THE STRATEGY FOR FORD TAURUS

Much of the planning for the Ford Taurus' marketing strategy occurred high atop a Renaissance Center tower in downtown Detroit, behind a door marked "Taurus War Room." There, Ford management developed and executed its strategy to get to the top of the domestic car market. Ford managers frequently worked the phones exhorting Ford dealers to sell more Taurus' before year's end. Their objective: to defeat Honda's Accord and make Taurus the best-selling car of 1992. As of November 1992, Taurus only trailed Accord by as few as 15,000 cars, with good prospects for topping the Accord by the end of the year.

However, victory would not come cheaply for either Ford or Honda because both were offering significant incentives to lure buyers into their showrooms in final weeks of 1992. Ford management believed that beating Honda would fire up employees and enhance its image as the leading competitor in the domestic car market. It would be the crowning achievement for the full-line auto division.

The Ford division's car sales rose 11 percent in 1992, despite a flat market. However, Ford's successes would be difficult to sustain because a large portion of its sales had been bought through dealing and discounting. But to ensure a Taurus victory, Ford had been using every marketing technique it could think of to win, including an ag-

TABLE 6.32–1 Taurus and Accord Ownership (decision making adults)

| | Ford Taurus | | Honda Accord | |
|---|---|---|---|---|
| | *%* | *Index* | *%* | *Index* |
| **Total** | **0.9** | **100** | **1.0** | **100** |
| *Gender* | | | | |
| Male | 1.1 | 124 | 1.1 | 108 |
| Female | 0.7 | 78 | 0.9 | 92 |
| *Age* | | | | |
| 18–24 | 0.4 | 42 | 1.2 | 122 |
| 25–34 | 0.9 | 106 | 1.2 | 120 |
| 35–44 | 1.5 | 179 | 1.1 | 108 |
| 45–54 | 0.8 | 95 | 0.9 | 93 |
| 55–64 | 0.7 | 84 | 1.0 | 97 |
| 65 and older | 0.5 | 55 | 0.5 | 48 |
| *Marital status* | | | | |
| Single | 0.5 | 57 | 1.0 | 100 |
| Married | 1.0 | 120 | 1.1 | 107 |
| Divorced, etc. | 0.7 | 87 | 0.8 | 78 |
| Parents | 1.3 | 151 | 1.0 | 99 |
| *Region* | | | | |
| Northeast | 1.6 | 193 | 1.1 | 105 |
| Midwest | 0.6 | 75 | 0.7 | 69 |
| South | 0.7 | 83 | 0.8 | 77 |
| West | 0.5 | 62 | 1.7 | 171 |
| *Income* | | | | |
| $75 + | 1.4 | 169 | 1.6 | 161 |
| $60 + | 1.7 | 203 | 1.7 | 165 |
| $50 + | 1.8 | 208 | 1.8 | 175 |
| $40 + | 1.5 | 170 | 1.6 | 153 |
| $30 + | 1.3 | 153 | 1.6 | 154 |
| $30–$39 | 0.9 | 106 | 1.6 | 157 |
| $20–$29 | 0.4 | 47 | 0.4 | 39 |
| $10–$19 | 0.2 | 22 | 0.4 | 40 |
| Less than $10 | 0.2 | 24 | 0.0 | 3 |
| *Presence of children* | | | | |
| Under 2 years | 1.1 | 130 | 1.7 | 167 |
| 2–5 | 1.3 | 151 | 1.2 | 115 |
| 6–11 | 1.1 | 126 | 0.6 | 58 |
| 12–17 | 1.1 | 128 | 0.4 | 42 |

Note: Index values above are computed by dividing the proportion in a particular grouping by their proportion of the population. For example, if an age group has 20.2% of the products users and represents 18.3% of the population, the index value for the grouping is 110. Index values over 100 signify above average usage and index values below 100 signify below average usage. However, values over 110 or under 90 are the most significant.

*Source:* Simmons Market Research Bureau, Inc., 1991.

gressive, $249 month, two-year lease deal that reduced the price of a well-equipped Taurus by up to $2,600. Ford was also offering cash incentives of up to $1,550 to prospective Taurus buyers.

Analysts estimated that the incentives would cost Ford tens of millions of dollars in 1992. But, with a surge in demand, Ford could still move solidly into the black. As the Big Three's low cost producer, Ford could break-even with its plants running at just 68 percent of capacity, with anything above that increasing profits dramatically. In 1992, Ford was running at 91 percent of capacity, putting it in a strong competitive position.

Ford continued to focus on its new model development activities with some new entries. It had cut a year off its five-year development cycle but needed to reduce that number by one more year. That would help it more quickly revamp aging models, such as the Mustang, which would be 14 years old when a new version comes out in Fall 1992. The new Mustang would be a fashionable, youth-oriented car, with enough nostalgia to attract the baby boomers who still had fond memories of the first Mustang. Already selling well was a new, sporty Probe that came out in mid-1992.

No other model was ready, though, to replace the Taurus as Ford's flagship, which was why the competition with Honda was so intense. Honda would not give up the top spot without a hard fight. Honda's marketing weapon: a $199-a-month, five-year lease on a stripped-down Accord. The company also offered a dealer incentive and a "Spin to Win" contest that awarded up to $500 to sales staff who sold Accords.

Ford spent about $100 million in measured media to launch the original Taurus and Sable. The car's jellybean like styling, considered radical then, was a hit with consumers and has been widely copied. Some industry observers question Ford's decision to stick with that styling. Ford would need an aggressive marketing push to convince consumers the new models were still state-of-the-art.

Ford planned to spend an estimated $100 million-plus in 1993 to publicize Taurus and Sable improvements, even though the cars did not look much different. That included a special effects laden television advertisement in which an old Taurus model reshaped into the new version, showing interior and exterior changes. A second commercial dramatized how designers were given the task of improving the car without dramatically changing it. The ads would carry the theme "Have you seen the 1990s taking shape?"

## WHAT'S NEXT FOR THE TAURUS?

The Taurus was and is a symbol of Ford's move to dominance in the American car market. The car embodies much of Ford's new consumer orientation and operational philosophy and Ford changed and benefited from the result. However, while it appears that the Taurus' success resulted from good market- and customer-oriented design and selling, others wonder if the Taurus' success is really more of an accident than the result of its systematic approach to meeting consumer needs.

One theory about why the Taurus has been such a hit is based on the idea that the car represents a product in the right place at the right time. This argument is analogous to the observation that Levi's success with jeans was the result of circumstances rather than foresight or good planning. Even if Ford produced the Taurus from insights into the desires of the car's target market, it is questionable as to whether that process is continuing. The new Taurus and Sable models had only minor design changes. And, there was no evidence that Ford was continuing to respond to customer desires by being willing to make significant changes in the car with future redesigns. Nevertheless, Taurus sales continue to grow because the car has tremendous appeal to a broad audience.

To plan future Taurus strategy, Ford needs to understand why the car continues to be such a big success and how the success can be continued. How would you explain the Taurus' continuing popularity? What situational factors do you think contributed to that popularity? And, how do you see the future unfolding? What marketing strategy would you recommend for the future, including specifics about pricing, product design, and promotion approaches?

## Sources

Bownes, Greg. "Taurus Goes For The Title." *Business Week* (May 18, 1992): 50–51.

Flint, Jerry. "Banzai With A Georgia Accent." *Forbes* (February 4, 1991): 58–59.

"Ford Motor Company," in *Contemporary Cases in Consumer Behavior* eds. Blackwell, Roger D., W. Wayne Talarzyk, and James F. Engel. (Chicago, IL: Dryden Press, 1990): 3–13.

*Ford Motor Company 1991 Annual Report.*

Kerwin, Kathleen, and Larry Armstrong. "Red Hot, Red Ink." *Business Week* (January 11, 1993): 26–27.

Kerwin, Kathleen, and Larry Armstrong. "Why Motown Is Going The Extra Mile In California." *Business Week* (October 12, 1992): 70–71.

Kerwin, Kathleen, and James B. Treece. "There's Trouble Under Ford's Hood." *Business Week* (November 29, 1993): 66–67.

Kichen, Steve. "Will The Third Time Be The Charm?" *Forbes* (March 15, 1993): 54.

"Road Test." *Consumer Reports* (March 1992): 191–198.

Serafin, Raymond. "$100M Back Ford Redesigns." *Advertising Age* (September 9, 1991): 41.

Simmons Market Research Bureau, Inc., 1991.

Treece, James B. "New Taurus, New Sable, Old Blueprint." *Business Week* (September 9, 1991): 45.

# Case Analysis Exercises

This appendix contains five sample case exercises. The exercises are designed to be done with the MPAS program described in Appendix B. The exercises are designed to provide an opportunity to structure your case analysis work within the MPAS program. Detailed instructions on how to do the exercises with the program are included through step-by-step instructions on how to do the work associated with the exercises and how to print the results. The exercises are an indication of the different assignments that can be created for the MPAS program and the cases in this book.

Every exercise can be used with any of the 32 cases in this book. However, only one example is given for each type of exercise, and the way that case is handled in the sample exercise is frequently specific to that firm and industry.

In addition to providing assignments for various parts of a course, the exercises provide training in how to use the MPAS program. Some instructors will want to assign the complete analysis of a firm by the end of a course. At that point, students should have accumulated enough experience with the features of the MPAS program to be able to do a complete case analysis without the kind of explicit instructions found in the sample case exercises.

## THE CONTENTS OF THIS APPENDIX

# *Exercise 1*
## *Deal-A-Meal USA*

This case exercise is used in conjunction with the "situation: macroenvironmental trends" portion of the course. It emphasizes the analysis of macroenvironmental trends relating an industry and a firm. Specifically, this assignment is to conduct a macroenvironmental analysis of the dieting and weight loss industry for Deal-A-Meal USA by analyzing the areas Table 7.1–1.

The best way to do this assignment is to specifically and literally follow the instructions on what to do during the MPAS program work. The format of your work will be defined by that computer program. You only need to submit the printouts described below to complete the assignment. **Submit ONE copy. But, keep a second copy handy to use in class discussions.**

## SCENARIO

### Deal-a-Meal USA Wants to Understand the Trends Impacting Its Business

Deal-A-Meal USA wants to understand the macroenvironmental trends that may significantly influence its marketing strategy. It needs to know more about those trends to better define the problems, opportunities, and threats it faces and develop marketing strategy objectives and alternatives consistent with those trends.

When doing the analysis, use a combination of the information in the case, the trends discussed in the casebook in chapter 3, and the trend related discussions in your course textbook.

### Assignment Steps

1. Once you start the program, you are in the main MPAS menu area . . . select **1. A–F** from the 1-Case menu.
2. Next, select **Deal-A-Meal** from the menu.

| for Case Analysis |
|---|
| is |
| nand |
| mand |
| ysis |
| ige |
| nmental trends |
| issues |

3. From the same menu, select **5. Name Entry** and select the **Edit** to enter your name(s). (You need to move the cursor to the appropriate line first.) When done your entering name(s), press **F10** to save your work and select **Return** to go the main MPAS menu area.

4. Next, move to the 3-Format main menu option and select **1. Situation analysis** from that menu. Select **5. Macroenvironment** from the 1-Situation menu. Select **1. Sociocultural.** Press **Enter** to begin typing your description of the sociocultural environment. When you are done writing, press the **Ctrl** and **S** keys simultaneously to do spell checking. When you are done spell checking, press **F10** to save your work. Next, select **Return** to go back to the 1-Situation menu.

5. Select **5. Macroenvironment** from the 1-Situation menu. Select **2. Demographic.** When you are done writing, press the **Ctrl** and **S** keys simultaneously to do spell checking. When you are done spell checking, press **F10** to save your work. Next, select **Return** to go back to the 1-Situation menu.

6. Select **5. Macroenvironment** from the 1-Situation menu. Select **3. Political and legal.** When you are done writing, press the **Ctrl** and **S** keys simultaneously to do spell checking. When you are done spell checking, press **F10** to save your work. Next, select **Return** to go back to the 1-Situation menu.

7. Select **5. Macroenvironment** from the 1-Situation menu. Select **4. Technological.** When you are done writing, press the **Ctrl** and **S** keys simultaneously to do spell checking. When you are done spell checking, press **F10** to save your work. Next, select **Return** to go back to the 1-Situation menu.

8. Select **5. Macroenvironment** from the 1-Situation menu. Select **5. Economic.** When you are done writing, press the **Ctrl** and **S** keys simultaneously to do spell checking. When you are done spell checking, press **F10** to save your work. Next, select **Return** to go back to the 1-Situation menu.

9. Select **5. Macroenvironment** from the 1-Situation menu. Select **6. Competitive.** When you are done writing, press the **Ctrl** and **S** simultaneously to do spell checking, press **F10** to save your work. Next, select **Return** to go back to the 1-Situation menu.

10. Next, move to and select **2-Return** to go to the main MPAS menu area.

11. Now, in the main MPAS menu area, move to 5-Results and select **3. Print plan reports.**

12. After the 1-Format menu appears, select **2. Situation analysis** and then select **1. Print all situation analysis reports.**

13. When the printing is done, move to and select **8-Return** to go to the main MPAS menu.

14. Select **7-Quit** and then **Yes.** You are done!

**NOTE: Never remove your diskette until you have completely left the MPAS program. If you get error messages while running the program, quit and restart it.**

# Exercise 2
## MicroProse

This case exercise focuses on "situation: competitive analysis." It emphasizes the analysis of the competitive forces operating on a firm. Use the MPAS program and the MicroProse case in your casebook to do this assignment.

The best way to do this assignment is to explicitly follow the instruction on what to do during the computer work. The format of your work will be defined by the MPAS program. You only need to submit the printouts described below to complete the assignment. **Submit ONE copy. But, keep a second copy handy to use in class discussions.**

## SCENARIO

### MicroProse Wants to Better Understand Its Competition in the Computer Game Market

As part of its marketing strategy development and planning, MicroProse wants to develop a better understanding of competition in the computer game market. To that end, it seeks answers to the following questions:

1. What is the competitive situation in the game market? Who are MicroProse's main competitors and why they are defined as competitors?

2. What are the competitive strengths and weaknesses of MicroProse and of its major competitors in each of the major functional areas, including marketing, production, organizational, and finance?

3. How does competition occur in the game market? That is, on what basis do the firms in the market compete for customers?

4. Given MicroProse's competitive situation, what are the problems, opportunities, and threats facing them?

The analysis should emphasize the competitors and the competitive industries most important to MicroProse. Also, it should consider the overall situation facing MicroProse and, especially, the macroenvironmental trends working for and against the firm (even though you will not be asked to explicitly describe those trends for this exercise).

When doing this analysis, use a combination of the information in the case, the competitive analysis ideas discussed in the casebook in chapter 3, and the competitive analysis discussions in your course textbook.

### Assignment Steps

1. Once you start the program, you are in the main MPAS menu area. Next, select **2. G–N** from the case menu.

2. Next, select **MicroProse** from the menu.

3. From the same menu, select **5. Name entry.** Then select **Edit** to enter your name(s). (You need to move the cursor to the appropriate line first.) When done, press **F10** to save your work and select **Return** to go to the main MPAS menu area.

4. Next, move to 3-Format and select **1. Situation analysis.** Select **5. Macroenvironment** from the 1-Situation menu. Select **6. Competitive** followed by **Edit** to begin typing your description of the competitive environment. When you are done writing, press **Ctrl** and **S** simultaneously to do spell checking. When you are done spell checking, press **F10** to save your work. Next, select **Return** to go to the 1-Situation menu.

5. Next, move to 3-Format and select **1. Situation analysis.** Select **5. Macroenvironment** from the 1-Situation menu. Select **7. Strengths** followed by **Edit** to begin typing your description. When you are done writing, press **Ctrl** and **S** simultaneously to do spell checking. When you are done spell checking, press **F10** to save your work. Next, select **Return** to go to the 1-Situation menu.

6. Next, move to 3-Format and select **1. Situation analysis.** Select **5. Macroenvironment** from the 1-Situation menu. Select **8. Weaknesses** followed by **Edit** to begin typing your description. When you are done writing, press **Ctrl** and **S** simultaneously to do spell checking. When you are done spell checking, press **F10** to save your work. Next, select **Return** to go to the 1-Situation menu.

7. Next, move to 3-Format and select **1. Situation analysis** from that menu. Select **5. Macroenvironment** from the 1-Situation menu. Select **9. Competition** followed by **Edit** to begin typing your description. When you are done writing, press **Ctrl** and **S** simultaneously to do spell checking. When you are done spell checking, press **F10** to save your work. Next, select **Return** to go to the 1-Situation menu.

8. Next, select **2-Return** to go to the main MPAS menu area.

9. Now, from the main MPAS menu area move to 3-Format option and select **2, POT analysis.**

10. Select **1. Problems** followed by **Edit** to begin typing your description. When you are done writing, press **Ctrl** and **S** simultaneously to do spell checking. When you are done spell checking, press **F10** to save your work. Next, select **Return** to go to the 1-Situation menu.

11. Next, again select **2. POT analysis.**

12. Select **2. Opportunities** followed by **Edit** to begin typing your description. When you are done writing, press **Ctrl** and **S** simultaneously to do spell checking. When you are done spell checking, press **F10** to save your work. Next, select **Return** to go to the 1-Situation menu.

13. Now, again select **2. POT analysis.**

14. Select **3. Threats** followed by **Edit** to begin typing your description. When you are done writing, press **Ctrl** and **S** simultaneously to do spell checking. When you are done spell checking, press **F10** to save your work. Next, select **Return** to go to the 1-Situation menu.

15. Now, in the main MPAS menu area, move to 5-Results and select **3. Print plan reports.**

16. After the 1-Format menu appears, select **2. Situation analysis.** Then select **6. Macroenvironmental trends** (all the macroenvironmental trends will be printed even though you only want the one on competition).

17. After the 1-Format menu reappears, select **2. Situation analysis.** Then select **8. Strengths and weaknesses.**

18. After the 1-Format menu reappears, select **3. POT analysis.**

19. When the printing is done, select **8-Return** to go to the main MPAS menu.
20. Select **7-Quit** and then **Yes.** You are done!

**NOTE: Never remove your diskette until you have completely left the MPAS program. If you get error messages while running the program, quit and restart it.**

---

# Exercise 3
## Foote, Cone & Belding

This exercise focuses on "formulating marketing strategies," with particular attention to the impact of industry dynamics and strategic change. It requires you to use the MPAS program to analyze business growth plans for Foote, Cone & Belding (FCB). Below you will find a business scenario and instructions on what you need to do in the computer portion of this case exercise.

The best way to do this assignment is to specifically and literally follow the instructions on what to do during the computer work. The format for what you do is defined by the computer program. You only need to submit the printouts described below to complete the assignment. **Submit ONE copy. But, keep a second copy handy to use in class discussions.**

## SCENARIO

### FCB Seeks New Business Based on Its Integrated Marketing Services Offering

As noted in the case, a new direction for advertising agencies is integrated marketing services. This offering is designed to bring in new clients and increase the loyalty of existing clients. The phrase "integrated marketing services" is defined in the Foote, Cone & Belding case.

For this assignment, the "trick" is to understand that advertising agencies bring in new clients in small numbers each year, but each does large (hopefully) amounts of business with the agency. For example, a new client might represent $45 million in billing, which translates to about $6.75 million in income if you assume a 15 percent commission rate. Additionally, there are other incomes from fees charged for services beyond the traditional advertising services. These out-of-pocket expenses by the agency are billable at 17.65 percent.

For this case assignment, you will be entering a combination of numbers and words. You must create the numbers that you enter, but suggestions are given. The words you use to describe what you are doing in the assignment are your responsibility.

Note that there is some lack of realism in the plan you are about to enter because it is over simplified. Many likely relevant expenses will not be entered by you, including initial investments and others for which MPAS does have entry screens. This is done so that you can more easily get experience with the numeric capabilities of the MPAS program.

## Assignment Steps

1. Once you start the program, you are in the main MPAS menu area. Select **1. Cases A–F.**

2. Select **Foote, Cone & Belding Communications** from the menu.

3. From the same menu, select **5. Name entry** and then **Edit** to enter your name(s). (You need to move the cursor to the appropriate line first.) When done, press **F10** to save your work and to go to the main MPAS menu area.

4. Next, move to 4-Analysis and select **1. Sales revenue** from that menu. Then, select **1. Sales estimates.** Then, select **2. Or Unit sales estimates less then 1000** because, as mentioned previously, advertising agencies get small numbers of new clients with each spending large amounts of money. Select **Edit** to begin entering your numbers.

   The unit sales (number of new clients for the agency) should be relatively small. These are only the incremental clients due to the integrated marketing services strategy for getting new clients. (In fact, some existing clients would probably spend more through the agency, but, for this exercise, ignore that contribution.) Enter **4** as the number of new clients for each of the 10 years. For average sales revenue unit (billings per client), enter **40000000** in each year to indicate that the average new client will have $40 million in bills per year. Next, enter **34000000**, which represents the average cost per unit (at 85 percent of billings per client for this exercise—but the price and cost numbers are actually more complicated because of other billable services). All the other calculations are done automatically.

   The net sales number is the amount of money available for running the office, etc., including profits. You need to use this number to determine how much money there will be for expenses (which are entered later in the MPAS program). One way to make that estimate is to take the net sales amount for the second year of your plan and multiple that amount by .80, using the resulting number as the yearly budget for your plan expenses. Normally, you would want to write that number on a piece of paper and subtract from that amount as you enter your specific expense amounts later in the MPAS program. In this example, you have $24,000,000 ∗ .8 or $19,200,000 to work with as an expenses total. The second year is usually better to use than the first year because some unit sales start slow in the first year and that first year amount may be only half of what is achieved in the second year.

5. When you are finished entering your sales revenue estimates, save your work by pressing **F10** (or by entering the last average cost per unit). Next, select **Return** to go to the main MPAS menu area.

6. Next, move to 4-Analysis and select **2. Marketing plan.**

7. From 1-Strategy, select **1. Marketing strategy.** Select **Edit** and enter a description of the integrated marketing services strategy for FCB. When you are done, spell check by simultaneously holding down the **Ctrl** and **S** keys. When satisfied, press **F10** to save your work. Select **Return** to go to the marketing plan menu area.

8. Next, move to 2-Target and select **3. Business target.** Select **Edit** and describe your business targeting and the types of firms you will attempt to get as new clients. (See step 9, below, for more on the actual numbers you will be entering.) When done, press **F10** to save your work and select **Return** to go to the marketing plan menu.

9. Next, move to 2-Target and select **4. Business data;** select **Edit** and enter your targeting information and data. The objective for this page is to enter some words under the business firm types and proportions under firm types, firm size, region, and number of employees so that each of the respective columns totals 100. For the business firm type, you should enter names of industries that will be the target of your marketing plan. As an advertising agency, you may want to get an automotive client, a supermarket client, a computer manufacturer client, a bank client, and an entertainment industry client. Enter those labels, or abbreviations in the business firms area. You would want to enter proportions next to those industry labels to show how much of your effort will be put against each. You might want to put 20 percent of your effort against getting an automotive client, 30 percent of your effort against getting a supermarket client, etc. until those proportions total 100. For the other columns, enter proportions to indicate how much of your effort will go against each of the categories so that each totals 100. For example, if you are only going to get new advertising clients from among the largest firms, then put 100 percent of your effort against firms with sales of $500+ million and with employees numbering more than 500. When done, press **F10** (or by entering the last demographic) to save your work and select **Return** to go to the marketing plan menu.

10. Move to 3-Product and select **1. Product strategy.** Next, select **Edit** and enter a description of the key elements of your Integrated Marketing Services. Spell check as necessary and press **F10** to save your work. Select **Return** to go to the marketing plan menu.

11. Move to and select **7-return** to go to the main MPAS menu.

12. Next, move to 4-Analysis and select **3. Other expenditures.**

13. Next, move to 2-Marketing and select **2. Marketing & sales personnel expenses.** Select **Edit** and enter some numbers in this spending area. This strategies requires that additional agency personnel be hired to manage the Integrated Marketing Services effort. Enter **5000** (meaning $5 million for each year). When done, press **F10** (or by entering a year ten number) to save your work and select **Return** to go to the other expenditures menu.

14. Move to 2-Marketing and select **3. Marketing research expenses.** Select **Edit** and enter numbers for research spending in support of getting new clients. It is a common advertising agency practice to conduct research to get and keep clients. The spending you are entering here is for research about the markets of prospective clients. If you assume that the agency gets a client for every 20 attempts it makes and that it spends $60,000 for research on each of the 20 prospects, you need 20 times 4 times 60000 or 4800000 (or $4.8 million) as your yearly research budget. Enter **4800** for each year. When done, press **F10** (or by entering a year ten number) to save your work and select **Return** to go to the other expenditures menu.

15. Move to and select **5-Return** to go to the main MPAS menu.

16. Next, move to 5-Results and select **1. View plan tables.** The MPAS program will process for awhile and stop at the plan tables menu.

17. From the 1-Plan tables, select **1. Net present value summary.** The net present value at the bottom has to be positive. If it were not, you need to go back and "adjust" your unit sales up and/or reduce your expenses and then come back and recheck the net present value. After you are done looking this table, press the **Enter** key on your keyboard to go to the 1-Plan tables menu.

18. Select **2. Sales revenue summary.** When you are done looking at the numbers and select **Return** to go to the 1-Plan tables menu.

19. Select **3. Income statement summary.** When you are done looking at the numbers and select **Return** to go to the 1-Plan tables menu.

20. Move to and select **3-Return** to go to the main MPAS menu.

21. Next, move to 5-Results and select **1. View plan graphs.**

22. Select **2. Net sales.** When you are done looking at the graph, select **Return** to go to 1-Graphs menu.

23. Select **b. Total expenses.** When you are done looking at the graph, select **Return** to go to 1-Graphs menu.

24. Select **c. Total expenses by net sales.** When you are done looking at the graph, select **Return** to go to 1-Graphs menu.

25. Move to and select **2-Return** to go to the main MPAS menu.

26. Now, in the main menu area, select **3. Print plan reports.**

27. After the next menu area appears, sequentially select each of the following for printing:
    **2-Sales, 1. Print revenue summary**
    **3-Strategy, 2. Marketing strategy**
    **3-Strategy, 3. Business target market**
    **3-Strategy, 5. Product strategy**
    **4-Expenses, 1. Print all expenses**
    **6-Summary, 1. Print all plan numbers**

28. Finally, move to and select **8-Return** to go to the main MPAS menu.

29. Next select **7-Quit** and **Yes.** You are done!

**NOTE: Never remove your diskette until you have completely left the MPAS program. If you get error messages while running the program, quit and restart it.**

---

*Exercise 4*
*White Castle Case*

This case exercise focuses on "market targeting and positioning." It requires you to use the MPAS program to create and analyze a marketing plan for White Castle that is designed to increment sales and profits.

Below you will find a description a business scenario and instructions on what you need to do in this case exercise. The best way to do this assignment is to specifically and literally follow the instructions on what to do during the computer work. The format for your work will be defined by the computer program. You need to submit the print-outs described below to complete the assignment. **Submit ONE copy. But, keep a second copy handy to use in class discussions.**

## SCENARIO

### White Castle Uses Market Targeting and Positioning to Increase Unit Sales

For this case, you are defining a consumer target market and promotional campaign designed to provide an incremental increase in White Castle's unit (individual burger) sales. The idea is to input into the MPAS program your sales increase, campaign characteristics, and associated expenses. It is your decision to determine how much sales will increase, what the promotion strategy will be, and what the media plan and promotion expenses you will include.

### Assignment Steps

1. Once you start the program and you are in the main MPAS menu area. Select **3. Cases O–Z**

2. Select **White Castle System** from the menu.

3. From the same menu, select **5. Name entry** and enter your name(s). (You need to move the cursor to the appropriate line first.) When done, press **F10** to save your work and select **Return** to go to the main MPAS menu area.

4. Next, move to the 4-Analysis main menu option and select **1. Sales revenue.** Next, select **1. Sales Estimates** and then select **1. Unit sales estimates greater than 1000** because this is a high volume business. Select **Edit** and enter the unit sales increase for your plan for each of the 10 years (without trailing zeros). Next, use an average unit price of .39 and the average cost per unit of .22 (which includes ingredients, facility, location employees, etc.). Enter the same average unit price and average cost per unit for each of the 10 years. Net sales is the amount of money left over for running the company (expenses above the level of the fast-food locations) and profits.

5. When you are finished entering the sales revenue related information, save your work by pressing **F10** (or by entering the last average cost per unit). Then select **Return** to go to the main MPAS menu area.

6. Next, select **2. Marketing plan.**

7. From the marketing plan area, select 1-Strategy, **1. Marketing strategy.** Select **Edit** and type your description of the marketing strategy. When you are done, spell check your work by simultaneously holding down the **Ctrl** and **S** keys: When satisfied, press **F10** to save your work. Then, select **Return** to go to the marketing plan menu area.

8. Next, move 2-Target menu, and select **1. Consumer target.** Select **Edit** and describe the target market in words. Spell check as necessary and press **F10** to save your work. Then, select **Return** to go to the marketing plan menu area.

9. Next, select **2. Consumer data.** Then select **Edit** and enter the targeting data. When done, press **F10** (or by entering the last demographic) to save your work and select **Return** to go to the marketing plan menu area.

10. Move to the 5-Promotion menu and select **1. Promotional strategy** Then, select **Edit** and enter the objectives for your campaign. Spell check as necessary and press **F10** to save your work. Select **Return** to go to the marketing plan menu area.

11. Next, select **3. TV media plan** followed by **Edit.** Enter the TV advertising dollars you want to spend for each year. When done, press **F10** (or by entering a year ten number) to save your work and select **Return** to go to the marketing plan menu area.

12. Next, select **4. Radio media plan** followed by **Edit.** Enter the radio advertising dollars you want to spend for each year. When done, press **F10** (or by entering a year ten number) to save your work and select **Return** to go to the marketing plan menu area.

13. Next, select **5. Magazine plan** followed by **Edit.** Enter the magazine advertising dollars you want to spend for each year. When done, press **F10** (or by entering a year ten number) to save your work and select **Return** to go to the marketing plan menu area.

14. Next, select **7. Sales promotion plan** followed by **Edit.** Enter the sales promotion dollars you want to spend for each year. When done, press **F10** (or by entering a year ten number) to save your work and select **Return** to go to the marketing plan menu area.

15. Move to and select **7-Return** to go to the main MPAS menu.

16. Now, from the main MPAS menu area, move to 5-Results and select **1. View plan tables.**

17. After 1-Plan tables appears, select **1. Net present value summary.** The net present value at the bottom has to be positive. If it is not, you need to go back and "adjust" your unit sales up and/or reduce your marketing expenses. Then come back and recheck the net present value. After you are done looking this table, press the **Enter** key on your keyboard to go to the 1-Plan tables menu. (At this point, you may want to also look at the other tables to see more about the sales and expense characteristics of your plan.)

18. Move to and select **3-Return** to go to the main MPAS menu area.

19. If your plan is making money, you are ready to print some reports. If you are not making money, go back to step (4) and redo your work. To print some reports, move to 5-Results and select **1. Print plan reports.**

20. In the printing area, sequentially select the following reports to print:
    **2-Sales, 1. Print revenue summary**
    **3-Strategy, 2. Marketing strategy**
    **3-Strategy, 3. Consumer target market**
    **3-Strategy, 7. Promotion strategy**
    **6-Summary, 1. Print all plan numbers**

21. Move to and select **8-Return** to go to **the main MPAS menu.**

22. Select **7-Quit** and **Yes.** You are done!

**NOTE: Never remove your diskette until you have completely left the MPAS program. If you get error messages while running the program, quit and restart it.**

# Exercise 5
# MTV Case

The case exercise focuses on "strategic marketing programs." It requires you to use the MPAS program to create and analyze a marketing strategy for MTV that is designed to provide incremental sales and profits.

Below you will find a description of the scenario and instructions on what you need to do in this case exercise. The best way to do this assignment is to specifically and literally follow the instructions on what to do during the computer work. The format of your work will be defined by the MPAS program. You only need to submit the print-outs described below to complete the assignment. **Submit ONE copy. But, keep a second copy handy to use in class discussions.**

## SCENARIO

MTV (The Music Channel) Uses a Strategic Marketing Program to Increase Its Advertising Revenues (Which Means Higher Sales)

For this case, you are defining a business target and marketing effort (because running a television channel is all about business-to-business marketing). It is designed to provide an incremental increase in MTV's money received per advertising space slot. Assume that the number of these spots is fixed. The idea is to input into the MPAS program your sales increase and associated expenses to produce a profitable plan. Assume $100 more per spot and 175,200 spots per year (that is, 20 spots per hour times 24 hours times 365 days).

## Assignment Steps

1. Once you start the program, you are in the main MPAS menu area.
2. Next select **2. G–N.** Then select **MTV Networks** from the menu.
3. Next, select **5. Name entry** and **Edit** to enter your name(s). When done, press **F10** to save your work and select **Return** to go to the main MPAS menu area.
4. Next, move 4-Analysis and select **1. Sales revenue.** Select **1. Sales estimates** followed by **1. Unit sales estimates greater than 1000.** Next, select **Edit** and enter your data. Put 175200 in each of the years for units (because you are going to get more money for a fixed number of spots) and put 100.00 in each of the price per unit slots and put 0.00 in each of the cost of goods slots (because it will not cost MTV for any goods to sell the advertising space at a higher cost).
5. When finished entering the sales revenue, save your work by pressing **F10** (or by entering the last average cost per unit). Then, select **Return** to go to the main MPAS menu area.
6. Next, select **2. Marketing plan.**

7. Next, select **1. Marketing strategy.** Select **Edit** and enter a description of your marketing strategy for MTV. When you are done, spell check your work by simultaneously holding down the **Ctrl** and **S** keys. When your are satisfied with your work, press **F10** to save your work. Select **Return** to go to the marketing plan menu area.

8. Next, move to 2-Target and select **1. Business target.** Then, select **Edit.** Describe the businesses you will attempt to get to spend more per spot with MTV and why they would do so. When done, spell check and then press **F10** to save your work. Select **Return** to go to the marketing plan menu.

9. Select **2. Business data** and then select **Edit** to enter the targeting data by describing the business categories you will be going after and what weight each will receive. When done, press **F10** (or by entering the last demographic) to save you work and select **Return** to go to the marketing plan menu.

10. Move to 3-Product and select **1. Product strategy.** Select **Edit** and enter a description of the key elements of the product strategy. For this MTV example, your product from an advertiser's perspective is the audience you can deliver but you should also mention how you intend to draw that audience by describing the programming you will be offering. Spell check as necessary and press **F10** to save your work. Select **Return** to go to the marketing plan menu.

11. Move to 4-Pricing and select **1. Pricing strategy.** Select **Edit** and enter a description of your pricing strategy (for your commercial spots). Spell check as necessary and press **F10** to save your work. Select **Return** to go to the marketing plan menu.

12. Move to 5-Promotion and select **1. Promotion strategy.** Select **Edit** and enter a description of your promotion strategy. Spell check as necessary and press **F10** to save your work and select **Return** to go to the marketing plan menu.

13. Next, select **7. Sales promotion plan** and then select **Edit.** Enter your sales promotion money in the dollars column. Press **F10** when done to save your work and then select **Return** to go to the marketing plan menu.

14. Move to and select **7-Return** to go to the main MPAS menu.

15. Next, select **3. Other expenditures.**

16. Move to 2-Marketing and select **2. Marketing & sales personnel expenses.** Select **Edit** and enter your numbers. When done, press **F10** (or by entering a year ten number) to save your work and select **Return** to go to the other expenditures menu area.

17. Select **3. Marketing research expenses.** Then select **Edit** and enter your spending for research. When done, press **F10** (or by entering a year ten number) to save your work and then select **Return** to go to the other expenditures menu area.

18. Move to and select **5-Return** to go to the main MPAS menu.

19. Now, move to 5-Results and select **1. View plan tables.**

20. After 1-Plan tables appear, select **1. Net present value summary.** The net present value at the bottom has to be positive. If it is not, you need to go back and "adjust" your unit sales up and/or reduce your expenses. Then, come back and recheck the net present value. After you are done looking at this table, select **Return** to go to the 1-Plan tables menu area.

21. Next, select 1-Plan tables, **2. Sales revenue summary.** When you are done looking at the numbers, select **Return** to go to the strategy tables menu area.

22. Next, select 1-Plan tables, **3. Income statement summary.** When you are done looking at the numbers and select **Return** to go to the strategy tables menu area.

23. Move to and select **3-Return** to return to the main MPAS menu.

24. Select **3. Print plan reports.**
25. After the printing menu appears, sequentially select the following to print:
    **2-Sales, 1. Print revenue summary**
    **3-Strategy, 1. Print all marketing strategy**
    **4-Expense, 1. Print all expenses**
    **6-Summary, 1. Print all plan numbers**
26. Move to and select **8-Return** to go to the main MPAS menu.
27. Select **7-Quit** and **Yes.** You are done!

**NOTE: Never remove your diskette until you have completely left the MPAS program. If you get error messages while running the program, quit and restart it.**

# *The Marketing Plan Analysis System (MPAS)*

This appendix describes the MPAS case analysis program. The program is specifically designed to work with each of the cases in this book, but it also has the ability to accommodate new cases that you may be assigned by your instructor. This program is unique because it allows you to work with a combination of words and numbers to produce a comprehensive description of your marketing strategy and plan showing its sales, expenses, and profit consequences. By explaining how the MPAS program works, this appendix will help you understand the capabilities it brings to the task of marketing strategy development and plan analysis.

## WHAT IS MPAS?

MPAS is an applications tool for the development and analysis of marketing strategies and plans. The logic of the program follows the format for case analysis detailed in chapter 3 of this book. MPAS is totally menu driven—you do not need to do any programming and you do not need to understand anything about Lotus 1-2-3 or similar programs. MPAS is designed to be as user friendly as possible so that you can concentrate on case analysis and not on learning new software.

The MPAS program has four main functions:

1. It provides a performance history for each case in this book. Your can view graphs of historical sales and/or net income from a menu in the program.

2. MPAS contains a fully functional word-processing environment, including a spell checker, that structures your descriptions of a case firm's situation, problems, opportunities, and threats. Given that background, it also allows you to describe your marketing strategy and plan objectives, alternative courses of action, and decision.

3. MPAS has screens that allow you to enter sales and expense estimates for your proposed plan. This process can be very detailed because you input sales and expense numbers for each of the next 10 years.

4. Once you have entered your strategy and plan, you will want to examine details about its likely performance. MPAS allows you to view numeric screens and graphics that summarize various aspects of your plan. If you are satisfied with how your plan will perform over the next 10 years, you can print reports. MPAS has an extensive list of reports to select from. All you have to do is pick the ones you want and they are automatically produced.

The MPAS program is the result of years of development and testing. Many students have successfully completed assignments using it. Do not try to second guess the program because it really is as easy as it looks. There are no tricks or special computer skills required. All you need to do is work your way through the menus, entering the words or numbers associated with the screens you see. In that sense, you should be concentrating on the content of what you want to do and not on the operations of the program.

The hardest part of using the MPAS program revolves around deciding what to enter in the places that accept words or numbers. The best approach is to have a good idea about what you want to enter before starting the program. The exercises in Appendix A are examples of what you might be asked to do by your instructor. Those exercises contain detailed descriptions on how to do sample assignments by specifying exactly which MPAS features to select. Your instructor may also create additional exercises for assignments.

Note that when using the MPAS program, you can get help by pressing the F1 key to bring up a list of help topics. You can also access this help system under the System menu. In that System menu, you will additionally find a small collection of hints on how to do well in entering and analyzing your marketing plan.

## HOW TO USE THIS MANUAL

This *appendix* is not designed around an expectation that the user wants to read it from beginning to end. Rather, it is a reference document that is best used to find specific information about parts of the MPAS program as needed. For example, if you want to know about installing the MPAS program, read that section of the appendix; if you want to get a good understanding of program functions, do the tutorial; and if you are interested in what you need to enter into a particular MPAS program screen, read about that specific screen.

Because this *appendix* is designed for references purposes, the wording in some sections is repetitive of what you find in other sections. This is necessary because an appendix user may start reading at any point or under any topic. Use the table of contents below to find the information you need and go to that specific section to get what you want.

## THE CONTENTS OF THIS APPENDIX

4.1.2. Analysis, Sales revenue, Other revenue
4.2.1.1. Analysis, Marketing plan, Strategy, Marketing strategy
4.2.2.1. Analysis, Marketing plan, Target, Consumer target
4.2.2.2. Analysis, Marketing plan, Target, Consumer data
4.2.2.3. Analysis, Marketing plan, Target, Business target
4.2.2.4. Analysis, Marketing plan, Target, Business data
4.2.3.1. Analysis, Marketing plan, Product, Product strategy
4.2.4.1. Analysis, Marketing plan, Pricing, Pricing strategy
4.2.5.1. Analysis, Marketing plan, Promotion, Promotional strategy
4.2.5.2. Analysis, Marketing plan, Promotion, Promotion theme
4.2.5.3. Analysis, Marketing plan, Promotion, TV media plan
4.2.5.4. Analysis, Marketing plan, Promotion, Radio media plan
4.2.5.5. Analysis, Marketing plan, Promotion, Magazine media plan
4.2.5.6. Analysis, Marketing plan, Promotion, Other promotion media plan
4.2.5.7. Analysis, Marketing plan, Promotion, Sales promotion plan
4.2.5.8. Analysis, Marketing plan, Promotion, Personal selling plan
4.2.5.9. Analysis, Marketing plan, Promotion, Public relations plan
4.2.6.1. Analysis, Marketing plan, Distribution, Distribution strategy
4.3.1.1. Analysis, Other expenditures, Startup, Startup expenses
4.3.2.1. Analysis, Other expenditures, Marketing, Distribution expenses
4.3.2.2. Analysis, Other expenditures, Marketing, Marketing and sales personnel expenses
4.3.2.3. Analysis, Other expenditures, Marketing, Marketing research expenses
4.3.2.4. Analysis, Other expenditures, Marketing, Other marketing expenses
4.3.3.1. Analysis, Other expenditures, Other, R&D expenses
4.3.3.2. Analysis, Other expenditures, Other, Personnel and administration
4.3.3.3. Analysis, Other expenditures, Other, Other strategy expenses
4.3.4.1. Analysis, Other expenditures, Investments, Capital investments
The MPAS Plan Results Screens:
5.1.1.1. Results, View plan tables, Plan tables, Net present value summary
5.1.1.2. Results, View plan tables, Plan tables, Sales revenue summary
5.1.1.3. Results, View plan tables, Plan tables, Income statement summary
5.1.1.4. Results, View plan tables, Plan tables, Net income by net sales ratio
5.1.1.5. Results, View plan tables, Plan tables, Expenses summary
5.1.1.6. Results, View plan tables, Plan tables, Expenses ratios
5.1.1.7. Results, View plan tables, Plan tables, Marketing expenses summary
5.1.1.8. Results, View plan tables, Plan tables, Advertising summary
5.1.1.9. Results, View plan tables, Plan tables, Promotion summary
5.1.1.0. Results, View plan tables, Plan tables, Promotion and advertising ratios
5.1.2.1. Results, View plan tables, Loan, Plan loan requirement
5.2.1.1. Results, View plan graphs, Graphs, Unit sales
5.2.1.2. Results, View plan graphs, Graphs, Net sales
5.2.1.3. Results, View plan graphs, Graphs, Net income
5.2.1.4. Results, View plan graphs, Graphs, Net income by net sales
5.2.1.5. Results, View plan graphs, Graphs, Total advertising
5.2.1.6. Results, View plan graphs, Graphs, Net sales by total advertising
5.2.1.7. Results, View plan graphs, Graphs, Total promotion
5.2.1.8. Results, View plan graphs, Graphs, Net sales by total promotion
5.2.1.9. Results, View plan graphs, Graphs, Total marketing
5.2.1.0. Results, View plan graphs, Graphs, Total marketing by net sales

5.2.1.a. Results, View plan graphs, Graphs, Total R&D by net sales

5.2.1.b. Results, View plan graphs, Graphs, Total expenses

5.2.1.c. Results, View plan graphs, Graphs, Total expenses by net sales

5.3.1.1. Results, Print plan reports, Format, Print all of case format

5.3.1.2.1. Results, Print plan reports, Format, Situation analysis, Print all situation analysis reports

5.3.1.2.2. Results, Print plan reports, Format, Situation analysis, Extent of demand

5.3.1.2.3. Results, Print plan reports, Format, Situation analysis, Nature of demand

5.3.1.2.4. Results, Print plan reports, Format, Situation analysis, Strategy analysis

5.3.1.2.5. Results, Print plan reports, Format, Situation analysis, Life cycle stage

5.3.1.2.6. Results, Print plan reports, Format, Situation analysis, Macroenvironmental trends

5.3.1.2.7. Results, Print plan reports, Format, Situation analysis, International issues

5.3.1.2.8. Results, Print plan reports, Format, Situation analysis, Strengths and weaknesses

5.3.1.2.9. Results, Print plan reports, Format, Situation analysis, Nature of competition

5.3.1.3. Results, Print plan reports, Format, POT analysis

5.3.1.4. Results, Print plan reports, Format, Objectives

5.3.1.5. Results, Print plan reports, Format, Alternatives

5.3.1.6. Results, Print plan reports, Format, Decision

5.3.2.1. Results, Print plan reports, Sales, Print revenue summary

5.3.3.1. Results, Print plan reports, Strategy, Print all marketing strategy

5.3.3.2. Results, Print plan reports, Strategy, Marketing strategy

5.3.3.3. Results, Print plan reports, Strategy, Consumer target

5.3.3.4. Results, Print plan reports, Strategy, Business target

5.3.3.5. Results, Print plan reports, Strategy, Product strategy

5.3.3.6. Results, Print plan reports, Strategy, Pricing strategy

5.3.3.7. Results, Print plan reports, Strategy, Promotion strategy

5.3.3.8. Results, Print plan reports, Strategy, Distribution strategy

5.3.4.1. Results, Print plan reports, Expenses, Print all expenses

5.3.5.1. Results, Print plan reports, Invest, Print capital investments

5.3.6.1. Results, Print plan reports, Summary, Print all plan numbers

5.3.6.2. Results, Print plan reports, Summary, Net present value

5.3.6.3. Results, Print plan reports, Summary, Sales revenue

5.3.6.4. Results, Print plan reports, Summary, Income statement

5.3.6.5. Results, Print plan reports, Summary, Ratio analysis

5.3.6.6. Results, Print plan reports, Summary, Promotion analysis

**E.** Producing and Submitting Your MPAS Work

**F.** Warnings, Errors, and Other Problems

Error Messages

Missing file and program will not start

Error reading drive A

Missing file during program operation

Out of environment message

Program Operating Speed

The program runs very slowly, particularly when doing work on the data diskette

Word Processing Problems

My word processing work looks strange when I print it

I get printing errors when I print my word processing work

Printing Problems
  The reports are not readable
  The reports produce a blank page after each report
System Configuration Problems
  The Help or Hint screens are out of aliment
  Because of the screen color combination, I am having trouble seeing some parts of the
    MPAS program
**G.** Getting Help

---

## A. HOW MPAS WORKS

MPAS takes the words and numbers you enter in a case analysis and produces reports you can submit to your instructor. Thus, MPAS is primarily a tool for completing case analysis assignments; it structures your work and makes easier the tasks associated with analyzing cases. However, it does not do any thinking for you; it only takes what you enter and analyzes that. You must decide what you want to say about a case firm and what marketing strategy and plan specifics you want to input. Although MPAS only makes your work easier, that is a really a big help if you think about how much work it would be to use Lotus 1-2-3 or a similar spreadsheet package to accomplish the same tasks at the same comprehensive level.

MPAS is essentially a database management system with a user-friendly interface (set of computer screens). Behind all the menus is a powerful data management system and analysis, display, and printing routines capable of very complex and detailed functions such as word processing, sales and financial analysis, **and** graphics and reporting.

---

## B. GETTING STARTED WITH MPAS

This section explains how to install the MPAS program. If you are installing MPAS on your own computer, you need to read the section below titled "Single Computer Installation." If you are a network supervisor who wants to install MPAS on a network, read the sections titled "Single Computer Installation" **and** "Network Installation" below.

**If you are going to use MPAS on a school's computer network or on an IBM-compatible computer where the MPAS program is already installed, you do not need to do any installation. Skip to the section on "Using MPAS" to read about using your data diskette (disk #3) and about how the MPAS program operates after it is installed.**

MPAS can be installed on a stand-alone machine or on a network. It will run under all the popular IBM-compatible computer operating systems, including DOS 5.0+, Windows 3.1, Windows for Work Groups, Windows 95, Windows NT, and OS2.

### Single Computer Installation

Hardware Requirements

To install and use MPAS on your computer, you need a 386 IBM-compatible computer or better with at least 4 megabytes of RAM. MPAS also requires MS-DOS or PC-DOS version 5.0 or higher or Windows 3.1 or higher and a 3 1/2″ high-density floppy as your **A** drive.

MPAS runs on a combination of your hard drive and a floppy disk. The program itself resides on your hard drive while your data is located on a high-density diskette in your A drive. The entire MPAS program requires about 10 megabytes of hard-disk space.

### Installing MPAS on Your Hard Disk

You should have three diskettes, labeled disk #1, disk #2, and disk #3. These three diskettes contain the MPAS program, with the third diskette also holding your data for doing assignments. After MPAS is installed, this third diskette is the one you will put in your A drive before you start the MPAS program (MPAS checks for this disk at startup). It is recommended that you make a copy the third diskette before you start using it just in case it gets damaged during frequent use. See your operating system manual about how to make a copy of a diskette.

Once you install the MPAS program on your hard drive and made a copy of disk #3, put all the original the diskettes in a safe place. You will not need them again unless you need to reinstall the program (a very unlikely event).

### Program Installation

Put disk #1 in your A drive. If you are installing the MPAS program under DOS, move to the A drive prompt A:> and type **INSTALL** and press **Enter** on your keyboard. If you are installing the MPAS program under Windows, either start the installation by double clicking the file name INSTALL in the file manager (Windows 3.1) or in the Windows Explorer (Windows 95). Or, you can open the run box in any version of Windows and type in **A:\INSTALL** followed by pressing **Enter** or selecting the **OK** button with your mouse.

Follow the instructions for installing the MPAS program as they come to the screen. The installation program will check to see that there is 10 megabytes of free space on your hard drive. If there is, it will continue. After disk # 1 is done, put each of diskettes, #2 and #3, in your A drive as requested during the installation process.

If something goes wrong during the installation, such as if it just stops by staying with the same diskette for 10 or more minutes (even if the drive light is still on), reboot your machine or just shut it off and restart it. Then, just start the installation process again with the first diskette (disk #1).

While the MPAS program will run under Windows, it was created for DOS. Thus, when it is installed under Windows, it does not create a Windows icon to start the program as Windows programs normally do. There are instructions below about how to start the MPAS program under either DOS or Windows.

### Setting Up the Program

To operate the MPAS program under DOS or Windows 3.1, you need to have the following commands in your computer's config.sys file:

Buffers = 30

(except for DOS 6.2 where it should be set to Buffers = 0)

Files = 50

You need to have a technical knowledge of DOS to know how to make these file changes. If you are not sure, ignore the need to make the file changes because the MPAS program will probably work anyway. If you get error messages about files when you start the MPAS program, speak to someone about how to make the above changes.

If you have a printer connected to your computer, you can use it to print reports of your work. The default printer is a HP laserjet. So, if you do not run the printer installation routine, that will be the printer the MPAS program expects to use. That printer setup works well with most laser printers, but, if you are using a dot matrix printer, you will definitely need to make a change. To tell the MPAS program what printer you are using, you need to do the following:

At the C:> prompt, type **CD\MPAS** (or just move to whatever drive you installed MPAS on and type **CD\MPAS**). Next, type **MPASSET** and the printer installation program will start. You can also start this file by double clicking it in the file manager (Windows 3.1) or in the Windows Explorer (Windows 95).

Choose **Configuration** from the menu. Choose the **RR.CNF** file. Choose **Printers**. At the **PRINTER 1 TYPE:** line, press **Enter** on your keyboard. Choose your printer from the list that appears (if it is there) by moving to highlight it and press **Enter**.

If your printer is not on the list, you will have to experiment by choosing a printer and trying to print with it from within the MPAS program. You cannot experiment with your printer settings from within the printer installation program. You can, however, select a different printer for each of the eight printer types.

After choosing a printer(s), select **SAVE** and next select **QUIT**. Then, select **EXIT**. Several screens will pass and you will get a message saying that the printer setup process is completed. You are now done with the printer installation routine.

If you installed multiple printers, these will appear as PRINTER A through PRINTER H on the printing menu in the MPAS program. When in the MPAS program, to get to the area where you can select among the printers that you installed, first select the sample case from the case menu and then go to the Results menu that contains the "Print plan reports" menu selection. Select it and you will go to another menu area where you will find a menu listing for Printer. Under that listing, there are eight printers to chose from. The first one you installed during the printer installation process is Printer A, the second one is Printer B, etc. You can test each printer you installed sequentially by selecting the printer from the printer menu and printing a report for the sample case. Try printing the Income statement under the Summary menu to see what it looks like. If it looks good, the printer you are testing is working. Note, however, that that printer will not be the default printer unless it is the first printer or PRINTER A. You will probably want to rerun the printer setup and make the printer that works the first one.

If you only installed one printer, the printer you installed is PRINTER A on the list of printers inside the printing menu of the MPAS program. During program operations, MPAS automatically selects PRINTER A unless you tell it to do otherwise.

## Network Installation

To install MPAS on a network, first install MPAS on a network workstation just as if you were doing a nonnetwork installation (except for the printer part described above).

Once the workstation installation is completed, copy the entire MPAS directory (and program) to where you want it to reside on your network.

Use the program printer setup routine to select the printers on your network. Type **MPASSET** at the DOS prompt in the directory in which you put the MPAS program to get the printer setup menu. The program will allow you to select from a database of printer drivers, automatically creating the appropriate printer driver(s).

Choose **Configuration** from the menu. Choose the **RR.CNF** file. Choose **Printers**. At the **PRINTER 1 TYPE:** line, press **Enter** on your keyboard. Choose your printer(s) from the list that appears (if it is there) by moving to highlight it and press **Enter** on your keyboard. If the printer(s) is not on the list, you will have to experiment by choosing a printer and trying to print from within the MPAS program. In experimenting, it saves time if you install as many of the printers as you think may work (noting which is 1 through 8) so that you can try each from inside the MPAS program because you cannot experiment with your printer settings from within the printer installation program.

If you installed multiple printers, these will appear as PRINTER A through PRINTER H on the menu on the printing menu in the MPAS program. When in the MPAS program, to get to the section where you can select among the printers that you installed, first select the sample case from the case menu and then go to the Results menu that contains the "Print plan reports" menu selection. Select it and you will go to another menu area where you will find a menu listing for Printer. Under that listing, there are eight printers to chose from. The first one you installed during the printer installation process is Printer A, the second one is Printer B, etc. You can test each printer you installed sequentially by selecting the printer from the printer menu and printing a report for the sample case. Try printing the Income statement under the Summary menu to see what it looks like. If it looks good, the printer you are testing is working. Note, however, that that printer will not be the default printer unless it is the first printer or PRINTER A. You will probably want to rerun the printer setup and make the printer that works the first one.

If you have only one type of printer on your network, you may want to select it as all eight of the printers the students may chose from (they can do this from a menu inside MPAS when it is running). If you make all eight selections the network printer, the students will not actually be able to change it, thus reducing potential confusion.

After choosing a printer(s), select **SAVE** and next select **QUIT**. Then, select **EXIT**. Several screens will pass and you will get a message saying the printer setup process is completed. You are now done with the printer installation routine. The first printer you installed is PRINTER A on the list of printers on the printing menu of the MPAS program. During program operations, MPAS automatically selects PRINTER A unless you tell it to do otherwise by going to the printer selection menu and explicitly choosing another printer.

Once you setup the printer(s), erase (or save elsewhere) the .EXE files that operate the setup program (RRCGMEM.EXE and RRSETUP.EXE). MPAS only needs one .EXE file, which is FOXR.EXE, to operate. There are also probably two compression related .EXE files in the MPAS directory that you may want to move or delete.

When MPAS is operating, avoid having memory resident programs present, if possible. For example, a memory resident program that allows the user at a workstation to press a key combination to change network printer functions may cause the MPAS program to lockup. Try disabling that program when MPAS starts, and reenabling it when MPAS closes.

Note that the MPAS program, and FoxPro 2.5 on which it is based, may want to write temporary files during normal program operations. In that sense, it is necessary to keep the MPAS program in a directory where it has read and write privileges, or it may lockup.

Also, because of the possibility of file corruption during day-to-day operations, you may want to "refresh" the program directory every night with an automated copying program so any damaged files are replaced. During this refresh, first erase the contents of the directory before you copy in a fresh set of files.

## Using MPAS

### Single Computer Operation

If you will be working on a single, stand-alone computer on which MPAS is installed, follow these instructions. If you will be working from a network workstation, skip to the section titled "Network Operation."

First, put your data diskette (disk #3) in the A drive of the computer. Next, to start MPAS under DOS, move to the directory in which the program is installed and type **MPAS** at the DOS prompt and then press **Enter** on your keyboard. Or, double click the file name **MPAS.BAT** in the Windows 3.1 file manager or the Windows 95 Windows Explorer to start MPAS.

After the startup checks your A drive diskette, the program begins, but it takes some time to load, so the first program screen you see asks you to be patient. The next screen is the copyright for the program, including the version number. Finally, the MPAS main menu area appears. There are seven selections across the top, each with its own menu. The section titled "The Main MPAS Menus" below describes those menus and summarizes what they do.

### Network Operation

If you are working from a network station, this is the section to read for understanding how to operate the MPAS program. If you installed MPAS on your own computer, go back and read the previous section titled "Single Computer Operation" instead.

First, put your data diskette (disk #3) in the A drive of the computer. Next, to start the MPAS program, you must know how it was installed on the network. Your instructor must provide you with that information. However, normally, MPAS is installed so that it appears on the network menu of programs available for your use. Once you select the MPAS program to start, the startup checks your A drive diskette and then it takes some time to load, so the first screen you see asks you to be patient. The next screen is the copyright for the program, including the version number. Finally, the MPAS main menu area appears. There are seven selections across the top, each with its own menu. The section titled "The Main MPAS Menus" describes those menus and summarizes what they do.

## THE MAIN MPAS MENUS

### The MPAS Cases Menu

This menu lists the 32 casebook cases, two new cases, and a sample case to choose from. It also has a selection for entering the names of case analysis team members. The 32 cases correspond to each of the cases in your casebook and are the basis for doing assignments about how to improve the performance of each firm. The two new cases provide spaces in which you can work on firms not in the casebook that your instructor may want to assign. The sample case data is used in the MPAS tutorial and, in general, for seeing how the features of the program operate. When you enter your name(s), it will appear on all the reports of your work that you print.

### The MPAS History Menu

You can look at the historical performance of each of the 32 casebook cases by viewing five year graphs of net sales and/or net income. These are the same numbers as you will find in each of the cases. The years covered by the graphs depend on when the events in the case occurred.

### The MPAS Format Menu

This is the area into which you enter the reasoning behind your marketing plan. The format for case analysis used here follows the outline for analyzing cases in chapter 3 of this book. In this section, you can enter your situation analysis; description of problems, opportunities, and threats; plan objectives; descriptions of marketing alternatives; and a summary of the decision you have made from among your alternatives. This program section emphasizes the entry of words; you are given the opportunity to type in descriptions of what you think or propose about each of the areas in the case analysis format.

### The MPAS Analysis Menu

In contrast to the word orientation of the previous menu section, this part of the MPAS program emphasizes numbers. There are places where you are expected to enter descriptions of parts of your marketing plan, but the primary focus is on entering the sales and expenses estimates associated with your plan. The results of your work in this section form the basis for a comprehensive financial analysis of your plan done by the MPAS program.

### The MPAS Results Menu

After you have finished entering the sales and expense information about your plan, you are ready to view and/or print the results of your work. Under this menu, you can view the impact of your plan as tables and/or graphs. Note that you cannot print these tables and/or graphs. However, you can print the formatted reports in this section of the MPAS program.

After viewing the tables and/or graphs, and if you are satisfied with the performance of your plan, you next move to printing all or some of the reports that describe the performance of your plan. Normally, most students input a plan and look at the results as tables and/or graphs only to find that the plan's performance is not what they expected. When that is true, they must go back to the plan input areas and change some or all of their sales and expenses expectations. Once these changes have been made, students again look at the plan results as tables and/or graphs.

This process of sales and expenses entry followed by viewing the results may take several iterations before you are satisfied. But when you are finally done, you are ready to print the reports summarizing your work. The **MPAS** program section for printing reports gives you hard copies of your work and/or what you need to submit to your instructor to show that you successfully completed an assignment.

The MPAS System Menu

This menu offers access to a list of hints on how to do well in marketing plan development; a menu of help topics, which provide information about some program functions; and a list of monitor configuration options, which represent different color combinations that can be used when operating the MPAS program. Note, however, that some of those color combinations may make it more difficult to see some program screens such as the word processing areas. You can also look at a calendar and/or an optional calculator, which can be used to do computations as you figure what numbers you want to enter as your marketing plan.

The MPAS Quit Menu

By selecting this menu option, you are indicating that you are ready to stop using the MPAS program. You will be asked to confirm that you are finished before the program closes. This is the best way to end when you are done working with the program because it insures that all your working files will be closed properly.

## C. MPAS TUTORIAL: EXPLORING MPAS USING THE SAMPLE CASE

Welcome to the MPAS tutorial. This section provides an introduction to the MPAS program and demonstrates many of its capabilities. The ten lessons offer a brief introduction to the features in the MPAS program that will make your marketing strategies easier to develop and understand. The lessons are best done sequentially. Note that each of the MPAS program screens is also described in detail in a separate selection titled "MPAS Screens Page-By-Page."

To start the MPAS tutorial, either type **MPAS** at the DOS prompt and press **Enter** on your keyboard while in the directory in which you installed the program. Or, double click the file name MPAS.BAT in the Windows 3.1 file manager or the Windows 95 Windows Explorer. As the program begins, you will see first screens asking you to wait. Finally, the MPAS main menu area appears.

## Lesson 1: Selecting a Case and Entering Your Name

In this tutorial, you will be using a sample case. So, select **New Cases** and **Sample Case** from the case selection menu. Next select the **Name entry** option followed by selecting **Edit** so that you can enter your name. Type in your name. If entering more than one name, use the keyboard arrow key to move from name entry area to name entry area. When you are done with name entry, press the **F10** key on your keyboard to stop and save your work. Next, select **Return** to go back to the main menu area of the MPAS program.

## Lesson 2: Viewing the History of a Case Firm

To view the historical information on the sample case, move to the **History** menu. Now you can make selections to view graphs of historical net sales and/or net income. First select **Net sales**. Next, you will see a graph of net sales in billions for each of five years. The 2.4 number in the lower right corner indicates that the longest bar is $2.4 billion. Note that the bottom of the screen shows the case you are working on and the market that firm operates in. To stop viewing this graph, select **Return** and you will find yourself back at the **History** menu. Next, select the **Net income** menu item. Again you will see a graph but this time of net income in millions. The number 240.0 in the lower right hand corner indicates that the longest bar represents $240 million. To stop viewing this graph, select **Return** and you will find yourself back at the **History** menu.

This same type of net sales and net income information is available for each of the 32 cases in your casebook. The numbers that you see in the MPAS program are the same as those found in the individual cases. Sometimes the graphs in the MPAS program may look somewhat different from those in the cases, but that is due to how the program shows graphs.

## Lesson 3: Using the Format for Case Analysis

This screen is where you do word processing to describe the your marketing plan. The format follows the outline for analyzing cases in chapter 3 of your casebook. Here you can enter descriptions of each topic in that outline, including a situation analysis; description of the problems, opportunities, and threats; marketing plan objectives; marketing plan alternatives; and your decision from among those alternatives.

As an example, you will do one of the topics in the format for case analysis. Assuming that you have just finished lessons 2 and 3 (if not, do at least lesson 1 before this to select a case), move to the **Format** menu item and select the first menu item **Situation analysis**. Next select the first item in **Situation** which is the **Extent of demand**.

After you select **Extent of demand**, you should see a box in the center of the screen. Below that box you will see information about what case you are working on and some instructions about entering and editing your word processing work.

You will now enter and edit words under **Extent of demand** as a way of understanding how to do the word processing for any of the topics in the format for case analysis, meaning that you will do this one topic to demonstrate how that process operates for all the other topics in the outline.

You are now ready to begin describing the extent of demand. Select **Edit** and the cursor will move into the box in the center of the screen at its upper left corner. The editing box is now ready to accept words. Type in: **This is a test of the extent of demand section. But I want to misspll something.** Note how the text automatically word wraps. You should not create any margins because the printing automatically ads margins, and you should not indent the first line of each new paragraph; rather, just create an empty line between paragraphs by pressing the Enter key on the keyboard at the end of each of your paragraphs. Note also that it is very important that you do not use certain symbols and characters as you type in your descriptions. (See "Warnings, Errors, and Other Problems" for more details.)

Normally, you would want to type in several paragraphs to describe the extent of demand. How much you actually write depends on what your instructor expects. You can type in much more than the size of the box you see on the screen because it will scroll down as you continue entering words, meaning that you can type in many pages of words if you so choose.

Assuming that you typed in: **This is a test of the extent of demand section. But I want to misspll something.,** you are ready to spell check your work with the built in spell checker. To activate that spell checker, simultaneously press the **Ctrl** and **S** keys on your keyboard. Make sure you firmly press the two keys or the spell checker will not activate.

When the spell checking box appears, it indicates what misspellings it has found and possible spellings for each of those words sequentially. If there are no misspelled words, the complete spell checking box will not appear when you simultaneously press the **Ctrl** and **S** keys on your keyboard. However, you should always see a box briefly in the upper right part of your screen indicating that spell checking has occurred. Note that the spell checker sometimes does a good job of suggesting the correct spelling of a word and, at other times, a very poor job, depending on the degree and type of misspelling.

Once the spell checker box appears, you have the options of ignoring the misspelling, editing the word, getting a suggestion about alternative spelling (which is done automatically), looking-up the word in a dictionary (if it is in the dictionary), or selecting **Done** to leave the spell checker completely. To select the correct word, move the highlight using the arrow key on your keyboard or a mouse to the word misspell under "Possible spelling" and press **Enter** on your keyboard. Next you can replace just this instance of the misspelling or all instances. Select **Replace**. Because there is only one misspelled word, selecting Replace takes you back to your working page. There you can see that the spelling mistake has been corrected.

Because what you entered under **Extent of demand** now looks good, you will press **F10** to stop editing and save your work. What you typed in is now saved to the data diskette in the computer's A drive. Each time you finish working on a section as you just did, all that work is saved at that time. This means that if the computer should stop working at any time, you would only lose the work being done at that moment and not what you had done before.

To leave the **Extent of demand** work area, select **Return**. At anytime, you can come back to this topic, or any other word processing area, to make corrections, additions, etc. After you select **Return**, you leave the word processing enter area and the situation analysis menu will appear. Select **Return** again to go to the main MPAS menu area.

All of the other word entry areas under the "Format For Case Analysis" operate in the same way as with the extent of demand.

## Lesson 4: Entering Sales Revenue Data

To begin entering your sales estimates, select **Sales** from the Analysis menu. Next select **Sales estimates** to enter information on unit sales, price per unit, and cost per unit. Before you can begin entering the estimates of impact for your plan, you must decide if you your plan will be selling unit volume greater than 1,000 units or less than 1,000 per year. This is important because the MPAS program treats the calculations differently in each circumstance. If you select the greater than 1,000 units option, the MPAS program assumes three zeros after each unit sales number you enter, and if you select the less then 1,000 option the program does not assume three zeros after each unit sales number you enter. Therefore, you cannot enter small numbers of unit transactions if you select the greater than 1,000 option.

**Note that everywhere else in the MPAS program when you enter dollar amounts it is usually assumed that there are three zeros after each number inputted. This fact is indicated on the screen into which you are inputting your numbers.**

As an example of a business for which you would chose the less than 1,000 units per year, consider an advertising agency that is fortunate if it gets several new clients per year with each amounting to $20 million in advertising spending. In contrast, a business with high unit volumes, such as retail clothing stores, might expect a new plan to contribute tens of thousands of additional unit sales at prices in the range of $40 per transaction.

For this tutorial, select the **Unit sales estimates greater than 1000** menu option. That will take you to a page where you can choose to edit the contents of a table by entering new data or by changing what is already there. Once the data entry table appears, you will see six columns, some of which have totals. For this example, the columns already contain data. However, if you were working on a case for the first time, the columns would contain either no values or zeros.

Examining the numbers in table, you can see that this plan will contribute 20,000,000 new units to the sales. However, only the number 20000 is entered because the MPAS program assumes the last three zeros. You can tell this is true by the designation of "(000)" above the column.

The numbers that you enter here are your plan for how your actions will add incremental sales for a case business. In that sense, you should only enter what sales you are adding and not the base business numbers, unless you are, for example, changing how much is charged (price per unit) for the number of units normally sold. In that example, you would enter the base business unit sales (See the MTV exercise in Appendix 1 for an illustration if this idea).

Sales increment strategies are all about increasing what is sold over what would have happened without your plan. So, to isolate the effect of your plan, you only enter what your plan adds to that business.

Note that plans that add 5 to 10 percent to the normal sales volume of a case firm are much more reasonable (and possible) than those expecting to get massive sales increases. Therefore, it is always safer to say that you will have a relatively small but important impact on a business than it is to say that you have found the answer to all its problems.

You can judge if the amount of sales increase that you are estimating is high by comparing the net sales amount you expect to get with the net sales of the firm as shown in the history part of the MPAS program or in the case itself. For example, if the case firm has net sales of $2 billion before your plan, it is reasonable to think that you could create a marketing plan that would increase sales by as much as $200 million.

When entering data into this form, you only need to input unit sales, price per unit, and cost per unit because all the other columns are figured automatically. Try to change the unit sales column first number from 20000 to 21000 to see what will happen. Select **Edit** and the cursor will automatically move to the first year of the unit sales numbers. Type in **21000** and use the down arrow key on the keyboard to move down to the next year. You can see the result immediately. The gross sales change as do the cost of goods and the net sales for that year. Now move the cursor down to year 10 using either the down arrow or by clicking there with your mouse. Change that number from 21000 to 22000 by entering **22000** and press the down arrow (or click the mouse on another location in the table). If you use the down arrow, you will find that the cursor moves to the first year of the price per unit column and the gross sales, cost of goods, and net sales numbers all change as a result.

With the cursor in the first year of the price per unit column, enter **21.11** to replace the 20.00 price number already there and press the down arrow on the keyboard. Note that the gross sales and net sales numbers change as a result. Next, move the down arrow on the keyboard down again until the cursor jumps to year one of the average cost per unit. Now you could change any of the cost per unit numbers, if you want to.

Note that if you plan calls for selling units of two different products, you must enter the total of the units you expect to sell for both of the products in each of the unit sales years. Then the average price per unit and the average cost per unit columns need to represent the average price and the average cost of the two types of products too. For example, if you expect to sell 10,000,000 units at $20 and 10,000,000 at $30, your total units is 20,000,000 (but you enter 20,000) and your average price per unit is $(10,000,000/20,000,000) \cdot 20 + (10,000,000/20,000,000) \cdot 30 = 25$, which you enter as 25.00.

After you are done entering your sales estimates for the next 10 years, you will need to enter estimates of the money you plan to spend to make those sales occur. One way to proceed from here is to take the net sales for the second year of your plan and multiple that amount by .80, using the resulting number as the yearly budget for your plan expenses. The second year is usually better to use than the first year because some unit sales start slow in the first year and that first year amount may be only half of what is achieved in the second year.

Write that number on a piece of paper and subtract from that amount as you enter your specific expenses later in the MPAS program. In this example, you have $210,000,000 \cdot .8$ or $168,000,000 to work with as an expenses total.

Normally, when you are ready to leave here, because you are done entering the sales estimates, you press the **F10** key on your keyboard to save your work. But in this example, press the **Esc** key to leave without saving your work or changes so that the numbers remain unchanged. You can see that when you press the **Esc** key the table numbers return back to what they were before you changed them. Now select **Return** and go back to the main MPAS menu area.

There is also another place for entering estimates of revenue as part of the sales forecast you are making. You get there by selecting **Sales** followed by **Other revenue**. Use this area to enter 10 years worth of information on sources of revenue that do not fit the format of the previous sales forecast entry area. Most of the time, you will not need to enter sales estimates in this additional area.

## Lesson 5: Entering Marketing Plan Expenses and Related Information

After doing the sales forecasts, you are ready to enter the details of your marketing strategy and plan. Select **Marketing plan** from the **Analysis** menu. You next find yourself at the marketing plan menu area. In this area, you are expected to enter words or numbers depending on which part of your plan you are addressing.

The first menu item is Marketing strategy. Select **Marketing strategy** and you will see a word processing box appear, which is the same kind of box described in Lesson 3. Leave the Marketing strategy description area by selecting **Return** (you will skip doing any word processing in this lesson).

Next look at the target market description and data input area. The Consumer target menu option allows you to enter a description of the target group who will be the focus of your marketing strategy. That section operates just as the other MPAS program parts where you can enter and edit words. The Business target section is also a word processing area. The Consumer data and Business data areas require the input of numbers, which result in a profile of the consumer or business segment at which your marketing strategy will be directed. Normally, you will target your strategy at a consumer or business group, but not at both.

Select **Consumer target.** The table you see operates in a manner similar to the area where you entered the sales estimates for your plan. The objective here is to enter proportions under age, income, social class, gender, household size, presence of children, and marital status so that each of the respective columns totals 100. For example, the numbers already entered in the table indicate that the sample case marketing plan will put 40 percent of its effort against 20 to 29 year olds and 60 percent of its effort against 30 to 50 year olds. By income, 50 percent of the effort will be against those with household incomes of 40–59 thousand and another 50 percent toward those with household incomes of 60–79. The other target demographics can be described in a similar fashion.

To see how this page of demographics operates, select **Edit** and the cursor will move to the 0–10 age group. Now, move the cursor down using the keyboard arrow key to the 20–29 age range and enter **50** followed by using the arrow key to move down to the 30–50 age range. The total for the age column is now 110, so enter **50** for the 30–50 group and use the arrow key to move down to the 50+ group. The total is 100 again. Now you can use the arrow key or the mouse pointer to move to any of the other consumer target demographics in this table.

Normally, you press F10 when you are done entering your demographic profiles, but because you do not want to save the changes you made, press the **Esc** key instead. As you can see, the numbers have returned to their original values. When working on the demographic information for an assigned case, you will not find any numbers in this table, and you will have to enter all of them while making sure that each demographic column totals 100. Now select **Return** and go back to the marketing plan menu area.

The next selection on the top menu line is Product. This is another word processing area as is the next menu item named Pricing. Each of these two areas require descriptions of strategy elements.

The Promotion section is considerably more complicated. It contains a combination of areas where you can enter words and other areas where you enter numbers. The ones that require words are Promotion strategy and Promotion theme. The rest are for inputting numbers. However, depending on you plan, you are likely to only want to spend money on some of the promotional tools rather than on each one.

Select the **TV media plan** and you will see a television advertising grid with several columns. You only need to enter the yearly spending numbers and the MPAS program will compute those for the other three columns. Select **Edit** and the cursor will move to the first year money amount. Remember that the number 70000 means that this plan will spend $70 million on television advertising in the first year because the last three zeros are assumed. To see how the grid works, type **72000** into the first year, replacing the 70000 number, and then use the arrow key to move the cursor down to the next year. Notice how the reach, frequency, and Gross Rating Points (GRPs), which are a measure of target audience impact combining the reach and frequency numbers, change automatically. Describing what the previous media terms mean is beyond the scope of this tutorial; they are normally learned in an advertising class. At this point, you only need to know that they indicate what you are getting for the money spent on television advertising.

Leave this grid by pressing the **Esc** key so that the changes you made are not saved, but remember that normally you would want to press F10 to save your work. Also, normally when you start this television grid, there are no numbers in it. Now select **Return** and go back to the marketing plan menu area.

The radio and magazine menu options operate in the same way as the television menu selection. The Other promotion media plan and the remaining items on the Promotion menu require that you enter spending levels for each of 10 years, but they do not provide any other information. That is, for those screens, you only enter numbers, and you do not see any other columns of information.

For example, select **Sales promotion plan** from the menu, and you will a table that follows the normal pattern of blank spaces for entering spending levels for each of 10 years. The sample marketing plan spends $20 million a year on sales promotion. If you select **Edit**, you can change the values which are entered under the sales promotion plan. However, skip changing any of the sales promotion numbers and select **Return** to leave the table so that you go back to the marketing plan menu area.

The last item on the top of the marketing plan menu is Distribution, which leads to a word processing area for describing the distribution strategy for the marketing plan. Now select **Return** and go back to the main MPAS menus area.

## Lesson 6: Entering Other Expenses Information

After entering the marketing plan information, you are ready to enter more details about other expenditures needed to make your marketing plan work. This next set of inputs is optional because not all plans need to spend additional money beyond what is described in the marketing plan expenditures sections (the previous lesson). To make entries into Other expenditures also requires a more sophisticated understanding of what must be done to make a marketing plan successful. However, most plans will not work without at least some spending beyond what you identified in the marketing plan spending area.

To begin with the Other expenditures area, select **Marketing plan** from the Analysis menu. You next find yourself at the Other expenditures menu area. In this area, you are expected to enter numbers about the money needed to startup your marketing plan and support it during its 10 years of operation.

Select **Startup expenses.** The next screen shows what is needed to be spent before the beginning of the first year to get the plan started. This spending is above and beyond what you identify as necessary spending during each of the 10 years of your plan's operation. The table works the same way as the other areas you have examined that require the entry of numbers. Now select **Return** and go back to the Other expenditures menu area.

Next select **Distribution expenses** under the Marketing menu item. This screen shows what needs to be spent on distribution during each of the 10 years of your marketing plan. The table works the same way as the other areas you have examined that require the entry of numbers. Now select **Return** and go back to the Other expenditures menu area.

All of the other menu items under Marketing, and those under Other, expect you to enter how much you want to spend on each type of marketing-related expense during each of the 10 years of your plan. However, not all plans require spending in each of the areas listed in the menus. Spending levels also vary considerably from plan to plan.

The last Other expenditures area is Investments and under that Capital investments. Next select **Capital investments** under the Investments menu item. This screen shows a list of items that represent possible capital investments in support of your plan. For example, your plan might require the construction of a new plant and the purchase of additional equipment. It might also require some initial R&D. The numbers you enter into this table are usually guesses about what needs to be spent. The table works the same way as the other areas you have examined that require the entry of numbers. Now select **Return** and go back to the Other expenditures menu area. You are done with the Other expenditures area. Now select **Return** and go back to the main MPAS menu area.

## Lesson 7: Examining Tables and Graphs of Your Work

You are now ready to look at the results of your plan work. With the MPAS program, you have the ability to look at tables that summarize the sales and expense information you entered and the expected financial results and/or you can look at graphs, which give much of the same information.

After you have finished entering the sales and expense information about your marketing plan, you should view the results of your work to confirm that your plan is performing correctly. This is best done by checking the tables.

From the main menu area, select **View plan tables**. The menu selections that appear next contain many tables you can view. You can look at any or all. The most important ones are the Net present value summary and the Income statement summary. Select the **Net present value summary.** A table of your plan's cash flows and net present value will appear on the screen. This sample plan has positive cash flows in all but the first year, and it has a positive net present value. If it did not have a positive net present value, you would have to go back to the sales forecast and/or expenses areas and make changes. Select **Return** to leave the plan net present value area.

Next select the **Income statement summary.** A summary of the plan's revenues and income will appear on the screen. This sample plan has pretax profits in all years but year one. Note that the loss in year one offsets the tax liability in later years. If this income statement summary showed poor plan performance, you would have to go back to the sales forecast and/or expenses areas and make changes. Select **Return** to leave the income statement summary area.

Now go and look at a graph. To leave the plan summary table area select **Return** and go back to the main MPAS menus area. From the main menu area, select **View plan graphs**. The list of graphs on the menu that appears next indicates what graphs you can view. You can look at any or all. Look at the unit sales graph. Select **Unit sales.** A graph appears showing the plan's unit sales for 10 years. This sample plan has a peak of 25 million unit sales per year. Select **Return** to leave the graph area. To leave the plan graphs area, select **Return** and go back to the main menu area.

## Lesson 8: Printing Reports About Your Work

After you have finished entering the sales and expense information about your marketing plan and you have viewed the results of your work to confirm that your plan is performing correctly, you are ready to print your work. From the main menu area, select **Print plan reports**. The menu selections that appears next contain many reports you can print. You can print all or some of these reports depending on what you want copies of and/or what your instructor told you to do. Thus, this printing gives you a hard copy of your work and/or the reports needed for your instructor. You can do printing at anytime because all your marketing strategy and plan work is always available on your diskette.

Assuming that there is a printer connected to your computer or there is a printer connected to the network that the computer is linked to, select **Consumer target market** under the Strategy menu. After the MPAS screen shows a box indicating that it is printing followed by a return to the menu, a two page report should appear on the printer. Note that there is very little on the first printed page because little was entered in the area of the MPAS program to describe the consumer target in words. That first page has the date and time, case identification, student team member names (if you entered some), and the words that were entered to describe the consumer target. The second page shows the target market numbers which describe the consumers who the plan is aimed at.

Next, do a more complicated report. Under the Summary menu, select **Income statement**. Again the screen will indicate that the computer is working on the report. When the program is done creating and printing the report, the menu will appear again. The income statement report is two pages long. It contains a great deal of information about the sales, expenses, income, and performance of the sample marketing plan over ten years. It is the most important financial report in the MPAS program. You are done looking at part of the printing area. Now select **Return** and go back to the main menu area.

## Lesson 9: Getting Hints and Help

There are two ways to get more information from within the MPAS program. The System menu offers access to a menu of hints on how to do well in marketing plan development and to a menu of help topics that provides information about some program functions. Both sources of information operate in the same fashion. To see how this works, select **Hints** on the System menu. A box will appear on the screen containing ten hints to chose from. Next select **Hint 1: INCREMENTALITY** by pressing **Enter** on your keyboard. The information on incrementality will next appear on the screen. You can use the arrow keys on the keyboard to move around this hint information or you can use your mouse by clicking the down arrow on the hint box. To move to the next hint topic, press the **N** key on your keyboard or click **Next** with your mouse. To get back to the list of hint topics, press the **T** key or click **Topics** with your mouse. To leave the hint area entirely and return to the MPAS main menu area, just press the **Esc** key on your keyboard. Both the hint and help areas operate in exactly the same way. Each is responsive to the same set of keyboard and mouse commands. Now select **Esc** to leave.

Note that sometimes the hint and/or help areas are hard to read because the inside part of the box has shifted. You can correct this by moving and/or resizing it as appropriate. To move the inside box, hold down the **Ctrl** key and press the **F7** key. The inside box will start flashing to indicate that it is ready to be moved. Use the arrow keys on your keyboard to move the box to the upper left corner of the double lined container box for the hint or help area. Then press **Enter** to indicate that you are happy with the location of the inside box. Next, to resize the inside box, hold down the **Ctrl** key and press the **F8** key. The inside box will start flashing to show that it is ready to be resized. Use the arrow keys on your keyboard to resize the box to the edges of the double lined container box for the hint or help area. Then press **Enter** to indicate that you are happy with the size of the inside box.

## Lesson 10: Changing the System Configuration

You can change the appearance of the MPAS program by picking from a listing of monitor configuration options that represents different color combinations that can be used when operating the program. The MPAS program normally starts with a blue, gray, and white set of colors, but you can chose from many other possibilities by selecting **Monitor** from the System menu. When you pick an alternative color combination, the entire appearance of the MPAS program changes. Note that some color combinations may make it more difficult to see parts of the program screens such as the word processing areas. Also note that if you are using the MPAS program on a network or on someone else's computer, you many need to change the appearance of the program each time you start it if you want to use a color combination other than the blue, gray, and white default.

## D. MPAS INPUT AND VIEWING SCREENS AND REPORTS PAGE-BY-PAGE

This section contains specific information about each major entry, viewing, or output area linked to menu selections in the MPAS program. To understand what item you are reading about, there is a labeling system to identify its MPAS menu location. It has the following meaning: the first number is the item's location in the main MPAS menus area; the second number is the location of that item as a member of a main MPAS menu; and, if there are further numbers, they represent continuations of subsequent locations. These numeric identifications are accompanied by labels that provide the same information as the numbers.

For example, the identifier "3.1.1.1. Format, Situation Analysis, Situation, Extent of Demand" means the number three item in the main MPAS menus area, the first item on that menu, the first selection in the next area the menu leads to, and the first item on that other area menu. This way of pointing to menu items is difficult in the abstract but is quite clear when you are operating the MPAS program.

### The MPAS History Screens

**2.1. History, Net sales:** This graph shows firm historical net sales for a five-year period. The range of years varies by which case you are working on. Net sales are the total revenue to a firm less the cost of goods. The numbers can be in thousands, millions, or billions as indicated on the top of the graph. The number in the lower right hand corner indicates what the longest bar represents in either thousands, million, or billions.

**2.2. History, Net income:** This graph shows firm historical net income for a five-year period. The range of years varies by which case you are working on. Net income is the pretax profits of a firm. The numbers can be in thousands, millions, or billions as indicated on the top of the graph. The number in the lower right hand corner indicates what the longest bar represents in either thousands, million, or billions.

### The MPAS Format for Case Analysis Screens

**3.1.1.1. Format, Situation analysis, Situation, Extent of demand:** In words, the task is to describe the extent of demand in a market by defining the actual size of that market and estimates of future sales potential. Use words and some numbers within what you write to provide information on customer demand for a category of products or services. To understand the extent of demand for a category, you need estimate the size of the market (units and dollars) now and in the future; competitor market shares and trends in units and dollars; and the market position of competitors in terms of sales and share, including forecasts of market segment growth, usually for the next five years, for the segments in which firms in the industry competes. In addition to considering differences in demand at the primary (category level demand), you will need to characterize selective demand (product or service specific demand) levels and make statements about related brand specific trends.

**3.1.1.2. Format, Situation analysis, Situation, Nature of demand:** Describe, in words, the category buyers and their purchase decision-making process by the consumer or industrial market segment. Include specifics about how those purchases are influenced by factors external to the customer or prospect, including any joint decision making that may occur in families or business organizations. The key to doing this is to be thinking about implications for alternative marketing strategies and programs.

Identify the target market(s). Are segments of the market growing? Is the case firm's target segment large enough to support its product or service? Can the market be more meaningfully segmented into several homogeneous groups on what customers want and how they buy? What are buyer segment demographics, psychological characteristics, and decision-making processes in the context of influences from other entities such as family, friends, society, business organizations, and government?

How has the market has been segmented by competitors and what is the basis for those segmentations. Identifying which segments have the most potential. What key competitors serve each customer group? Are there segments currently not being served? Can the case firm successfully serve those markets? Think about whether a more effective marketing program might be developed for each segment versus having an overall program for all segments. Will tailoring a marketing plan to a specific segment provide a competitive advantage?

Describe the *who, what, where, when, why,* and *how* of the purchase decision. How do buyers (consumer or industrial) purchase existing products or services? What are the more important types of behavior patterns and attitudes? In connection with decision making, how many stores are shopped or industrial sources considered in making a purchase, what is the degree of information seeking, what is the level of brand awareness and loyalty, what are the sources of product or service information, and who makes the purchase decision?

How frequently is the purchase decision made or repeated? What is the buyer's involvement in the decision-making process? Is it a routine decision made frequently (such as buying toothpaste) or is it a decision that occurs infrequently (for example, buying a car)? What is the risk or uncertainty level associated with the purchase and what are the consequences of making a poor choice? What are the reasons for purchase behavior? What needs do buyers satisfy by purchasing the product or service? Are they emotional or rational? What are the most important sources of information used to make a decision and what criteria are used to evaluate the product or service?

**3.1.1.3. Format, Situation analysis, Situation, Strategy analysis:** In words, explain the case firm's strategy and the strategies of major competitors. Start by delineating the objectives of the various marketing strategies. For each firm you analyze, provide specific answers to the following questions:

1. What are the firm's objectives?
2. Have/are they being successfully achieved?

As you describe the marketing strategy of each firm, you should also address a series of specific questions about the case company and its major competitors: Does the firm (or major competitor) have an integrated marketing strategy made up of individual product, channel, price, advertising, and sales force strategies? Is the role selected for each mix element consistent with the overall program objectives, and does it complement other mix elements? Are adequate resources available to carry out the marketing strategy? Are resources committed to sell to individual targets consistent with the importance of each one?

To describe a firm's product or service marketing strategy, you need to delineate what it is doing with each product, promotion, price, and distribution. Is the product mix geared to the needs that the firm wants to meet for each market? What branding strategy is being used? Are products properly positioned against competing brands? Does the firm have a sound approach to product planning and management, and is marketing involved in product decisions? Are additions to, modifications of, or deletions from the product mix needed to make the firm more competitive in the marketplace? Is the performance of each product evaluated on a regular basis?

Has the firm selected the type and intensity of distribution appropriate for each market it wants to serve? How well does each channel access its market target? Is an effective channel mix used? Are channel organizations carrying out their assigned functions properly? How is the channel(s) of distribution managed? Are improvements needed? Are desired customer service levels reached, and are the costs of doing this acceptable?

How responsive is each market target to price variation? What roles does price have in the marketing mix? Is price an active or passive part of the product or service positioning strategy? How do the firm's price strategy and tactics compare with those of competitors? How are prices established? Are there indications that changes should be made in price strategy or tactics?

What are the roles and objectives for advertising and sales promotion in the marketing mix? Is the creative strategy consistent with the positioning strategy? Is the budget adequate to carry out the advertising and sales promotion objectives? Do the promotional plans represent the most cost-effective means of communicating with market targets? Do advertising copy and content effectively communicate the intend message? How well does the promotional program meet its objectives?

**3.1.1.4. Format, Situation analysis, Situation, Life cycle stage:** In words, provide a description of your assumptions about where the product or service market is in its life cycle. This is important because the effectiveness of specific marketing options and approaches tend to vary by stages of that life cycle.

In what stage of the life cycle is the product or service category? What market characteristics support your life-cycle stage evaluation? Be sure to describe the category in which the case firm is competing and not just the specific product or service the firm is selling. The product life cycle is a description of a whole category of products or services and not just of the offerings of individual firms in a category.

**3.1.1.5.1. Format, Situation analysis, Situation, Macroenvironment, Sociocultural:** In words, elaborate on the sociocultural environment in terms of the cultural, attitudinal, and behavioral aspects of the macroenvironment. Focus on changes such as those in individual values, family structure, leisure-time activities, and expectations about the future. These changes affect the sale of personal consumer goods; the advertising of products and services; the marketing of political candidates; and almost every other area of social, economic, and political life related to business activities.

**3.1.1.5.2. Format, Situation analysis, Situation, Macroenvironment, Demographic:** Describe, in words, any demographics that are important to this industry and case firm. For example, what impact does America's aging population have on industry and on firm prospects? Is there any need for concern over changes in the income and social structure of the United States as they may impact the nature of consumer or industrial demand in this industry?

**3.1.1.5.3. Format, Situation analysis, Situation, Macroenvironment, Political and legal:** In words, describe the political and legal environment factors controlled by public authorities, interest groups, and other forces that influence this industry and firm. Describe the regulatory environment within which businesses must operate. Be sure to characterize the political and legal constraints on industry operations and on the behavior of customers and prospects. As with any other external force, this environment presents both opportunities and threats to an industry and to a particular firm. Describe both, particularly the major elements of that environment that have a potential impact on marketing activities through government regulation, consumer protection legislation, and other politically driven influences.

**3.1.1.5.4. Format, Situation analysis, Situation, Macroenvironment, Technological:** Describe the technological driving forces behind developments in this industry and firm in words. How does technology influence existing products and new product development? What is the timing between ideas, invention, and commercialization?

**3.1.1.5.5. Format, Situation analysis, Situation, Macroenvironment, Economic:** Throughly describe the economic situation as it impacts this industry and firm. How is any recession or growth phase influencing the prospects for this industry and firm?

**3.1.1.5.6. Format, Situation analysis, Situation, Macroenvironment, Competitive:** In words, explain the effects of United States and international competition on this industry and firm. Does the industry and/or firm still enjoy a competitive advantage? In the United States, is competition between firms for customers and market share resulting in major industry shakeouts?

**3.1.1.6. Format, Situation analysis, Situation, International issues:** Delineate in words, the international issues relevant to the case firm's business and marketing activities. This may include a discussion of products and services from international competitors; changes in international market opportunities, including shifts in demand; international competitive trends that have implications for the case firm; and others.

**3.1.1.7. Format, Situation analysis, Situation, Strengths:** In words, describe the firm's internal strengths and strengths of its major competitors. Develop a profile of the case firm's strengths by examining each of that firm's functional areas and identify those that are strong. A full list of firm strengths might include product lines, market coverage, manufacturing competence, marketing skills, materials management, R&D, information systems, human resource, product cost or differentiation, and financial position among many others.

Overall, cover whether the case firm and its key competitors have the skills and experience to perform the functions necessary to compete in their product or service category. During your analysis, look especially at each of the following areas:

1. Marketing skills.
2. Production skills.

**3.** Management skills.

**4.** Financial skills.

**5.** R&D skills.

How do the case firm's skills compare with those of competitors? Does the firm in the case have the funds to support an effective marketing program and the resources to successfully execute that plan?

**3.1.8. Format, Situation Analysis, Situation, Weaknesses:** Describe the firm's internal weaknesses and the weaknesses of its major competitors, in words. Develop a profile of the case firm's weaknesses. Examine each of that firm's functional areas and identify those that are weak. A list of weaknesses might include an obsolete or narrow product line, manufacturing costs, inadequate R&D innovations, poor marketing skills, poor materials management systems, poor customer service, inadequate information systems, loss of brand loyalty, poor financial management, and others.

Overall, cover whether the case firm and its key competitors have the skills and experience to perform the functions necessary to compete in their product or service category. During your analysis, look especially at each of the following areas:

**1.** Marketing skills.

**2.** Production skills.

**3.** Management skills.

**4.** Financial skills.

**5.** R&D skills.

How do the case firm's skills compare with those of competitors? Does the firm in the case have the funds to support an effective marketing program and the resources to successfully execute that plan?

**3.1.1.9. Format, Situation Analysis, Situation, Competition:** In words, describe the present and future nature of competition in the case firm's industry. The key is to write about how buyers evaluate alternative products or services relative to their needs by characterizing the critical success factors in a market and whether the case firm is strong in those areas. The firm's probability of success in a particular market depends on whether its business strengths (i.e., distinctive competencies) not only match those key success requirements but also exceed those of its competitors. The best-performing company will be the one that is strong on what customers value and can sustain a differential advantage in that competence over time. Thus, having a competence is not enough; the firm must bring a superior competence in order to attain a sustainable competitive advantage.

**3.2.1. Format, POT analysis, Problems:** Describe the problems facing the case firm. Be sure not to describe just symptoms. Problems are causes while symptoms are effects. Symptoms are usually declines in sales, profits, and/or market share. You want to emphasize why sales are declining or why profits are down. The key question is "why." What is the cause or causes? If you have identified two or more problems that are not directly associated with one another, describe them in the order of their importance.

**3.2.2. Format, POT analysis, Opportunities:** Explain each opportunity for the case firm in which it might have a competitive advantage. Each opportunity should be characterized according to its attractiveness and possibility of being achieved. Do not confuse opportunities with taking action. You can recognize an opportunity but not take any action related to it. You may decide not to compete for an opportunity due to a lack of resources or skills, or the existence of strong competition. It is one thing to identify attractive opportunities in the environment, it is another to have the necessary competencies to succeed in those opportunities. Your analysis of firm strengths and weaknesses in the marketing, financial, manufacturing, and organization of the case firm forms the basis for determining if opportunities can and should be pursued.

**3.2.3. Format, POT analysis, Threats:** Elaborate, in words, the major threats challenging the case firm that are an unfavorable trend or development in the external environment. These threats would lead, in the absence of purposeful marketing action, to an erosion of the firm's position. The various identified threats should be described according to their seriousness and likelihood of occurrence. Potential environmental threats to the firm include domestic competition, increased foreign competition, changing consumer tastes, new or substitute products, new forms of competition, changes in demographics, changes in economic trends, government legislation, consumer pressure groups, recession, slower market growth, and many others.

**3.3. Format, Objectives:** In words, describe the objectives of your marketing strategy. These objectives should be specific and explicitly point to where you expected the case firm to be at a particular time in the future, for example, in 10 years. These objectives must be explicitly stated because they are the standards against which the success or failure of your particular strategy will be evaluated.

When describing your objectives, make them as measurable as possible. Make sure that the objectives are feasible and attainable. Moreover, because strategic marketing is futuristic and no one can predict the future with complete accuracy, your objectives should always be adaptable to the changing conditions taking place in the organization, marketplace, and industry.

Objectives are usually classified in terms of sales, market share growth, and/or financial targets, which are symptoms of successful marketing efforts. For example, you may decide that the firm needs to grow sales by 10 percent per year for each of the next 10 years, with a market share growth of 5 points at the end of that 10-year period. At the same time, you expect pretax profits to increase by 12 percent annually. Other objectives are also appropriate, including an increase in consumer advertising awareness and brand preference.

In general, there are two types of objectives. The *quantifiable behavioral objectives* are invariably behavioral. They concern responses such as orders for a product, requests for information, or sales calls. These objectives should be specific about actionable results to accomplish such as the number of orders or number of units sold. *Unquantifiable nonbehavioral objectives* are the nonbehavioral objectives for marketing, which include product image enhancements or attitudinal changes.

**3.4.1. Format, Alternatives, A Alternative:** Describe, in words, your first marketing alternative or strategic option or action that represents one viable solution to the problem(s) that you have identified while also pursuing opportunities and avoiding threats. Be sure that your descriptions of problems, opportunities, and threats and this alternative are consistent. To help avoid any mistake, be explicit in describing the connections between the situation analysis, the problems, opportunities, and threats, and your alternative. Include an assessment of the advantages and limitations associated with the alternative.

Your alternative should address as many topic areas as appropriate in terms of strategy-related marketing mix and program decisions. They should cover product line breath and depth, positioning, and branding issues; price points and discounting; promotion mix in terms of advertising, sales promotion, and personal selling; and distribution channels, including intensity and types (wholesalers and retailers).

**3.4.2. Format, Alternatives, B Alternative:** Explain, in words, your second marketing alternative. (See 3.4.1. for more details.)

**3.4.3. Format, Alternatives, C Alternative:** In words, describe your third marketing alternative. (See 3.4.1. for more details.)

**3.5.1. Format, Decision, Recommendation:** Provide a description, in words, of your decision (choice of marketing alternatives) and associated recommendations. Pick one alternative and not a mixture of two or more. Address what actions should be taken and why. State the main reasons you believe your recommended course of action is best, but avoid rehashing what you wrote in the other sections of the MPAS program. It is important that your recommendations be specific and operational. Such recommendations often includes several parts such as an increase in spending on the introduction of a new product and promotional efforts. Avoid recommending a course of action beyond a the case firm's means. Be realistic. No organization can possibly pursue all the strategies that could potentially benefit it. Reach a clear decision.

**3.5.2. Format, Decision, Implementation and control:** Address plan implementation and control issues. The aim here is to describe what control systems to use when executing and monitoring your recommended plan.

## The MPAS Plan Analysis Screens

**4.1.1.1. Analysis, Sales, Sales estimates, Unit sales estimates greater than 1000:** For this screen, you need to enter data on unit sales, price per unit, and cost per unit. By selecting the greater than 1,000 units option, the program assumes three zeros after each unit sales number you enter. Therefore, because you select unit sales estimates greater than 1000, you cannot enter small numbers of unit transactions. Businesses with high unit volumes are retailers such as clothing stores, which might expect a new plan to contribute tens of thousands of additional unit sales at unit prices in the range of $110 per transaction (average register transaction amount).

(Note that almost everywhere else in the MPAS program when you enter dollar amounts it is assumed that there are three zeros after each number you input. This fact is indicated on the screen into which you are entering your numbers.)

On this screen, you can see six columns, some of which have places for totals. The numbers that you enter are your plan for how your marketing plan will add incremental sales to the case business. In that sense, you should only enter what you are adding due to your plan and not the sales that would occur without the effect of your plan. Sales increments from marketing strategies are all about increasing what is sold over what would have happened without your plan.

Plans that add 5 to 10 percent to the normal sales volume of a case firm are much more reasonable (and possible) than those that expect to get massive sales increases.

Therefore, it is always safer to assume that you will have a relatively small, but important, impact on a business than it is to assume you will have a massive impact on the amount normally sold.

You can judge whether the amount of sales increase that you are estimating from your plan is high by comparing the incremental sales amount you expect with the net sales of the firm as shown in the history part of the MPAS program or in the case itself. For example, if the case firm has net sales of $2 billion before your plan, it is reasonable to think that you could create a marketing plan that would increase sales by as much as $200 million.

When entering data into this form, you only need to supply the unit sales, price per unit, and cost per unit. All the other columns are figured automatically. When you are ready to leave, press the **F10** key on your keyboard to save your work. If you press the **Esc** key to leave, your work or changes will not be saved.

Note that if your plan calls for selling units of two different products, you must enter the total of the units you expect to sell for both of the products in the unit sales column. Then the average price per unit and the average cost per unit columns represent the average price and the average cost of the two types of products. For example, if you expect to sell 10,000,000 units at $20 and 10,000,000 at $30, your total units is 20,000,000 (but you enter 20,000) and your average price per unit is $(10,000,000/20,000,000) \cdot 20 + (10,000,000/20,000,000) \cdot 30 = 25$, which you enter as 25.00.

After you are done entering your sales forecasts for the next 10 years, you will later need to enter the estimates of the money you plan to spend to make those sales occur in expenses part of the MPAS program. Take the net sales amount for the second year of your plan and multiply that amount by .80 for have an estimate of your yearly money available for expenses. Write that number on a piece of paper and subtract from that amount as you enter your expenses later in the MPAS program. For example, if you have $200 million in net sales, then the calculation is $200,000,000 \cdot .8$ or $160,000,000 to work with for expenses. Note that the second year net sales are usually better to use than the first year because some unit sales start slow in the first year and that first year amount may be only half of what is achieved in the second year.

**4.1.1.2. Analysis, Sales, Sales estimates, or Unit sales estimates less then 1000:** For this screen, you need to enter information on unit sales, price per unit, and cost per unit. By selecting the less than 1,000 units option, the program assumes that you will enter the exact number of units per year you plan to sell. Businesses with low unit volumes are, for example advertising agencies, which may get several new clients per year each contributing $20 to $30 million.

(Note that everywhere else in the MPAS program when you enter dollar amounts it is usually assumed that there are three zeros after each number inputted. This fact is indicated on the screen into which you are entering your numbers.)

You can see six columns, some of which have totals. The numbers that you enter are your plan for how you will add incremental sales to the case business. In that sense, you should only enter what you are adding and not the numbers for sales that would occur in the absence of your marketing plan. Marketing strategies are all about increasing what is sold over what would have happened without your plan. So to see the effect of your plan, only enter what your plan adds to the business.

Plans that add 5 to 10 percent to the normal sales volume of a case firm are much more reasonable (and possible) than those that expect to get massive sales increases. Therefore, it is always safer to say that you will have a relatively small but important impact on a business than it is to say that you have found the answer to all its problems.

You can judge if the amount of sales that you are getting is high by comparing the sales increase you expect to get with the net sales of the firm as shown in the history part of the MPAS program or in the case itself. For example, if the case firm has net sales of $1 billion before your plan, it is reasonable to think that you could create a marketing plan that would increase sales by as much as $100 million.

When entering data into this form, you only need to supply the unit sales, price per unit, and cost per unit. All the other columns are figured automatically. When you are ready to leave, press the **F10** key on your keyboard to save your work. If you press the **Esc** key to leave, your work or changes will not be saved.

Note that if your plan calls for selling units of two different products or services, you must enter the total of the units you expect to sell for both of the products in the units column. Then the average price per unit and the average cost per unit columns represent the average price and the average cost of the two types of products. For example, if you expect to sell 100 units at $2 million and 100 at $3 million, your total units is 200 and your average price per unit is $(100/200) \cdot 2 + (100/200) \cdot 3 = 2.5$, which you enter as 2.5 million (or 2500000, with all the zeros).

After you are done entering your sales forecasts for the next 10 years, you will then need to enter the estimates of the money you plan to spend to make those sales occur in another part of the MPAS program. Therefore, you need to make an estimate of how much money you will have for expenses in support of your plan. Do this by taking the net sales amount for the second year of your plan and multiply that amount by .80. Use the result as the yearly budget estimate for expenses. Write that number on a piece of paper and subtract from it as you enter your expense amounts in the MPAS program. For example, if you have $100 million in net sales, then the calculation is $100,000,000 \cdot .8$ or $80,000,000 to work with for expenses. Note that the second year net sales are usually better to use than the first year because some unit sales start slow in the first year and that first year amount may be only half of what is achieved in the second year.

**4.1.2. Analysis, Sales, Other revenue:** This is a place for entering estimates of sales revenue that are separate from the unit sales forecast for your plan. Use this area to enter 10 years worth of sales revenue that does not fit the format of the sales estimates entry area (either 4.1.1.1. or 4.1.1.2.). However, most of the time you will not enter sales estimates in this additional area.

**4.2.1.1. Analysis, Marketing plan, Strategy, Marketing strategy:** Use this area to provide a summary of your marketing strategy. Enter a description of the major aspects of what you are trying to do. If you did the "Format for Case Analysis," you can enter here the decision information you typed in that part of the MPAS program because the decision you made is the marketing strategy you selected to pursue.

In writing your marketing strategy description, address what actions should be taken and why. Describe the outstanding aspects of your strategy and the main reasons why you believe it is the best course to take. Be specific and operational by indicating what the strategy is intended to do and how it will operate.

**4.2.2.1. Analysis, Marketing plan, Target, Consumer target:** In this area, you need to describe the consumer target group who will be the focus of your marketing strategy. There is a separate place to characterize or profile your target market with numbers, so in this area write a general description of your consumer target.

**4.2.2.2. Analysis, Marketing plan, Target, Consumer data:** For this form, your objective is to enter proportions under age, income, social class, gender, household size, presence of children, and marital status so that each of the respective columns totals 100. For example, the numbers you entered on the page can indicate that your marketing plan will put 40 percent of its effort against 20 to 29 year olds and 60 percent of its effort against 30 to 50 year olds. By income, you may have 50 percent of the effort against those with household incomes of 40–59 thousand and another 50 percent toward those with household incomes of 60–79. The other target demographics can be described in a similar fashion.

**4.2.2.3. Analysis, Marketing plan, Target, Business target:** In this area, you need to describe the business target group who will be the focus of your marketing strategy. There is separate place to characterize or profile your target market with numbers, so in this area write a general description of your business target.

**4.2.2.4. Analysis, Marketing plan, Target, Business data:** The objective for this page is to enter some words under the business firm types and proportions under firm types, firm size, region, and number of employees so that each of the respective columns totals 100. For the business firm type, you should enter names of industries that will be the target of your marketing plan. For example, as an advertising agency, you may want to get an automotive client, a supermarket client, a computer manufacturer client, a bank client, and an entertainment industry client. Enter those labels, or abbreviations in the business firms area. You would want to enter proportions next to those industry labels to show how much of your effort will be put against each. You might want to put 20 percent of your effort against getting an automotive client, 30 percent of your effort against getting a supermarket client, etc., until those proportions total 100. For the other columns, enter proportions to indicate how much of your effort will go against each of the categories so that each totals 100. For example, if you are only going to get new advertising clients from among the largest firms, then put 100 percent of your effort against firms with sales of $500+ million and with employees numbering more than 500.

**4.2.3.1. Analysis, Marketing plan, Product, Product strategy:** In this area you need to describe your product (or service) strategy. What attributes will you focus on? How will you package your product (or service)? What needs will your product (or service) address?

**4.2.4.1. Analysis, Marketing plan, Pricing, Pricing strategy:** For this area, describe your pricing strategy. Indicate how much you intend to charge for your product(s) or service(s) and why. Be specific about what you think that pricing approach will accomplish versus any other pricing you could have selected.

**4.2.5.1. Analysis, Marketing plan, Promotion, Promotional strategy:** For this area, describe your promotion strategy. Indicate what your strategy is and how you intend it to operate. Be specific about what you think that this promotional approach will accomplish versus any other promotional approach you could have selected.

**4.2.5.2. Analysis, Marketing plan, Promotion, Promotion theme:** Describe the promotion theme or creative focus of your marketing strategy. This is the place to indicate the benefit(s) your promotion, particularly advertising, will focus on and how that information will be communicated.

**4.2.5.3. Analysis, Marketing plan, Promotion, TV media plan:** This television advertising grid has several columns, but you only need to enter the yearly spending numbers and the MPAS program will create those for the other three columns. Note that the spending levels per year that you enter should be inputted without the last three trailing zeros because those last three zeros are assumed. If you enter a number in the spending column for any year, the reach, frequency, and GRPs are automatically computed after you use the arrow key on your keyboard to move down a year. Describing what the media terms reach, frequency, and GRPs mean is beyond the scope of this manual; they are normally learned in an advertising class. At this point, you only need to know that they indicate what you are getting for the money spent on television advertising.

**4.2.5.4. Analysis, Marketing plan, Promotion, Radio media plan:** This radio advertising grid has several columns, but you only need to enter the yearly spending numbers and the MPAS program will create those for the other three columns. Note that the spending levels per year that you enter should be inputted without the last three trailing zeros because those last three zeros are assumed. If you enter a number in the spending column for any year, the reach, frequency, and GRPs are created automatically after you move to the next year on the grid by pressing the arrow key on your keyboard. Describing what the media terms reach, frequency, and GRPs mean is beyond the scope of this manual; they are normally learned in an advertising class. At this point, you only need to know that they indicate what you are getting for the money spent on radio advertising.

**4.2.5.5. Analysis, Marketing plan, Promotion, Magazine media plan:** This magazine advertising grid has several columns, but you only need to enter the yearly spending numbers and the MPAS program will create those for the other three columns. Note that the spending levels per year that you enter should be inputed without the last three trailing zeros because those last three zeros are assumed. If you enter a number in the spending column for any year, the reach, frequency, and GRPs appear automatically after you move to the next year on the grid by pressing the arrow key on your keyboard. Describing what the media terms reach, frequency, and GRPs mean is beyond the scope of this manual; they are normally learned in an advertising class. At this point, you only need to know that they indicate what you are getting for the money spent on magazine advertising.

**4.2.5.6. Analysis, Marketing plan, Promotion, Other promotion media plan:** This area requires that you enter other promotion media spending levels for each of the 10 years, but you do not need to provide any other information. Enter the yearly dollar amounts you want to spend for such marketing tools as direct mail, telemarketing, billboards, etc. If you want to use more than one of the aforementioned tools, total the spending for each by year and enter those totals for those years in this area.

**4.2.5.7. Analysis, Marketing plan, Promotion, Sales promotion plan:** Enter your sales promotion spending by year in this area for each of the 10 years, but you do not need to provide any other information.

**4.2.5.8. Marketing plan, promotion, Personal selling plan:** Enter your personal selling spending by year in this area for each of 10 years, but you do not need to provide any other information.

**4.2.5.9. Analysis, Marketing plan, Promotion, Public relations plan:** Enter your public relations spending by year in this area for each of the 10 years, but you do not need to provide any other information. Enter the yearly dollar amounts you want to spend.

**4.2.6.1. Analysis, Marketing plan, Distribution, Distribution strategy:** For this area, describe your distribution strategy. Indicate what your strategy is and how you intend that strategy to operate. Be specific about what you think that distribution approach will accomplish versus any other distribution approach you could have selected.

**4.3.1.1. Analysis, Other expenditures, Startup, Startup expenses:** In this area, you can enter marketing and additional expenses associated with spending in support of your plan before year one. You can also think of this spending as expenses incurred just before your product or service is launched in its first year. For convenience, these expenses are deducted from the first operational year of your strategy. For example, you may want to do some marketing research before your first year of sales or you may want to do some promotional spending to load the distribution channel. You may also want to hire some personnel or do some extra pre-year one R&D work.

**4.3.2.1. Analysis, Other expenditures, Marketing, Distribution expenses:** Enter your distribution expenses spending by year in this area for each of the 10 years. Enter the additional yearly dollar amounts you want to spend on distribution. If you expect to enter a new distribution channel or expand in a channel already serviced by the case firm, you may need to spend extra money to make that happen.

**4.3.2.2. Analysis, Other expenditures, Marketing, Marketing and sales personnel expenses:** Enter your spending for additional marketing and sales personnel. Many strategies require that additional marketers be hired to manage a product or service plan and that more sales people be recruited to reach a greater number of distribution channel or new distribution channel members.

**4.3.2.3. Analysis, Other expenditures, Marketing, Marketing research expenses:** Marketing research spending is important to understanding what is happening in the marketplace and with customers and prospects. Research is useful in a very large number of ways, including product or service improvement studies (product testing), attitude surveys, store product movement audits, pricing manipulation experiments, and much more. Almost all marketing plans require that money be spent for an ongoing program of marketing research. Enter the yearly dollar amounts you want to spend.

**4.3.2.4. Analysis, Other expenditures, Marketing, Other marketing expenses:** Enter dollar amounts here for spending on things not covered under the spending categories noted above. Enter the yearly dollar amounts you want to spend.

**4.3.3.1. Analysis, Other expenditures, Other, R&D expenses:** This is ongoing spending for R&D designed for product or service improvement. Almost all offerings can benefit from an ongoing improvement program, which involves research on different configurations for a product or service. This budget is separate from the marketing research budget because it involves the money needed for making changes to the product or service in response to customer and prospect research. Some changes may also made to obtain production efficiencies or to respond to management judgments about how to improve sales performance with the target audience. Enter the yearly dollar amounts you want to spend.

**4.3.3.2. Analysis, Other expenditures, Other, Personnel and administration:** In this area, enter the money you want to spend or are required to spend on company overhead. That overhead is the money charged to most marketing plans to support the functioning of the entire firm. This is frequently some fixed percentage of product or service net sales increment. If you are unsure about what to put here, try 2 to 5 percent of your net sales. That net sales number is available in the place where you entered your sales estimates (see 4.1.1.1. or 4.1.1.2.). Enter here the yearly dollar amounts you must allocate for personnel and administration.

**4.3.3.3. Analysis, Other expenditures, Other, Other plan expenses:** Enter here the plan expenses that you could not, so far, find any appropriate place for (keeping in mind that the last section of this expense input area allows you to itemize your capital investments—see 4.3.4.1.). This is a good place to input spending on miscellaneous items, which you are not sure about in the sense that the money can be used as a contingency fund for unexpected expenses related to your plan. Thus, enter the yearly dollar amounts you want to hold for miscellaneous expenses.

**4.3.4.1. Analysis, Other expenditures, Investments, Capital investments:** Capital investments are frequently required to support the enhancement of an existing product or service or for the creation of a new one. In this table, enter your estimates of the expenditures you need to make to have the capacity to produce your product, the additional office space for those who will work on your product, and whatever computer systems and other equipment they may need to do their jobs. This money is spent before the introduction of your product or service and then depreciated over the 10 year life cycle of your plan.

## The MPAS Plan Results Screens

**5.1.1.1. Results, View plan tables, Plan tables, Net present value summary:** This screen shows a summary of your plan's cash flows and net present value. You want your plan to have positive cash flows in most years, and a positive net present value. If it does not have a positive net present value, you have to go back to the sales estimates and/or expenses areas of the MPAS program and make changes.

**5.1.1.2. Results, View plan tables, Plan tables, Sales revenue summary:** This summary shows your plan's net sales, other revenues, and totals of the two for each of the 10 years. It also shows what percent each year's total revenues is of all of the 10 years. This display of sales percentages by year is interesting because it shows how concentrated your sales are by year.

**5.1.1.3. Results, View plan tables, Plan tables, Income statement summary:** This screen shows a summary of your plan's revenues and income. It itemizes the revenues, expenses, income, and much of the other information associated with your plan, including after tax profits. Note that losses in any one year offset tax liabilities in later years. If this income statement summary shows poor plan performance, you have to go back to the sales estimates and/or expenses areas of the MPAS program and make changes.

**5.1.1.4. Results, View plan tables, Plan tables, Net income by net sales ratio:** This page shows the ratio of net income divided by net sales for each of the 10 years. A good target for the ratio is where net income is at least 10 percent of net sales. However, if the ratio is much greater than 20 percent, that may mean that you are being too optimistic about how well your plan will perform. If you see any problems with the ratio (it is too high or too low), go back to the sales estimates and/or expenses areas of the MPAS program and make changes.

**5.1.1.5. Results, View plan tables, Plan tables, Expenses summary:** This expenses summary for your plan shows how much of what you are spending on your product or services is for marketing, including advertising, sales promotion, etc., versus for additional expenses such as R&D, personnel and administration, and others by year for the 10 years.

**5.1.1.6. Results, View plan tables, Plan tables, Expenses ratios:** These ratios of R&D to net sales, total marketing expenses to net sales, and total expenses to net sales provide a good indication of the relative allocation of your marketing plan effort versus the amount of sales revenue your plan will be bringing in over the 10 years.

**5.1.1.7. Results, View plan tables, Plan tables, Marketing expenses summary:** For this table, total promotion is the sum of all money spent on advertising (television, radio, magazines, and other promotion media), sales promotion, personal selling, and public relations. The table also shows what your plan spends on distribution, marketing and sales personnel, marketing research, and other marketing for each of the 10 years.

**5.1.1.8. Results, View plan tables, Plan tables, Advertising summary:** This table itemizes the amount of money spent per year on specific advertising media, including television, radio, magazines, and other media (such as direct mail, telemarketing, billboards, etc.). It also shows a total for all these media for each of the 10 years.

**5.1.1.9. Results, View plan tables, Plan tables, Promotion summary:** The promotion summary table shows how much money is spent on each form of promotion by your plan for each of the 10 years and in total. It lists specific spending on sales promotion, personal selling, public relations, and media advertising (the total of television, radio, magazines, and other media).

**5.1.1.0. Results, View plan tables, Plan tables, Promotion and advertising ratios:** This table shows the ratios between net sales and total promotion and net sales and total advertising for media, plus the actual dollar amounts used to create the ratios. These ratios are of interest because they indicate how much is spent on either total promotion and/or on total advertising to produce a certain number of dollars in net sales. For example, your plan may produce three dollars in net sales for every dollar spent on total promotion. In that case, the ratio of net sales to total promotion would be 3.0.

**5.1.2.1. Results, View plan tables, Loan, Plan loan requirement:** This table indicates the business loan and equity requirements of your marketing plan. The loan amount is automatically computed and is based on your money needs for initial capital investments and for initial startup expenses. This loan is assumed to come from a bank or from investments made by the case firm. Loans are also made to you for your plan based on your year-to-year cash flows. If your plan cash flow becomes negative in any year, you are automatically loaned money to pay your expenses. However, what you borrow determines a yearly loan payment, which can hurt your profitability in future years. This supplemental money is loaned to you at the interest rate indicated in the table and the yearly loan payment amount is also shown.

**5.2.1.1. Results, View plan graphs, Graphs, Unit sales:** When you select Unit sales from the list of graphs, a bar graph appears showing your plan's unit sales for each of the 10 years. With the title of the graph at the top, you can see if the bars are in thousands, millions, or billions. The number in the lower right is the height of the largest bar on the same scale as indicated in the title of the graph.

**5.2.1.2. Results, View plan graphs, Graphs, Net sales:** When you select Net sales from the list of graphs, a bar graph appears showing your plan's net sales for each of the 10 years. From the title of the graph at the top, you can see if the bars are in thousands, millions, or billions. The number in the lower right is the height of the largest bar on the same scale as indicated in the title of the graph.

**5.2.1.3. Results, View plan graphs, Graphs, Net income:** When you select Net income from the list of graphs, a bar graph appears showing your plan's net income for each of the 10 years. From the title of the graph at the top, you can see if the bars are in thousands, millions, or billions. The number in the lower right is the height of the largest bar on the same scale as indicated in the title of the graph.

**5.2.1.4. Results, View plan graphs, Graphs, Net income by net sales:** When you select Net income by net sales from the list of graphs, a bar graph appears showing your plan's ratio of net income to net sales for each of the 10 years. This bar graph shows ratios either less than or greater than one. A preferred ratio is between .10 and .20, with any plan producing less than .10 not profitable enough, and any plan producing a ratio much greater than .20 is suspect as to its ability to deliver what it promises. The number in the lower right is the ratio value for the largest bar.

**5.2.1.5. Results, View plan graphs, Graphs, Total advertising:** When you select Total advertising from the list of graphs, a bar graph appears showing your plan's total advertising spending for each of the 10 years. From the title of the graph at the top, you can see if the bars are in thousands, millions, or billions. The number in the lower right is the height of the largest bar on the same scale as indicated in the title of the graph.

**5.2.1.6. Results, View plan graphs, Graphs, Net sales by total advertising:** When you select Net sales by total advertising from the list of graphs, a bar graph appears showing your plan's ratio of net sales to total advertising for each of the 10 years. This bar graph shows a ratio either less than or greater than one. A preferred ratio is between 3 and 5 for many consumer goods cases, indicating that between three and five dollars in net sales is produced for every dollar spent on total advertising. Business-to-business marketing normally expends considerably less on total promotion, specifically 10 to 20 dollars in net sales for every advertising dollar. The number in the lower right is the ratio value for the largest bar.

**5.2.1.7. Results, View plan graphs, Graphs, Total promotion:** When you select Total promotion from the list of graphs, a bar graph appears showing your plan's total promotion spending for each of the 10 years. From the title of the graph at the top, you can see if the bars are in thousands, millions, or billions. The number in the lower right is the height of the largest bar on the same scale as indicated in the title of the graph.

**5.2.1.8. Results, View plan graphs, Graphs, Net sales by total promotion:** When you select Net sales by total promotion from the list of graphs, a bar graph appears showing your plan's ratio of net sales to total promotion for each of the 10 years. This bar graph shows ratios either less than or greater than one. A preferred ratio is between 3 and 6 for many consumer goods firms, indicating that between three and six dollars in net sales is produced for every dollar spent on total promotion. Business-to-business marketing normally expends considerably less on total promotion, specifically 10 to 20 dollars in net sales for every promotional dollar. The number in the lower right is the ratio value for the largest bar.

**5.2.1.9. Results, View plan graphs, Graphs, Total marketings:** When you select Total marketing from the list of graphs, a bar graph appears showing your plan's total marketing spending for each of the 10 years. From the title of the graph at the top, you can see if the bars are in thousands, millions, or billions. The number in the lower right is the height of the largest bar on the same scale as indicated in the title of the graph.

**5.2.1.0. Results, View plan graphs, Graphs, Total marketing by net sales:** When you select Total marketing by net sales from the list of graphs, a bar graph appears showing your plan's ratio of total marketing to net sales for each of the 10 years. This bar graph shows ratios either less than or greater than one. The number in the lower right is the ratio value for the largest bar.

**5.2.1.a. Results, View plan graphs, Graphs, Total R&D by net sales:** When you select Total R&D by net sales from the list of graphs, a bar graph appears showing your plan's ratio of R&D to net sales for each of the 10 years. This bar graph shows a ratio either less than or greater than one. The number in the lower right is the ratio value for the largest bar.

**5.2.1.b. Results, View plan graphs, Graphs, Total expenses:** When you select Total expenses from the list of graphs, a bar graph appears showing your plan's total expenses for each of the 10 years. From the title of the graph at the top, you can see if the bars are in thousands, millions, or billions. The number in the lower right is the height of the largest bar on the same scale as indicated in the title of the graph.

**5.2.1.c. Results, View plan graphs, Graphs, Total expenses by net sales:** When you select Total expenses by net sales from the list of graphs, a bar graph appears showing your plan's ratio of total expenses to net sales for each of the 10 years. This bar graph shows ratios either less than or greater than one. The number in the lower right is the ratio value for the largest bar.

**5.3.1.1. Results, Print plan reports, Format, Print all of case format:** Selecting this option prints all of the "Format for Case Analysis" reports. (See the following for individual descriptions of those reports.)

**5.3.1.2.1. Results, Print plan reports, Format, Situation analysis, Print all situation analysis reports:** Selecting this option prints all of the word processing you did in describing the situation for the case firm and industry. This report has multiple pages, which will include whatever you wrote on extent of demand, nature of demand, strategy analysis, life cycle stage, macroenvironmental trends (all six of them), international issues, strengths and weaknesses, and the nature of competition. Almost all the pages have the date and time, case name identification, and student team member names.

**5.3.1.2.2. Results, Print plan reports, Format, Situation analysis, Extent of demand:** Selecting this option prints all of the word processing you did to describe the extent of demand. The page has the date and time, case name identification, and student team member names.

**5.3.1.2.3. Results, Print plan reports, Format, Situation analysis, Nature of demand:** Selecting this option prints all of the word processing you did to describe the nature of demand. The page has the date and time, case name identification, and student team member names.

**5.3.1.2.4. Results, Print plan reports, Format, Situation analysis, Strategy analysis:** Selecting this option prints all of the word processing you did to describe the strategies of the case firm and its major competitors. The page has the date and time, case name identification, and student team member names.

**5.3.1.2.5. Results, Print plan reports, Format, Situation analysis, Life cycle stage:** Selecting this option prints all of the word processing you did to describe the industry life cycle stage. The page has the date and time, case name identification, and student team member names.

**5.3.1.2.6. Results, Print plan reports, Format, Situation analysis, Macroenvironmental trends:** Selecting this option prints all of the word processing you did to describe the macroenvironmental trends. The report has multiple pages showing what you wrote about the sociocultural, demographic, political and legal, technological, economic, and competitive environments. The first page has the date and time, case name identification, and student team member names.

**5.3.1.2.7. Results, Print plan reports, Format, Situation analysis, International issues:** Selecting this option prints all of the word processing you did to describe the international issues. The page has the date and time, case name identification, and student team member names.

**5.3.1.2.8. Results, Print plan reports, Format, Situation analysis, Strengths and weaknesses:** Selecting this option prints all of the word processing you did to describe the strengths and weaknesses of the case firm and its major competitors. The first page has the date and time, case name identification, and student team member names.

**5.3.1.2.9. Results, Print plan reports, Format, Situation analysis, Nature of competition:** Selecting this option prints all of the word processing you did to describe the nature of competition. The page has the date and time, case name identification, and student team member names.

**5.3.1.3. Results, Print plan reports, Format, POT analysis:** Selecting this option prints all of the word processing you did to describe the problems, opportunities, and threats facing the case firm. The first page has the date and time, case name identification, and student team member names.

**5.3.1.4. Results, Print plan reports, Format, Objectives:** Selecting this option prints all of the word processing you did to describe the objectives of your marketing plan. The page has the date and time, case name identification, and student team member names.

**5.3.1.5. Results, Print plan reports, Format, Alternatives:** Selecting this option prints all of the word processing you did to describe the three marketing strategy alternatives you proposed to address the problems, opportunities, and threats facing the case firm. The first page contains the date and time, case name identification, and student team member names.

**5.3.1.6. Results, Print plan reports, Format, Decision:** Selecting this option prints all of the word processing you did to describe the decision you made about which marketing strategy and plan alternative to pursue. The page has the date and time, case name identification, and student team member names.

**5.3.2.1. Results, Print plan reports, Sales, Print revenue summary:** This report summarizes the unit sales and pricing numbers you entered into the MPAS program. The report shows unit sales, average price per unit, gross sales, average cost of goods per unit, cost of goods, and net sales for each of the 10 years, with totals where appropriate. The first page has the date and time, case name identification, and student team member names.

**5.3.3.1. Results, Print plan reports, Strategy, Print all marketing strategy:** Selecting this option prints all of the marketing plan reports, including those based on your word processing work and the numbers you entered. (See the following for descriptions of the individual reports.) Almost all the pages have the date and time, case name identification, and student team member names.

**5.3.3.2. Results, Print plan reports, Strategy, Marketing strategy:** Selecting this option prints all of the word processing you did to describe your marketing strategy. The page has the date and time, case name identification, and student team member names.

**5.3.3.3. Results, Print plan reports, Strategy, Consumer target:** This two page report prints all of the word processing you did to describe your consumer target, and a page of numbers that profile your target market by age, income, social class, gender, household size, presence of children, and marital status. The first page has the date and time, case identification, and student team member names.

**5.3.3.4. Results, Print plan reports, Strategy, Business target:** This two page report prints all of the word processing you did to describe your business target, and a page of numbers that profile your target market by firm types, firm size, region, and number of employees. The first page has the date and time, case identification, and student team member names.

**5.3.3.5. Results, Print plan reports, Strategy, Product strategy:** Selecting this option prints all of the word processing you did to describe your product strategy. The page has the date and time, case name identification, and student team member names.

**5.3.3.6. Results, Print plan reports, Strategy, Pricing strategy:** Selecting this option prints all of the word processing you did to describe your pricing strategy. The page has the date and time, case name identification, and student team member names.

**5.3.3.7. Results, Print plan reports, Strategy, Promotion strategy:** Selecting this option prints all of the word processing you did to describe your promotion strategy. The page has the date and time, case name identification, and student team member names.

**5.3.3.8. Results, Print plan reports, Strategy, Distribution strategy:** Selecting this option prints all of the word processing you did to describe your distribution strategy. The page has the date and time, case name identification, and student team member names.

**5.3.4.1. Results, Print plan reports, Expenses, Print all expenses:** This two page report summarizes all the expenses in support of your marketing plan. It provides details on marketing expenses and additional expenses by year for each of the 10 years and totals. It also itemizes your startup expenses, and it provides data on your yearly interest expense and your depreciation amount. The first page has the date and time, case name identification, and student team member names.

**5.3.5.1. Results, Print plan reports, Invest, Print capital investments:** This one page report itemizes the capital investments you made in support of your plan. The page has the date and time, case name identification, and student team member names.

**5.3.6.1. Results, Print plan reports, Summary, Print all plan numbers:** By selecting this option, you print all of the reports in this section covering the plan numbers you entered, including reports on the net present value of your plan, a summary of your sales revenue, an income statement, ratios analyses, and a promotion summary. (See the following for descriptions of the individual reports.) Almost all the pages have the date and time, case name identification, and student team member names.

**5.3.6.2. Results, Print plan reports, Summary, Net present value:** This report shows a summary of your plan's initial investment, yearly cash flows, total cash flow, and net present value. You want your plan to have positive cash flows in most years, and a positive net present value. The page has the date and time, case name identification, and student team member names.

**5.3.6.3. Results, Print plan reports, Summary, Sales revenue:** This report summarizes your plan's net sales, other revenues, and a total of the two for each of the 10 years, and in total for all 10 years. It also shows what percent each year's total revenues is of all of the 10 years. This information about sales percentages by year is interesting because it shows how concentrated your sales are by year. The page has the date and time, case name identification, and student team member names.

**5.3.6.4. Results, Print plan reports, Summary, Income statement:** This two page report provides a summary of nearly all aspects of your marketing plan, including sales revenue, expenses, income, cash flow, and profits. This report is the best summary of how your plan is expected to perform on an overall basis over all 10 years of your plan. The first page has the date and time, case name identification, and student team member names.

**5.3.6.5. Results, Print plan reports, Summary, Ratio analysis:** This one page report contains ratios of R&D to net sales, marketing spending to net sales, total expenses to net sales, and net income to net sales ratios for each of the 10 years. The page has the date and time, case name identification, and student team member names.

**5.3.6.6. Results, Print plan reports, Summary, Promotion analysis:** This is a two page report. The first page contains by media advertising spending information for television, radio, magazine, and other tools such as direct mail and telemarketing for each of the 10 years and in total. It also shows spending for sales promotion, personal selling, and public relations for each of the 10 years and in total. And, it shows the total of all promotion spending for all promotion tools. The second page has ratio information, showing net sales divided by total promotion and net sales divided by total advertising. The first page has the date and time, case name identification, and student team member names.

---

# E. PRODUCING AND SUBMITTING YOUR MPAS WORK

As evidence that you have done an assignment, most instructors require that you submit reports printed by the MPAS program. These reports provide the instructor with the concrete information needed to grade your performance. When each reports prints, it also places your name(s) at the top, and it shows what case you worked on.

Producing your work with the MPAS program involves inputting your marketing plan information and printing the results. Your instructor should tell you what to enter and which of the reports to print. If you are in doubt, print those reports directly related to the inputs you made into the program; if you only entered words to describe the industry and case firm situation, only print those reports; and if you only entered the numbers and words related to describing and quantifying your marketing plan, only print those and related reports.

## F. WARNINGS, ERRORS, AND OTHER PROBLEMS

### Error Messages

**Missing file and program will not start:** If you get an error message about a missing file when the MPAS program starts, that means that there is one or more files missing from your data diskette in your A drive. Or, it can also mean that you have the wrong diskette in the A drive. If the problem is missing files, you can use your backup copy of the data diskette (disk #3) to create a new copy of the data diskette. However, that new copy will not contain the information that was on the old diskette.

**Error reading drive A:** This error message usually means that your data diskette is defective (or it may not be firmly placed in the A drive). If your data diskette is defective, you will lose all the work on that diskette. This is not a MPAS program problem, but rather it is due to a malfunction associated with the diskette you are using for your MPAS work. Hopefully, you made a copy of the original diskette (disk #3) so that you can create a new data diskette.

**Missing file during program operation:** If you get an error message about a missing file, that message will contain a place to send an e-mail message on what file is missing (but you will most likely be told to reinstall the MPAS program). You can do that or you can also try reinstalling the MPAS program (which will not effect your data diskette). First, you must delete the old copy of MPAS before doing the installation again. It is easiest to delete MPAS from Windows but you can also use DOS to delete the contents of the MPAS directory followed by deleting the directory itself. (See DOS manual for more details.) For information on installation, read that section.

If you are working on a network, the network supervisor should have set up the MPAS program to automatically refresh itself at the end of the day. So come back another day and the error message should not appear when you use the MPAS program again.

**Out of environment message (at MPAS startup).** You need to change your config.sys file line defining environment parameters if you are running the program under DOS or Windows 3.1 or Windows 3.51 or less. If this is a network installation, tell the supervisor about the problem.

### Program Operating Speed

The Program Runs Very Slowly, Particularly When Doing Work on the Data Diskette

MPAS operates five to ten times faster if you load SMARTDRV, the disk caching program, or some other disk caching software, before you begin using the MPAS program. You can get the same effect when running MPAS as a DOS program under Windows 3.1+, Windows 95, or Windows NT 3.51+ because each normally loads SMARTDRV or some other caching program before it starts. The primary difference between operating just under DOS and DOS with SMARTDRV, or under some version of Windows, is disk access speed.

Note that many network installations do not use SMARTDRV with DOS and sometimes not even with Windows. If that is the case at your school, you have no choice but to wait for long periods of time as the MPAS program accesses your data diskette in the A drive.

## Word Processing Problems

### My Word Processing Work Looks Strange When I Print It

The word processing part of the MPAS program works better if you do the following:

Only type your entries in single space (and NOT double space).

Do not try to indent your paragraphs as when someone would indent the first line of the paragraph. Separate your paragraphs with a space and it will be clear that you are moving to your next topic.

Do not try to create margins for your paragraphs. The margins are already there; you will see them when you print your work.

Do not use any of these characters in your documents: &, @, " (i.e., do not use quotes), - (i.e., do not use hyphens)

### I Get Printing Errors When I Print My Word Processing Work

Read the information in the previous section.

## Printing Problems

### The Reports Are Not Readable

This usually means that the printer is not defined correctly. Either you did not setup the printer when you installed the MPAS program or you installed it incorrectly. Reread the section of this appendix on installing your printer. If you are experimenting with which printer setup to use, you need to try another one.

If you did not install the MPAS program on the computer you are using or if you are using a workstation on a network, you need to contact the person who owns the computer about the problem you are having or the person responsible for the network.

### The Reports Produce A Blank Page After Each Report

This is done to insure that the printing clears out the pages which MPAS is producing, and it is, therefore, a normal part of printing a report.

## System Configuration

The Help or Hint Screens Are Out of Alignment

Sometimes the hint and/or help areas are hard to read because the inside part of the box has shifted. You can correct this by moving and/or resizing it as appropriate. To move the inside box, hold down the **Ctrl** key and press the **F7** key. The inside box will start flashing to indicate that it is ready to be moved. Use the arrow keys on your keyboard to move the box to the upper left corner of the double lined container box for the hint or help area. Then press **Enter** to indicate that you are happy with the location of the inside box. Next, to resize the inside box, hold down the **Ctrl** key and press the **F8** key. The inside box will start flashing to show that it is ready to be resized. Use the arrow keys on your keyboard to resize the box to the edges of the double lined container box for the hint or help area. Then press **Enter** to indicate that you are happy with the size of the inside box.

Because of the Screen Color Combination, I am Having Trouble Seeing Some Parts of the MPAS Program

You can change the appearance of the MPAS program by picking from a listing of monitor configuration options, which represent different color combinations that can be used when operating the program. The MPAS program normally starts with a blue, gray, and white set of colors, but you can chose from many other possibilities by selecting **Monitor** from the **System** menu. When you pick an alternative color combination, the entire appearance of the MPAS program changes. Note that some color combinations may make it more difficult to see parts of the program screens such as the word processing areas. Also note that if you are using the MPAS program on a network or on someone else's computer, you may need to change the appearance of the program each time you start it if you want to use a color combination other than the blue, gray, and white default.

## GETTING HELP

For help on how to do your assignments, look first to what your instructor gave you on how he or she wants you to do the work. If you want help on how to do well in doing the number parts of the MPAS assignments, look at the hints under the **System** configuration and **Help** menu. There is also a help with some information about the general functioning of the MPAS program menus in help under the **System** configuration and **Help** menu. You can also see the general help information from most parts of the program by pressing **F1**. In addition, see http://www.winstonms.com/mpas.

If you have trouble installing or operating the MPAS program, check with your instructor first about your problem and any possible solutions. You can also send an e-mail message to MPAS@winstonms.com if you have an installation or operations related question. However, questions about how to do assignments cannot be answered. If you send e-mail, you should receive a reply within 24 hours. All replies are made to e-mail addresses only. No phone calls can be made because of associated expenses.

# INDEX